A HISTORY OF BRITISH INDIA

A HISTORY OF BRITISH INDIA

BY

SIR WILLIAM WILSON HUNTER, K.C.S.I. M.A. LL.D.,

A Vice-President of the Royal Asiatic Society

VOLUME II

TO THE UNION OF THE OLD AND NEW COMPANIES UNDER THE EARL OF GODOLPHIN'S AWARD

GYAN

Published by

Gyan Publishing House
5, Ansari Road
Daryaganj, New Delhi-110002
Phone: 011-47034999, 9811692060
E-mail: books@gyanbooks.com

Distribution Network
gyanbooks.com
India, USA, Canada, UK, Australia, France

ISBN : 978-81-212-3500-6 (Set)
ISBN : 978-81-212-4728-3 (HB)
First Published, 1900

2nd Impression 2020

Printed at: Gyan Press, Delhi.

A History of British India Vol. II
Author: Sir William Wilson Hunter

A HISTORY of BRITISH INDIA. By Sir William Wilson Hunter, K.C.S.I., M.A., LL.D., a Vice-President of the Royal Asiatic Society

VOLUME II.

TO THE UNION OF THE OLD AND NEW COMPANIES UNDER THE EARL OF GODOLPHIN'S AWARD

LONGMANS, GREEN, AND CO.
LONDON, NEW YORK, AND BOMBAY
1900

CONTENTS

OF

THE SECOND VOLUME

INTRODUCTION

THERE is something pathetic in the publication of a posthumous work. The pathos is deepened in the case of a writer suddenly called away in the midst of apparent health and vigour, as he stands on the threshold of a great literary undertaking. When Sir William Hunter, on January 24, 1900, penned the last words of Chapter VIII. in the present volume it was little realised, either by himself or his friends, that the shadow of death had already fallen across his path. Yet so it was. A fortnight later he was lying dead—his end so sudden, so calm, and so mercifully wrapped in the sleep of unconsciousness that he had no time to give more than a bare hint of his wishes as to the book he had left incomplete.

Of the man himself and his work this is not the place to speak. Innumerable tributes to his memory, both in the English and Indian Press, are still fresh in the public recollection. Moreover, a 'Life' is in preparation, which has been entrusted to the capable hands of Mr. F. H. Skrine, late of the Bengal Civil Service, and it would therefore be at once premature and unnecessary to anticipate the task he has undertaken.

It remains to say something as to the publication of this volume. In the original scheme of the work it was to end with the battle of Plassey; but gradually this plan was modified. As the darkest period of the Company's history, that of the seventeenth century, was reconstructed and illuminated from the manuscript records of the India Office, Sir William Hunter determined that the results were of sufficient interest and importance to justify a narrative on a more extended scale. The exact date for the conclusion of the volume had not been finally fixed when death stayed the hand of the writer. Chapters I. to VII. were already set up in proof, while Chapter VIII. existed in manuscript only. At first it was decided to publish the volume as it stood, without the addition of a single word; but Sir William Hunter had left a rough outline sketch of what the next chapter was to be, together with abundant material, either collected by himself or amassed under his immediate direction, and eventually it was resolved to use that material so far as to carry on the history to a convenient terminal date. Such a date was obviously afforded by the union of the two Companies under the provisions of the Earl of Godolphin's Award in 1708, and Chapter IX. has therefore been added to round off the volume. For the form and arrangement of that concluding portion Sir William Hunter is in no way responsible, and any imperfections of style or matter that may be found (of which there are probably only too many) are not to be attributed to his pen.

Though he unhappily only lived to carry out a fragment of his original design, yet it may be said that Hunter has left a complete account of one great section of our history in India—the struggle for and attainment of commercial supremacy in the seventeenth century. Speaking generally, this was the achievement of the old London Company. The work of the great United Company, founded in 1708, was to establish our political ascendency. But there would have been no political ascendency for us at all, had not the humbler task been well and thoroughly performed. Nor must we attempt to draw too dogmatically the line of demarcation between the periods thus roughly characterised. The one shades into the other by almost imperceptible gradations, and we shall find that, even in the early period covered by this volume, the English in India were not without occasional premonitions of the great destiny awaiting them.

The once firmly-rooted conviction that our real history in India began about 1746 is dying hard. It was due partly to an accidental cause. The events of that time were related with marvellous accuracy of detail and unique charm of style by a consummate military historian. But the bright light focussed by the genius of Orme on the Anglo-French struggle in India of the eighteenth century has not only somewhat lifted that period out of its proper perspective, but has deepened by contrast the shadow on the years that went before.

We have too long fostered the notion that our Indian Empire was an unconscious lapse into greatness. The historian who attempts to work from primary sources has frequently to combat generalisations, more brilliant than sound, which have crystallised into hard-and-fast traditions. Thus the late Professor Seeley writes: 'Our acquisition of India was made blindly. Nothing great that has ever been done by Englishmen was done so unintentionally, so accidentally as the conquest of India.' It seems an invidious task to breathe even a word of criticism against a writer from whom we have all learnt so much. But fallacy must inevitably lurk in the attempt to sum up in a single sentence the motives and tendencies of a century and a half. To prove how seriously this statement needs qualification, we have only to point to the fact that as early as 1687 the Court of Directors hoped, in their own words, to lay the foundation of a 'large, well-grounded sure English dominion in India for all time to come.' Of course they by no means always wrote or acted up to the full height of this conception. They aimed, as Seeley truly points out, at a commercial rather than a political ascendency; but in no sense did the Company act 'blindly.' It set itself from the first most consciously and deliberately to acquire the bulk of the Indo-European trade.

The truth is better expressed in Captain Mahan's description of the English and Dutch colonial and mercantile policy as a whole. Both peoples, he says, 'in their native country and abroad, whether settled in the ports of civilised nations or of barbarous Eastern rulers or in colonies of their own foundation . . . everywhere strove to draw out all the resources of the land, to develope and increase them.' This is eminently true of our work in India; we strove *to draw out all the resources of the land.* But the political and economic condition of the Mughal Empire was such that a domination over the Indo-European trade inevitably brought with it a large measure of political and territorial power. It would have been madness to grasp the sceptre too soon. That was the fatal rock on which the French Companies were lured to destruction. Though a trading company might acquire an empire, we may be sure it could only do so by trading, *i.e.* by a vigorous and unimpeded exercise of its own proper function. Militarism is a dangerous weapon in the hands of a Chartered Company—at least, in the early stages of its history.

In the main therefore the Directors, that much-abused body of men, were moved by a sound instinct in their determination to avoid the acquisition of territory and political power as long as possible. Naturally they clung too tenaciously to a policy in itself wise and prudent. In many ways, and the fact is hardly surprising, they lamentably failed to realise the conditions which determined the actions of their representatives in India. By a strange fatality they saw only a check or a repulse in each great forward step made in the East. The advance to the peninsula appeared as a flight from the Spice Islands. Each of the three great capitals of British India was founded in their despite. They entered the name of Francis Day, builder of Madras, in the Company's Black Book. They received Bombay from the King as relieving him of an onerous burden. Gerald Aungier, its real founder, they snubbed and neglected. They only acquiesced in the establishment at Calcutta 'because we cannot now help it.'

But the Court never failed so disastrously as when for a time it abandoned its normal attitude and sent a hot-brained sea captain with a few hundred men to wage war on the majesty of the Mughal Empire. After the dismal failure of that ill-conceived project they reverted with the chastened wisdom of experience to their older policy; and though they undoubtedly 'made mistakes and failed and blundered, the important thing is that they never gave up, they never once relaxed their grim and often despairing hold on the India trade, whether mocked and befooled by the tortuous scheming of Charles I., or plunged headlong and against their will into the fierce conflict of the Civil War, or swamped in the party strife of the period of the Revolution.

Nor while we admit that the policy of the Court at this time was essentially a commercial one, need we on that account contemn the period itself as insignificant or the men it produced as beneath the notice of history. There are many names of the seventeenth and eighteenth centuries better known with less reason than those of Josia Child, Gerald Aungier, and Thomas Pitt. In comparing these men with some of their contemporaries we may recall the words of Burke, 'I have known merchants with the sentiments and abilities of great statesmen; and I have seen persons in the rank of statesmen with the conceptions and character of pedlars.' The same writer in one of those flashes of historical intuition which light up even his most fugitive productions realised that as early as the reign of Charles II. the East India Company was something more than a mere association of traders. They seemed, he said, to be 'not . . . merely a Company formed for the extension of British commerce, but in reality *a delegation of the whole power and sovereignty of this kingdom sent into the East.*'

Bearing this aphorism in mind, we shall no

longer make the mistake of underrating the first century of our Indian history. It is, indeed, a period of no mean importance, if we wish to understand the organic growth of our Eastern Empire. From the home aspect it reveals the slow and painful birth of a world-commerce in an age that had not yet emancipated itself from semi-mediæval notions as to the pernicious nature of foreign trade and the necessity of cramping and confining it by repressive laws. From the Eastern aspect it affords a wonderful spectacle of the advance of a Western civilisation into the vast dominions of an Oriental empire—an advance as gradual, yet as irresistible, as the surging-in of the ever-moving ocean through the tidal creeks and lagoons of the Indian shore.

The first volume related the history of the Company from its foundation to the expulsion of its servants from the Spice Archipelago. From that point this volume takes up the thread of the narrative. Driven from the far eastern islands, we were constrained to develope our settlements on the Indian continent. Widely different political conditions influenced the growth of our factories in the three great Presidencies. On the Bombay coast—*i.e.* in the newly-acquired Imperial province of Gujarat—we were shielded in our early efforts by the protecting power of the Delhi dynasty. By the time that the forces of disruption had impaired the vitality of the empire we had acquired the strength to stand alone. On the Coromandel coast we lurked secure behind the walls of Madras, and consolidated our power amid the ceaseless strife waged between the Moslem Kings of Golconda and Bijapur and the local coast Rajas, the remnants into which the great Hindu kingdom of Vijayanagar had been shattered. In Bengal our early settlements were dominated and controlled by the individual caprice of semi-independent Viceroys, till in time we learnt to use that personal factor to wrest privileges and powers from the Mughal Emperor.

But the Company had also a home history which profoundly modified its policy in the East. It could not, though it would fain have done so, stand apart from clashing interests and parties in England. It had not only to secure its position in Asia; it had also to justify its title to existence at home. Hence the space devoted in this volume to the relations of the Company with Charles I., the Commonwealth, the Protector, the restored Charles II., and the Parliaments of William III. and Anne. It was only slowly and tentatively that the great corporation which wielded the resources of the India trade found its appropriate place in the social and political structure of the English nation.

Under Charles I. the Company reached the verge of ruin. The cataclysm of the Civil War caused the only real break in the continuity of their trade from 1600 till 1813, when the monopoly of the commerce of India was finally abolished. In the Protector they found a champion, though one who exacted a full compliance with his wishes. Under Charles II. they entered upon a long period of commercial prosperity which raised up bitter rivals to their pretensions both at home and abroad. Galled by a persevering and active opposition, the Directors determined on a policy of offensive resistance. They shut the door of admission to the Company on the numerous and influential body of mercantile England that clamoured for a share in the India trade. They formulated and attempted to carry out a policy of armed industrialism in India. In both cases they failed. The opposition at home, in spite of organised corruption on a gigantic scale, developed into a great antagonistic company based on a Parliamentary sanction. The war against the Mughal Emperor resulted in a ruinous and humiliating defeat.

But the Court was never more admirable than in the hour of disaster. 'No great good was ever attained in this world without throes or convulsions,' wrote Sir Josia Child; and the Directors resolutely set themselves to save what was left. They succeeded at any rate in maintaining the continuity of the trade, and in forcing upon the new association the most characteristic features of their traditional policy. Though in point of material advantages the battle between the two Companies was a drawn one, yet the older association might justly claim that it had triumphantly carried its great principle, 'no nation can thrive by an East

India trade or support it long and to public advantage without one entire . . . Company armed with forts and fortifications.' The theory of maintaining a resident ambassador at the Imperial Court was finally discredited by the failure of Sir William Norris. The regulated basis of the 'General Society' was swept away in the settlement of 1708. The great United Company, which in that year entered upon a future fraught with immense possibilities for good or ill, was in effect the old London Company, with a far larger body of proprietors, a Parliamentary charter, and a closer connection with the State.

The materials for the period 1600-1708 are now far more accessible than was at one time the case. When the standard historians Mill and Thornton were writing, most of the documents necessary for the right comprehension of the time were mouldering to decay in India or lying neglected and unread in the cellars of Leadenhall Street. The very names of the men who faced European rivals, Hindu Rajas, and Mughal Generals on the field of battle, and who warred with the more deadly and intangible foes of disease and death, had passed into the limbo of forgotten things. But the dim memories of these early pioneers of empire have now been rescued from unmerited oblivion. Forty and fifty years ago the Rev. Philip Anderson and J. Talboys Wheeler ransacked the secretariats of Bombay and Madras.

Both men did valuable work, but work that was necessarily somewhat partial and incomplete, for each dealt only with the records of a single settlement. It was Sir George Birdwood who first effectively stimulated interest in the early history of the East India Company. His *Report on the Old Records of the India Office*, originally published by Government in 1878 and reprinted in 1889 and 1891, not only called attention to the vast body of historical documents stored in the India Office archives, but also by its comprehensive summary of their contents revealed, perhaps for the first time, the true meaning and characteristics of the period as a whole, and indicated the lines on which further research could most advantageously proceed. The tireless industry and indefatigable zeal of Sir Henry Yule carried on the work more thoroughly and more systematically than was possible to his predecessors and inspired others to follow in his footsteps. The work of G. W. Forrest, C. R. Wilson, and A. T. Pringle gives us almost a daily record of the lives lived by our countrymen two hundred years ago in Bombay, Bengal, and Madras. The historian is now, so far from being at a loss, rather in danger of being overwhelmed by the multiplicity and variety of his authorities.

Something may profitably be said here as to the series of records in the India Office and MSS. in the Bodleian Library, Oxford, which have been used in the compilation of this volume. The records in the India Office are very voluminous for the whole period. Among the most important are the Court Books, containing the Minutes of the Courts of Directors as well as those of the General Courts of the Company. They extend without a break from 1639 to 1858. From 1628 to 1639 they are complete, with the exception of the years July 1629–July 1630, July 1631–July 1632, July 1637–July 1639. This series has proved a veritable mine of information in working out the home history of the Company, especially under the first Stuart Kings, the Commonwealth, and the Protectorate; and as far as I know it is a mine as yet comparatively unexplored.

Two other series—the Letter Books or copies of despatches sent out by the Court of Directors to India, and the immense collection of papers known as 'Original Correspondence' (O. C. records), consisting of letters home from India and letters sent from factory to factory in the East—have also been carefully examined. But both sets of records were laid under contribution by Sir Henry Yule for his edition of Hedges' 'Diary,' and it is rare indeed to find anything of importance that has escaped him. An exhaustive search in these collections only strengthens and confirms the impression of his wonderful accuracy and acute discernment.

Besides these three main series of records, others dealing with particular periods have been examined. The letter-book of Sir William Norris from February 15, 1699 to August 22, 1700 is contained in Volumes 19 and 20 of the 'Miscellaneous Factory Records,' and has been the main authority for the account given of his embassy. Volumes 5 and 6 in the same collection contain abstracts of letters received from the servants of the Old and New Company in India, and have afforded details of considerable interest. A few references will also be found to the India Office transcripts of Dutch records at The Hague.

Much valuable material for this period is preserved in the Bodleian Library, Oxford, especially amongst the Rawlinson MSS. so admirably calendared and catalogued by the Rev. W. Dunn Macray. The East India Company's papers are mostly contained in two volumes known as Rawlinson MSS. A. 302, 303. The first volume consists mainly of records relating to the struggle between the two Companies. Among the most important are copies of the numerous memorials, petitions, and counter-petitions of the two associations to Parliament, the proceedings of the committees appointed to bring about a union, and copies of letters between the Old Company's servants and the New, upon their arrival in India from July 1699 to January following. The originals of these letters are to be found as a rule among the O. C. records of the India Office, but the collection preserves transcripts of one or two which have been lost; *e.g.* John Beard's answer to Sir Edward Littleton's letter of July 29, 1699, which Sir Henry Yule could not find (see his Hedges' 'Diary,' vol. ii. p. 208), and an important letter of Littleton's to Beard, dated July 28. The second volume also contains papers relating to the two Companies, both printed and in MS.; but perhaps the most interesting are a set of original autograph letters of Sir Josia Child, addressed to various persons, but mostly to Robert Blackborne, secretary to the London Company. These letters, dated 1692–1694 and written at Wanstead, illustrate the strong control exercised by this masterful man over the counsels of the Company.

Many volumes of the Historical Manuscripts Commission have been laid under contribution; amongst these, two may be especially noticed. First, the report on the Dropmore Papers (Thirteenth Report, Appendix III.), which contains many letters of Thomas Pitt. Most of them had been already given to the world by Sir Henry Yule, but some are here printed for the first time. Secondly, the Tillard Manuscripts (Fifteenth Report, Appendix X., pp. 78–91), a diary kept by William Tillard, servant of the new Company in Masulipatam. Though containing nothing of great importance, the diary affords means of comparing facts and dates with the India Office records.

I have to acknowledge my deep indebtedness to Sir George Birdwood and Mr. William Foster for many valuable suggestions and much help in passing the proofs through the Press. It was hoped that Sir George Birdwood would have been able to write the Introduction, but he was unhappily compelled by ill-health at a critical time to relinquish the task. Finally, I only wish it were possible for me adequately to express my sense of the obligations under which I labour to Lady Hunter. To her, of course, is wholly due the fact that this book has been finished at all, and that her husband, though dead, 'yet speaketh' with the old familiar voice. Her extraordinarily intimate and sympathetic knowledge of his work, her fine judgment and suggestive criticism have been invaluable to me, not only in preparing the whole volume for the Press, but also in writing the concluding portion.

P. E. Roberts.

Oxford:
August 14, 1900.

CHAPTER I

THE COMPANY AND THE KING

1623–1649

IN 1628, while the Petition of Right was giving shape to the conflict between the King and the Commons, the fortunes of the Company reached a low ebb. During the preceding five years one blow after another had fallen upon it, at home and abroad. In the Far East its servants only saved their lives by abandoning their settlements in Japan.[1] In the Spice Archipelago we have seen them tortured and slain at Amboyna, and driven forth from the Clove Isles. In the Javanese Straits they had been decimated by disease at their ocean-refuge of Lagundy, and were brought back by the clemency of the Dutch to Batavia, only to quit it again after a further struggle with misery.[2] On the Bay of Bengal, the native governor was inflicting on them the 'foul injuries'[3] which were to force them out of Masulipatam. On the opposite or western coast of India, their warehouses were ransacked and their chiefs at Surat 1623 to 1628

[1] *Calendar of State Papers*, East Indies, 1622–1624, Nos. 146, 415, *sub anno* 1623.

[2] *Ante*, vol. i. pp. 424–5.

[3] *Calendar of State Papers*, East Indies, 1625–1629, No. 716, p. 548.

imprisoned in irons; 'to be,' in the words of their President, 'the shameful subjects of daily threats, revilings, scorns and disdainful derisions.'[1]

At home, the finances of the Company threatened a collapse. Notwithstanding the profits of individual voyages, the value of its capital had in
1626 1626 fallen over twenty per cent., and 100*l*. of stock were not worth 80*l*.[2] Its shipping had decreased by one-third. The affrighted adventurers, seeing no end to their losses, would contribute but one-fifth of what they had formerly provided for the annual voyage,[3] and in 1628 the Company could not obtain a subscription for a new joint-stock.[4] It had already borrowed so heavily that no one would lend it more money on its common seal, and its managers had to carry on business by pledging their private credit.[5] Internal dissensions rose high, and
1627 in 1627 the Company was constrained to 'battulate' a brawling member, that is, to forbid him any more to come to its meetings or to trouble its house and courts.[6]

From outside it could hope for little support. To the country gentlemen the East India Company was a monopoly which drained England of its bullion in order to buy spices, luxuries, and

[1] *Calendar of State Papers*, East Indies, 1625–1629, No. 56. Letter dated Swally Road, February 1625.

[2] *Idem*, No. 288.

[3] 40,000*l*. instead of 200,000*l*. *Idem*, No. 786. Statement by the Company dated January 1629.

[4] *Idem*, No. 679.

[5] *Idem*, No. 786. The Company's debt amounted to 230,000*l*. in June 1628, further increased to 300,000*l*. by March 1629, and the yearly interest to 20,000*l*.

[6] *Idem*, No. 567. The member was Mr. Thomas Smethwike, of whom we shall hear further.

toys. This 'canker of the commonwealth,' on (1601)
which Malynes had laid a rough finger,[1] with the threatening motto *sublatâ causâ tollitur effectus*, became a stock theme for patriotic eloquence. The delusive reports of the India trade were, accord-
ing to another writer, but 'the pleasing notes of (1615)
the swans in Meander flood,' which would in reality prove, like theirs, the dismal croaking of 'greedy ravens and devouring crows.'[2] The Company, it was said, had cut down the oaks that should have built the royal ships; it had raised the price of timber for merchant vessels by five shillings a load; it was in truth 'a parricide of woods.'[3] Its gains, 'the price of blood,' 'bought with so many men's lives,' had, the nation was assured, killed and worn out the mariners who formed the defence of England, and left a multitude of widows and orphans to an unhappy fate.[4] 'The whole land'[5] was called to protest against the drain of bullion that 'causeth the body of this commonwealth to be wounded sore.'[6] As the Portuguese 'were the enemies of Christendom, for they carried the treasure of Europe to enrich the heathen,'[7] so the Company was the enemy of England, which,

[1] *A Treatise of the Canker of England's Commonwealth*, by Gerard de Malynes, pp. 3, 68, &c. London 1601.

[2] *The Trades Increase*, p. 14, by J. R., London 1615. J. R. is identified doubtfully with Robert Jenison, more probably with John Floyd. Neither the British Museum Catalogue nor that of the Bodleian Library gives the name in full.

[3] *Idem*, p. 18.

[4] *Idem*, pp. 27–32.

[5] *Idem*, p. 32.

[6] *Free Trade, or the Means to Make Trade Flourish*, by Edward Misselden, 1622, pp. 13, 19, 20, 29.

[7] *The Trades Increase*, p. 32, 1615.

1622 between the export of coin and the Dutch, had become a blind Belisarius begging by the wayside.[1]

To these popular denunciations, many of them ill-founded, some of them insincere,[2] the Company opposed an array of facts, convincing to the modern economist. But the English political economy of that day was a compound of mediæval tradition and national prejudice; the true principles of currency and commerce only emerged in the following century. Meanwhile the enemies of the India trade had mediæval tradition and national prejudice on their side. The fact that the Company's defence had to be conducted by its own servants or members deepened the popular distrust.
1615 It was in vain that Sir Dudley Digges, in 1615, proved that the statements about the consumption of timber, the loss of mariners, and the export of coin were exaggerated, or compensated by counter-benefits to the nation. For Sir Dudley Digges had been a candidate for the governorship of the Company in the preceding year. He did not help his case by insulting contrasts between 'the idle drone and the greedy caterpillars' who live at ease in England, and the 'laborious bees' in the East who 'bring the honey to the hive.' Nor did the

[1] Misselden's *Free Trade*, p. 14, 1622.

[2] Misselden changed his tone in *The Circle of Commerce or Balance of Trade*, published in the following year 1623, when replying to Gerard de Malynes' *Lex Mercatoria* of 1622. But he had meanwhile been secured to the Company's interests as its Commissioner to Amsterdam, 1623, and he remained its agent until 1628.

public take seriously his metaphor, which was 1615
destined to prove so true, of the Company as a 'Hercules yet in the cradle.'[1] We must, indeed, distinguish between the young Sir Dudley Digges of 1615 dabbling in the City, and the mature Sir Dudley Digges who stood forth for the Commons in the impeachment of Buckingham, and gave voice to the nation on the Petition of Right. Yet Sir Dudley Digges of the East India Company, under the first Stuart king, came near to the principles by which Sir Dudley North of the Turkey Company, under the last Stuarts, anticipated the doctrines of Adam Smith. In the case alike of the earlier and the later Sir Dudley, the actual facts of our Eastern commerce supplied the basis for sounder economics.

Thomas Mun's 'Discourse of Trade,' in 1621, 1621
formed by far the ablest statement of the case on behalf of the adventurers.[2] But to his contemporaries Mun appeared as a wealthy director of the Company, who was rewarded for his advocacy by the offer of the inspectorship of its factories in India.[3] His arguments were in advance of the age, and as we shall find them reiterated in the Company's petition to Parliament in 1628, I need not pause over them here. On the public they had

[1] *Defence of Trade*, pp. 2, 3.

[2] *A Discourse of Trade from England into the East Indies*, 1621, and reprinted in 1621 and 1625. The edition which I use of this remarkable book is that in the *Select Collection of Tracts of Commerce*, London, 1856.

[3] For notices of this early economist, see the *Calendar of State Papers*, East Indies, 1617–1621, No. 1023: 1622–1624, Nos 425, 433, &c.; and 1625–1629 in *multis locis*.

1625 little effect. The Company still continued to be the Jason that had stolen away England's golden fleece of bullion.[1] 'The clamourous complaints,'[2] which induced Mun to come forward in its defence, continued as 'loud as before;' 'the only remedy' being 'to put down this trade.'

Nor could the Company hope much from the King, to whose act of prerogative it owed its existence. The Crown had commenced anew the encroachments which James on more than one occasion effusively relinquished. How far the royal aggression can be excused we shall presently examine. To the despondent adventurers it seemed to threaten the finishing stroke. It was bad enough that their interests should be the sport of an evasive foreign policy: thrown over in favour of Portugal when His Majesty sought a Spanish marriage; and sacrificed to a Dutch alliance when Prince Charles returned angry and sore from his wooing at Madrid. It also rankled that the Company should be bidden[3] by a courtier and the groom of the Prince's bedchamber to carry to India two emissaries whom it believed to be rivals in trade. But when King James arrested its ships and stigmatised the directors as 'pirates' because, under legal advice, they refused to comply with certain demands of the Crown, the situation grew well-nigh intolerable.[4] The end came when Charles was

[1] *A Discourse of the Sea and Navigation*, by John Hagthorpe, 1625, p. 16.

[2] Mun's *Discourse*, pp. 6, 37.

[3] By Sir William Heydon and Endymion Porter, April 1622. *Calendar of State Papers*, East Indies, 1622–1624, Nos. 81, 96, 136.

[4] *Calendar of State Papers*,

found conniving at the opposition within the Company's own courts, and encouraging the 'battulated' member to raise the whole question of the Indian trade before His Majesty's Council.[1] Meanwhile the Company, on the flood-tide of popular feeling which bore forward the Petition of Right, appealed in 1628 to Parliament.

Its 'Remonstrance' begins almost in the lan- 1628
guage of despair. It prays the House that 'if the said trade be found unprofitable to the Commonwealth it may be suppressed, and if otherwise that then it may be supported and continued by some Public Declaration.'[2] But it presently takes a higher tone. Drawn up by Thomas Mun and revised by Sir John Coke,[3] the Memorial answers one by one the objections that had been urged during the past twenty-eight years against the Company. It is in fact Mun's 'Discourse of Trade,' reduced to language of precision, and developing economic arguments which Mun's book of 1621 had more timidly wrapped up.

So far from weakening the nation, the Company urged that its fleets[4] formed a vast training school for the English marine, a magazine from which

East Indies, 1622–24. Nos. 303, 413.

[1] *Idem*, 1625–1629. No. 784, January 1629. Smethwike, after long resistance, was obliged in 1640 by a 'Court of Honour' to make a public submission to the Company. MS. Court Book, No. 17, p. 86.

[2] *The Petition and Remonstrance of the Governor and Company of Merchants of London, trading to the East Indies.* Exhibited to the Honourable the House of Commons. *Anno* 1628.

[3] *Calendar of State Papers*, East Indies, 1625–1629, Nos. 633, 635, 648, &c.

[4] 15,000 tons of shipping re-

1628 the royal navy could draw both men and munitions of war. That so far from decreasing the national wealth, it brought to England a store of Indian products of which only a portion was consumed at home, while the greater part was re-exported to other countries, at a large profit to the realm. Of 208,000*l.* worth of pepper imported in 1627, no less than 180,000*l.* worth was re-exported to foreign States. That while the Crown thus secured an increase to its customs, the people were enabled to buy spices at much lower rates; although in some articles the Dutch interference had again doubled the prices.[1] That the gentry gained by the increased exportation of wool, and woollen stuffs, 'which doth improve the landlords' rents.' That the Company was in fact become a defence of the Commonwealth, 'to counterpoize the Hollanders' swelling greatness by trade, and to keep them from being absolute Lords of the Seas.' It had also deprived Spain of the 'incredible advantage of adding the traffique of the East Indies to the treasure of the West.' That if the English trade with the Indies shall fail, then other English

duced by losses to 10,000 in 1628. *The Petition and Remonstrance*, pp. 1–3, 1628.

[1] Thus when the Indian wares had to come *viâ* the Levant, the price of pepper was 3*s.* to 3*s.* 4*d.* per lb. and of indigo 6*s.*, reduced by the Company's direct trade with India to 1*s.* 8*d.* for pepper and 4*s.* for indigo. If the finer spices were again high (cloves 11*s.*, mace 10*s.*, and nutmeg 5*s.* per lb), it is because 'the Hollanders . . . have now three years past, and still do keep us by force from the trade of those spiceries.' Before the Dutch interference the Company had reduced the prices to 6*s.* per lb. for mace, 5*s.* 6*d.* for cloves, and 2*s.* 6*d.* for nutmegs. *Idem*, pp. 9, 10.

commerce will fail with it, and pass into the hands of the Dutch.[1] 1628

The Company thus grounded its first appeal to Parliament on a broadly national basis. But the charge of draining the country of its bullion was more difficult to meet. In 1621, Mun had exposed the exaggerated character of this complaint, and shown that during the previous twenty years the Company shipped only half a million sterling, not in English coinage but in Spanish reals, while licensed to export three-quarters of a million.[2] He now in the Remonstrance to the Commons takes a bolder stand. The Company declares that this export of bullion, to buy Indian wares which it resells to foreign nations at a great profit, is a good employment for the national treasure. England can only acquire bullion, since she hath neither gold nor silver mines, 'by making our commodities which are exported, to over-balance in value the foreign wares which we consume.' 'It is not . . . the keeping of our money in the kingdom which makes a quick and ample trade, but the necessity and use of our wares in foreign countries, and our want of their commodities which causeth the vent and consumption on all sides.'[3]

'For,' as Mun privately wrote: 'if we only behold the actions of the husbandman in the seed-

[1] *The Petition and Remonstrance*, pp. 13, 17, 19, 22, 24, 25.

[2] 548,090*l.* from 1601 to July 1620, instead of 720,000*l.* Mun's *Discourse of Trade with the East Indies*, 1621, p. 18.

[3] *The Petition and Remonstrance of the Governor and Company of Merchants of London, trading to the East Indies*, 1628, pp. 27, 28, 32.

time when he casteth away much good corn into the ground, we will rather accompt him a madman than a husbandman: but when we consider his labours in the harvest, which is the end of his endeavours, we find the worth and plentiful encrease of his actions.'[1]

1628 This early enunciation of the Mercantile System, which anticipated Colbert's acceptance of it by a quarter of a century, fell flat in 1628. Parliament was too busy with the Petition of Right to spare time for the complaints of the Company.[2] But even if it had had the leisure, it was too deeply ingrained with the old prejudice against exporting bullion, to be enticed by new-fangled economics. Four years previously, on a motion 'to search the East India ships for money,' the Company's friends were answered by tumultuous cries of 'stay the money that they send out of the land,' 'search the books.'[3] Cheap pepper and cloves mattered little to the country-gentlemen of England, battling for their liberties with the Crown.

To the people at large the Company represented the survival of a Royal prerogative, which had

[1] Mun's *England's Treasure by Forraign Trade*, 1664, p. 50. Written probably between 1628 and 1632, but not published till twenty-three years after his death in 1641.

[2] Its *Petition and Remonstrance* was on May 7, 1628, read and referred to the Committee for Trade (*Commons Journal*, i. 893), but amid the greater matters of the prorogation of Parliament in 1628, and its dissolution in March 1629, we hear no more about it. No Parliament met again in England for eleven years.

[3] *Calendar of State Papers*, East Indies, 1622–1624, No. 425, 8th March, 1624.

grown unpopular even under Elizabeth, become intolerable under James, and was in 1624 sternly curtailed by statute.[1] A monopoly might be needful for the armed trade which was then the only trade possible in the East. Yet to the rising spirit of the nation, the exclusive privileges granted to the Company by the King seemed scarcely more bearable than those granted by the Borgian Pope to Portugal and Spain. Its sufferings, with the exception of the Amboyna outrage, touched no chord of popular sympathy. Up to 1628, books for or against the Company were published at intervals. But from its appeal to Parliament in 1628 onwards until 1640, I do not find that a single book or pamphlet in its interests issued from the press.[2] Parliament and the nation left the Company severely alone to the King.

The aggressions of the early Stuarts on the

[1] The East India Company had not been specially exempted in 1624 from the Statute 21 and 22, Jac. I. cap. III. for the abolition of monopolies, but was held to come under clause 9 of general exceptions—a title to existence afterwards found susceptible of dispute.

[2] *A Transcript of the Registers of the Company of Stationers of London*, 1554 to 1640, edited by Edward Arber. Privately printed 1875-1877, vol. iv. In addition to the works already cited, three important publications issued shortly before the Company's petition of 1628. *A Sermon called the Stripping of Joseph*, by Dr. Robert Wilkinson, with a *Consolatory Epistle to the East India Company*, by Thomas Myriall, February 1625. *A Discourse of the Sea and Navigation*, by John Hagthorpe, July 1625. *A Reply to the Remonstrance of the Bewinthebbers* (or Dutch Directors), March 1627, one of the Amboyna Pamphlets. The only work touching on the India trade entered between 1628 and 1640 is Thomas Herbert's *Itinerary of some yeares Travale through divers parts of Asia and Affricke*, 1634, reprinted in 1638 and 1667. I thank Mr. P. E. Roberts for examining the Stationers' registers for me.

1603 to 1640 Company, often denounced as mere acts of extortion, are disclosed by a dispassionate inquiry in a somewhat different light. The Crown regarded the Company as its own creation, and knew it to be in continual need of its support. It had made over to the Corporation a privilege of a highly marketable value—the monopoly of the Indian trade—which it could have sold and resold at large prices to successive groups of adventurers. The King also armed the Company with powers of military aggression on sea and land, and he had to maintain it by the royal power in what went near to a piratical warfare on the ships of friendly Christian nations.

The Crown expected in return, not only the stipulated customs which it would in any case have received from successive groups of adventurers, but also a complaisance to its creatures, and loans or gifts of money. This necessity for paying for what was in fact a curtailment of the trade-liberties of the nation, continued long after the power of curtailment passed from the Crown to Parliament. Such payments grew, indeed, from rare and grudging benevolences to the first Stuart kings, into large and frequent loans to the constitutional government.

In dealing with the Company James I. might scold, Charles I. might sigh, and Charles II. might laugh; but they all understood their power and were equally resolved to profit by it. 'Did I deliver you from the complaint of the Spaniards and do you return me nothing?' James I. replied angrily to the directors when they refused the two-tenths of the 100,000*l.* worth of booty seized at Ormuz. The directors took legal advice, wriggled long on the hook, but in the end paid the 20,000*l.* to His Majesty and the Lord High Admiral.[1] James, indeed, was as ready to share the misfortunes of the Company as he was determined to profit by its successes. During the darkest days of Amboyna he offered to become a freeman of the Company,[2] and to support it with the royal authority, and the right of carrying the royal flag. The Company foresaw, however, that with so high a personage among them they would lose 'the free election' of their own officers, who must in the end become the nominees of the King and Court. They also feared being 'drawn into actions of war' and costly enterprises of State. They thus avoided the rocks on which the French Companies afterwards suffered shipwreck, and humbly declined His Majesty's proposal.[3] 1622–4 1624

The kingcraft which James I. naïvely professed, Charles I. feebly practised. His release, in 1628, of the Dutch ships which he had promised to hold fast as the sole means of securing redress for Amboyna, came like a stab in the dark to the Company.[4] Nor did his unprecedented complaisance in sending the Lords of his Council to 1628

[1] The proceedings, spun out from the capture of Ormuz from the Portuguese in 1622 to 1624, will be found in the *Calendar of State Papers*, East Indies, 1622–1624, Nos. 303, 413, &c. *Vide ante*, vol. i. p. 329.

[2] *Ante*, vol. i. p. 406.

[3] *Calendar of State Papers*, East Indies, 1622–1624, Nos. 511, 527. The arguments are set forth in the India Office MSS.

[4] *Ante*, vol. i. p. 414.

1628 Leadenhall Street to explain away the transaction avail more than to tinge resentment with contempt. The Directors knew perfectly that it was the royal revenge for their Petition and Remonstrance to Parliament in the preceding spring. But Charles, unlike James, kept his temper and did not use bad words. Swallowing his wrath at the Directors' appeal to Parliament, he assured them in July 1628, that such was his love to commerce in general and to the Company in particular that he would not have them doubt of his protection, and meanwhile he would feel obliged for a loan of 10,000*l.*[1] As the loan was not forthcoming, he transferred his civilities to the Dutch. In the following month he was said to have taken their bribe of 30,000*l.*, and he certainly let their ships go.[2]

Charles thus learned early in his reign that the Company, while ready to gratify the Royal love of 'varieties' by the gift of a leopard or other strange Indian beast, was not to be squeezed of hard cash. But his courtiers discovered more subtle means. The Company imported saltpetre, and this could not be sold till His Majesty's pleasure was known as to whether he might want it for gunpowder,[3] or until payments had passed secretly to the Court. As the royal distresses increased he acted more vigorously, and in 1640, the Company having no money to lend him, he forced it to sell him on credit 65,000*l.* worth of

[1] *Calendar of State Papers*, East Indies, 1625–1629, Nos. 677, 678, July 1628.

[2] *Idem*, 699, 706, August 1628.

[3] *Idem*, Domestic Series, 1637–1638, p. 19, 12th December, 1637.

pepper, which he promptly resold for cash at a 1640
loss of 6,000*l*. His Majesty's profit on the transaction was nevertheless a handsome one, as all that the Company received from him seems to have been 13,000*l*., certain disputed exemptions from customs-dues, and the privilege of taking timber from the Forest of Dean.[1]

So ingenious a device would not bear repetition. Charles, however, had already hit on a surer plan for making money out of the Indian trade. The Charter of James I. granted the monopoly to the Company for ever. But it contained a proviso for the resumption of the privilege, on three years' notice from the Crown, if the grant should not prove profitable to the realm. On this matter the King was the sole judge. He was surrounded by courtiers with their salaries in arrears, and by adventurers eager to show him a more excellent way, and to pay secret money for the permission to do so. How could he be sure that a Company, which constantly paraded its losses, was carrying on a trade profitable to the realm, unless he allowed others to try their hand? He had done many things for the Company, encouraged its efforts to raise fresh capital, issued royal proclamations to help it against its servants' private trade,[2] written letters to Eastern potentates, nego-

[1] *Calendar of State Papers*, Domestic, 1640, p. 654; 1640–41, pp. 271, 324; 1641–1643, p. 67, &c. It is right to add that the King gave securities for repayment; but in the end, 1663, the Company compounded at a loss of 31,500*l*.

[2] The second Proclamation, February 19, 1632, condescends

1625 to 1640 tiated with Spain and Holland on its behalf, offered to send an envoy to the Great Mogul, and was he to get nothing for his pains? By some such casuistry Charles seems to have felt justified in allowing his courtiers and their City friends to experiment in the Indian trade.

The records of the Company during his reign are full of the ignominious struggle which ensued. The King commenced cautiously by compelling
1630 the Company in 1630 to find a passage for the Earl of Denbigh, who had been seized by a desire to visit India and Persia; not altogether without an eye to business, as, on his return, he was reported to have landed sixty bales of indigo and other goods secretly at Dover, and conveyed them in carts to Southwark.[1]

Four years after Denbigh's return, Prince Rupert, aged eighteen, appeared as the figure-head of a Court clique for colonising Madagascar, then regarded as a half-way house to India, and
1637 within the limits of the Company's Charter.[2] The Company's protests might have availed little. But the young adventurer's mother, the Queen of Bohemia, laughed at the scheme as a Quixote's isle of Barataria, 'neither feasible, safe, nor honourable.' So in spite of a servile poem by

to the feet and inches of the chests which commanders and factors were allowed to ship on their own account, and specifies every commodity in which they might trade. *Calendar of State Papers*, East Indies, 1630–1634, No. 263.

[1] *Idem*, Nos. 49, 490. The Earl of Denbigh was brother-in-law to the late favourite Buckingham.

[2] MS. Court Book, No. 16, p. 294, March 20, 1637.

Davenant, Prince Rupert, or 'Prince Robert' as 1637
he appears in the Company's records, went off to the siege of Breda instead. Lord Arundell, who succeeded to the leadership of the project,
not only proposed to plant a colony in Mada- 1639
gascar, but asked for a contract 'to transport the Company's pepper and other commodities from thence to England.' The Company politely thanked his Lordship, said that it had enough ships of its own, and firmly refused a passage for him or his friends.[1]

But it was not with noble and princely personages that the Company had mainly to strive. Wealthy merchants were now willing to stake their fortunes on breaking down the Company's monopoly, and they found gentlemen about the King's person ready, for a consideration, to gain His Majesty's ear. The most famous of these
cabals of the City and Whitehall was Courten's 1635
Association; it had lasting consequences on the India trade, and it illustrates the hostile combinations to which the Company, as long as it depended on the royal favour, was exposed. The chief actors in the drama were Sir William Courten and Sir Paul Pindar, two London merchants, who between them 'lent' the King 200,000*l.*; and Endymion Porter, groom of the bedchamber and His Majesty's factotum for secret affairs.

William Courten started as a plain London trader, the son of a Flemish Protestant clothier who had found refuge in England under Elizabeth,

[1] MS. Court Book, No. 17, pp. 25, 27, Sept. 27, and Oct. 9, 1639.

and prospered beneath her protecting rule. William learned business at Haarlem, and began usefully by marrying the deaf and dumb daughter of a Dutch merchant who brought him 60,000*l.* Returning to London he grew into a great merchant with ships trading to Portugal, the African coast and the West Indies. He had the distinction in 1619 of being fined 20,000*l.* by the Star Chamber for exporting gold—an experience sweetened after three years by a knighthood from James. This mingled taste of royal discipline and kingly favour led him to seek closer relations with the Court, and in 1625 he modestly applied for a grant of the 'Terra Australis Incognita' or Unknown South of the World. Three years later, letters patent, more limited in scope and discreetly addressed to the Earl of Pembroke—the late King's gentleman of the bedchamber, and a spirited company-promoter for Virginia, the North-West Passage, South America and elsewhere —were granted 'in trust for Sir William Courten.' The project failed, and Sir William, with a purse ever
1635 open to His Majesty's needs, obtained in 1635 a more promising license for the East Indian trade.

His principal partner in the adventure was Sir Paul Pindar, a man of good family, born after Elizabeth's accession and educated for the University, but with a natural genius for commerce. He learned the secrets of the Eastern trade during fifteen years of profitable business in Venice and Italy, and practised them for nine years more as James's envoy, and the nominee of the Levant Company, in Turkey. He brought home so great a fortune that Buckingham fitted out Prince Charles for his wooing trip to Madrid with Pindar's diamonds, saying he would talk about payment afterwards. One fine jewel, valued at 35,000*l.*, Pindar was wont to lend James I. to wear on State occasions; and in two transactions alone he handed over diamonds to the value of 26,000*l.* on the payment-deferred system to Charles. His loans to His Majesty were reckoned at 100,000*l.*, besides moneys to the Queen and royal children; for 'this Sir Paul never fails the King when he has most need.'[1] To so generous a financier a Stuart king could not stint his favours by scruples as to chartered rights.

The two merchants took into partnership an 1635
ally more influential than either. Endymion Porter, poetaster, courtier, speculator, virtuoso, patron of the Muses and of the Olympic Games on the Cotswold Hills, was a sort of Jacobean echo of Elizabethan Philip Sidney, with Zutphen left out. We have seen Sidney himself a defaulting subscriber to North-Western Passages.[2] Porter married the niece of Buckingham, accompanied the favourite and Prince Charles to Spain, and on Charles's succession to the Crown became groom of the King's bedchamber. His portrait shows a tall and graceful dilettante, with a face full of

[1] Carew's *Hinc illæ lachrymæ*, 1681, p. 23, quoted in the *Dictionary of National Biography*, xlv. 311. But his *Fraud and Violence Discovered and Detected*, London, 1662, should also be studied. Pindar's estate was valued in 1639 at 236,000*l.*

[2] *Vide ante*, vol. i. p. 204.

interest and intrigue.[1] On more than one occasion he had acted as go-between to the Court and the Company; and in 1635, certain drainage projects
1635 of his on a royal grant of land in Lincolnshire having failed, he was on the look out for some means of mending his fortunes.

The confederates, Courten, Pindar and Porter, commanded a greater capital than the Company could then raise, and they wielded an influence with which it could not cope. In 1628 it had asked Parliament either to uphold it or to abolish the trade. Parliament had vouchsafed no answer, and the Company had ever since been wearying the King with tales of its losses. A trade so disastrous to its conductors could scarcely be profitable to the Realm, within the meaning of the Charter, especially when new capitalists were willing to take it up with more energy and spirit. The three allies formed the bold design of erecting
1635 themselves into a rival Company, with the King as their partner—a partner who should bring in no money, but earn his profits by his secret support.

Charles had a plain course open to him. He had only to give the East India Company the three years' notice required by the Charter, and either resume its monopoly, or force it to come to terms. Some of its members were quite ready for a compromise, and indeed preferred the 'Regulated' system of separate ventures[2] to a Joint

[1] In the National Portrait Gallery. Another portrait of him in the National Gallery displays a stouter sylvan hero elaborately accoutred for the chase.

[2] A system practically adopted

Stock. Others were so despondent that they desired nothing better than to have three years allowed for bringing home their ships and property.[1] In 1635 the King granted a license to his three friends on the ground that the Company had consulted only its own interests, neglected those of the nation, and broken the conditions on which its exclusive privileges had been bestowed.[2] Instead, however, of giving the three years' notice Charles assured the Company that the new association would not trade within its jurisdiction, but was to 'be employed on some secret design which His Majesty at present thought not fit to reveal.'[3] 1635

In vain the dismayed Governor waited in the Whitehall antechamber all forenoon. He only succeeded in thrusting a petition into the King's hand as His Majesty passed forth after dinner, but got not a word in reply.[4] News soon arrived that two of Courten's ships which sailed 'without any cargoes' almost as undisguised privateers, had plundered an Indian vessel in the Red Sea; and that the Company's servants at Surat were in prison for the piracy.[5] Other of Courten's captains so outraged the Canton magistrates that the English 1636

by the East India Company in 1628 and on other occasions. Macpherson's *History of the European Commerce with India*, p. 111, 4to. 1812. For the 'Regulated' system *vide ante*, vol. i. pp. 254 *et seq.*

[1] Macpherson, p. 113.

[2] Preamble to the first grant to Sir William Courten, dated December 12, 1635.

[3] MS. Court Book, No. 16, p. 109, January 15, 1636.

[4] *Idem*, p. 147, March 1636.

[5] Bruce's *Annals of the Honorable East India Company*, vol. i. p. 341, 1810. See also Macpherson's *History of the European Commerce with India*, p. 113, 1812.

1636 were declared enemies of the Chinese Empire, and were to be for ever excluded from its ports.[1] Projects by interlopers for plantations in Madagascar and the Mauritius;[2] armed settlements by Courten's agents on the Malabar coast; and their open hostility to the Company's servants at Surat and elsewhere, now become the staple of the India Office records. The Company's factors in the East vainly begged for orders as to whether they were to obey the Charter of King James, or the letters of King Charles which the newcomers flourished in their faces.

Charles had another chance given him. On Sir William Courten's death in 1636 his grant lapsed, and the King had only to enforce the three years' notice clause of the Company's Charter in order to compel its despondent and wearied shareholders to a coalition. But his secret bonds forbad open methods, so he desired the Company not to trouble the dying man about the ships, and presently issued a new license to his son, William Courten, and his associates.[3]

The remaining years of freedom left to Charles form a record of subterfuges to conceal his real relations to the rival companies. If the old Company arrested a servant of the new one for infringing its Charter, the King did not defend him, but merely ordered his release.[4] If the old

[1] *Macartney's Embassy to China*, by Sir George Staunton, i. 5–12. 1797.

[2] MS. Court Book, No. 16, p. 294, No. 17, pp. 44, 77, &c.

[3] June 1, 1637. *Fœdera*, vol. xx. p. 146.

[4] February 1, 1637. MS. Court Book, No. 16, p. 250.

Company stayed by process of law the interlopers' ships, His Majesty or the Lords of his Council arranged to let them go. He was prodigal of good wishes to the Directors, dangled wider privileges before their eyes,[1] and pressed on them the good offices of his Government to compose the disputes which his own action had stirred up. But their attendance on the Privy Council only resulted in royal rebukes delivered by the Archbishop of Canterbury, and reproaches from Lord Arundell.[2] The Company was in no humour to be harangued by Howard, or to be lectured by Laud. His Majesty's request that if the Earl of Southampton, 'who is a noble and brave Gentleman, shall make any offer or proposition to the Company' (needless to say for the brave gentleman's own benefit), 'that they shall be pleased to hearken unto it,'[3] fell on deaf ears. The Company had tried His Majesty's courts in vain; it had tried His Majesty's Privy Council in vain; it had tried the King in person in vain. Slowly and very reluctantly it resolved once more to try the House of Commons. 1640

Charles became afraid. The same need of money which had tempted him into a confederacy against the Company now compelled him to summon a Parliament.[4] Within four days of its meeting in April, 1640, the Company was con-

[1] As 'this trade is of so great consequence and importance to His Majesty and the Kingdom.' March 1640. MS. Court Book, No. 17, p. 78.

[2] *Idem*, No. 17, p. 32, &c.

[3] *Idem*, p. 77*a*. March 12, 1640.

[4] Assembled April 13, 1640; dissolved by the King in anger, May 5, 1640.

1640 sidering whether it should not lay its wrongs before the Commons.[1] Mr. Recorder, however, counselled it not 'to make His Majesty's proceedings notorious,'[2] and the abrupt dissolution of Parliament, after a three weeks' wrangle with the Crown, seemed to put an end to the project. The Company's stock fell so low that 100*l.* of it sold for 60*l.*[3] But in November of the same year the King, with a mutinous army and the Scotch war on his hands, was forced again to call together the estates of the realm. The Long Parliament met in wrath at the King's creatures, and promptly arrested
1641 Strafford. In January 1641 the Company, once more on the flood-tide of popular feeling, petitioned Parliament against Courten and Endymion Porter, His Majesty's groom of the bedchamber.[4]

The King, in great trouble, sent hurried messages to the Governor of the Company to attend at Whitehall.[5] The counsellors, on whose audacity Charles had relied, were themselves trembling; Strafford and Laud impeached, Mr. Secretary Windebank and Lord Keeper Finch soon to take flight, the Star Chamber and the Court of High Commission doomed. The King at length confessed to the Governor of the Company 'that Mr. Porter had nothing to do in the business, his

[1] 17th April, 1640, MS. Court Book, No. 17, pp. 84*a*, 85.

[2] *Idem*, p. 88*a*.

[3] Macpherson's *History of the European Commerce with India*, p. 117, 1812.

[4] MS. Court Book, No. 17. pp. 191, 193. The petition was to be presented on the 7th Jan., but was delivered on Friday, the 8th Jan., 1641.

[5] On Sunday night the 10th, and Monday the 11th January, 1641. India Office Records.

name only being used; that what was done was His Majesty's act.' [1] The petition, therefore, must not go forward. The Governor feared it was too late: the petition had been delivered to the House on Friday night. 1641

The King astutely replied that it was not too late, as the petition had not yet been read; and that he had in view a very fine thing for the Company, but that 'without him they could never get a penny.' With a spark of the royal spirit which flickered up in his worst distresses, Charles declared that if the petition were pressed he would publicly own that Porter was only a screen for himself. In the end the Governor sent round to the House of Commons, recovered the petition, and begged the Company to believe he had acted for the best, although 'as yet he durst not divulge the reasons thereof.' [2]

Charles was grateful for his escape. His thanks to the Company, and those of his groom of the bedchamber,[3] were the prelude to a real effort to afford it redress. Courten supposed, however, that he still had the King secretly on his side, and insisted on terms which put an end to the negotiations.[4] The Company now gave up further hopes from Charles. In June 1641 it petitioned Parliament, and thenceforward boldly laid its grievances before the Commons.[5]

[1] MS. Court Book, No. 17, p. 193, January 1641.

[2] *Idem*, pp. 193–5.

[3] *Idem*, p. 197.

[4] The proposals and counter-proposals are set out in the MS. Court Book, No. 17, pp. 211–218, February 1641.

[5] MS. Court Book, Nos. 17, 18, 19, 20, 1641 to 1649.

1641 But Parliament regarded the Company as the creation of the royal prerogative, and was by no means ardent on its behalf. It forbad the re-printing of the Amboyna Book against the Dutch,[1] although Courten's 'Red Sea Pyrate' Captain was
1642 at length lodged in prison.[2] To the Commons, indeed, the Company seemed one of the secret sources of money which had helped Charles to do without their constitutional supplies.[3] The Company now threw itself on their mercy, and in 1646
1646 attempted to re-incorporate itself on a Parliamentary basis, under the form of an 'Ordinance for the Trade,' which practically reaffirmed the provisions of its royal Charter. The Commons, after a good deal of money had been spent, agreed, and gave Courten three years to withdraw from India.[4]
1647 But the House of Lords rejected the bill, in spite of the report of their own committee in its favour.[5] The Company was at the end of its resources, and a new joint stock could not be raised. In 1646 the Governor, in despair, advised the shareholders to 'draw home their factors and estate,' yet the Court determined to go on for another year. In

[1] March 1642. MS. Court Book, No. 18, p. 69.

[2] *Idem*, p. 154*a*.

[3] According to popular tradition (Baker's *Chronicle*, p. 440, ed. 1679), the Company 'lent' 80,000*l*. to help Charles to go on without a Parliament in 1627 (Macpherson, *History of the European Commerce with India*, p. 116). I find no mention of this transaction in the Calendars of State Papers, or in Bruce's *Annals*, compiled year by year from the India Office Records; nor does Gardiner refer to it.

[4] MS. Court Book, No. 20, p. 13.

[5] September 4, 1646 to March 19, 1647, MS. Court Book, No. 20, pp. 13, 45, &c.

1648 it resolved to abolish seven of its Indian 1648
factories.[1]

The Company was a loyal body, but Charles wore out its loyalty. The fines and sequestrations afterwards laid on its stubbornly royalist members by Parliament and the Commonwealth fill many documents. Indeed, the sole great act of betrayal perpetrated by a servant of the
Company was committed in the King's cause. 1645
Captain Mucknell treacherously carried his ship into Bristol, then held for His Majesty, and made her over for the support of the war against Parliament at a loss of 20,000*l.* to his masters.[2] It was a useless crime, and only added resentment to the Directors' distrust of the King. Whatever His Majesty might say, the Company had always found that he left something unsaid, and that the royal prerogative, which he professed to exercise on its behalf, was at the secret service of its rivals.

Yet if these records disclose Charles I. in an 1625 to 1649
unheroic light, they also enable us to understand how he salved his own conscience. The Kings of Portugal and of Spain had drawn large profits from the Indian trade, the King of France was about to try to do so, and why should Charles alone among the sovereigns of Europe deny himself? Nor is it by any means clear how far his early connivance with the opposition inside the Company, or with its 'battulated' member, was his own act

[1] MS. Court Book, No. 20, pp. 45, 45*a*, 58, 103*a*.

[2] *Idem*, No. 19, pp. 128*a*, 129, 130, 144, 144*a*. January to May 1645.

1625 to 1649 or that of the creatures about him. To force the Company to sell him its pepper, and then quickly to resell it a loss without paying for it, would be called by an ill name in a modern law-court. But the King had given bonds for the amount, and when they could not be realised, there is a pathos in his momentary earnestness to make restitution, even by the sale of the royal parks.[1] When he violated the Charter by a license to, and his secret partnership in, Courten's Association, he half believed that he secured the Company from damage by the condition that the new adventurers should not trade to its disadvantage. India was surely wide enough for both, and the King fancied that he could partition the Indian markets between the two without loss to either.[2]

To all this there is a plain answer. Charles was not an absolute monarch like the Kings of Spain, or Portugal, or France, and his very twinges of conscience show that he knew it. Even if he had been an absolute sovereign, his father had limited the exercise of the royal prerogative by the Charter granted to the Company. He might have withdrawn that Charter by giving the three years' notice to the Company and firmly facing its oppo-

[1] He desired that the very first money which could be procured should be paid over to the Company. *Calendar of State Papers*, Domestic Series, 1641–1643, p. 67. Bruce's *Annals*, quoting the India Office Papers, trace the ineffectual results. Vol. i. p. 389, &c., 1810.

[2] The King's commission to Courten's Captain, John Weddell, as 'Commander of the fleet, whereof the Dragon is admiral, employed by His Majesty to the Indies.' *Calendar of State Papers*, Domestic Series, 1637–38, p. 306, March 14, 1638.

sition. But to this straightforward course Charles could never make up his mind. Elizabeth, imperious, wayward, yet sensible, had maintained the royal prerogative of monopolies by surrendering its abuses. Under James I., a genuine although foolish person, that prerogative had received a rude shock; under Charles I. it became a discredited legend. His high pretensions and low expedients wearied out the Company, as they had wearied out the nation; and the Company's appeal to Parliament was the commercial counterpart of the nation's appeal to the sword. 1625 to 1649

CHAPTER II

OUR FIRST SETTLEMENTS ON THE BOMBAY COAST

1607–1658

AMID the discomfitures and distresses of the Company at home resolute groups of Englishmen were making their presence felt in India. The sites of their settlements were at first determined by political rather than by commercial considerations. During centuries the natural meeting marts of the Indo-European spice trade had been the ports of Malabar; but the monopoly of those marts was secured to Portugal by her fortress-capital at Goa, and the coast Rajas were on too small a scale to afford protection to newcomers. If our captains
1601 to 1612 of the 'Separate Voyages' were to find a footing in India, it must be under the shelter of a strong native government. The march of the Mughal Empire southwards, at the end of the sixteenth century, gave them their chance. Leaving the direct route from Africa to Malabar, they struck north-east to the Gulf of Cambay, on whose coasts the Mughal Emperor Akbar had lately imposed
1593 his rule.[1]

[1] Akbar the Great, born 1542; reigned 1556–1605, the contemporary of Elizabeth; conquers and reconquers Gujarat and the provinces on the shore of the Gulf of Cambay, 1572–1592;

Surat, the emporium of this ocean inlet and the capital of Gujarat, lies on a bend of the Tapti where the stream sweeps abruptly westward towards the sea. Chief maritime city of India in ancient times,[1] the silt-bearing currents of its river and sand-laden ocean tides had blocked its approach to mediæval shipping, but had formed a roadstead protected by mud-banks at Swally, near the river mouth. Gujarat was cut off from the 1572 to 1592
Mughal base in Northern India by mountains and deserts, and its annexation to the Mughal Empire cost twenty years of war. The work of conquest was rudely interrupted by revolts, which flared up afresh in the early years of the seventeenth 1600 to 1607
century; but the long arm of the Empire at length prevailed, and just as the anarchy ended the English came upon the scene.

In 1607, Captain William Hawkins, of the 1607
third 'Separate Voyage,' landed at Surat with a letter from James I. to the Mughal Emperor,[2] and proceeded to the court at Agra. But the magnificent monarch of India did not take seriously the

finally annexes them to the Mughal Empire in 1593.

[1] Ptolemy *circ.* 150 B.C. speaks of the trade of Pulipula, which has been identified with Phulpada, the old sacred part of Surat town. Surat is, however, the modern representative of the ancient province of Surâshtra which, at one time included not only Gujarat but part of Kathiawar. Before the Gulf of Cambay silted up, some of the chief ports and seats of civilisation were on the Kathiawar side of the bay. General Alexander Cunningham's *Ancient Geography of India*, pp. 316–324, and particularly 324–326. The shallowing of the Gulf of Cambay was one of the great factors in the commercial geography of ancient and mediæval India.

[2] Jahangir, literally 'The Conqueror of the World,' reigned 1605–1627.

1607 proffers of an unknown island-king brought by a ship's captain. Such European influence as then existed at the Mughal capital was entirely Portuguese; and, after four years, Hawkins returned to Surat with a native wife but without any grant for trade.[1] Meanwhile the local Governor of Surat had allowed some of Hawkins' followers to remain there, apparently as a set-off to the Portuguese, who formed an unruly element at the roadstead.
1609 In 1609 a shipwrecked crew of our fourth 'Separate Voyage' also claimed shelter.[2] This the Mughal Governor, whether 'bribed by the Portugals' or merely afraid lest he should have too many of the European Infidels on his hands, discreetly refused. Our poor sailors had to make their way home, part of them *viâ* Lisbon, by the clemency of the Portuguese, who were only too glad to get rid of them.[3]

The accounts which thus reached England from Surat, of its settled government under the *ægis* of the Great Mogul, and of its opportunities for trade, determined the Company to effect a settlement at its port. In 1611 Sir Henry Mid-
1611 dleton, of the sixth 'Separate Voyage,' landed at Swally in spite of the Portuguese, although they

[1] *Letters received by the East India Company*, vol. i. 1602–1613. Anderson's *English in Western India*, p. 12, 1856.

[2] Their story was written by one of the survivors, Captain Robert Coverte, in his *True and almost Incredible Report of an Englishman that (being cast away in the ship called the 'Assention' in Cambaya the farthest part of the East Indies) travelled by land through many unknown kingdoms and great cities.* London, 1612.

[3] Coverte's *True and almost Incredible Report*, pp. 25, 67.

had compelled him to do business by exchanging 1611
cargoes in the roadstead. The Mughal Governor, while still refusing us a factory, allowed some trade.[1] Next year, 1612, Captain Best with the 1612
old 'Red Dragon' and the little 'Hosiander' routed the Portuguese squadron that commanded the approaches to Surat, while the Mughal Governor looked on from the shore. A month's hard fighting destroyed for ever the Indian legend of the Portuguese supremacy over other Europeans.[2] The gallant Captain Best would have been satisfied with his victory, but he had with him a man who was resolved that England should reap its full results. Thomas Aldworth, factor and merchant, improved the momentary congratulations of the Mughal Governor into a grant for our first settlement in India.[3]

'Through the whole Indies,' Aldworth wrote to 1613
the Company, 'there cannot be any place more beneficial for our country than this, being the only key to open all the rich and best trade of the Indies.'[4] With a handful of English merchants in an unfortified house he struggled through the reaction against us which followed the departure of Best's ships, until Downton's sea fight two

[1] *Letters received by the East India Company*, vol. i. 1602–1613. Introduction, xxxiv.

[2] November 29 to December 27, 1612. *Vide ante*, vol. i. 300–304.

[3] 'The greatest cause and means of our settling here was Mr. Aldworth, for our General (Captain Best) would have been gone three or four times and left this place.' *Letters received by the East India Company*, vol. i. 1602–1613, p. 301, and vol. ii. 1613–1615, p. xxi.

[4] *Idem*, vol. i. p 238, January 25, 1613.

1615 years later established for ever our superiority at Surat over the Portuguese.[1]

Downton's feat of arms proved, unexpectedly, to be a great strategic victory. He had cut in half the Portuguese line of communication along the Indian coast. That line was held by Goa as its southern, and by Diu as its northern, base; and between the two by a squadron, which assured to Portugal the traffic of Surat and the Gulf of Cambay. This trade now passed to the English, and it became necessary to secure it by no mere grants of local Mughal governors, but by an instrument from the Imperial Court.[2] In January 1615, while Downton was battering the Portuguese fleet off Surat, James I. issued his commission to Sir Thomas Roe 'to be ambassador to the Great Mogul,' the Company to pay all expenses and to reap any results that might accrue.

Roe reached Surat in September 1615, and proceeded to the Mughal Court, then at Ajmir. Surat was the chief starting place for Mecca, and the Portuguese squadrons had troubled the ocean path of pilgrimage. The Imperial Court, too happy that one infidel fleet should destroy another, granted to Sir Thomas Roe an 'Order' for trade.

[1] January 20 to February 13, 1615. *Vide ante*, vol. i. pp. 321–326.

[2] The Company's records over-estimate the authority of the trade-permits of the local governors or the more doubtful sanctions hitherto obtained under the alleged Imperial authority. Captain Best won such a grant, if ever man did, by his sea-victory over the Portuguese in 1612. Yet in 1614 a servant of the Company, writing from the Imperial Court, declared that 'none here will take notice of it.' *Letters received by the East India Company*, 1613–1615, vol. ii. p. xxi.

These 'Orders' we sometimes called 'grants' or 'licenses,' and sometimes dignified with the name of 'treaties.'[1] The truth is that as our power in India increased they gradually developed from mere permits into grants, then into treaties, and finally into *de jure* confirmations of conquests which we had *de facto* won. The treaty as drafted by Sir Thomas Roe would have allowed the English to found factories at all ports of the Mughal Empire, particularly in Gujarat, in Bengal, and in Sind; and exempted them from inland transit tolls, 1616

[1] Farmána, variously spelt Phirmaund, Firman, &c., in the Company's records. Under the strongly centralised system of the Mughal Empire every authorisation, whether for succession to an office or to an estate, or for the levying of a toll, or for trade, or for industrial enterprises (from the manufacture of salt to the reclamation of waste lands and the cutting down of the jungle), required an order from the Throne or its local representative. The word 'treaty' is misapplied to such grants. From the native point of view they divide themselves into four not strictly demarcated classes. (1) *Parwánas*, permits issued by an executive officer, the governor of a port, or sometimes a mere customs house subordinate. (2) *Nisháns*, literally a 'sign,' in the form of a sealed document, or flag, or other emblem, from the local authority of a district or province. (3) *Farmánas*, issued by the Emperor or his Viceroys or Deputies. A farman was literally an 'Order' conferring title, rank, command, office, or privileges, and was essentially of the nature of an imperial command. It had the wide sense which attaches to our term 'Order,' from a General Order in the Field to an Order in Council or a Local Government Order, or Order by the Board of Trade. (4) *Sanads*, or grants for land, money, inheritance, or high administrative office, under the Imperial seal, and serving as a discharge to the treasury for payments, allowances, or exemptions of revenue. The early servants of the Company in India had to content themselves with the inferior classes of permits, *parwánas*, and *nisháns*; then followed *farmánas*, and finally *sanads*. But during their first century and a half in India, for 'treaty' or 'grant,' it is generally safe to substitute the word 'order.'

on payment of a fixed import duty of 3½ per cent.
1616 on goods and 2 per cent. on treasure. But these proposals, although they figure as 'Roe's Treaty' in Anglo-Indian histories,[1] never passed beyond the draft stage and were rejected by the Imperial Court.[2] Roe obtained, however, a permit for the English to reside at Surat and to travel freely into the interior, together with an order for the redress of the injuries inflicted on them by the local officials.[3] He afterwards received a farman
1618 or grant,[4] in similar although somewhat handsomer terms, from the heir-apparent, then Viceroy of Gujarat, the province of which Surat was the chief port. The prince[5] allowed the English to hire, although not to buy or build, a house for their trade at Surat, and promised the assistance of boats in case they were attacked by the Portuguese. Sir Thomas Roe lingered long enough among the Mughal grandees to find that he was by no means regarded as the Ambassador of an equal sovereign. But his presence at the Imperial Court, and the heir-apparent's viceroyalty of Gujarat, gave prestige to the English at Surat.

[1] Even in Bruce's *Annals*, i. 176–7.

[2] *The Embassy of Sir Thomas Roe*, by William Foster, 1899, vol. i. pp. xli–xliii; 152, 260, &c., where the question is discussed with a complete knowledge of the records.

[3] *Idem*, pp. 159, 162. April 1616.

[4] Sept. 1618. No copy of this farman exists, but Mr. Foster has pieced together its provisions from the India Office MSS.

[5] Prince Mirza Khurram, afterwards the Emperor Shah Jahan, 'fifteenth Viceroy of Gujarat,' 1618–1622. *History of Gujarat*, p. 276. Govt. Press: Bombay, 1896.

Meanwhile Captain Keeling, the 'General' of the squadron which had brought out Roe, resolved to carry the war against the Portuguese into Southern India. Keeling was a sailor of taste with a wide outlook into the possibilities of his times. On a previous voyage, while detained at Sierra Leone, he and his crew had played 'Hamlet' and 'Richard II.' by way of private theatricals.[1] He believed in India as a career, and wanted to carry his wife with him—but gave up his request on compensation of 200*l*. from the Company.[2] He now, in 1616, sailed boldly to Malabar, and tried to turn the flank of the southern Portuguese base at Goa, by a treaty with Calicut further down the coast. The allies were to drive out the Portuguese from Cochin, which was then to be made over to the English.[3]

This project failed, but a halcyon period opened to the English at Surat. The crop-fields of Gujarat, with their miracle of two harvests a year, seemed a paradise to our storm-tossed mariners, as they rowed up the smooth channels of the Tapti. 'Often of two adjoining fields,' they wrote, 'one was as green as a fine meadow, and the other waving yellow like gold and ready to be cut down.'[4] They might regret that spices did not grow so far

[1] September 1607.

[2] *Calendar of State Papers*, East Indies, 1513–1616, No. 827. Court Minutes, December 10, 1614.

[3] Captain Keeling's Treaty with the Zamorin of Calicut, dated 10th March, 1616.

[4] Letter of Mr. Copland, dated 24th December, 1613. *Gazetteer of Bombay Presidency*, vol. i. part i. p. 224, Bombay Government Press, 1896.

north, but they found substitutes in the fine cotton fabrics and dyes of upper India. Small English agencies, thrown out into the interior,[1] collected the muslins of the neighbouring provinces, and the indigo of Agra, for shipment at Surat.

The titular viceroyalty of the heir-apparent to the Empire, left the real administration of Gujarat in the hands of the Governor who had seen us shatter the Portuguese fleet. Indeed the Emperor Jahangir complains in his 'Memoirs' that this too liberal official bought from the Europeans a turkey and other curiosities quite regardless of the price.[2] An annalist makes the transaction take place at Gogo, in whose safe anchorage on the opposite side of the Cambay Gulf, our ships, when driven from the Swally roadstead, could always find shelter.[3] The only drawbacks to the Company's success at Surat were the 'voluntaries,' or private traders from England, who began to creep in, and who, when their speculations failed, became a burden on

[1] In Gujarat, Ahmadabad, Kathiawar, especially the Kathiawar coast of the Gulf of Cambay, and Sind.

[2] The turkey seems to have been introduced into India by the Portuguese. Its present Hindustani name, *piru*, is identical with the Portuguese perû, derived from Peruana (Peru) in its old wider sense. Peruana and Guyana were used to denote Spanish America at least as late as the almanacs of Charles II.'s reign; and the turkey, probably brought by Cortez to Spain, was for long called the Guinea fowl. In Hindustani it preserves the other old name of Spanish-America, Peruana. Bluteau, in his *Vocabulario Portuguez e Latino*, 1720, gives no certain sound.

[3] Elliot, *History of India as told by its own historians*, vi. 331, footnote. But the *Tuzák-i-Jahángiri* (p. 105, Aligarh ed. 1864) clearly says Goa not Gogo.

the factory, or turned Muhammadans 'to keep them from starving.'[1]

More formidable rivals soon came upon the 1616
scene. In 1616 a Dutch ship under Van den Broeck appeared in the roadstead, but was not allowed to establish a factory. Next year two Dutch ships got wrecked off the coast, and ten of the survivors remained at Surat. In 1618 they 1618
received a license from the Mughal government, notwithstanding the efforts of Sir Thomas Roe to 'turn them out,' and in 1620 Van den Broeck 1620
returned to Surat as Director of Dutch trade.[2] But the Dutch, accustomed to barbarian island chiefs, did not realise that they had come under an Empire which insisted on good behaviour, and could crush the petty infidel settlements by a stroke of the pen. Even the English, backed by the Imperial order for trade, had to rest satisfied with the protection assured to all residents within the Mughal Empire, and were not allowed to fortify their house at Surat.[3] The Dutch attacks on native vessels now involved us in the common disgrace of the European name, and while the Dutch were slaughtering us at Amboyna, in 1623, 1623
the English at Surat were held responsible by the Mughal Governor for the piracy of their most bitter enemies.[4] He seized upon our warehouses,

[1] Letters from Surat and Ajmir to the Company, 31st December, 1616, to 4th March, 1617 : Bruce's *Annals*, i. 183.

[2] *Surat and Broach Districts*, p. 79, Bombay Government Press, 1877 ; Anderson's *English in Western India*, pp. 16, 37, 38. 1856.

[3] Bruce's *Annals*, *sub anno* 1617–18, vol. i. p. 196.

[4] *Idem*, vol. i. pp. 236, 243.

1623–4 threw our President and factors into irons, and let them hold their consultations 'in prison'[1] for seven months, amid the revilings of 'whole rabbles of people.'[2]

The Mughal Government, however, soon learned to discriminate. It ceased, at any rate, to confound the peaceable English traders, who paid their customs punctually and abhorred images, with the Portuguese, who prostrated themselves like Hindus before a tinsel goddess, and plundered the True Believers on the holy voyage to Mecca. In 1622 our factory at Surat had organised the fleet which destroyed the Portuguese power in the Persian Gulf,[3] and so outflanked the northern base of the Portuguese at Diu, which had controlled the entrance to the Gulf of Cambay. The English, having thus freed the approaches at Surat from the menace of the Portuguese, came to be regarded by the Mughal Viceroy as a useful sea-police.

But the Portuguese, although beaten out of the Gulf of Cambay and the Persian Gulf, still harassed the route to the Red Sea. Surat was the main exit of the Empire to Mecca, and the Mughal Government hit upon the device of employing one nation of the Infidels against another to keep open
1629 the pilgrim ocean highway. In 1629 it granted letters of marque to our President at Surat to make reprisals on all Portuguese ships, whether at sea

[1] *e.g. Calendar of State Papers*, East Indies, 1622–1624, No. 438.

[2] *Idem*, 1625–1629, No. 56.

[3] *Persian and Persian Gulf Records*, 1620–1697. India Office Report, pp. 17–19, 76. For our capture of Ormuz, in 1622, *vide ante*, vol. i. pp. 310, 328–330.

or in harbour.[1] Next year a Surat Governor again 1630
witnessed a repulse of the Portuguese from his river, 'our English' driving the landing parties pell mell into the sea, and 'not fearing to run up to the chin in water, even to the frigates' sides.' We rescued the Viceroy's son in the sight of the whole people, 'to their great admiration and our nation's great honour.'[2] In the following winter, December 1630, the treaty of Madrid declared that thenceforth the English and Portuguese should dwell at peace in the Indies, and enjoy a free commerce open to both—a consummation not to be attained by parchment alliances.[3]

The English at Surat thus early won for themselves a recognised position as trustworthy payers of revenue and as a maritime patrol for the Mughal Empire. On shore the Empire was, within its limits, all powerful, but at sea it depended on mercenary fleets. As it held in check the pirate nests along the western shores of India by subsidising the Abyssinian chiefs who had settled on that coast, so it looked to the English at Surat to keep open the ocean path of pilgrimages to the holy cities of the Red Sea. The Mughal

[1] Farman or 'order,' of the 5th April, 1629.

[2] *Calendar of State Papers*, East Indies, 1630–1634, No. 87, October 17, 1630.

[3] 'Abstinebunt in futurum ab omni præda, captione, offensione et spolio,' with 'liberum commercium' for the two nations. Treaty between Charles I. and Philip IV., Nov. 15, 1630. When, however, the Governor of the E. I. C. attended on Lord Dorchester to learn its precise force, the league was explained to mean little more than the articles of 1604—*i.e.* sea-fighting beyond the Cape at the Company's own risk. *Calendar of State Papers*, East Indies, 1630–1634, No. 134.

1630 supremacy was essentially of land origin. It had started from Central Asia, spread from the mountain passes across the Punjab, forced its way through the Aravalli deserts to Gujarat, and followed the courses of two mighty rivers, the Indus and the Ganges, to the opposite shores of India. From the vast hinterland of Hindustan the Mughal Emperors were constrained to find an outlet to the ocean. But the great distance of their capitals in North-Western India from the coast rendered it impossible, when they had found an outlet, to exercise an effective sea-control.

On the east, Portuguese buccaneers and Arakanese pirates swept the Bay of Bengal, and the Mughal Viceroy had, by a special tax, to maintain an armed flotilla to keep open the mouths of the Ganges. On the west, the royal galleons and frigates of Portugal blocked the approaches to the Indus and the Gulf of Cambay. What the river fleet of the Bengal Viceroy did for the Gangetic delta, the Indian Emperors resolved that the English at Surat should do for the Arabian Ocean. Our squadrons formed, in fact, the naval complement to the land-conquest of Gujarat by the Mughal Empire. The anarchy which had ended just as we arrived gave place to a period of prosperity unexampled in the history of the province. Caravans came and went to all the inland capitals of India—Golconda, Agra, Delhi, Lahore; the products of Asia, from the Straits of Malacca to the Persian Gulf, were piled up on the wharves of the Tapti. Merchants flocked in such

numbers to Surat that during the busy winter 1630
months lodgings could scarcely be had.[1] A succession of able men directed the English factory; and soon after 1616 a Surat chaplain[2] commenced those liberal researches into the native customs and religions, which are among the most honourable memorials of our Indian rule, and which have done much to mould that rule to the needs of the people.

The Company saw the position which its little band of servants had won on the Gulf of Cambay, and recognised the President at Surat as the chief of the English in India. After Amboyna the hopes of reviving the trade in the Spice Archipelago flickered out, and in 1630 even Bantam, its headquarters in Java, was declared subordinate to
Surat.[3] In the same year a calamity fell upon 1630
Gujarat which enables us to realise the terrible meaning of the word famine in India under native rule. Whole districts and cities were left bare of inhabitants.

In 1631 a Dutch merchant reported that only 1631
eleven of the 260 families at Swally survived. He found the road thence to Surat covered with bodies decaying 'on the highway where they died,

[1] *Imperial Gazetteer of India*, vol. xiii. pp. 121–2, 1887.

[2] Henry Lord, in 1616, 'left one of the English ships for a charge of souls on shore,' and after fourteen years published *A Display of two Forraigne Sects, the sect of the Bannians, the ancient natives of India, and the sect of the Parsees, the ancient inhabitants of Persia, together with the religion and manners of each Sect.* London, 1630. 4to. Sir Thomas Roe also made a considerable collection of oriental MSS. on his travels.

[3] Bruce's *Annals*, i. 304.

1631 [there] being no one to bury them.'[1] In Surat, that great and crowded city, he 'could hardly see any living persons;' but the corpses 'at the corner of the streets lie twenty together, nobody burying them.' Thirty thousand had perished in the town alone. Pestilence followed famine. The President and ten or eleven of the English factors fell victims, with 'divers inferiors now taken into Abraham's bosom'[2]—three-fourths of the whole settlement. 'No man can go in the streets without giving great alms or being in danger of being murdered, for the poor people cry aloud, "Give us sustenance, or kill us."'[3] 'This, that was in a manner the garden of the world, is turned into a wilderness.'[4]

The Dutchman estimated that it would take three years before the trade could revive at Surat. Indeed, one striking contrast between native and British rule was the slowness of recovery from famine in the Mughal Empire. But the English at Surat clung to the wreck of their settlement, and their new jurisdiction over our other factories in India placed at their command the whole of the Company's ships in the Indian seas. A strong naval force thus came under the centralised control of Surat. The Company had from twenty to twenty-five vessels employed in the East Indies, chiefly in port to port trade.[5] In 1629, it declared

[1] *Calendar of State Papers*, East Indies, 1630–1634, No. 242.

[2] *Idem*, No. 257, January 23, 1632.

[3] *Idem*, No. 242.

[4] *Idem*, No. 241.

[5] Twenty-two in 1623. *Calendar of State Papers*, East Indies, 1622–1624. Introduction, lix.; 23 in 1628, including those going out and

that during the past twelve years it had 'sent out fifty-seven ships containing 26,690 tons, besides eighteen pinnaces, to be worn out by trading from port to port in The Indies.' [1] 1617 to 1629

To this scattered fleet, strongly armed and always eager to fight, the Surat factory added a local flotilla of stout sea-going craft, carrying two to six guns apiece, and charged with the defence of the Tapti estuary and Gulf of Cambay. Ten of these Surat 'grabs and gallivats' are said to have existed in 1615, during Captain Downton's six weeks' battle with the Portuguese, and from that year the permanent establishment of our Indian navy has been reckoned.[2] In 1622, four of them accompanied the squadron which drove the Portuguese from Ormuz and the Persian Gulf.[3] These Surat cruisers were greatly superior to the Portuguese 'frigates.' [4] Yet the Portuguese 'frigates' sufficed to make it unsafe for Dutch ships to lie in at the Malabar roadsteads.[5] The broad lateen sails, light draught, and hardy rowers of the Surat 'grabs' enabled them to outmanœuvre both the Dutch and the Lisbon galleons along the shore. When combined with the heavily armed English ships engaged in the port to port trade, they made up a formidable force.

coming home. *Idem*, 1625–1629, No. 726.

[1] *Idem*, 1625–1629, No. 786.

[2] According to Low's *History of the Indian Navy*, vol. i. pp. 16, 24.

[3] *Idem*, pp. 37, 38.

[4] These Indo-Portuguese 'frigates' mark an intermediate stage between the original Spanish *fragata*, or row-boat, and the final development of the frigate into a war-ship of 50 to 60 guns.

[5] Dutch MS. Records, Report and Balance Sheet of the Trade at Surat, June 20, 1634, *vide ante*, vol. i. pp. 320–1.

1630 The Viceroy at Goa now found his whole line of communication on the west coast of India dominated by our Surat factory. The English at Surat, on their side, felt the necessity for a direct trade with the pepper districts and spice ports of Malabar, which also remained the Indian marts of exchange for the more precious cloves and nutmegs of the Eastern Archipelago. European diplomacy had failed to secure peace between the
1634 Christian nations in Asia. So in 1634, the Viceroy of Goa and the English President at Surat took the matter into their own hands and entered into direct negotiations. They signed a formal
1635 truce, which in 1635 they developed into a commercial convention on the basis of the ineffective Madrid treaty of 1630. Two English ships were annually to obtain a cargo at Goa, two more might load at other Portuguese factories. The long promised *liberum commercium* between the English and Portuguese in India became an accomplished fact.[1]

It was this talent of isolated groups of Englishmen for making their power felt in distant regions, that carried the Company through the dark days of Charles I. They turned their factory at Surat into a sea-defence of the Mughal Empire, convoyed noble and imperial devotees to the Persian Gulf on their way to Mecca, and guarded

[1] The India Office Records (quoted by Bruce, i. 334, footnote) indicate January 1635-6 as the date of this Surat-Goa convention. But Clause xii. of the Anglo-Portuguese treaty of 1642 expressly gives the date as 'le 20 Janvier, 1635, nouveau stile.'—Dumont's *Corps Universel Diplomatique*, vol. vi. part i. p. 240.

the pilgrim route. Their Dutch rivals, although much stronger in men and ships in Asiatic waters, found themselves on the Gujarat coast in the grip of the Mughal power. Nor did the Hollanders, secure of the Spice Archipelago, care so much to come to terms with the Indian Portuguese.

But while our Surat factors thus secured a strong position and earned large profits for their masters, they also, in spite of their masters, did a lucrative trade on their own account. The Company viewed with mixed emotions the rising power of its servants in the East. It had seen its President
at Surat commission a squadron to wage open war 1628
on the Portuguese.[1] But for a local factory to make a treaty on its own account with an independent European Power was a dangerous audacity. Yet, in spite of the home Directors'
alarm [2] and half-heartedness, this convention of 1636
the Goa Viceroy with the President at Surat became the basis of the settlement of the Indies.

Even Holland began to realise that, notwithstanding her Spice Island supremacy, the English understood the greater game of Indian politics better than her own servants in the East. The Dutch factors at Surat contrasted their insignificance with the strong position which the English, by the favour of the Mughal Sovereign, enjoyed.[3]

[1] Bruce's *Annals*, p. 294, vol. i. Commission dated 12th Dec., 1628. *Calendar of State Papers*, East Indies, 1625–1629, No. 763.

[2] Letter of the East India Company to the Secretary of State, and from the Governor to Lord Aston, 3rd March, 1636, Bruce's *Annals*, p. 336, vol. i.

[3] MS. Dutch Records; Letter from Surat to the Directors at Amsterdam, August 30, 1631, &c.

1634 'We have no real power in these countries,' they lament, 'while the (Mughal) Governors can always revenge any real or pretended affront, by laying an embargo on the Company's property.'[1] The truth is that the Dutch Governors-General at Batavia, domineering over their petty island chiefs, had the very worst training for the direction of distant factories under the irresistible Mughal Emperors. 'The English get daily a firmer footing in India,'
1634 'we should act in concert with the English,' 'a good understanding with the English is the best guarantee of our commerce in India'—the Dutch factors at Surat reiterated in vain.[2]

From their height of prosperity the handful of
1636 English at Surat were suddenly cast down. In 1636, arrived Captain Weddell of Courten's Association, with a letter from King Charles to our President, intimating that under His Majesty's authority six ships 'had been sent on a voyage of discovery to the South Seas,' and that 'the King himself had a particular interest' in the expedition.[3] Presently came news that two of these ships 'to the South Seas' had turned pirates in the Red Sea, and plundered an Indian vessel. The Mughal Governor at once seized our factory at Surat, threw the President and Council into prison for two months, and only released them on payment of 18,000*l.*,[4] and on their solemn oath (in spite of

[1] MS. Dutch Records; Letter from Surat to the Governor-General at Batavia, April 30, 1634.

[2] MS. Dutch Records; Report and Balance Sheet of the Trade at Surat, 20 June, 1634, &c.

[3] Bruce's *Annals*, i. 340.

[4] Rs. 170,000.

their protestations of innocence), never again to 1636
molest a Mughal ship.

As in 1623 the Mughal Government had held the Company's servants responsible for the piracy of their public enemies the Dutch,[1] so in 1636 it punished them for the piracy of Courten's interlopers. 'Wee must beare the burthen,' says a sorrowful despatch, 'and with patience sitt still, until we may find these frowning tymes more auspicious to us and to our affayres.'[2]

A still heavier blow was about to fall on the poor prisoners at Surat. While the piracies of Courten's Association brought them into disgrace with the Mughal Government, the ablest Captain of the interlopers, Weddell, resolved to snatch the fruits of the Surat President's convention with the Portuguese Viceroy. He sailed to Goa, and, on the
strength of a letter from King Charles, got leave to 1637-8
hire a house and to land his goods.[3] After forcing himself, by the same authority, on the Company's struggling factories from the Bay of Bengal to near the Straits of Malacca, he fixed his headquarters at Rajapur on the Bombay coast. The site was well

[1] *Ante*, p. 55.

[2] Chaplain Anderson, relying on the Surat Records, quotes these words as coming from the factors. *The English in Western India*, p. 90. Bruce ascribes them to instructions from the Directors, without specifying his authority. *Annals*, i. 349. The General Instructions of the Court, however, sometimes recapitulated the contents of 'letters home.' The draft of this letter from the Court may now be read in Letter Book, i. pp. 162–3, India Office MSS. It refers primarily to Cobb's piracies (another of Courten's captains), but immediately adds: 'The like wee saie of Captain Weddell and his Companie.'

[3] Bruce's *Annals*, *sub anno* 1637–1638, p. 352, vol. i.

1638 to 1640 chosen. It lay up a long tidal creek, in the independent Kingdom of Bijapur,[1] about half way between Goa and the modern city of Bombay. It thus cut in two the Company's line of communication between Surat and Goa, as the Company's settlement at Surat had cut in two the Portuguese line of communication between Goa and Diu. The Mughal Empire had not then advanced so far down the coast, and Rajapur[2] formed a chief inlet of the Arabian commerce for the yet unconquered kingdoms of the South. In vain the Company's servants at Surat protested, and tried to found a rival station in the South. Captain Weddell secured by lavish gifts the support of the King of Bijapur, and began to plant factories along the coast.[3] The sagacity of his selection is proved by the part which these factories played in the subsequent annals of the Company.

From home the Surat factory could get no succour, nor any certain sound from their distracted masters, then in their desperate struggle with the Court cabal. We have seen that fifty-seven ships besides eighteen pinnaces had been sent out for port-to-port trade alone, during the twelve years ending 1629. The Company's Records, which during the same period abound in journals of voyages to and from India, only preserve eight

[1] *Vide ante*, vol. i. pp. 152–153. Bijapur was not finally annexed to the Mughal Empire till 1686.

[2] In the present district Ratnagiri, and 30 miles S.E. of Ratnagiri town, lat. 16° 39′ 10″ N., long. 73° 33′ 20″ E.

[3] Particularly at Carwar and Baticala. For Baticala, which has dropped out of modern maps, *vide ante*, vol. i. p. 109, footnote.

such documents for the thirteen disastrous years 1640 to 1649
from King Charles' grant to Courten's Association in 1635 to His Majesty's death in 1649.[1] But the Surat factors, thus left to ruin, asserted their vitality in a wholly unexpected manner. They practically kept up the trade on their own account, continued to patrol the pilgrim highway, and maintained an attitude at once so reasonable and so resolute, that the Mughal Government repented of having punished them for the piracy of their rivals.

As the Emperor used the English to check the piracy of the Portuguese, so he employed them to bring it to an end. The Portuguese had continued to plunder Mughal ships, subject to such reprisals as the English could inflict on them. But the English President at Surat had now made a treaty on his own account with the Goa Viceroy: Why should he not also include in it the Indian
Government? In 1639, the Surat Council found 1639
themselves raised into negotiators between the Mughal Governor and the Portuguese.[2] The degenerate successors of Albuquerque and the half-breed corsairs of Goa transferred for a time their piracies from the Mecca route to the Bay of Bengal, and the cold shadows which had fallen on the Surat factory were again warmed into prosperity under the sunshine of the Mughal Court.[3] However low the fortunes of the Company sank under King or

[1] List of Marine Records, India Office, Folio, p. 4—evidently incomplete, however, for these years.

[2] Bruce's *Annals*, i. 358.

[3] Summarised from the India Office Records and Bruce's *Annals*, 1638–1640, vol. i. 358, &c.

Commonwealth in England, the Surat factory grew
1657 with a strength of its own. In 1657 the Company decided that there should be but one Presidency in India—and that Surat.[1]

I have narrated at some length the rise of the Surat factory for several reasons. It formed the first headquarters of the English in India—a centre of English control in the East which had a vitality in itself apart from the Company in London, and which won by its Persian Gulf victory our first revenue grant—the Customs of Gombroon[2]—and profoundly influenced our later settlements on the Indian continent. It also illustrates the position which the English quickly secured in the economy of the Mughal Empire: as a sure source of revenue, a sea-police for the coast, and the patrol of the ocean path to Mecca, gradually developing into negotiators on behalf of the native Government. Surat forms the type of an early English settlement under the strong hand of the Mughal Emperors.

[1] MS. Court Book, No. 24, p. 18. December 1657.

[2] *Vide ante*, vol. i. 330.

CHAPTER III

OUR FIRST SETTLEMENTS ON THE MADRAS COAST

1611–1658

THE problem which lay before the English on the East coast of India was a more complex one. The Mughal Empire had not yet reached those distant shores. Instead of the firm order which it imposed on its provinces, the conflict of dynasties and races still raged. The inland Moslem Kings of Golconda advanced their boundaries to the Madras coast after the destruction of the Hindu Suzerainty of Vijayanagar at the battle of Talikot in 1565. But the remnants of that ancient Hindu dynasty had sought refuge, and again gathered strength, in its eastern maritime provinces. There, backed by the shore-Rajas, its feudatories in more prosperous times, the descendants of the Hindu over-lords still disputed with the Golconda Moslems the hill tracts, the river deltas, and tidal lagoons.

The Madras coast looked out towards the Eastern Archipelago as the Bombay coast looked out towards Africa and the Cape. The Portuguese, advancing eastwards from their African base, formed their first and most lasting settlements on the Bombay side; the Dutch, reverting westwards from their Spice Island dominions, established themselves chiefly on the Bay of Bengal. In 1609 they obtained a settlement at Pulicat, a long, low isle with the surf breaking on its outer shores, and a sheltered lagoon stretching inwards to the mainland, about twenty-three miles north of Madras city.[1] Its great backwater, or 'Pulicat Lake,' formed by the sea bursting through the sand dunes of the coast in some ancient cyclonic storm, afforded a haven for the shipping of those days.

1609

1611 In 1611 Captain Hippon and Peter Floris in 'The Globe' of our seventh Separate Voyage[2] essayed a landing at Pulicat. Floris was a Hollander who had learned the secrets of the Indian trade while in the Dutch service. Captain Hippon, with the knowledge thus obtained, resolved to strike into the port-to-port trade, which bartered the calicoes of the Madras coast for the spices of the Eastern Archipelago. Not unnaturally, the Dutch, who had meanwhile built a fort at Pulicat, 'did beare a hard hand against them.' The Queen of the place refused even to see our Captain, saying that a grant had already been given to the Hollanders.[3] But Hippon although cast down was not dismayed. He sailed further up the coast, and landed at Pettapoli, at the mouth of a southern channel of

[1] Pulicat, lat. 13° 25′ 8″ N. and long. 80° 21′ 24″ E., now part of Chengalpat District, and has a population of about 5,000. Its lagoon was afterwards connected with Madras town by a canal. *Imperial Gazetteer of India*, vol. xi. p. 239. Ed. 1886.

[2] *Vide ante*, vol. i. pp. 291, 297.

[3] *Calendar of State Papers*, East Indies, 1513–1616. No. 578; *Letters Received by the East India Company*, 1602–1613, vol. i. pp. 133–136.

the Kistna delta: more exposed to the monsoon 1611
than Pulicat, yet sufficiently sheltered for a ship to ride out a storm.[1] There he arrived on August 18, 1611, was well received by the local Governor, and left two supercargoes to found our first shore settlement on the Bay of Bengal.[2] Of its fortunes presently.

In 1614 another captain of the English Com- 1614
pany cast longing eyes on Pulicat. The Dutch 'Rector of all the factories upon that coast' and his lieutenant, who was 'English-born,' feasted the visitors in their 'castle,' but firmly refused to let
them trade.[3] The Anglo-Dutch treaty of 1619 1619
at length gave us this right, and at the same time compelled us to pay half the charges of the garrison. A band of English factors accordingly
landed at Pulicat in 1620, and for a year their trade 1620
went 'roundly forward.'[4] But the Dutch opposition,[5] which was to culminate in the tragedy of Amboyna, soon rendered our position untenable at Pulicat,. and in 1623, shortly after that tragedy,

[1] *Manual of the Kistna District*, pp. 39, 130, compiled for the Government. Madras 1883.

[2] Captain Hippon landed his goods apparently on the 26th August. Pettapoli, from the Telugu, *pedda*, great, and *palli*, village, is the modern Nizampatam in Kistna District, lat. 15° 54′ 30″ N., long. 80° 42′ 35″ E., with a population of between 4,000 and 5,000. *Imperial Gazetteer of India*, vol. x. p. 338. Ed. 1886. See also the India Office *List of Factory Records*, p. xxiii., folio 1897.

[3] Voyage of John Gourney and Thos. Brockedon in the 'James.' Letter of 28 July, 1614; *Calendar of State Papers*, East Indies, 1513–1616, No. 756; *Letters Received by the East India Company*, vol. ii. pp. 80–87.

[4] *Calendar of State Papers*, East Indies, 1617–1621. Nos. 884, 1129.

[5] Dutch MS. records in India Office, 1620–23.

1623 we had to quit the lagoon-haven for a refuge further north.[1] Later English projects to re-occupy Pulicat[2] came to nothing, and our first attempt at a settlement on the Madras coast ended in failure and a heavy loss.

The mud-creeks of Pettapoli, where Captain
1611 Hippon had found shelter in 1611, promised, under the protection of the powerful Golconda Kings, a
1614 better fortune. In 1614 Peter Floris built a half-fortified factory at Pettapoli with a lofty flagstaff. But its mangrove-swamps were deadly, the trade
1621 was small, and the factory was dissolved in 1621; a solitary merchant being left to collect country cloths from the fever-stricken delta of the Kistna.
1633 In 1633 the English again settled at Pettapoli, and the factory lingered on to 1687, when it was finally broken up by orders from home. What the Dutch were to us at Pulicat the pestilence proved to us at Pettapoli. A local writer in 1687 describes the whole region as depopulated and the trade 'wholly ruined,' 'there being scarce people left to sow and reap their little harvest.'[3]

Thus perished our first two settlements on the Madras coast. But Captain Hippon, although he sought shelter at Pettapoli in 1611, seems to have suspected its unhealthiness, and after a halt sailed

[1] *Calendar of State Papers*, 1622–1624, Nos. 43, 54, 85, 110, 264, 352, 368, &c.

[2] *Idem*, 1625–1629, No. 716, and 1630–1634, No. 91.

[3] Records of Fort St. George, 5th October, 1687. For its miserable plight at an earlier period, see the Memorial of Streynsham Master, 19th March, 1679; reprinted in the Government *Manual of the Kistna District*, p. 130. Madras, 1883. Cf. for the dates the India Office *List of Factory Records*, pp. xxiii. and 50, folio 1897.

a few days northward, to Masulipatam.[1] This 1611
ancient port lay north of the great projection of fen-lands and mud-banks formed by the mouths of the Kistna (as Pettapoli lay to the south) and was to that extent better protected from the Monsoon. Around it stretched a dreary expanse of sand, flooded into swamps during the months of the rains. To seawards, silt-bars and sand deposits make it unsafe for large modern ships to anchor within five miles of the shore, and from October to December the monsoon often renders it unapproachable. Yet it formed a coveted roadstead on the open coast-line of Madras, and became the scene of bitter rivalries—English, Dutch, and French. Its earliest surviving tombstone commemorates the 'Chief by Water and by Land of the Dutch India Company on the Coromandel Coast. Died August 29, 1624.'[2] 1624
A later but more romantic memorial of the English settlers long shaded their dusty evening drive, and was known as 'Eliza's Tree;' after Sterne's 'Eliza,'[3] who here solaced an uncongenial Indian marriage by a sentimental correspondence with the author of 'Tristram Shandy.'

On August 31, 1611, Captain Hippon, and his

[1] Factory Records of the late East India Company, India Office, folio 1897, p. xxi. The name Masuli-patanam = Machli-patanam, 'Fish-town;' and its harbour is still known as Machli-bandar, 'Fish Port.' *Imperial Gazetteer of India*, p. 352, vol. ix. 1886. Cf. Sir George Birdwood's *Report on the Old Records of the India Office*, p. 88, 1891.

[2] Government *Manual of the Kistna District*, p. 100. Madras, 1883. (The Jacob Dedel of *ante*, vol. i. p. 379, footnote 2.)

[3] More strictly 'Elizabeth' Sclater or Mrs. Draper. The tree was washed away by the cyclone wave of 1864. *Kistna District Manual*, p. 128, footnote.

1611 Dutch lieutenant Peter Floris, cast anchor at Masulipatam, loaded up 'The Globe' with the local calicoes, and sailed eastwards to exchange them for spices at Bantam and the rich products of Siam.[1] They left behind a few Englishmen to collect more 'white cloths' pending their return. From that date an English trade went on; at first between Masulipatam and Sumatra or Java, but gradually throwing out offshoots along the Bay of Bengal, and eventually doing business with Surat and direct with England. Masulipatam was the chief seaport of the Moslem Kings of Golconda, who were not subdued by the Mughal Empire until 1687.[2] It formed the outlet for the Golconda diamonds and rubies, for the marvels of textile industry which had developed under the fostering care of that luxurious inland Court, and for the commoner 'white cloths' woven on the coast. The profits from their barter for the gold, camphor, benzoine ('benjamin') and spices of the Eastern Archipelago and Siam were immense. In 1627 our Council at Batavia recommended their Honorable Masters in London to send out each year 67,500*l.* in specie to Masulipatam to be invested in country cloths, which would be exchanged in Batavia for spices at a profit of 135,000*l.*[3]

In Masulipatam the English found a half-way mart between the West and the Far East, scarcely

[1] Government *Manual of the Kistna District*, p. 88. Also *Calendar of State Papers*, East Indies, 1513–1616, Nos. 578, 596.

[2] *Imperial Gazetteer of India*, p. 143, vol. v. 1885.

[3] 300,000 and 600,000 reals of eight respectively at 4*s.* 6*d.* per real. Bruce's *Annals*, p. 279, vol. i. 1810.

less lucrative than the Portuguese seats of the Indo-European trade on the Malabar coast. We thus turned the eastern flank of the Portuguese in Southern India, as our Surat factory had turned the western flank of the Portuguese in Northern India and the Persian Gulf. But from the first, or almost from the first, our captains had to struggle with the Dutch for Masulipatam. The inland Court of Golconda,[1] however, knew the advantages of keeping the port open to all comers, and here as at Surat the English seem to have understood the greater game of Indian politics better than their Dutch rivals accustomed to trample upon island chiefs.
In 1613 the English obtained a grant for a fortified factory, 'written on a leaf of gold,'[2] from the Hindu authorities in the interior—although not yet from the Golconda Kings; while the Dutch made 1613

[1] Golconda is now a ruined village and fortress seven miles west of Haidarabad, the capital of the Nizam. Lat. 17° 22′ N., long. 78° 26′ 30″. Originally a stronghold of the Hindu Raja of Warangal, it passed to the Musalman Bahmani dynasty in 1364, and in 1512 gave its name to one of the five Musalman Kingdoms of the South which arose on the breaking up of that dynasty. The independent Golconda kingdom, thus founded under the Kutab Shahi line in 1512, increased its dominions by the downfall of the great Hindu suzerainty of Vijayanagar on the field of Talikot in 1565, and reached the height of its splendour about 1611. But it had long to struggle with the remnants of the Hindu dynasty of Vijayanagar and with their feudal chiefs for the distant districts on the Madras coast. This struggle was going on when we made our first settlements, and did not end till about 1644. In 1687 the kingdom of Golconda was itself conquered by Aurangzeb and annexed to the Mughal Empire. *Imperial Gazetteer of India*, vol. v. pp. 143, 144, &c. 1885.

[2] Government *Manual of the Kistna District*, pp. 88, 89. Madras 1883. Captain Hippon had received a 'cowle' or license to trade from the native port-officer or 'governor' at Masulipatam in 1611.

1614 the local Governor their friend. Next year the English felt strong enough to give a severe lesson to this petty magnate; who seems to have been unpopular in his own city. As he refused to pay a sum of money due to them, they seized his son and, in their own words, 'carried him aboard our ship prisoner in spite of one thousand of his people, to the Company's benefit, the honour of our King and country, and to the great content of all the Moors.'[1] Soon afterwards the local Governor was dismissed and heavily fined, while the English obtained leave to trade at Masulipatam as freely as the Dutch or any other nation.[2] 'No factory
1619 in India,' says a report in 1619, 'hath been so fortunate and thrifty.'[3]

But the control of Golconda over its distant provinces was very different from the firm grasp of the Mughal Empire. We must bear in mind that the old Hindu rulers, whom the Golconda Kingdom displaced, still exercised an authority on the coast; and it was from them and not from the Golconda Court that we received our first grants at Masulipatam.[4] The confusion was scarcely less wild than

[1] November 24th, 1614. *Letters Received by the East India Company*, vol. ii. 1613-1615, pp. 292-295. Cf. *Calendar of State Papers*, East Indies, 1513-1616, Nos. 877, 1004.

[2] Letter of Wm. Nicolls to the Company, dated 15 January, 1616, *State Papers, ut supra*, No. 1084.

[3] *State Papers, ut supra*, 1617-1621, No. 782.

[4] *e.g.* From the King of Narasingha or 'Viseapore' (*i.e.* the Raja of Vijayanagar), the 'Queen of Paleakate,' Jaga Raja, Tima Raja, &c., Government *Manual of the Kistna District*, p. 89, &c., Madras 1883. The ancient Hindu dynasty of Vijayanagar, although shattered by the battle of Talikot in 1565, resettled in one of its outlying coast-provinces in 1594, and exercised an authority over its Hindu feudatories and the petty

the scramble of rival native claimants on the same coast, into which the English and the French plunged a century later. The retreat of a rebel son of the Mughal Emperor through the district[1]
in 1624 added to the disorder. The Dutch again 1624
won over the local Governor, who made our position 'insufferable.' Unable to resist or revenge his 'foul injuries,' our factors resolved in despair to abandon Masulipatam. They declared they would never return except under a grant from the King
of Golconda direct.[2] On September 27, 1628, they 1628
stole out of their factory, leaving all behind, and secretly set off in a small boat for Armagaon.[3]

Their hard experiences in that wild roadstead further down the coast, I shall presently relate.
In 1630, finding it impossible to collect a sufficient 1630
supply of the 'white cloths' at Armagaon, they crept back to Masulipatam.[4] They returned to a city silenced by death, with no one either to help or hinder them. The great famine which desolated Surat, had stretched across the whole Indian continent. At Masulipatam, our returned factors reported that 'the major part of weavers and washers are dead and the country almost ruinated.' 'The living were eating up the dead, and men durst

chiefs or Naiks of the Madras seaboard for half a century longer, in spite of the claims and the efforts of the Mussulman Kings of Golconda. *Vide post*, p. 80, footnote 3.

[1] Prince Mirza Khurram, afterwards Emperor Shah Jahan. *Manual of the Kistna District*, p. 35.

[2] Bruce's *Annals*, i. 295.

[3] *Calendar of State Papers*, East Indies, 1625–1629, Nos. 668, 716.

[4] *State Papers, ut supra*, 1630–1634, Nos. 88, 103.

1630 scarcely travel in the country for fear they should be killed and eaten.'[1]

As the final annexation of Gujarat to the Mughal Empire had put an end to anarchy on the North-western coast of India, and enabled the English to settle securely at Surat, so the gradual establishment of the Golconda Musalman dynasty on the East coast gave us an assured position at Masulipatam. In both cases we commenced with permits from subordinate coast authorities, and were eventually forced to seek a guarantee from the inland sovereign power.

What the Prince Imperial's grant to Sir Thomas Roe had been to our Surat factory, the 'Golden Phirmaund' of the King of Golconda in 1632 proved to the English settlement at Masulipatam.[2] 'Under
1632 the shadow of Me, the King, they shall sit down at rest and in safety.'[3] In return, our factors engaged to import Persian horses for His Majesty of Golconda. Next year they were strong enough to
1633 send out a trading party northwards to attempt a settlement in Bengal. The importance of Masulipatam factory declined on the growth of the more southern settlement which it founded at Madras in
1639 1639. But in spite of the confusions arising from the struggle of the coast-Rajas with the inland kingdom of Golconda, and of the subsequent

[1] *Letters to the Company*, January 1632, January 1633. *State Papers, ut supra*, Nos. 262, 384.

[2] Dated November 1632, and renewed 21st February, 1634. Translations of the Farmans, or Trade Orders, may be read in the India Office, 'Bundle D,' Birdwood's *Report on the Old Records of the India Office*, p. 81. 1891.

[3] *Calendar of State Papers, East Indies*, 1630–1634, No. 349.

collapse of Golconda itself beneath the advancing power of the Mughal Empire, Masulipatam remained, and still remains, an important seat of Indo-European trade.[1]

Armagaon, the roadstead in which our fugitive factors from Masulipatam sought shelter in 1628, 1628
lay a few days' sail down the coast, and about forty miles north of our first attempted settlement at Pulicat. Armagaon now figures as 'a shoal and lighthouse' on modern charts, and its port[2] is but a poor village with some solar salt-pans and no commerce. In 1626 the English Council at Batavia had obtained leave from the petty coast chief at Armagaon to erect a factory.[3] The flight of our factors from Masulipatam, two years later, made Armagaon, miserable as it was, our sole shelter on the East coast. Resolved to hold it to the last, they landed twelve cannons from passing ships, and formed themselves into a small militia of twenty-three soldiers and merchants, against 'the depredations of the natives and of the Dutch'[4]— 1629
our first fortified garrison in India. But the place

[1] Government *Manual of the Kistna District*, p. 90, &c. Bruce's *Annals*, i. 454. Birdwood's *Report on the Old Records in the India Office, in multis locis*. The continuous Masulipatam papers from 1640 to 1700 are catalogued in the India Office Folio of Factory Records, pp. 41–42. 1897.

[2] Locally known as Durgarayapatnam or Durgaraz-patanam, lat. 13° 59′ N., long. 80° 12′ E. Population, 2,123 in 1881. *Imperial Gazetteer of India*, vol. iv. 326, and vol. i. 331. 1885.

[3] Letters from the President and Council at Batavia, 3rd August 1625, and 25th February, 1625–26. Bruce's *Annals*, i. 269. The date is usually given as 1625, as the month of February came within that year, Old Style.

[4] Bruce's *Annals*, i. 290, 295. *Calendar of State Papers*, East Indies, 1625–1629, No. 865. Armagaon fort was built in 1628–29.

1629 was too poor for ought save a temporary refuge. Country cloths could not be bought in sufficient quantity. Most of our factors flitted back to
1630 Masulipatam in 1630, and Armagaon was practically abandoned for a new settlement further
1639 south in 1639. Again the Company lost, in the end, the outlay on buildings and fortifications.[1]

The new settlement was Madras. In 1639
1639 Francis Day, a member of the Masulipatam Council and Chief at Armagaon, proposed to get free of the struggle with the Dutch by founding a factory to the south of their Pulicat settlement.[2] He discovered the place he wanted, thirty miles down the coast from Pulicat, with a practicable roadstead, and a friendly Portuguese colony on shore. The local Hindu chief welcomed the English and obtained for them from his inland Raja (the descendant of the once great Hindu Suzerains of Vijayanagar) a grant for a piece of land on the shore and the right to build a fort.[3] The local chief piously directed that the new settlement should be called after his father, and the natives know it by his name[4] to this day; but the English

[1] The expenditure on the fort alone in 1634 was 1000 pagodas, £333. *Calendar of State Papers*, East Indies, 1630-1634, No. 616.

[2] *Madras Government Manual of Administration*, vol. i. p. 161, folio. Madras Government Press, 1885. Bruce's *Annals*, i. 368.

[3] Dated 1st March, 1639. J. Talboys Wheeler's *Madras in the Olden Time, compiled from the Official Records*, vol. i. p. 25. Madras 1861. The remnants of the Vijayanagar dynasty had settled in 1594 at Chandragiri (in North Arcot District, about seventy miles south-west from Madras), whence its descendant, Sri Ranga Raya, 1639, issued to us the grant.

[4] Chennappa, whence Chennapatanam, the native name for Madras. This local chief was the Naik of Chengalpat. The English

called it Madras, probably from a Hindu shrine or legend of the place.

Without waiting for permission from home, Day built an embrasured factory and christened 1639-40 it Fort St. George in honour of England. The Company, uneasy about the money already sunk in fortified factories on the Madras coast, viewed the new settlement as another hazardous experiment, but left the Council at Surat to decide whether it should go forward. The Surat Council realised the advantages of a stronghold on the Bay of Bengal as a half-way house for the trade with Java, and gave their sanction. But six years later the Company at home had not forgiven its servants at Madras for the new expenses into which they had plunged. In 1645 it summoned one of them before its Court 'to answer the charge of the building of Fort St. George.' It only let him off on the ground that 'it was the joint act of all the factors;' and 'if it should not prove so advantageous for the Company hereafter, it can be charged upon no man more justly than upon Mr. Day.'[1]

The little isolated group of Englishmen mean-

name is probably derived from a legendary Sanskrit King of the Lunar Race, corrupted in Telugu to Mandaraz, and would be in full Mandaraz-patanam, on the analogy Durgaraz-patanam (Qy. Dugaraz-patanam), the alternative name of Armagaon. The Raja of Chandragiri (descendant of the Vijayanagar dynasty) had ordered it in the grant to be called Sri-ranga-raya-patanam, after his own name, Sri Ranga Raya. The Musalman derivation from *Madrissa* cannot be accepted. *Madras Government Manual of Administration*, i. 161, 1885.

[1] Proceedings against Mr. Cogan, May 13, 1645. MS. Court Book, No. 19, p. 146.

while pushed on the works, and, in spite of their Honorable Masters, founded the future capital of Southern India. The first General Letter from
1642 Fort St. George, dated November 5, 1642, announced that the chief settlement on the Coromandel Coast had been transferred from Masulipatam to Madras.[1] It humbly tried to argue away the displeasure of the Company at home, but with little success, for
1644 by 1644 the cost of the fortifications had mounted up to 2,294*l.*; and it was found that another 2,000*l.* with a garrison of a hundred men would be required.[2]

The Madras grant gave us our first piece of Indian soil, apart from the mere plots on which our factories were built. It was but a narrow strip running about a mile inland for six miles up the shore, north of the Portuguese monastic village around the shrine of Saint Thomas.[3] It contained, however, a little island formed by two channels of the Cooum backwater—a swampy tidal patch, about 400 yards long by 100 broad, which could be defended against the attacks of predatory horsemen. Mr. Day built a wall round this river-girt eyot, with a fort in its northern corner, and laid out the enclosure in lanes or alleys. As only Europeans were allowed to live within the walled isle, it became known as White Town, while the weaving hamlets which grew up outside, under the

[1] Bruce's *Annals*, i. 393.

[2] *Madras Government Manual of Administration*, i. 162.

[3] Saint Thomé or Saint Thomas Mount, *vide ante*, vol. i. p. 99, and *Imperial Gazetteer of India*, vol. xii. 142–144. 1887.

shelter of its guns, were called Black Town. The whole was included under the name of Madras.

The English had from the first secured their position by grants from the superior inland kings, while the Dutch preferred the facile support of the petty coast rulers, who more resembled their island chiefs in the Spice Archipelago. An English merchant penetrated to Golconda as early as 1617, and in 1634 the importance was recognised of keeping 'a continual residence' there, in order 'to have an able man at all times so near the King's elbow.'[1] In 1645 the sovereign of Golconda re- 1645
newed the grant for Madras, and thus gained the goodwill of our young settlement in his struggle with the feudal fragments of the Vijayanagar empire.[2] But two years later a terrible famine added to the calamities of the perpetual war 1647
between the Moslem Court of Golconda and the Hindu coast chiefs. Trade came to an end, and our Surat factory had to send round a ship with provisions to save the Madras settlement from starvation. The Golconda King, perhaps struck by such a display of distant resources, became eager for a closer alliance. In 1650–51 he even 1650–1
proposed to form a Joint Stock with the English Company for trading between the ports of his kingdom and those of other Indian Powers.[3]

This dangerous honour, like the proffered

[1] *Calendar of State Papers*, East Indies, 1617–1621, No. 220; 1625–1629, No. 716; 1630–1634, No. 616, and MS. Court Books.

[2] *Madras Government Manual of Administration*, i. 162; Bruce's *Annals*, i. 415.

[3] Bruce's *Annals*, vol. i. pp. 424, 430, 455.

F 2

partnership of James I.,[1] was prudently evaded.
But the Company in London perceived that a new
future had opened for it on the Bay of Bengal.
Hitherto Madras ranked as a subordinate agency
1653 to Bantam in Java. In 1653 it was raised to an
independent Presidency. Presently the Honorable
Masters at home, in terrible straits to maintain their
position from day to day, took fright at the cost of its
1654 new fortified factory, and in 1654 reduced the staff
at Madras to two factors, with ten soldiers for their
guard. The native Powers at once detected this
change of front; the Dutch, with superior forces
on sea and land, seized upon the trade; and English
interlopers flocked to the Madras roadstead. Then
the Company, its courage revived by Cromwell's
charter of 1657, resolved to make Madras its
effective headquarters in Eastern India, and in
1658 1658 declared all its settlements in Bengal and
the Coromandel coast subordinate to Fort St.
George.[2] Thenceforward Madras stood as the
type of the system of fortified factories, which
the conflicts of the native Powers in South-
eastern India rendered indispensable for the safety
of European trade.

[1] In 1624; *ante*, p. 29.

[2] *Madras Government Manual of Administration*, i. 162. Folio 1885.

CHAPTER IV

OUR FIRST SETTLEMENTS ON THE BENGAL COAST

1633–1658

In North-western India the English had adapted themselves to the settled order of the Mughal Empire, and won an honourable position as a coast-police and the patrol of the pilgrim ocean highway. In South-eastern India they had secured their settlements by grants from the inland kings, and by forts, amid the perpetual struggle between those kings and their half-subdued coast-rajas. In Bengal we were to be confronted by a different set of political conditions.

The great satrapy of the Lower Ganges, including Bengal Proper and Orissa, was in itself so affluent, and lay so far from the Imperial Court, as to render it almost a separate sovereignty. Only by long wars, and after repeated revolts, had it been completely annexed to the Mughal Empire. When the Afghan Kings of Bengal went down before the Emperor Akbar in 1576, they found a refuge in the adjoining province of Orissa. Their slow subjugation amid its hill-fastnesses and network of rivers I have narrated in another work.[1] The

[1] *Orissa, or the Vicissitudes of an Indian Province under Native and British Rule*, vol. ii. chapter vi. 1872.

Mughal governors who succeeded them were so remote from the Imperial control that they could oppress on their own account; yet could call in the whole force of the Empire to crush resistance to their oppression. This semi-independence of the Gangetic Viceroys dominated our position in Bengal. It was a personal element which the Imperial Court kept under strict subjection in its nearer province of Gujarat. But it influenced our whole history on the Bengal seaboard, from our first gracious reception in Orissa, to the caprices of the half-mad youth infamous for the Black Hole of Calcutta.

The popular story of our settlement in Bengal is a pretty one. A patriotic ship-surgeon, Mr. Gabriel Boughton, having cured an imperial princess of a severe burn in 1636, would take no fee for himself, but secured for his countrymen the right to trade free of duties in Bengal.[1] It is true that Mr. Boughton obtained an influence at the Mughal Court, but he did not go there until 1645, and meanwhile the English had fixed themselves on the Bengal seaboard by no romance of Imperial favour, but by sufferings and endurance of a deeper pathos.

The draft-treaty proposed by Sir T. Roe in 1616[2]

[1] Major C. Stewart's *History of Bengal* from Native Sources, pp. 251–3, 1813; Orme's *History of the Military Transactions of the British Nation in Indostan*, book vi. vol. ii. and so forth. 'It has become the staple of the popular historian,' says Sir Henry Yule dryly, 'but I cannot trace it to any accessible authority.' *Diary of William Hedges*, edited by Sir Henry Yule, vol. iii. p. 168. Hakluyt Society, 1887–1889.

[2] *Ante*, p. 52.

had mentioned the ports of Bengal as places free to the English, and visions of trade with that distant province flitted before the Company's servants of Surat.[1] Bengal was to be opened to us, however, not by any plunge of the Surat Council into the Eastern *terra incognita*, but by the gradual advance of the English up the Madras coast. The 'Golden Phirmaund' of the Golconda King in 1632[2] 1632
encouraged the Masulipatam factory to send a trading party northward. Accordingly in March 1633, eight Englishmen started in a native 'junk,' 'with a square sail, an oar-like rudder, and a high poop with a thatched house built on it for a cabin,' and rolled up the Bay of Bengal till they reached the mouths of the Great River[3] of Orissa.

There, on April 21, Easter Day, 1633, they 1633
cast anchor inside the mud-banks of the Mughal customs-station of Harishpur.[4] The Hindu Port-officer or 'Rogger' (our sea-captain's rendering of Raja) behaved with Indian courtesy to the strangers. But presently a Portuguese frigate steered into the haven, anchored close to our half-decked boat, and got up a scuffle on shore, 'where our men being oprest by multitudes had like to have been all slaine or spoyled, but that Lucklip

[1] Grants from the Mughal Governor of Surat, Nov. 12, 1623, and Sept. 7, 1624, Hedges' *Diary*, *ut supra*, vol. iii. pp. 173–175.

[2] *Ante*, p. 78.

[3] The Mahanadi literally 'The Great River.'

[4] Harishpur-Ghar, or Harishpur-Kila; see my *Statistical Account of Bengal*, vol. xviii. p. 226. Harishpur lies on one of the old mouths of the Devi River, which is a bifurcation of the Katjuri River, which is the main southern branch from the Mahanadi River, striking off from it at the delta head near Cuttack.

1633 the Rogger [*i.e.* Lakshmi the Raja] rescued them with two hundred men.'[1]

Ralph Cartwright, the chief merchant, leaving the boat in the joint protection of its crew and the friendly Port-officer, proceeded with a small deputation inland to the Moslem Governor of Orissa at Cuttack, at the delta-head of the Mahanadi or Great River. Their mission was to 'the Nabob of Bengal,' but our simple explorers looked on one native ruler as much the same as another, and they thought that the Governor of Orissa would serve their purposes equally well. The kindness which they met with on their few days' journey up the delta—kindness which Hindu hospitality showed to any stranger from a distant land who came in peace—impressed them deeply. The imposing etiquette of the Court at Cuttack[2] quickly brought them back to a sense of their position.

The Moslem Governor[3] of Orissa was merely

[1] I take the narrative chiefly from *Newes from the East Indies, or a voyage to Bengalla,* written by William Bruton . . . . . now lately come home in the good ship Hopewel, of London. Imprinted at London by J. Okes, 1638. Reprinted in Osborne's *Collection of Voyages and Travels,* vol. ii. Also from Mr. C. R. Wilson's *Early Annals of the English in Bengal, being the Bengal Public Consultations for the first half of the eighteenth century,* Calcutta 1895—an admirable piece of research, my obligations to which will abundantly appear in the following pages.

[2] In the fort of Malcandy, at the bifurcation of the Mahanadi and Katjuri Rivers, close to the modern Cuttack.

[3] Agha Muhammad Zaman, born in Tahran, in Persia, a distinguished soldier and administrator of the Mughal Empire, whose career is worked out by Wilson from the native records. *Early Annals, ut supra,* p. 8, footnote.

a deputy of the Mughal Viceroy of Bengal. But he was a polite Persian who knew how to combine courtesy with state, and with a certain simplicity, half military half religious. By day the lord of a magnificent fortress-palace, at night he slept like a soldier in his tent, 'with his most trusty servants and guards about him.'[1] He received the three Englishmen in his Hall of Public Audience amid oriental splendour; affably inclined his head to Mr. Cartwright; then slipping off his sandal offered 'his foot to our merchant to kiss, which he twice refused to do, but at last he was fain to do it.' Cartwright presented his gifts. Before, however, he could finish his petition for trade, 'the King's almoner' gave the signal for prayer, the glittering Court knelt down with their faces to the setting sun, and business ended for the day. Meanwhile the palace had been lighted up with a blaze of countless tapers, and the English returned to the quarters assigned to them in the adjacent city of Cuttack. 1633

The picturesque negotiations which followed read like a tale out of the 'Arabian Nights.' Cartwright came with two distinct objects; redress for the Portuguese attack within a Mughal harbour, and a license for trade. The Portuguese Captain lodged a counter-complaint against our crew, and each of the litigants purchased the aid of powerful officials. Cartwright asserted his title to seize the frigate on the bold ground 'that all such vessels as did trade on the coast and had not a pass either

[1] The quotations are (unless otherwise mentioned) from Captain Bruton's *Newes from the East Indies.* 1638.

1633 from the English, Danes or Dutch, were lawful prize.' The Portuguese Captain could only produce a pass from his own nation, which availed nothing, as the Mughal Government looked on the Portuguese as pirates, and had in the preceding autumn
Oct. 1632) sacked their chief settlement in Bengal. Accordingly the Governor 'made short work with the matter, and put us all out of strife presently; for he confiscated both vessel and goods all to himself.' This was too much for the English temper. To the astonishment of the courtiers 'our merchant rose up in great anger, and departed, saying that if he could not have right here, he would have it in another place. And so went his way, not taking his leave of the Nabob or of any other. At which abrupt departure they all admired.'

The Governor, rather amused than offended by his audacity, gave him three days to cool down, and then ordered him into the Presence. Cartwright knew that his life and those of his companions depended on a nod from the State Cushion. Yet 'with a stern undaunted countenance' he declared that His Highness 'had done his masters of the Honorable Company wrong, and by his might and power had taken their rights from them, which would not be so endured.' This was a new language to the polite Persian. He inquired of the Indian merchants before him what sort of a nation it was that bred a man like that. They answered that it was a nation whose ships were such that no 'vessel great or small' could stir out 'of His Majesty's dominions; but they would take

them.' 'At these words the King said but little, 1633
but what he thought is beyond my knowledge to tell you.'[1]

The result soon appeared. The Governor or 'King' kept the Portuguese frigate, but on May 5, 1633, he sealed an order giving the English an ample license to trade. It was addressed to 'Ralph Cartwright, merchant,' and granted him the liberty to traffic and export, free of customs, at any port of Orissa, and to purchase ground, erect factories, and build or repair ships. We had now, by the circuit of the Indian coast, re-entered the provinces of the Mughal Empire and there is no question of fortifications, as on the unsettled seaboard of Southern India. All disputes were to be brought before the Governor in person and decided by him in open darbar, 'because the English may have no wrong (behaving themselves as merchants ought to do).'[2]

[1] *Newes from the East Indies*, *ut supra*.

[2] The text of the Order is given in full by Mr. C. R. Wilson, *Early Annals of the English in Bengal*, pp. 11, 12. The beginning of our trade with Orissa is usually ascribed to a farman granted to the English a year later by the Emperor Shah Jahan, received at Surat 2nd February, 1634, and confining them to Pippli, near an old mouth of the Subarnarekha River ('The Streak of Gold'), on the Orissa coast. The only evidence for this farman is a letter from the Surat Council, dated 21st February, 1634. Exhaustive inquiry renders it doubtful whether such a farman was ever issued; and whether any English factory was built at Pippli under its authorisation. Sir Henry Yule's *Hedges' Diary*, pp. 175, 181, vol. iii.; C. R. Wilson's *Early Annals*, pp. 12, 13, vol. i. Captain Alexander Hamilton, however, who knew the Indian coast well between 1688 and 1723, speaks of an English factory as formerly existing at Pippli, whose river had by that time silted up. *A New Account of the East Indies*, vol. ii. p. 3.

1633 Next day the Governor feasted the Englishmen and sent them contented away. They built a house of business at Hariharpur,[1] on a channel half way down the delta, and, as they fondly hoped, beyond the malaria of the swamps. Next month, June 1633, Cartwright founded the factory of Balasor further up the coast, and near the present boundary between Orissa and Bengal.[2] The Masulipatam Council gave loyal support, by sending on to him the 'Swan' with her whole cargo, just arrived from England; and on July 22, 1633, she anchored off the Mughal customs-station of Harishpur. There she broke the silence of the swamps by firing three guns, but receiving no answer, sailed up the coast till she found Cartwright at Balasor.

Everything seemed to smile on the adventurers, and they projected outlying factories at Puri[3] in the southern extremity, and at Pippli on the northern

1727. The explanation probably is that our Balasor factory had for a time an agency at Pippli, which, as we shall see at p. 94, it soon abandoned.

[1] Where they had halted on their journey from the coast to Cuttack. This was our first factory within the present Lieut.-Governorship of Bengal. It then formed an important seat of native trade on a deltaic distributory of the Katjuri branch of the Mahanadi; it now gives its name to a *pargana* or fiscal division. Hunter's *Statistical Account of Bengal*, vol. xviii. p. 226. 1877.

[2] Balasor, on the right bank of the Burabalung River (literally, 'The Old Twister'), seven miles from the sea in a straight line, and now about 16 miles by river, which has silted up new land in various stages of formation around its mouth. See my *Statistical Account of Bengal*, vol. xviii. pp. 280–283, where the traditional account of the settlement (which I now correct) is followed.

[3] Puri, literally 'The City,' and temple centre of the worship of Jagannath ('The Lord of the World'), by whose name it is known in the early records; 'Gugernat,' 'Guggurnot,' 'Juggernauth,' &c. For Pippli, *vide ante*, p. 91, footnote 2.

boundary, of the Orissa seaboard. But their brief 1633
prosperity ended in disaster and death. The cargo of the 'Swan,' chiefly broadcloth and lead, found no purchasers at Balasor, and lay for nearly a year unsold. The luscious fruits and cheap arrack of Orissa formed temptations which the English sailors could not resist, and during the rainy season the deadly malaria of the swamps crept round their factory[1] in the mid-delta as round a beleaguered city.

Before the end of the year, five of our six factors in Orissa perished; the mortality among the sailors was terrible; and a second English ship sent thither had to make her way back to Madras with most of her crew stricken down by fever.[2] It is difficult for us now to realise the miseries which our countrymen, with their English habits of eating and drinking, suffered in the stifling forecastles and cabins of their ships, and in the mat-huts which formed their sole shelter on shore. Even a third of a century later, when they had learned in some measure to accommodate their dress and manner of living to the climate, two large English ships, after one year of the climate of Balasor, were unable to put out to sea 'because most of their men were lost.'[3]

With their goods unsaleable and factors and seamen dying around them, the survivors clung through the rainy season of 1633 to the footholds they had won on the Orissa coast. But two new

[1] At Harihărpur.

[2] Hedges' *Diary*, vol. iii. p. 180.

[3] In 1666. Bernier's *Travels*, vol. ii. p. 334. Amsterdam edition.

1634 to 1641 scourges were added to their miseries. The Portuguese pirates from the other side of the Bay of Bengal[1] swooped down on the river mouths: a Dutch fleet from the Madras coast and the Eastern Archipelago blockaded the roadsteads with pinnaces of ten to sixteen guns strengthened by an occasional ship. Cartwright had to give up the idea of planting agencies at the northern and southern extremities of Orissa[2]; his central factory midway down the delta fell into decay, due in part to the silting up of the river[3]; and soon all that remained to the English in Orissa was the unhealthy settlement at Balasor. The parent factory at Masulipatam had enough to do to keep its head above the all-engulfing wars between the inland King of Golconda and his half-subdued coast-rajas. The Company at home, in the grip of Court cabals, looked on the Orissa settlements as a new and unprofitable burden which had been thrust upon it. 'No one cared about them; they
1641 were distant, unhealthy, dangerous.'[4] In 1641, the ship 'Dyamond' was ordered thither to pay off their debts and bring away the factors.[5]

1642 But in the summer of 1642, after nine years' despairing struggle for existence, the tide began to turn. Francis Day, who had just founded Madras, visited Balasor and protested that it 'is not to be totally left.'[6] After all, it lay within the Mughal Empire, whose settled order contrasted with the

[1] On the Arakan and Chittagong seaboard.

[2] At Pippli and Puri.

[3] Hedges' *Diary*, vol. iii. pp. 179, 180, 181, &c.

[4] Wilson's *Early Annals*, p. 31.

[5] Hedges' *Diary*, vol. iii. 181.

[6] *Idem*, p. 182.

wild dynastic confusion further down the coast. 1642
The Madras Council shrank, however, from the risk, and referred the question home. Meanwhile the Company in London was exchanging the makeshift rule of Charles for the control of Parliament. In 1650 it .resolved to follow the 1650
example of the Dutch and to found a settlement in Bengal itself. Yet the perils of the Húgli river, then unsurveyed and without lights or buoys, rendered it unsafe for large vessels. The Madras Council resolved therefore to make Balasor a port of transhipment, whence cargoes should be carried in native boats round to the Gangetic delta, and so up its south-western channel, the Húgli, to Húgli town, about a hundred miles from the sea.[1]

There, on the bank of a deep pool formed by the current whirling round a bend of the river, the Portuguese had built a factory more than a century before.[2] But having incurred the displeasure of the Emperor Shah Jahan, when Prince Imperial,[3] that sovereign soon after his accession resolved to root them out. On a petition to the throne 'that some European idolaters who had been allowed to establish factories in Húgli, had mounted their fort with cannon, and had grown

[1] In this it followed the analogy of its first settlement in Orissa—Hariharpur—which lay at some distance up a deltaic channel, so that goods had to be transhipped into native cargo boats at the port of Harishpur, where the deltaic estuary merged into the sea.

[2] Probably in 1537–38. Major Charles Stewart's *History of Bengal*, from native sources, pp. 153–4, footnote. Calcutta reprint, 1847.

[3] Prince Mirza Khurram, *ante*, pp. 52, 77, footnotes.

(1632) insolent and oppressive,' he took the city by storm in 1632; slew (according to the native tradition) one thousand of the Portuguese, and carried off four thousand prisoners to his capital in Northern India, where the most beautiful of the girls were distributed among the harems of his nobility. It is said that of sixty-four Portuguese ships and 257 smaller craft anchored opposite the town, only three small vessels escaped to sea.[1]

A remnant lingered around their old monastery at Bandel, a mile higher up the Húgli, while the Dutch had a factory at Chinsurah, a little way down.[2] The Dutch site was well chosen, for it marked the most inland point of the Gangetic delta then accessible to sea-going ships. The ancient royal port of Bengal,[3] on a creek which entered the river not far above Húgli town, had lately silted up, and the Mughal Government, after destroying the Portuguese settlement in 1632, made Húgli the imperial port for the Gangetic provinces. Húgli remained the chief seat of the maritime trade of Bengal until the founding of Calcutta, half a century later.

1650 The arrival of the English at Húgli in 1650 promised an accession of trade to the new imperial port, and an increased customs-revenue to the Mughal Governor. They came as four peaceable

[1] Hunter's *Statistical Account of Bengal*, pp. 299, 301, vol. iii.—reproducing the traditional account and numbers as given by Major Stewart from native sources, *History of Bengal*, p. 153. Ed. 1847. Cf. Bernier, i. 236.

[2] Hunter's *Statistical Account of Bengal*, pp. 301, 307, vol. iii. Chinsurah and Húgli now form one municipality.

[3] Satgaon, *idem*, pp. 307–310.

merchants who had left their ship the 'Lyoness' 1650 far off in the Balasor roadstead, and only asked leave to sell the goods brought up the river in small native boats. The letter of instructions drawn up for their guidance mingled religious admonition with shrewd commercial advice. 'Principally and above all things,' runs its opening paragraph, 'you are to endeavour with the best of your might and power the advancement of the glory of God, which you will best do by walking holily, righteously, prudently and christianly in this present world,' that so, 'you may enjoy the quiet and peace of a good conscience towards God and man.'[1] In the next place they were to buy in the cheapest markets a cargo of Bengal sugars, silks and 'Peter' (saltpetre); to 'enquire secretly' into the business methods of the Dutch; and above all to procure a license for trade which 'may outstrip the Dutch in point of privilege and freedom.' They carried with them an able Hindu[2] who had been the 'Company's broker' since our first settlement in Orissa in 1632, and who now repaid its confidence in the face of intrigues against him, by rendering good service to us in Bengal.

They also found a friend at the Viceregal Court then held at one of the shifting Gangetic capitals,[3]

[1] Instructions from Captain Brookhaven of the 'Lyoness' in Balasor to James Bridgeman, chief merchant, Stephens, second, and Blake and Tayler, assistants, sent forward to Húgli, December 1650. The text is given in Hedges' *Diary*, vol. iii. pp. 184–186.

[2] Narayan (or 'Narrand') by name.

[3] At Rajmahal, then on the banks of the Ganges, afterwards left high and dry by a change of the river-bed.

1650 above the point where the mighty river splits up into its network of deltaic channels. Gabriel Boughton, doctor of the Company's ship 'Hopewell,' had in 1645 been lent to a nobleman in the imperial service, and was in 1650 Chirurgeon to the Mughal Viceroy of Bengal.[1] In or about the latter year he obtained from his patron a license[2] for free trade by the English in Bengal in return for 3,000 Rs. judiciously expended at the Viceregal Court.[3] But the document was soon afterwards lost,[4] and whether it confined our trade to the seaports or sanctioned it also in the interior, remains doubtful. The Masulipatam factory rewarded Mr. Boughton with a gift
1651 'of gay apparel,'[5] and from 1651 onward the English were established as traders alike on the seaboard and in the interior of Bengal.[6]

[1] Letter from the Surat factory to the Company dated 3 January, 1645, Hedges' *Diary*, vol. iii. pp. 182, 185; Wilson's *Early Annals of the English in Bengal*; and Dow's *History of Hindostan*, where a clue to the popular story of Boughton's being sent to cure the Princess Jahanara, daughter of Shah Jahan, may be found. More than one surgeon rose to high administrative office under the Mughals. Thus Mukarrab Khan, who had effected a cure of the Emperor Akbar, was fourteenth Viceroy of Gujarat, and preceded Prince Mirza Khurram (afterwards the Emperor Shah Jahan) in that appointment.

[2] Technically a 'nishan' or sealed permit as a 'sign' to subordinate officers.

[3] Bruce's *Annals*, vol. i. pp. 463, 464. Shah Shuja, then Viceroy of Bengal, was a son of the reigning Emperor, Shah Jahan.

[4] By Mr. Waldegrave on his land journey to Madras in 1653, or 1654. The subject is discussed in Wilson's *Early Annals*, footnote, pp. 27–8, and referred to in Hedges' *Diary*, vol. iii. 188. Bruce quoting a Madras letter of 14 January 1652 specifies Pippli as a seat of the trade, *Annals*, i. 464.

[5] A dress of honour suitable to a high personage in attendance on the Viceregal Court, February 1651. Hedges' *Diary*, vol. iii. 187.

[6] At Balasor, and perhaps Pippli on the Orissa coast; at Húgli, Kasimbazar near Murshidabad, and one or two out-stations in the Gangetic delta; and at

It soon appeared that this advance northward exceeded the still feeble powers of the Company. The Bengal factories lay beyond effective control. Their staff, in spite of all pious instructions, plunged into irregularities which ended in two[1] of them deserting the Company's service, in the death of a third ruined by debt, and in the return of a fourth to Madras with a story that he had lost the Company's papers. The good surgeon Boughton was also dead, and his widow, who had married again, was clamouring for a reward for his services. In 1656–7 the Madras Council for the second time withdrew, or resolved to withdraw, their factories from the Bengal seaboard.[2] 1651 1657

But once again we were saved from the counsels of despair. In October 1657, Cromwell reorganised the Company on a broader basis. A commission to Bengal put down malpractices and re-established the trade. Húgli became the head agency in Bengal, with two others[3] under its control in the Gangetic Delta, and Patna on the higher Ganges in Behar; besides out-stations or local houses for buying goods. Each factory had a Chief, with three assistants or councillors, a regular subordination of authorities, and a code of rules for the conduct of life and of business. In the lowest grade of the new staff appears the name of a youth, Job Charnock—the future founder of Calcutta. 1657–8

Patna and subordinate agencies higher up the Ganges, in Behar.

[1] Including James Bridgeman, the Chief. Hedges' *Diary*, iii. 187–194.

[2] Bruce's *Annals*, i. 525–6. *Ante*, p. 94.

[3] At Balasor, on the Orissa coast, and at Kasimbazar near Murshidabad.

1658 Bengal thus took its rank as one of the five important seats of the Company's trade, and was placed, together with Bantam and the Persian factories, under the control of Madras, itself subordinate to the presidency of Surat.[1] The year 1658, the last of the Protector's life, saw the Company's affairs in the East remodelled upon a system of graduated dependence and control, under which its factories were to grow into settlements and finally into the British Indian Empire. The same year saw the deposition of the Indian Sovereign by his rebel son Aurangzeb, and the commencement of the half-century of bigot rule under which the Empire of the Mughals slowly declined towards its fall.

[1] Bruce's *Annals*, i. 532.

CHAPTER V

THE COMPANY AND THE COMMONWEALTH

1649–1660

In 1650 the Company, by command of the Council of State, effaced the King's arms still remaining on one of its ships.[1] After the Restoration in 1660, it sought in like manner to hide the memorials of the Commonwealth, and the great charter of Cromwell disappeared from the India House. Its official historiographer, the only annalist who has made a careful use of its archives, holds up the events of the intervening period as 'an awful example' of a King and Government 'subverted by factions,' 'duped' by a 'Usurper,' and the 'victim' of 'guilty ambition.'[2] To the general historian those years appeared as a disastrous 'scramble for the trade of India.'[3] Cromwell's own life was so full of great English interests,

[1] Court Book, No. 20, p. 264, 1st May, 1650. India Office MS. Records.

[2] Bruce's *Annals*, vol. i. pp. 416, 426, 447, 501, &c. Quarto, 1810.

[3] Macpherson's *History of the European Commerce with India*, p. 123, which is the next best authority to Bruce, gives $5\frac{1}{4}$ pages to the period from 1650 to 1660, in a quarto of 440 pages dealing with only two centuries of the Company's history: pp. 119–124 (1812). Mill and Wilson's nine volumes, with their 5,425 pages, can only spare 15 pages to a somewhat discursive account of the same period at home and in the East, vol. i. 77–91. Ed. 1840–1848.

and so crowded by European events, that his biographers have found no leisure for his dealings with the East India Company.[1]

Yet the manuscript records attest how decisive those dealings were. The East India trade ceases to be a pawn sacrificed to kings and queens in the game of royal marriages. It begins to stand out as a national interest, to be maintained by European treaties and enforced by a European war.
1640 In 1640, when the Governor of the Company had rebuked 'the generality' for their slack subscriptions notwithstanding the King's promises, they replied: 'Until they shall see something *acted* by the King and State, men will not be persuaded to underwrite a new stock.'[2] They were now to come under a ruler chary of promise but in action intrepid.

1649 Cromwell found the Dutch triumphant in Europe and Asia, our Indian relations with the Portuguese still left to the haphazard of local conventions on the Bombay coast, and Amboyna unavenged. He enforced from Portugal an open trade for the English in the East; from Holland he wrung the long-denied redress for the torture and judicial slaughter of Englishmen in 1623, together with the restoration of the island then seized by the Dutch. Chief of all, he definitely

[1] Even in the admirable article in the *Dictionary of National Biography*, extending over 32 pages of closely printed double columns, the name of the East India Company does not occur, and the only passing reference to Eastern commerce, is in connection with the Dutch treaty of 1654, vol. xiii. pp. 155–186.

[2] MS. Court Book, No. 17, pp. 84–5, April 17, 1640.

imposed on the Company the principle of a permanent joint stock, on which it continued until its trade was thrown open in the nineteenth century. Under Cromwell's Charter of 1657 was raised the 1657 first subscription destined not to be dissolved, but to grow into the permanent capital of the East India Company. The corporation passed, with little recognition of the change at the time, from its mediæval to its modern basis.

Born in 1599, the year when the London merchants met in Founders' Hall to project an East Indian voyage, Cromwell entered the House of Commons in 1628, the year of the Company's first appeal to Parliament. His Charter of 1657 inaugurated the three cyclic dates of Great Britain in the East. It was fitly commemorated by the Battle of Plassey in 1757, and by the reconquest of India after the Sepoy Revolt, exactly one hundred years later.

But before his strong hand could make its weight felt, a period intervened when there was no King in Israel. From the Battle of Edgehill, in October 1642, to the last scene outside Whitehall in January 1649, Charles, whatever may have been his faults, cannot be held accountable for the distresses of the East India Company. One Parliament, with the King, a majority of the Lords, and a minority of the Commons, sat at Oxford. Another Parliament, with a majority of the Commons and a minority of the Lords, sat at Westminster. It was with this London Parliament that the Company had to reckon. The Houses at Westminster

1643 could levy contributions in the capital, they collected the customs, and controlled the shipping in the Thames. In 1643 they put a curb on the Royalist members of the Company by demanding a forced loan of its ordnance, 'for the fortifying of the bulwarks, now in preparation for the security of the City.'[1] On its refusal, the Commons declared they would grant an order to the Committee of Fortifications to take them. So the cannon had to be given up, and next year the Company is still petitioning for payment or their return.[2]

The London Parliament was, in truth, in no mood to tolerate a King's faction within the liberties of the City. In 1643, it cashiered the Company's Governor, sequestrated moneys due to Royalists at the India House, and forbad any dividends to be paid until the Directors had an interview with a Committee of the Lords and Commons.[3] Later in the year, the Parliamentary Government demanded a loan of 10,000*l.*, and the Company was glad to get off for half that sum.[4] By 1644 the Royalist party in the Company
1644 was cowed and the chief officers of its ships had taken the Solemn League and Covenant.[5]

This coercion cost the Company dear. It had lately opened houses in Italy[6] to dispose of its Indian goods, almost unsaleable amid the troubles

[1] March 28, 1643, MS. Court Book, No. 18, p. 153*a*.

[2] *Idem*, No. 19, pp. 51*a*, 60.

[3] *Idem*, p. 21*a*.

[4] November 1643. On the security of an excise on flesh and salt. *Idem*, No. 19, pp. 41, 41*a*.

[5] *Idem*, p. 74, March 22, 1644. Again in 1646, p. 200*a*.

[6] At Leghorn, Messina, Genoa, and Venice. *Idem*, No. 18, pp. 85, 151; No. 19, pp. 104, 110, 212.

at home, and one of its Royalist members[1] re- 1645
venged his sequestrations in England by seizing 300 bags of its pepper in Venice. Its captains, when clear of the Thames, were sometimes difficult to control. We have seen that one[2] of them carried his ship into Bristol and delivered it to the King's general. He then sallied forth with three armed vessels to waylay other Indiamen, and the Company was advised to despatch two nimble pinnaces to scout among the Western Islands or Azores and warn its homeward-bound vessels of their danger.

Amid this confusion, the Company still tried to make a show of trade. With no hope from the King, by whose Charter it existed, and in little favour with Parliament, it found its position almost as isolated as that of its servants in India. Like them, it evoked from the sense of desertion a resolve to rely upon itself. It entered, as we shall see, into direct negotiations with the Portuguese ambassador in London, and it almost succeeded in coming to an arrangement with the Dutch. It also began to strike out new trade methods. In 1640, with the help of royal promises, it had tried to raise fresh capital under the name of the Fourth Joint Stock. But the public had lost confidence, and with the shares selling as low as sixty per cent., the money could not be obtained.[3]

[1] Sir Peter Rychaut by name, MS. Court Book, No. 19, pp. 16, 142, August 1643 and April 1645.

[2] Captain Mucknell, of the ship 'John.' *Idem*, pp. 128*a*, 129, 130, 144, 144*a*, January 24 to May 2, 1645.

[3] Macpherson, pp. 116, 117.

1641 to 1647 Yet individual expeditions, if conducted without a dead outlay on factories, forts, and a permanent staff in India, yielded large profits. Laying aside for the time the project of a Fourth Joint Stock, some of its members subscribed in 1641 for a Particular Voyage, which should engage no servants in the East, but pay a commission to the Third Joint Stock for selling its goods and collecting a return cargo. Others began to take heart and got together a small nucleus for the Fourth Joint Stock. This double organisation of individual voyages and a general stock led to grave difficulties, as it tried to combine the early plan of Separate Voyages[1] with the Joint Stocks, or series of voyages, which had superseded them. Yet it enabled the Company to struggle through the civil wars without altogether losing its continuity of trade.

1647 That fate was narrowly averted. In 1647, when the House of Lords rejected the 'Ordinance for the Trade,' which the Commons had passed as a Parliamentary Charter for the Company,[2] the Governor called together the shareholders. He explained to them that, while they had lost the privileges, they remained subject to the responsibilities of the royal grant. 'Every man had liberty to go to India,' but the Indian princes held the Company 'liable for what depredations' any Englishman might there commit. In this way they had already lost 100,000*l.*, besides another 100,000*l.* from Courten's trading. Courten's Association, having reached the end of its resources, was carry-

[1] *Ante*, vol. i. pp. 277-305. [2] *Ante*, p. 42.

ing on business with counterfeit coin, pagodas and 1647
rials, which it manufactured on a great scale at Madagascar, and so brought the English name into disgrace throughout the East. The Indian princes made the Company responsible for this and similar offences. The Governor advised the brethren, therefore, 'to draw home their factors and estate,'[1] and the Company decided to wind up the Fourth Joint Stock. 'In regard to the troubles of the times,' they abandoned the idea of forming a new Joint Stock, but in order that the trade might not be wholly lost, they decided to find money for another voyage.[2]

Cromwell viewed the India trade from a national 1649
standpoint, and regarded the Company as one of several alternative methods for conducting it. When a protracted inquiry convinced him that it was the method best suited to the times, he strongly supported it. But throughout he had the interest not of the Company, but of the nation, in mind. As he set himself, while still a cavalry colonel, to form an army of victory at home, so he resolved, as head of the Commonwealth, to create a marine which should give England predominance abroad.
The Navigation Act of 1651 served as his New 1651
Model for winning the supremacy of the seas. The East India Company, its charters and its rivals, were merely instruments for carrying out this great design.

Yet if Cromwell long stood aloof from the

[1] March 19, 1647. MS. Court Book, No. 20, pp. 45, 45*a*.

[2] *Idem*, p. 58.

1650 to 1652 Company in its domestic distresses, he lost no time in dealing with its foreign enemies. In 1650 it petitioned 'the Supreme Authority of this Nation, the High Court of the Parliament of England,' for help against Holland. After a list of Dutch injuries, involving an alleged loss of two millions sterling during the past twenty years, it declared that it had repeatedly laid its wrongs before the King and Council, and had prayed in vain 'that satisfaction should be demanded from the States-General.'[1] Parliament received the petition with favour, and on the same day voted that it be referred for consideration by the Council of State. But Cromwell had Scotland on his hands, and he intended, if a Dutch war must come, to wage it on
1651 wider issues. So next year, 1651, the Company twice brought its Dutch grievances before the Council of State, and again in January 1652.[2] Cromwell was now ready, and the wrongs of the East India Company furnished one of the causes of the war with
1652 Holland declared in the following summer.[3] Next year the Company supplied saltpetre for the navy, and offered to equip a fleet of its own, which, with the aid of a few ships to be lent by the Government,
1653 would turn the Dutch flank by carrying the war into the Indian seas.[4] The proposal was not

[1] Bruce's *Annals*, i. pp. 447–449.

[2] *Idem*, pp. 458–460.

[3] 8th July, 1652.

[4] Petition of the East India Company to the Council of State, 9th September, 1653; and Preamble to a Subscription for reprisals against the Dutch, of same date. Ordinance of the Council of State to pay 10,670*l.* to the East India Company for saltpetre, 28th January, 1654.

accepted, but compensation to the East India 1653
Company figured largely among the final spoils of victory. In 1653 a Dutch fleet threatened our factory at Surat. The Mughal Government, however, did not allow private wars of Europeans within its dominions, so the Hollanders sailed to the Persian Gulf, where they captured three English ships. The Company's trade at Bantam was also suspended during the war.

By the treaty of 1654, which restored peace, 1654
Holland pledged herself 'that justice should be done upon those who were partakers or accomplices in the massacre of the English at Amboyna, as the Republic of England is pleased to term that fact,' and sent commissioners to London to settle all money claims.[1] By this time the torturers and the tortured had alike passed away; it only remained to offer some solatium to the heirs of the victims and to compensate the Company for its losses. Twelve years previously the Company,
hopeless of action by the King, was willing to (1642)
compound privately with the Dutch for a payment of 50,000*l.*, and the negotiations had only broken down as the Dutch demanded the relinquishment of its rights in the island of Pularoon.[2] It now produced a swollen bill of 2½ millions sterling for Dutch injuries perpetrated from 1611 to 1652. The Dutch gravely replied by counter-claims amounting to nearly three millions.

[1] Treaty of Westminster, ratified by the Protector, 5 April, 1654. Articles 27, 30.

[2] MS. Court Book, No. 18, p. 72. 1642.

1654 But the Protector was not to be trifled with, and had resolved that any questions left open at the end of three months should be referred for arbitration to the Protestant Swiss Cantons. So the Commissioners made short work of the huge totals, and, striking a balance, declared that the Dutch Company must pay 85,000*l.* to the London Company, besides 3,615*l.* to the heirs or executors of the Amboyna victims, and must restore Pularoon to the English.[1] The sum thus awarded to the London Company was more than half as much again as that for which it would, in its despondency, have settled privately with the Dutch in 1642. Oliver sternly let it know, however, that it held Pularoon only in trust, and must 'plant and manage the island so that it may not be lost to the nation.'[2]

1654 In the same summer of 1654, Cromwell put an end for ever to the exclusive claims of Portugal in the East—claims based on the Papal Bull of 1493, but embodied during a century and a half in the public law of Europe.[3] With regard to this matter also the Company had tried to accomplish by private negotiation what the royal diplomacy failed to effect. The commercial convention between its President at Surat and the Goa Viceroy in 1635[4] seemed to open the door to an international settlement of the Indies. When the instrument reached England, the Company applied to King Charles

[1] Award of the English and Dutch Commissioners, dated August 1654. The English claim was 2,695,999*l.* 15*s.*, and the Dutch counter-claim 2,919,861*l.* 3*s.* 6*d.*

[2] Through Secretary Thurlow, MS. Court Book, No. 23, p. 245.

[3] *Ante*, vol. i. pp. 81, 216, &c.

[4] *Ante*, p. 62.

and to his Minister at Madrid with this end in view, as usual without practical result.[1] After the separation of the crowns of Spain and Portugal in 1640, our Surat President again entered into negotiations on his own account with the Goa Viceroy, and obtained from him letters to the Portuguese Ambassador in London.[2] The Directors in England also addressed his Excellency. But the Portuguese ambassador distrusted their amateur diplomacy, and would grant no settled peace in the Indies; indeed, only a further truce for two years.[3] In 1642 Charles I., while arranging for freedom of trade between England and Portugal, agreed that their relations in India should remain for three years more on the basis of the local Surat-Goa Convention.[4]

Cromwell had no liking for such private negotiations. Resenting the shelter given by Portugal to Prince Rupert's fleet, he prepared the way for peace by Blake's cannon, and three months after the Dutch submission he extorted a final settlement from Portugal. His Portuguese treaty of July 1654 placed on an international basis the right of English ships to trade to any Portuguese possession in the East Indies.[5] 1654

[1] Letters of the East India Company to the Secretary of State, and to Lord Aston, Minister at Madrid, 1636.

[2] Or to be forwarded thence to Lisbon. Letter from the President and Council at Surat to the Company, 27th January, 1642.

[3] MS. Court Book, No. 17, p. 235*a*, June 1641.

[4] Treaty between Charles I. and John IV. of Portugal, ratified by Charles at York, 22nd May, 1642. Article xii.

[5] For the text *vide ante*, vol. i. p. 331. Dumont's *Corps Universel Diplomatique*, vol. vi. part ii. p. 83. Amsterdam, 1728.

1654 In all this Cromwell made no pretence of special favour to the Company. To him the India trade was one of the great English interests to be subserved by the treaties which followed European wars. Yet as the Company was a chief gainer from the national successes, he thought it should contribute to their cost. In 1649 the Commissioners of the Navy constrained it to lend 4,000*l.*; in July 1655 Cromwell borrowed from it 50,000*l.*;
1655 and in October of the same year another 10,000*l.* to pay Blake's seamen.[1] These loans were strictly applied to public purposes and faithfully repaid.

But Cromwell expected from the Company not money alone. In 1652 the Council demanded from it, without success, two ships of war 'for Defence of the Right and Honour of this Nation.'[2] To secure Pularoon the Company was called, in
1656 1656, to provide 30,000*l.* for fortifications, guard-pinnaces, and cannon, together with a garrison of eighty Englishmen and over two hundred native soldiers.[3] As the Dutch rooted up the spice trees before they even pretended to deliver over the island, no speedy return could be expected. Indeed, the money had to be levied by a contribution from the shareholders of twenty per cent. on their original ventures. When, therefore, the Protector started, also in 1656, his project of a volunteer fleet, the Company found itself compelled to hold aloof. He ordered it to send representatives to

[1] MS. Court Books, No. 22, p. 43, and No. 23, p. 236*a*; also Bruce's *Annals*, i. 504.

[2] MS. Court Book, No. 21, p. 100.

[3] *Idem*, No. 23, pp. 245*a*, 248, &c.

arrange with other trading bodies and himself for 1656 the equipment of thirty-nine men-of-war as convoys.[1] The wearied Directors replied that the existing dues already amounted to ten per cent., and that they could not possibly pay more.[2]

By this time Cromwell had inquired into the affairs of the Company, and knew that it could not bear further burdens. But while considerate to its distresses, he brooked no private diplomacy such as the Company had carried on during the late reign with the Dutch and Portuguese. In the moment of granting his Charter of 1657, the Protector called it sharply to task for 1657 attempting to negotiate on its own account with Holland. The Directors had sought redress from the Dutch ambassador in London for a fresh infringement of their rights in the East. His Excellency, like most foreign representatives under Cromwell's rule, proved gracious. But the Protector intimated his displeasure at the Company's approaching a foreign minister without his knowledge, and commanded it to submit all grievances to himself.[3]

While Cromwell thus alike strengthened and controlled the Company in regard to its foreign enemies, he intervened with reluctance between it and domestic rivals. For several years after the death of King Charles the task of constructing a government in England, and of defending it by

[1] MS. Court Book, No. 23, p. 248*a*. February 29, 1656.

[2] *Idem*, p. 249.

[3] 2nd September, 1657, *Idem*, pp. 292, 293*a*, 295*a*.

1649–50 arms, left him no leisure for trade wrangles. The Council of State, which meanwhile carried on the civil administration, found itself besieged by three sets of applicants for the Eastern traffic. Foremost among them was the Company, founding its monopoly on a royal charter, but on a royal charter so tampered with by royalty itself as to have lost much of its value. Next came Courten's Association, which also based its claims on a royal grant. In the background the great merchants of London and Bristol, belonging to neither of these societies, clamoured for an open trade in the joint interests of themselves and the nation. We have seen that the attempt in 1647 to embody the Company's charter into an Act of Parliament failed; as the Ordinance for the Trade, although it passed through the Commons, was rejected by the House of Lords. After the King's death in 1649, therefore, the Council of State had to face the whole question anew.

It did so in no revolutionary spirit. Without going into constitutional questions as to how far a trade-charter from King James held good under the Commonwealth, it took up the matter as it was left by the abortive action of Parliament in 1647. It counselled the Company to come to terms with Courten's Association, and it refused to interfere until they themselves arrived at a settlement. Both the rivals had reached the brink of ruin. Courten's Association, or the Assada Merchants as they were now called from their plantation on Assada Isle at Madagascar, were almost bankrupt. We have seen them reduced to carrying on their trade by a manufacture of counterfeit coin, and they had offered to surrender their factories[1] on the Indian coast to the Company's President at Surat. In 1651, they made a similar offer of their Madagascar settlement, Assada itself.[2] The East India Company, on its part, found it impossible either to raise a new Joint Stock or to go on with its old capital, and had to fall back on another 'Particular Voyage.'[3] Indeed, in 1649, it passed a resolution of despair not to send out any more ships, either upon the Joint Stock or Separate Voyage system after April of that year.[4] 1649-50

Yet only after long strife could the disputants come to terms. In 1649 they agreed that the two societies should work together as regards the general Indian trade; that Courten's Association should retain its Assada factory at Madagascar and have liberty to traffic thence to all Asiatic and African countries; while the port-to-port trade in India should be reserved to the Company. The business in gold and ivory on the coast of Guinea should be open to both.[5]

Their compact was embodied in a petition to

[1] Karwar in 1645-6; Rajapur in 1649.

[2] Bruce, i. 452.

[3] September 27, 1649. This 'Particular' or 'General' Voyage, for both terms are applied to that class of subscription, did not take place, as an agreement with Courten's Association was announced next day, September 28, 1649. MS. Court Book, No. 20, pp. 201, 202, &c.

[4] MS. Court Book, No. 20: January 24, 1649, p. 159 *a*.

[5] Agreement between the East India Company and the Assada Adventurers, 21st November, 1649. Bruce, i. 439.

1650 Parliament, and on January 31, 1650, the House of Commons resolved: 'That the trade to the East Indies should be carried on by one Company, and with one Joint Stock, and the management thereof to be under such regulations as the Parliament shall think fit, and that the East India Company should proceed upon the articles of agreement made between them and the Assada Merchants on the 21st November, 1649, until further orders from the Parliament.'[1] This coalition of the rival bodies under a Parliamentary sanction formed the basis on which the India trade continued until Cromwell's charter towards the close of the Commonwealth.

At first all was concord. The day after the Parliamentary vote, the two associations proposed to form a 'United Joint Stock,' which should take over the factories in India, and continue to trade for three years.[2] But in vain the Company's beadle went round to the freemen with the subscription book. Money would not come in, and extraordinary methods were employed to raise capital. The Company sent letters to thirteen of the port-towns of England inviting them to join; and blank subscription books, with a preamble setting forth the nature of the adventure, were humbly laid before the Parliament and Council of State. The members of these honourable bodies would not venture a penny; and even the offer of the freedom of the Company, once so valued, failed

[1] Vote concerning the East India Trade, 31st January, 1650. Bruce, i. 440.

[2] MS. Court Book, No. 20, pp. 235, 235*a*, 236, &c. 1st February, 1650.

to tempt the general public. The thirteen port- 1650
towns were equally unresponsive. The Governor had to announce that replies had been received from only Bristol and Exeter; and there seemed no likelihood of money being obtained from that source.[1] The Assada Merchants having barely the funds to carry on their own business, could furnish but little to the new Joint Stock. With such sums as its own exhausted members might subscribe, the Company struggled on.[2]

How hard was the struggle abundantly appears in the records. The continued existence of the Company depended not on the continuity of its trade or on its sending out a yearly succession of ships. As long as it elected in each July a Governor and the other officers named in the Charter of James I. it preserved its existence as a body corporate in the eye of the law. In July
1651 the question arose whether it was worth 1651
while to keep up this formality. The General Court decided, however, to proceed with the election of officers, although 'hereafter there will be little use of any governor, in regard they are to set no ships out, nor much other business but to pay their debts.'[3]

[1] MS. Court Book, No. 20, pp. 240, 253, 254, &c.

[2] On February 6, 1650, the East India Company after much debate agreed that the adventurers in the Fourth Joint Stock should contribute 26,000*l.* to the United Joint Stock (MS. Court Book, No. 20, p. 238*a*) and other sums were raised or brought into account, making a total, it is said, of 191,700*l.* Macpherson's *History of the European Commerce with India*, p. 119, 1812. But two ships alone required bullion to the value of 60,000*l.* for export.

[3] MS. Court Book, No. 21, p. 58, July 2, 1651.

1649 to 1651 The fact is that the union of the Company and the Assada Merchants failed to cope with the situation. For outside these societies a body of capitalists had grown up, who protested against the monopoly of the India trade as a relic of the royal prerogative no longer suited to the times. They claimed that the Eastern traffic should either be organised on the Regulated system, under which each member of a trade guild or association might traffic on his own account, as in the Turkey Company, or that it should be thrown open to the nation. This feeling had at first expressed itself in a demand for increased State protection of foreign trade. 'It is not our conquests, but our commerce,' runs a powerful appeal just after the
(1641) meeting of the Long Parliament, 'it is not our swords but our sayls, that first spred the English name in Barbary, and thence came (*sic*) into Turkey, Armenia, Moscovia, Arabia, Persia, India, China, and indeed over and about the world. It is the traffic of their merchants and the boundless desires of that nation to eternize the English honour and name, that hath enduced them to saile and seek into all the corners of the earth.'[1]

Under the Commonwealth the desire for an open trade to India gained strength. The Navigation Act of 1651 gave it a decisive impulse. Next year —the very year after the Company had declared that thenceforth 'there will be little use of any

[1] *The Treasure of Traffike, or a Discourse of Forraigne Trade*, by Lewes Roberts, 1641. Reprinted in 'A Select Collection of early English Tracts on Commerce,' 1856, p. 108.

governor, in regard they are to set no ships out'—a new voice rang aloud to the nation: 'That with all possible conveniency we enlarge our Forraign Plantations, and get further footing in Barbarie, East and West Indies.' Forasmuch as 'a little spot of ground, as England is, with its Dominions, if it do not enlarge them,' will strive in vain against the growing trade of Holland and the other European powers.[1] Men of rank once again joined with men of the city in ventures beyond the seas. Indeed in 1649 the Company had complained that the name of Lord General Fairfax stood first in the draft of a patent for the Assada Merchants which it was intended to submit to Parliament.[2]

1652

The outside capitalists hoped that after the three years for which the United Joint Stock of 1650 was formed, a broader basis might be adopted. But on the expiry of that period in the summer of 1653 the Company found itself too weak to attempt any new departure, and the existing arrangement continued, although no ships could be sent out.[3] Forthwith it appeared that the outsiders had strong supporters within the Company itself. The standard of revolt was raised at a Court meeting in the following December, when one of the generality proposed that individual members should, as under the Regulated system, be allowed to trade on their

1653

Dec. 1653

[1] *Certain Proposals in order to the People's Freedom and Accommodation in some Particulars, with the Advancement of Trade and Navigation of this Commonwealth in General*, by Henry Robinson, London, 1652, p. 11.

[2] MS. Court Book, No. 20, p. 205.

[3] *Idem*, No. 23, pp. 128, 183, &c.

1653 own account. The traffic was passing into the hands of interlopers, and if the Company could not send forth ships itself, why should it preclude its members from doing so? [1]

The governing body found it difficult to answer this argument, and temporised by allowing private members to trade to India on a payment to the Company for the privilege. But the concession amounted to a change from the Joint Stock to the Regulated system, in opposition to the terms of the late Parliamentary settlement of 1650. So in March
1654 1654 the governing body took a firmer stand. They decided that 'it is not in the power of this Court to give liberty to any private persons to trade to India; but if any do it, it is at their own peril. And thereupon the votes of Parliament were read, concerning the carrying on of the trade in a Joint Stock.' [2]

Issue was thus definitely joined between the two great parties which have always divided mercantile opinion in England with regard to the Indian trade. Under the first Stuarts the conflict was waged between the Company and individuals or associations licensed, in infringement of the Company's charter, by the King. Under the Commonwealth it widened into a struggle between the conservative section of the Company and a forward party within itself, but allied to the outside capitalists who claimed an open trade to India. Under the Restoration it became a war of lawsuits between the Company and the independent

[1] MS. Court Book, No. 23, p. 159*a*, &c. December 1653.

[2] *Idem*, p. 176.

mercantile community at large; a war only ended by the great Parliamentary amalgamation after the Revolution. That settlement lasted down to our own century, when even its broad basis was found too narrow for the expansive forces of British commerce, and the Act of 1813 threw open the India trade to the nation. The records of the East India Company form a concentrated history of the English hatred of monopoly; of the Company's efforts to maintain exclusive privileges by from time to time widening its doors, as long as the country believed exclusive privileges necessary for the India trade; and of their abolition as soon as the country thought them no longer required.

Meanwhile the Parliamentary settlement of 1650, in subjecting the trade to further regulation by the Commons, provided for such difficulties as arose under the Commonwealth. The Council of 1654 to 1656
State recognised the claims of the outside merchants by a cautious yet liberal issue of licenses for private trade to India.[1] Cromwell's name begins to appear in connection with these grants,[2]

[1] I note the following entries in the State Papers from October 1654 to February 1656, and there may be others. October 6, 1654 Thomas Barnardiston, Thomas Bludworth and William Love and company petitioned the Council for leave to ship 6,000*l.* in rix dollars for a voyage to the East Indies. November 30, 1655, Thomas Kendall and company beg leave of the Protector to carry out 3,500*l.* free of custom, as they have prepared the 'Marigold' for the South Sea in the East Indies. February 1656, Ant. Fernandez Caravajal, merchant of London, requested permission to export 2,000*l.* in Spanish money to the East Indies, a request which was granted on payment of 5 per cent. customs. *Calendar of State Papers*, Domestic Series, 1654, p. 374; 1655–6, pp. 42, 161.

[2] Not only to individuals, but also to the Merchant Adventurers

1654 to 1660 and to onlookers both at home and abroad the Company seemed doomed. Nine months after it had taken up its rigid attitude against private trading by its own members in 1654, the Amsterdam
1655 burghers received 'advice that the Lord Protector will dissolve the East India Company at London, and declare the navigation and commerce to the Indies to be free and open.'[1] The mere rumour of the nationalising of England's Eastern trade sent a thrill of apprehension through Holland.

Meanwhile the expansive forces within the Company burst forth beyond control. In the
1654 autumn of 1654 the section of its freemen in favour of private enterprise had petitioned the Council of State that the East India trade be still carried on by a company, but with liberty for the members individually to trade with their own capital and ships in such way as they may deem most to their advantage.[2] The Company urged in reply that the experience of forty years proved that the India trade could only be conducted by an association strongly bound together by a series of Joint Stocks, and that the plan of Separate Voyages had been given up after a full trial; that the Company had now factories beneath fourteen native sovereigns, together with a costly equipment necessary for the protection of so distant a trade; and that, under its engagements with the Indian Powers, it was

working on a subscription of 46,000*l.*, and with a committee of management.

[1] January 1655, J. Thurlow's *State Papers*, vol. iii. p. 80, 1742.

[2] Petitions of the 21st September, and 14th November, 1654.

held responsible by them for depredations or misconduct of all Englishmen in the East. It accordingly prayed the Protector to grant it a new and wider charter, to the exclusion of private trade. 1654 to 1656

In 1654, therefore, Cromwell found himself called on to decide between the three sets of applicants: the outside capitalists who desired that the commerce with India should be thrown open to the nation; the governing body of the Company who asked for wider privileges upon the basis of a series of exclusive Joint Stocks; and the section of its members who desired that the Company should be transferred from the Joint Stock to the Regulated system. His clear eye saw that if the India trade were to be thrown open to the nation, it must be protected by the national arms. He realised that neither the navy nor the land forces of the Commonwealth were adapted for such a task. He accordingly eased the situation by granting trade licenses to individual outsiders, and referred the main question as to the future constitution of the Company to the Council of State.

The Council soon found itself plunged in a quagmire of irreconcilable claims. A question even arose as to which of the several sets of adventurers really represented the Company. When the Dutch compensation of 85,000*l.* came to be distributed, the survivors or heirs of the Third Joint Stock, of the Fourth Joint Stock, and of the United Joint Stock asserted their several rights to it. The Council could only find a way out of its bewilderment by referring their titles to arbitration,

1655 and meanwhile lodged the money with trustees.[1] Cromwell hastened a decision by borrowing 50,000*l.* of the compensation fund for the State.

If such a confusion of claims existed within the Company itself, the conflict on the wider issue as to the future management of the India trade may be imagined. During two years the Council of State laboured for a settlement in vain. The governing body of the Company lost hope, and
1656 its Court of Committees resolved in 1656 to sell its 'privileges and houses in India . . . to some Englishmen,'[2] at a valuation of 14,000*l.*, retaining, however, a share with the purchasers in the future trade. But the General Court overruled this decision, and on October 20, 1656, sent up one more petition to Cromwell.[3]

On the very same day the Protector, under his own hand, referred the petition to the Council of State, and took care that that body now appointed a committee which should carry his own vigorous resolve into its task. While great names and high office gave weight to its deliberations,[4] the actual

[1] Sir Thomas Vyner and Alderman Riccard. The arbitrators were five in number, including three Doctors-in-Law and an Alderman.

[2] MS. Court Book, No. 23, p. 272, October 14, 1656.

[3] *Idem*, p. 272*a*, and Bruce, i. p. 514.

[4] The members were the Lord President Lisle, Lord Commissioner Fiennes, the Earl of Mulgrave, Sir Charles Wolseley, Lord Strickland, Colonel Sydenham, the Lord Deputy of Ireland, and Colonel Jones. How strongly the Committee represented the personal views of Cromwell, a scrutiny of the members attests. Lisle had long been a submissive follower of the Protector, and was raised to the peerage in the following year in Cromwell's new House of Lords (December 1657). Fiennes, a warm personal friend of Cromwell, was in the fol-

work was entrusted to a man in whom he placed 1656
complete confidence. Colonel Philip Jones, after suffering much and fighting hard on behalf of the Parliament, became a leading member of the Council of State and filled important offices under the Commonwealth. In the previous year, 1655, Oliver selected him as sole arbiter in a delicate question between England and Portugal; in 1657 he was one of the Committee appointed to offer to Cromwell the Crown: and as controller of the household he superintended the Protector's funeral in 1658.[1] It was on this tried friend that Oliver chiefly leant for advice 'in what manner the East India trade might be best managed for the public good and its own encouragement.' Colonel Jones was specially charged 'to take care thereof.'

His prompt action indicates that Cromwell had already made up his mind on the evidence before him. In six weeks Colonel Jones and his colleagues accomplished what the Council of State had failed to do during two years—they arrived at a settlement for the India trade. The Committee's report[2] was only signed by three members: one of

lowing year (April–May 1657) deputed to argue him into the acceptance of the Crown. Walter Strickland, popularly called Lord Strickland, was in both the Councils of State under the Protectorate, Captain of Cromwell's grey bodyguard at Whitehall, a member of his new House of Lords in Dec. 1657. And so forth, with one exception, down the list.

[1] Colonel Philip Jones must be distinguished from John Jones the regicide, sometimes also styled Colonel. An examination of the Order of Reference, dated 3rd November, 1656, preserved in the State Paper Office, has now made this clear.

[2] Dated 18th December, 1656. *East Indies Papers*, vol. v., Nos. 59 and 71, Public Record Office. The original documents have been

1656 whom [1] had lately stood forth in Parliament as Cromwell's mouthpiece for religious toleration; another was the controller of his household [2]; while the third [3] was his most intimate confidant. They were of opinion that the India trade should be carried on by one company on the basis of a United Joint Stock, yet they sent the matter back to the Council of State as being too high for them to decide. The Council of State again procrastinated, but under severe pressure, as we shall see, adopted the report, and referred it for final orders to the Protector.

To the decision of this great issue Cromwell brought a slow but effective training. He had been a member of the Commission of Trade and Plantations in 1643, at the moment when the commercial prerogatives of the Crown passed in reality from the King to the Parliament. Years of war and internal struggle followed. But as soon as Cromwell firmly established the Common-

kindly re-examined for me by Mr. William Foster under instructions from Mr. Wollaston, Superintendent of Records, India Office; and I take the opportunity of expressing my thanks to both these gentlemen for their unfailing courtesy and aid.

[1] Colonel William Sydenham, one of the Council of Thirteen in 1653 and a chief promoter of the Protectorate, held high office under Cromwell and brought the Parliament back to reason when the Protector's intervention on behalf of the Quaker Naylor led to a question of breach of privilege. He became one of Cromwell's peers in 1657.

[2] Colonel Philip Jones, aforesaid.

[3] Sir Charles Wolseley, who married Anne, youngest daughter of Lord Saye and Sele. This Sir Charles Wolseley was an ancestor of the present Field Marshal Viscount Wolseley, to whom I am indebted for information regarding him from the Wolseley Family Papers.

wealth, his mercantile policy took a definite shape. The Navigation Act of 1651 laid the foundation of England's mercantile ascendency, and formed a chief cause of the Dutch war in the following year. Even before Cromwell granted peace to Holland, he seems to have resolved on a similar assertion of power over the Catholic nations. From Portugal he enforced the English liberty of trade in the East Indies; and his West Indian expedition against Spain, in 1654–5, had its origin in mercantile not less than in political reasons.[1] Not only in European waters, but throughout all the ocean-world from Malabar to Hispaniola, Oliver determined to make England supreme. In 1655 the chief economic writer of the time presented to the Protector his mature work,[2] and in the same year Cromwell appointed the Committee of Trade—'a great concernment of the Commonwealth,' says Carlyle, '"which His Highness is eagerly set upon."'[3]

Cromwell perceived that, as the time had not yet come for an open trade to India, to be sup- 1657
ported by a national fleet in Asiatic seas, the real question lay between a Regulated Company, the members of which might trade on their individual

[1] Mr. Frank Strong throws light on these trade aspects in his monograph on 'The Causes of Cromwell's West Indian Expedition,' *American Historical Review* for January 1899, pp. 228–245.

[2] 'Great Britain's Remembrancer,' by Sir Ralph Maddison, London, 1655. A reprint, with few alterations, of his earlier work of 1641, and based on Gerard Malynes' *Consuetudo vel Lex Mercatoria* of 1622 and 1629.

[3] *Oliver Cromwell's Letters and Speeches*, p. 396, vol. ii. Ed. 1845.

1657 account, and a Joint Stock Company. The analogy of the Turkey Company, confidently relied on by the advocates of the Regulated system, did not bear scrutiny. For the dealings of the Turkey Company were chiefly with the Mediterranean Powers—Venetians, Spaniards, Barbary Corsairs, and Turks—within the reach of English diplomacy and of English reprisals. When the Doge laid prohibitive customs on our Levant trade, Elizabeth forbad the Venetian import into England of the raisins of Corinth and the wines of Candia, until the Adriatic Republic should take off its imposts. Cromwell had just given sharp proof to Spain and the Barbary Corsairs that they were both within range of his guns. As regards Turkey, the very year after James I. granted a Charter in perpetuity to the merchants of England in the Levant, it was found necessary to appoint an English envoy to the Grand Seignior, and to establish consuls within his dominions. International relations sprang up and eventually developed into a system of consular jurisdiction for the protection of English subjects in the eastern Mediterranean. It is said that in 1685 the only English diplomatic agent with the title of ambassador[1] resided at Constantinople, and was paid in part by the Turkey Company. But no statesman believed, in 1657, that the Mughal Empire could be called to a reckoning

[1] I make this statement on the authority of Lord Macaulay, *Works*, i. 241. Ed. 1866. We have seen Sir Paul Pindar in the double capacity of Turkey merchant and English representative at the Porte. *Ante*, p. 34.

by English diplomacy or arms, or that the Common- 1657
wealth should maintain a permanent embassy at Agra, and a cordon of consuls around the Indian coast. The plea for a Regulated East India Company from the analogy of the Regulated Turkey Company proved to be no argument at all.

The real evidence which confronted Cromwell lay in the history of the East India Company itself. Even before Elizabeth granted her charter, its founders had declared in 1599 'that the trade of the Indias being so far remote from hence cannot be traded but in a joint and united stock.'[1] Yet the actual charters of Elizabeth and James contained no reference to the subject, nor was a continuous joint stock ever raised. The truth is that the term 'Joint Stock' had to the founders in 1599 a very different meaning from that connoted by its modern development, the 'Joint Stock Company.' It signified only a subscription for a joint voyage, whose accounts were to be wound up and the capital repaid when the ships came home. The East India Company was a body corporate with an exclusive grant of the India trade from the Crown, and it conducted its business by forming successive groups among its own members for raising joint stock subscriptions for successive and distinct ventures.

At first, indeed, it differed but slightly from the Turkey and other Regulated Companies of mediæval commerce, except that the right of separate trading passed from the individual freemen to

[1] *Court Minutes*, 25th September, 1599.

1657 successive groups of freemen.[1] On this basis it equipped its first nine voyages.[2] When the system of Separate Voyages proved too weak to cope with its Portuguese and Dutch rivals in the East, it raised a series of 'joint stock' subscriptions, each of which supplied the capital for a distinct series of voyages. But the 'joint stock' subscription was designed only for a limited number of years, at the end of which it was to be wound up—in short, the original system of Separate Voyages gave place to a system of separate series of voyages. Every new joint stock was intended to take over at a valuation the factories of its predecessor in India. In this rudimentary form of joint stock the group of members took the place of the individual freeman, as the group of voyages took the place of the individual venture, in a 'Regulated' association like the Turkey Company.

Amid the troubles of the Civil War the system of separate series or groups of voyages broke down. But although money could not be raised for a series of voyages, there were, as we have seen, men both inside and outside the Company ready to stake a sufficient sum for a single voyage, if freed from the burden of the capital sunk in India. Such attempts to combine the original system of Separate Voyages with that of Joint Stock series of voyages led to a demand for the individual freedom of each member of the Company to trade on his own account—in

[1] This sentence must be taken subject to the full explanation given in the chapter on the Constitution of the Company in the preceding volume, i. pp. 236–276.

[2] *Ante*, vol. i. 291 (1601–1612)

short, for a reversion from the successive and distinct series of Joint Stocks back to the old Regulated system. The resistance of the governing body of the Company to this demand produced the petitions and counter-petitions on which the Council of State had so long been unable to decide. 1657

Colonel Jones' report was presented to the Council of State on December 18, 1656. That body renewed its old hesitations, and the Company, in anger and despair, resolved on January 14, 1657, that unless a decision were received within a month, it would make sale of its factories, rights, and customs in India 'to any natives of this commonwealth to and for their own proper use.'[1] There is now no mention of its taking a share with the purchasers, and it evidently contemplated a complete withdrawal from the trade. It ordered bills of sale to be hung up in the London Exchange. The Council of State, thus galvanised into action, summoned the Company and the rival merchant adventurers for a final hearing, and advised the Protector 'that the trade of India be managed by a United Joint Stock exclusive of all others.' Forthwith, on February 10, 1657, Cromwell directed that a committee should sit to draw up a charter, which on October 19 passed the Broad Seal of England. 19 Oct. 1657

After the Restoration the Company hastened to purge itself of complicity with the Commonwealth, and the document disappeared. A diligent inquiry now leaves no hope that a copy survives in

[1] MS. Court Book, No. 23, p. 277*a*.

1657 England, Holland, or the East.[1] But although the charter has perished, I have been able, from contemporary documents,[2] to piece together its main provisions. It ratified the Charter of James I. with slight modifications, and gave additional privileges.[3] As new coast towns had sprung into vigour, the original three ports (London, Dartmouth, and Plymouth), from which bullion might be exported, were to be increased to

[1] Cromwell's Charter has been repeatedly sought for in the Company's records, the last time by Mr. William Foster. I am also indebted to this gentleman, under instructions from Mr. Wollaston, Superintendent of Records at the India Office, for a fresh inquiry in the Public Records Office (supplementary to that by Mr. Noel Sainsbury), the Privy Council Office, and the House of Commons' Archives. I thank Sir Henry Howard, Her Majesty's Minister at the Hague, for a renewed search of the Dutch records. A letter from the Dutch East India Company, dated April 16, 1658, shows that a copy was sent out to Batavia for their Governor-General's information. But a thorough search of the Java records, courteously made for me by order of Mr. Van Riemsdyk, proves that this copy no longer exists. The Marquis of Lansdowne has kindly enabled me to examine the Lansdowne MSS. containing summaries of the East India Company's Charters. Their only document bearing on the subject is a summary of the Preamble for the subscription issued by the Company in 1658. Through the courtesy of Mr. St. Loe Strachey I have also ascertained that no information is forthcoming from the paper referred to by the Historical Manuscripts Commission as Packet 8, Doc. F, in the Strachey collection. I also thank Mr. J. H. Reddan, of the Foreign Office, for most ungrudging and valuable help.

[2] Namely (1) A short report by the Attorney-General to the Council of State, dated 28th February, 1657. Public Record Office. (2) Resolutions passed by the Privy Council. *Calendar of State Papers*, Domestic, 1657–58, p. 115. (3) MS. Court Book, No. 24, 19th October and 11th November, 1657. (4) The Company's advertisement of the subscription for the New Stock, in the *Mercurius Politicus*, No. 387, October 22–29, 1657. Bodleian Library. (5) The Lansdowne MSS. 'East India,' vol. lxxxix. (6) *Hollantse Mercurius*, October 1657, p. 101. ff. (Hague Archives).

[3] Lansdowne MSS. vol. lxxxix. p. 12.

seven.[1] On the other hand, the clauses granting the 1657
powers of Law Martial and immunity from customs, tonnage, and poundage, and certain other privileges, were to be omitted, and left to be dealt with by special orders from the Protector, who should also have the right to recall the charter if he saw cause.[2] Cromwell's Charter, in fact, combined the substance of the Royal Charter of 1609 with the more continuous Government-control provided by the Parliamentary grant of 1650.[3] The Protector promised that his settlement should in the next session be confirmed by Act of Parliament.[4]

Cromwell died the following year before a Parliamentary sanction could be obtained, and his charter formed the last word of the Commonwealth on the three sets of proposals which had so long divided English merchants: namely, for an open commerce to India, for a Regulated Company, and for a Joint Stock Company. He reconstituted the India trade on the basis of 'One Joint Stock.'[5] The words 'Joint Stock' do not occur in the Charters of Elizabeth or James I., nor, indeed, in any Royal Charter until that of 1686.[6] The Company's

[1] Attorney-General's Report on the Proposed Charter, 28th February, 1657.

[2] Resolutions of the Privy Council, *Calendar of State Papers*, Domestic, 1657-58, p. 115.

[3] *Ante*, p. 116.

[4] Lansdowne MSS. and *Mercurius Politicus*, 1657.

[5] 'Whereas his Highness, Oliver Lord Protector of England, Scotland and Ireland, &c., with the Advice of his Right Honourable Council, through their desire to promote the East India trade, for the honour and benefit of this nation, have been pleased to think fit and declare, that the trade shall be managed in the way of One Joint Stock.' Preamble by the Company to the new subscription, *Mercurius Politicus*, October 22-29, 1657.

[6] I find these words used for

1657 so called 'Joint Stocks' had been merely successive subscriptions for separate sets of voyages; each set being a distinct and several adventure to be wound up at the end of a fixed number of years. The idea of a united joint stock, which emerged in the Parliamentary settlement of 1650, developed under Cromwell's Charter of 1657 into a united and continuous joint stock.

The change was wrought not by Cromwell alone, but by Cromwell representing the spirit of the times. If the Protector prescribed unity, the Company interpreted unity to imply also continuity and permanence. The very day that the charter passed the Broad Seal, a General Court held at the India House laid down the conditions under which it should be carried out.[1] These conditions, as finally settled, threw open the freedom of the Company to the public for the nominal sum of 5*l*.[2] They admitted not only the members of the various groups who had made up the old East India and Assada Companies, their servants and apprentices, but also the Merchant Adventurers and private traders in India who might be willing to throw their possessions, at a fair valuation, into the common stock.

That stock was not to be dissolved after the expiry of a few years, as had always been provided in former subscriptions. An appraisement of the

the first time in any Royal Charter to the East India Company, in that of James II., 1686. They recur incidentally in William and Mary's Charter of 1693.

[1] 19th October, 1657, Lansdowne MSS.

[2] MS. Court Book, No. 24, p. 13, December 1657.

Company's property was to be made at the end of 1657
seven years, and thereafter at the end of every three years, so that any shareholder who wished to retire might do so, and receive the current value of his original subscription.[1] But the joint stock was to continue as the common capital of the Company, and the money drawn out by retiring members was to be made good by 'any other persons' who chose to join the Company. As a matter of fact, these triennial appraisements resolved themselves into periodical statements of assets by which the members and the public might regulate their dealings in the stock.

Cromwell thus laid the groundwork of the modern constitution of the East India Company. Under the regulations based on his Charter, it cast its mediæval skin, shook off the traditions of the Regulated system, and grew into one united, continuous, and permanent Joint Stock Corporation in the full sense of the words.[2]

These new conditions of unity and permanence drew forth a large capital of 739,782*l.*—of which only one half was called up. The minimum subscription was fixed at 100*l.*; a contributor had a vote for each 500*l.* of his holding; and 1,000*l.* qualified for election to the Committee. Small adventurers might club together to make up 500*l.*,

[1] *Mercurius Politicus*, October 22-29, 1657.

[2] Some clauses of the Preamble to the Subscription Book of 1657 read almost like the prospectus of a modern Limited Liability Company. The book was to lie open till the 10th November for all persons within a radius of 20 miles of London, and until the 25th for country subscribers.

1657 and appoint one of their number to vote for them. The actual management of the Company was vested, as under the Royal Charters, in a Governor, Deputy-Governor, Treasurer, and a Committee of Twenty-four. With the ample funds at its disposal, the new association bought up the factories, forts, customs and privileges of the old Company in the East,[1] including the island of Pularoon, for 20,000*l.*; arranged for taking over the properties of individual adventurers in India at a valuation; and resolved to unite the Guinea traffic in gold and elephant tusks with the India trade.[2]

While thus amalgamating the various conflicting interests into one permanent Joint Stock, the new Company provided ample safeguards for its own monopoly. Outside traders continued subject to the same penalties as those laid down by King James' Charter—the confiscation of their ship and cargo. Members inside the Company, who might still hanker after the Regulated system and be tempted to trade on their own account, were to forfeit their whole stock or holding to the rest of the shareholders.[3] Fair consideration was extended to all actually engaged, under whatever show of title, in Indian ventures in the past; but there was to be no mercy for private traders, whether inside the Company or outside it, in the future.

[1] Practically of the so-called 'United Joint Stock' formed under the Parliamentary settlement of 1650.

[2] *Mercurius Politicus*, October 1657.

[3] *Idem*, and the Lansdowne MSS.

Although resolved on a firm control of its individual members, the Company made provision for a steady flow of new men from the generality to its governing body. That body consisted, as I have said, of a Governor, Deputy-Governor, and Committee of Twenty-four. But eight members of the Committee were to retire in rotation each July, and no Governor or Deputy-Governor was to serve for more than two successive years.[1] The freemen were also to be relieved of the old inconvenience of having to receive their individual shares of the profits in pepper, calicoes, or other Indian commodities, and all dividends were henceforth to be paid in cash.[2] In the East the New Company received in return for its 20,000*l.* the Old Company's factories at Surat, with dependencies on the Bombay coast; at Fort St. George, with dependencies on the Madras coast and in the Bay of Bengal; at Bantam, with dependencies at Jambi, Macassar, and Pularoon; and Gombroon on the Persian Gulf. 1657

The small price paid for these acquisitions is explained by the circumstances of the times. On the Persian Gulf the Agents of the Old Company had struggled on amid oppressions and exactions, not because they hoped to do any trade, but merely on the chance of reasserting, at some future day, the English right to half the customs of Gombroon under the treaty of 1622.[3] Bantam seemed again to be passing under the power of the Dutch, English ships were intercepted in the narrow seas,

[1] MS. Court Book, No. 24, p. 12, December 1657.

[2] *Idem.*

[3] *Ante*, vol. i. p. 330.

1657 and the port was about to suffer a regular blockade.[1] Nor did the political state of India itself warrant any large price for English possessions on that continent.

The military convulsions, amid which Aurangzeb seized the throne, rudely interrupted the order that the Mughal Empire had during a century imposed. Surat castle was seized and the town pillaged on behalf of one of the claimants; and our distracted President complained 'that it was equally dangerous to solicit, or to accept of, protection, it being impossible to foresee who might ultimately be the Mogul.'[2] In Southern India, the first great act of Maratha hostility to the Mughals took place in May 1657.[3] On the East coast, the Madras Council in despair resolved for the second time to withdraw the factories from Bengal.[4] Their own existence was threatened by the war between the Golconda King and his dependents, and by the still more dreaded approach of the Maratha hordes.

Thus in the very year that Cromwell's Charter reconstituted the Company on its permanent basis at home, the English in the Eastern seas, from the Persian Gulf to the island of Java, stood face to face with ruin. In India itself, the firm Mughal

[1] Petitions of the East India Company to the Lord Protector, dated 19th January and 12th August, 1658. Bruce, i. pp. 531, 539.

[2] Letters from the President and Council of Surat to the Company, dated 5th November, 1657, and 16th January, 1658.

[3] *History of the Mahrattas*, by Captain James Grant Duff, vol. i. p. 119. Bombay reprint, 1863.

[4] *Ante*, p. 99.

rule, under whose shelter our settlements on the 1657
continent had grown up, was for the first time assailed by that combination of Moslem disunion and Hindu confederate force which, during the next fifty years, broke up the Empire.

The new Company went courageously to work. December
It decided that Surat, then in the grip of civil war, should be its sole Presidency in India, and that the factories at Madras, Bengal, Bantam, and the Persian Gulf should be distinct agencies subordinate thereto.[1] All these settlements were destitute alike of money and men. On the Persian Gulf the bare subsistence of the factory consumed the customs of Gombroon and the whole profits of the trade.[2] The late Company had ordered the establishment at Madras to be reduced to two factors with a guard of ten soldiers, and to a single factor at Masulipatam. From every English settlement in the East came the same story of decay. The new Company at once resolved to send out such a staff as never had sailed to India.

In January 1658 it selected seventeen of the 1658
late Company's most likely stations in the East, from China to the Persian Gulf, and appointed to them ninety-one factors and assistants,[3] well

[1] MS. Court Book, No. 24, p. 18, &c.

[2] Letters from the President and Council of Surat to the Company, dated 16th October, 1658, 15th January, and 12th April, 1659. Bruce, i. 543.

[3] MS. Court Book, No. 24, p. 23. The following staff was elected under Cromwell's charter of 1657 at a General Court of the Company in January 1658. The numbers include, apparently, both the strictly commercial establishment of factors, &c. and supernumeraries, such as chaplains and surgeons. To the Presidency of Surat, 20; to Ahmadabad, 3; to

1658 supplied with goods and bullion for the re-establishment of the trade. When an adventurer,[1] under plea of a license from the Commonwealth, shipped mortars and shells for one of the rival claimants to the Mughal throne, the Company firmly remonstrated with Cromwell, and at the same time despatched a consignment to undersell the interloper. On the west coast of Africa it bought up Fort Comantine, together with the charter, rights, and trade of the Guinea Company, for the modest sum of 1,300*l.*[2] In the mid-ocean it resolved to fortify St. Helena, as a half-way house for the Indian fleets.[3] In the Far East it projected a place of strength at Pularoon, and applied to Richard Cromwell for letters to the Emperors of China and Japan.[4] From the charter of 1657 the Company drew a new life, whose pulsations reached its furthest factories in Asia. Against European aggressors it boldly claimed the aid of the Commonwealth. More than once it invoked Cromwell's intervention against Holland; and the

Tatha in Sind, 5; to the coast factories of the south-west coast (Malabar, &c.), 5; to the Persian Gulf and inland Persian agencies, 6; to Fort St. George or Madras, the factory in India next in importance to Surat, 6; to Masulipatam, 4; to 'Verasheroone,' 3 (*i.e.* Víravásaram in the Godavari District; *Imperial Gazetteer of India*, vol. xiii. p. 478, ed. 1887); to Pettapoli, 2 (*ante*, p. 73); to Húgli, 5; to Balasor, 5; to Kasimbazar, 4; to Patna, 4; to Bantam in Java, 6; to Maccassar, 4; to Jambi (a Malay state on the north-east side of Sumatra), 4; to China, 5. MS. Court Book, No. 24, pp. 27, 27*a*, 28.

[1] Mr. Rolt by name, associated with Colonel Rainsford, probably one of Cromwell's old officers, but then at Surat.

[2] MS. Court Book, No. 24, p. 14, December 1657.

[3] *Idem*, p. 81, 1658.

[4] October 1658, just after Cromwell's death. *Idem*, No. 24, pp. 71*a*, 72.

Company's last transaction with the Protector was 1658
still another petition against the Dutch.[1] Three weeks later the strong ruler was dead, and about to be laid with royal pomp in Westminster Abbey.[2]

After the Restoration men dug up his body from its sepulchre among kings, hung it on a gallows, and shovelled the headless trunk into a felon's grave. But though they might tear out his laws from the statute-book and hide away his charters, there was one part of his life's work which they could not destroy. He found the English in the East struggling, humiliated, in despair. He left them with their future assured. He was the first ruler of England who realised that the India trade was no private preserve of the sovereign and his nominees, but a concern of the nation, to be maintained by national diplomacy and defended by the national arms. His union of conflicting Anglo-Indian interests in 1657 anticipated the great Parliamentary fusion of those interests fifty years later. Under his charter the East India Company transformed itself from a feeble relic of the mediæval trade-guild into the vigorous forerunner of the modern Joint Stock Company. A large and continuous capital, always capable of automatic increase, took the place of a succession of uncertain subscriptions, each of them intended to be dissolved at the end of a few years.

[1] Dated 12th August, 1658.

[2] Cromwell died 3rd September, 1658. Buried in Henry VII.'s chapel, November 1658. Exhumed 26th January, 1661, and the corpse hung at Tyburn on 30th January, 1661—the twelfth anniversary of the execution of Charles I.

1658 While Cromwell thus renewed the East India Company and placed it on its permanent basis at home, abroad he secured for England the recognition of her right to a free expansion in the East. The arrogant claims of the Catholic Powers in Asia he blew from the cannon's mouth. Our great Protestant compeer had to learn that similarity in religion formed no excuse for commercial wrong-doing. Cromwell's sea-rivalry with Holland hardened and set into a national tradition, which dominated the feeling of the English trading classes for thirty years; and in the end led to the overthrow of the Dutch supremacy in Asia and to the establishment of our own. The head which planned these great designs was set to shrivel on a pole. But if the grandson of Cromwell's secretary, Milton, died as parish clerk in Madras, both the grandson and great-grandson of the Protector lived to be Governors of Bengal.[1]

[1] Sir John Russell, Governor of Bengal, 1711–1713, son of Cromwell's youngest daughter, Frances; and Sir Henry Frankland (second son of Elizabeth, daughter of the said Frances), Governor of Bengal, 1726–1728. Another great-grandson of Cromwell, Sir Francis Russell, 7th Bart., was a member of the Bengal Council; and the Protector's descendants long formed one of the powerful family connections of the East India Company. I am indebted chiefly to Mrs. Frankland-Russell-Astley of Checkers Court, the present representative of this branch, for the verified pedigree. Caleb Clarke, the grandson of Milton, says Professor Masson, 'rose to what seems to have been his highest position in life, that of Parish Clerk of Madras.' He died there, 26 October, 1719. Masson's *Milton*, vol. vi. pp. 754–758. Ed. 1880.

CHAPTER VI

THE COMPANY'S SERVANTS AND TRADE

TO 1660

THE reader must sometimes have wondered how the Company lived on, in spite of its failures to raise fresh capital, and of its repeated resolves to send forth no more ships. Its legal existence depended, however, not on the continuity of its trade, but on the annual election of certain officials named by the Royal Charters. Neither Elizabeth nor James acknowledged the subscribers as a body corporate. Each of their grants vested privileges not in the Company, but in 'The Governor and Company of the Merchants of London trading into the East Indies.'[1] They could not contemplate the existence of the Company apart from the Governor, nor did they recognise any lawful conduct of its business except through the Governor or his Deputy, acting conjointly with the Committee of Twenty-four as constituted by both the Royal Charters.[2]

In this nucleus of permanent officials lay the

[1] *India Office Library Quarto of Charters:* Elizabeth's, p. 8; James I., p. 33.

[2] A treasurer—more vaguely referred to in Elizabeth's grant, *Idem*, p. 23—and a secretary, accountant, &c., were also elected.

1599 to 1658 secret vitality of the corporation. How permanent they tended to become may be seen from the fact that three men practically governed the Company from its foundation by Elizabeth to the death of Cromwell. Sir Thomas Smythe[1] ruled, except during accidental disabilities, from 1600 to 1621; Sir Morris Abbot from 1624 to 1637; and William Cockayne from 1643 to 1658.[2]

The office proved a burden to its holders, from which they sometimes prayed in vain to be released. The Governor had to preside in person or by his Deputy at all Court Meetings, especially at the election of officers,[3] and as early as 1614 stress was laid on his daily attendance in Parliament 'to answer any imputations that may be cast upon the Company.'[4] He had not only to superintend the details of a great import and export business,

[1] Sir Thomas Smythe was named Governor in both the charters of Elizabeth and James. The breaks (1601–2) were due to his imprisonment for alleged complicity in Essex's rebellion, and to his absence in 1606. But he was promptly re-elected in 1603 and in 1607.

[2] The whole number of Governors from 1600 to 1658, including temporary appointments, only amounted to nine: namely, (1) Sir Thomas Smythe, 1600, 1603–6, 1607–21; (2) Alderman Watts, and (3) Sir John Hart, during Sir T. Smythe's troubles about the Essex rebellion, 1601–2; (4) Sir William Romney, owing to Sir Thomas Smythe's absence, 1606; (5) Sir William Hallidaie, 1621–24; (6) Sir Morris Abbot, 1624–37; (7) Sir Christopher Clitheroe, 1638–41; (8) Sir Henry Garraway, on Sir C. Clitheroe's death, November 1641 to July 1643; (9) William Cockayne, 1643–58. Compiled from the MS. Court Books and *Calendars of State Papers*.

[3] In certain cases this duty was imposed by the Charter (as in that of James I., p. 39, of the *India Office Library Quarto*), and in others by the Company's bye-laws.

[4] *Court Minutes*, April 9, 1614; *Calendar of State Papers*, East Indies, 1513–16, No. 709.

to set on foot new subscriptions, to reconcile the 1599 to 1658
conflicting 'Voyages' or joint-stock groups, and to wind up their accounts; he had also to be in constant and confidential communication with the Government, something of a courtier to the Stuarts, and a good deal of a saint under the Commonwealth. At the same time he had to be placed by his wealth above the suspicion of using his office for his private ends, and to possess an influence which assured him of a seat in the House of Commons.

Of the first of the three merchant-princes who ruled the Company from 1600 to 1658, I gave some account in the preceding volume of this history.[1] The second, Sir Morris Abbot,[2] who governed from 1624 to 1637–8
1624 to 1637 or 1638,[3] was the son of a Guildford clothworker, and was born in 1565. He early rose to eminence as a London merchant, and appears as a founder of the East India Company in both the Charters of Elizabeth and James.[4] Besides conducting a large business of his own in cloth, jewellery, spices and indigo, he took a leading part in many foreign ventures of the day; as a Turkey merchant, a director of a North-West

[1] *Sir Thomas Smythe*, vol. i. pp. 242–3, 248, 250, 270, 277, 288.

[2] *Calendar of State Papers*, East Indies, 1630–34, p. vii. &c.

[3] Abbot was elected Governor on the death of Alderman Hallidaie in March 1624. Some doubt exists regarding the date on which his tenure of office ceased, as the MS. minutes for 1637 and 1638 are missing. He certainly held office in 1636, and Clitheroe was *re*-elected in 1639. MS. Court Books.

[4] As one of the grantees or founders in Elizabeth's charter, and as both a grantee and a 'Committee' or Director in that of James. *India Office Quarto of Charters*, pp. 4, 31, 35.

1624 to 1637–8 Passage exploration, an adviser in the proposed expedition against the Barbary Corsairs, a projector of Persian voyages, and a member of the Council for the Virginia colonisation scheme.

After serving the East India Company for some years as a member of the Committee of Twenty-four, he was in 1615 elected Deputy-Governor, and secured a safe seat in Parliament before becoming Governor in 1624. Nor were his brothers less distinguished in their own calling; as the elevation of one to the Archbishopric of Canterbury, and of another to the Bishopric of Salisbury, attests. He himself was among the first subjects knighted by King Charles, and he retired from the Governorship of the Company, still apt for public service at seventy-three, to become Lord Mayor of London.

This life, so crowned with riches and honours, appears in the Company's records as a hard struggle against fate. To Abbot it fell, as Deputy-Governor, to conduct during eight years (1615–1623) the hopeless negotiations with Holland which ended in a worthless treaty and our expulsion from the Clove Archipelago. In vain he bewailed his 'base usage' to the fickle James. The first year of his governorship was darkened by the news of Amboyna. Sir Morris, calm amid the panic, counselled moderation to the Company and trust in the King. But James' indignation, quite genuine at first, spent itself in tears and inkhorn threats; while Charles' promises ended in his letting go the Dutch ships for a bribe. Not without reason did the generality murmur at their Governor's confidence in the royal word. He indeed served the King but too faithfully: now at the risk of a Star Chamber prosecution for resistance to illegal demands, then at the hazard of the Parliament's vengeance for obeying his Majesty in the matter of ship-money. At last it came to the faithful white-haired man waiting all forenoon in the royal ante-chamber to supplicate Charles against his infringement of the Company's Charter, and the King passing him without a look.[1] 1624 to 1637–8

But although the generality did not spare Abbot reproaches, they could not do without him. In vain he begged to be relieved of his thankless task. They realised that his influence had softened many blows, and stood between them and worse dangers. Already in 1630 he longed for release. Next year he reminded the malcontents 'that he had not made suit at any time to be continued Governor,' and 'had laboured to be eased of this burden.' In 1632 he told the General Court that 'he never had so little comfort in all his time,' 'yet could never go out with more honour than now, having endured the touch and withstood the malice of his adversaries.' Again in 1633 he bade them 'think of some other more able and worthier' than himself.[2] The Company, unlike the King, knew a good servant, and would not let him go. Charles had driven Abbot's elder brother, the Archbishop, in disgrace from Lambeth, for holding

[1] *Ante*, p. 37.

[2] *Calendar of State Papers*, East Indies, 1630–34, Nos. 40, 196, 281, 465.

1624 to 1637–8 aloof from the royal attacks on the liberties of the nation, with as little compunction as he left the loyal old merchant standing among the lackeys of Whitehall.

William Cockayne, Governor from 1643 to
1643 to 1658 1658, carried the Company through the Civil Wars and the Commonwealth to the haven of safety provided by Cromwell's grant. During those fifteen perilous years it was no longer a question of nibbling at the charter by Court and City cabals, but of the abolition of the Company, and the throwing open of the India trade to the nation. Governor Cockayne, who is often confused in the Calendars of State Papers with his kinsman Sir William the magnificent Lord Mayor of London, was a Turkey merchant. As far back as 1623 he had been elected a Director or 'Committee' of the East India Company, but had begged to be excused the honour. After serving in that office from 1629 onwards, the post of Deputy-Governor was forced on him in 1639; and upon the removal of the Royalist Governor by order of Parliament in 1643, William Cockayne was elected Governor of the East India Company.[1] He saw that Charles I. had not the power to help, nor any stedfast purpose even if he should regain the power. Under his guidance

[1] Compiled from the MS. Court Books. Sir Henry Garraway, the Royalist Lord Mayor, and Governor from November 1641, was dismissed from that office in both the Turkey Company and the East India Company, by order of the House, in April 1643. William Cockayne presided as Governor from that year until July 1658, when he reverted to his old position as a Director of the New General Stock under Cromwell's charter.

the Company threw in its lot with the Long Parliament, and in 1647 just failed to obtain a new charter from it. His indomitable resistance to opposition within the corporate body, and to attacks from without, supplied the one element of continuity in its history under the Commonwealth. The reconstitution of the Company on a wider and more permanent basis by Cromwell forms the best memorial of Cockayne's governorship. 1643 to 1658

In his long task he had the aid of a man of wider experience, and a more buoyant nature than his own. William Methwold, nephew of the Lord Chief Baron of the Exchequer in Ireland, served his apprenticeship in Middleborough, and went out to Surat as a servant of the East India Company, in 1615. Indefatigable in trade and in travel, he visited the factories on the Bay of Bengal, and was the first Englishman who explored the mines of Golconda.[1] During seven[2] critical years he guided the English fortunes in India as President at Surat. His letters nerved the disheartened Company to plant itself firmly on the Bengal coast. As a young man he wrote encouraging words from the storm-tossed roadstead of Masulipatam.[3] In

[1] *Relations of the Kingdome of Golchonda and other neighbouring Nations within the Gulfe of Bengalas*, by Master William Methold, printed pp. 993 seq. of Purchas his Pilgrimage, 1626.

[2] Officially from 1633 to 1638, but Methwold probably reckoned from 1631, as John Hopkinson (1631–33) was only President *pro tem.* In his evidence before the General Court Methwold declared he had been president for the last seven years of his Indian service. MS. Court Book, No. 17, p. 78*a*.

[3] *Calendar of State Papers*, East Indies, 1617–21, No. 782, *ad finem.*

high office he calmly faced the fact that the trade of Surat, after the great pestilence and famine, must take four or five years to revive; and before the end of that period he restored it to prosperity.[1] His treaty with the Goa Viceroy in 1635 became the basis of the free intercourse between

1640 to 1653 the English and the Portuguese in the East. On his return to England, after twenty-five years of service, Methwold took an important part in the home control, and, both as a shareholder and when Deputy-Governor, opposed the counsels of despair.[2] Hitherto the potent voices in the Company's courts had been those of city magnates, like Sir Thomas Smythe and Sir Morris Abbot. William Methwold was the first of its servants who brought home a great fortune from the East. His stately abode in Kensington, Cromwell House,[3] was only pulled down to give place to the Exhibition of 1851, and its name survives in a noble line of mansions.

1657 Cromwell's Charter marks the triumph of the permanent officials of the Company over the section which desired individual liberty of trade. It also marks the beginning of their decline. The basis of a lasting Joint Stock supplied a new element of stability. Continuity of capital took the place of the permanence of the governing body. Seven

[1] *Idem*, 1630–34, No. 607. Also MS. Court Books.

[2] For example, in his evidence before Lord Cottington and the General Court in the spring of 1640, and again in October of the same year. MS. Court Book, No. 17, pp. 78*a*, 165; and again in 1646.

[3] Originally Hale House. Methwold bought it in 1648, erected alms-houses near it for six poor women, and died in 1653. *Dict. National Biography*, xxxvii. p. 309, *s.n.* Methold.

weeks after the charter passed the Broad Seal, 1657
the Company resolved that no Governor or Deputy-Governor should serve more than two years in succession, and that eight of the twenty-four Directors, or 'Committees,' should retire annually in rotation.[1]

The task of distributing the profits to the shareholders was at the same time simplified. Formerly a complicated division of the imports often took place.[2] The United Company under the new charter determined that the cargoes should be sold for the general benefit, and all dividends paid in cash.[3] The office of treasurer, which had also tended towards a too powerful permanence, was abolished, or, rather, placed in commission; and the 'trust of the treasure' made over to a sub-committee of three.[4]

The Governor, Deputy-Governor, and Committee of Twenty-four, or Directors, received no salaries. But the General Court voted them 'gratifications,' which grew into a right.[5] When an attempt was made to obtain Directors without payment, Sir Morris Abbot plainly told the gene-

[1] At a General Court held 10th–13th December, 1657 (MS. Court Book, No. 24, p. 12). A movement in favour of a new Governor being elected each year had taken place among the generality as far back as 1631–32, but was frustrated by Sir Morris Abbot's influence.

[2] Thus on July 7, 1641, a dividend of 25 per cent. was announced to be paid, five-eighths in silk, two-eighths in calico, and one-eighth in cloves. MS. Court Book, No. 18, p. 3.

[3] *Idem*, No. 24, p. 12.

[4] *Idem*, No. 24, p. 13.

[5] The total of these 'gratifications' to the 'Governor, Deputy, Treasurer Committees, with all their principal officers and servants at Crosby House and Blackwall, amounts not to $1\frac{1}{2}$ per cent. upon the stock sent out and returned whereas no merchant allowed his

1631 rality 'that if such men be chosen,' he should 'get his estate out of their hands as soon as he could.' For they must 'have some further end than the good of the Company.'[1] Under Cromwell's Charter, a regular scale of salaries, although not extended to the Governor, Deputy and Directors, was drawn up.[2]

If the Company declined to leave the undivided trust of its money in any one man's hands, it also took steps to save its servants from the temptations incident to misspent time and bad company. Under the Commonwealth it demanded from them a godly life; amid the orgies of the Restoration it forbad all clerks of the India House to 'go to play-houses, dancing schools' or taverns, under pain of dismissal.[3] For its workmen, and

factors abroad for factorage and storage less than 2 and 2½ per cent.' Minutes of a General Court held 2nd July, 1630. *Calendar of State Papers*, East Indies, 1630-1634, No. 40. Sir Thomas Roe, on his return from his embassy, was allowed 200*l.* a year for a time as a Director or 'Committee.' But the arrangement seems to have been an exceptional one. Court Minutes, 1619–1621. Mr. Wm. Foster's *Embassy of Sir Thomas Roe*, vol. ii. pp. 529–30, and Introd. 1899.

[1] Court Minutes, 1631. *Calendar of State Papers, ut supra*, No. 196.

[2] With effect from 1659. The officials elected in July 1660, and nominally subject to annual re-election, were as follows: Accomptant-General, salary 220*l.*; his assistant, 80*l*; Writer of Letters and Keeper of Calicoe Warehouse, 150*l*; Cashier, 150*l.*; his assistant, 80*l.*; Husband and Keeper of Saltpetre Warehouse, 80*l.*; Surveyor of Shipping, 50*l.*; Paymaster of the Mariners, 30*l.*; Beadle and Porter, 30*l.*; Keeper of Pepper Warehouse, 140*l.*; Solicitor, 20*l.*; Keeper of the Blue (*i.e.* indigo) Warehouse, 80*l.* In 1661 the date of election was altered from July to April. MS. Court Book, No. 24, p. 184*a*; *Idem*, No. 24, p. 139.

[3] MS. Court Minutes for January 17, 1679. A batch of clerks was summoned before the General Court, and admonished by the Governor for these offences.

the population which grew up around its docks and warehouses at Blackwall, the Company voted 200*l.* for a chapel to be built at Poplar; as owing to their distance from Stepney Church 'most of them are deprived of the means of Grace for their precious souls.'[1] Nor did it forget its worn-out servants or their widows and orphans in its almshouses, but provided that the Psalms and Lessons be read twice a day 'with one of the prayers at the end of the Bible.'[2]

The Company celebrated the departure and the return of its ships by a solemn service and a special 1634 sermon. In 1634, long before the reign of the saints, members declared on the Exchange that in the guidance of their affairs they saw 'the finger of God.' The General Court sometimes opened its proceedings with thanks to the Almighty for the safe arrival of vessels, and it was at least on one occasion called together chiefly for that purpose.[3] The Company thus took on the Puritan colour of the times; but it was a Puritanism content to abide by the ritual of the Church until stirred into resistance by Laud.

Over its factors in India it kept a paternal eye. It sent out to them good books for Sunday and Ministers of the Word. Yet the theology 'of that worthy servant of Christ, Mr. William Perkins,'[4]

[1] MS. Court Book, No. 23, p. 65.

[2] *Idem*, No. 19, p. 133*a*, February 7, 1645.

[3] *Calendar of State Papers*, East Indies, 1630–1634, Nos. 184, 281, 622, and many other documents.

[4] *First Letter Book of the East India Company*, Birdwood and Foster, 4th April, 1611, p. 419. The works selected at a later period, under Cromwell's Charter, were entirely

as he is styled in the records, proved dry reading in the tropics; and the chaplains, although sometimes keen traders, did not always command the respect
1617 of their little flocks. Thus in 1617, while Chaplain Lesk wrote bitterly of the 'luxurious and hare-brained youths'[1] at Surat, and calumniated the President,[2] a pious merchant of the same place was praying the Company to send them true preachers 'to break unto the factors the blessed manna of the heavenly Gospel.'[3] Chaplains there were of high merit,[4] backsliders there doubtless were among English lads suddenly set free from the restraint of public opinion and of home life. But the chance notices of travellers give a fairer picture of the habits and morals of the early servants of the Company in India than their own recriminations, clerical or lay.

1623 In 1623, Pietro della Valle visited Surat under circumstances not calculated to bias him in favour of the English. He had brought his young wife, and he offended our President[5] by refusing the hospitality of the factory where there were only men. Yet he acknowledged that the English chief

books of 'practical divinity' by Dr. Reynolds, Mr. Baxter, Mr. Perkins again, Dr. Downham, &c., quite a little theological library at a cost of 40*l.* March 19, 1658. MS. Court Book, No. 24, p. 46.

[1] *Calendar of State Papers*, East Indies, 1617–1621, No. 54.

[2] Thomas Kerridge, whose 'integrity and ability were unquestionable,' says a more impartial witness: Chaplain Anderson's *English in Western India*, p. 42, ed. 1856.

[3] *Idem*, p. 54.

[4] For example, the good Henry Lord. *Idem*, pp. 51, 53. Chaplains were chosen with care; the Company assigning a text to the clerical candidates, and attending in a body to hear them preach on it.

[5] Thomas Rastell, President of Surat, 1622–1624, again in 1631.

proved himself in all things a person accomplished and generous, with a mastery of the Italian tongue, and that their difference ended in good-fellowship.[1] About fifteen years later (1638) Albert de Mandelslo gives a detailed account of the little English community at Surat. The strict order observed, the deference to the President, the collegiate life of the factory, the common table with the Chaplain to say grace, above all the Divine Service held twice daily, and on Sundays three times—made a deep impression on the traveller. 1638

Then as now the eyes of the exiles turned wistfully towards home. 'On Fridayes after prayers, there was a particular assembly,' writes Mandelslo, 'at which met with us three other merchants, who were of kin to the President, and had left as well as he their wives in England, which day being that of their departure from England, they had appointed it for to make a commemoration thereof, and drink their wives' healths. Some made their advantage of this meeting to get more than they could well carry away, though every man was at liberty to drink what he pleas'd, and to mix the sack as he thought fit, or to drink Palepuntz, which is a kind of drink consisting of aqua vitæ, rose-water, juice of citrons and sugar. At our ordinary meetings every day we took only Thé.'[2]

[1] *The Travels of Pietro della Valle in India*, edited by Edward Grey, 1892, vol. i. pp. 19, 26, 28, 29. Hakluyt Society.

[2] 'Which,' continues Mandelslo, 'is commonly used all over the Indies, not only among those of the country, but also among the Dutch and English, who take it as a Drug that cleanses the stomach, and digests the superfluous humours, by a temperate heat

1600 to 1660 India constrains to temperance, and the English factors soon found that deep potations, even in honour of absent wives, had to be too dearly paid for. Some among them were men of great ability,[1] skilful negotiators with the native Powers, vigilant traders in the Company's interests and their own, masters of a lucid business style, and not less ready with the pen on shore than with broadsides against the Dutch and Portuguese at sea. What the Company most dreaded was 'intemperate living,' meaning thereby not drunkenness alone, or even chiefly, but 'pride and gorgeous apparell,' the 'wearing of gold lace,' the use of umbrellas by the younger men,[2] 'profane oaths,' irregular attendance at morning or evening prayers, and coming in after the factory gate was locked for the night.

Their worst crime was gambling, a failing common in all times to bachelor groups of English-

particular thereto.' *The Voyages and Travels of J. Albert de Mandelslo . . . into the East Indies.* Translated by John Davies. London 1662, p. 18. The 'Palepuntz' was of course punch (from the Maráthi *pánch* = five), compounded of five ingredients, viz. arrack, sugar, lime-juice, spice, and water. Sir Henry Yule accused Schiller of sacrificing truth to trope in his *Punschlied* by omitting the spice and making the elements four. But Mandelslo and others also reckoned them at four, perhaps because they assumed spice to be common to all Indian drinks and dishes.

[1] Mr. Noel Sainsbury thus sums up from his exhaustive examination of the records: 'Most of the factors were, indeed, thoroughly competent and well-fitted for their posts and deserved well of the Company, but'—there were black sheep among them. *Calendar of State Papers*, East Indies, 1630–1634. Introduction, p. xvi.

[2] For an umbrella implied a servant to carry it, and was regarded as a piece of Portuguese ostentation. *Ante.* vol. i. p. 158, last lines.

men from the East to the Far West. In vain the 1600 to 1660
Company commanded that all who indulged in games of chance should be sent home. One President went so far as to reply that he did not know of any gamesters or dicers remaining at any factory. Yet there were youths who lost at 'dice, lance, knight, or cards' two or three years' salary in as many hours—not a difficult feat, as a writer's pay was but 20*l.* per annum. One famous delinquent is said to have parted with 1,000*l.* in a single night.[1]

The stigma attached to such individual cases,[2] and the prominence given to them, prove the reality of the Company's efforts to enforce an orderly life. The Portuguese had made an even more ample provision for public religious observances. But while the Government at Goa raised a revenue from licenses to gambling saloons, where the gamesters ate and slept for days together, the Company visited the frequenters of 'China houses' with severe penalties, and sternly cut off dicers and card-players by dismissal and deportation. It
struck fearlessly at offenders in high places, and 1631
recalled its President at Bantam for his bad example to the youth.[3]

The family life of the factory enabled the President to exercise a control not less strict than

[1] The above details are collected chiefly from the MS. Court Books and the Calendars of State Papers, 1600 to 1660.

[2] I only find three very bad ones between 1630 and 1634, and two of them were denounced as much for their private trade as for gambling or intemperate living. *Calendar of State Papers*, East Indies, 1630–1634, pp. 417–628. 'The ancient order' by the Company against gaming was repeatedly renewed, *e.g.* p. 501.

[3] *Idem*, No. 142, February 1631.

1600 to 1660 that of the Head of a House at Oxford. The youth who stayed out at night, or who came in after the gate was shut, had to pay forty shillings (or five weeks' salary) to the poor. For absence from prayers the fine was 2*s.* 6*d.* on weekdays and 5*s.* on Sundays; for an oath, 1*s.*; for being drunk, and 'thereby prostituting the worthiness of our nation and religion to the calumnious censure of the heathen,' 2*s.* 6*d.*; for striking or abusing persons not in the Company's service, 'three days' imprisonment in irons.'[1] The factory formed a large trade-household, in which the President exercised all the authority of the mediæval master-craftsman over the apprentices and men under his roof. The Company itself kept up a 'Black Book' for offenders,[2] and a 'White Book' for faithful services.[3]

These efforts to enforce 'temperate living' were powerfully aided by the climate. The Indian sun makes no allowance for human frailty; exposure and lack of the modern adaptations to a tropical life killed off even the most temperate of the early English by scores. We have seen five out of six pioneers die in the Orissa swamps in one autumn; two ships with their crews destroyed by disease in harbour and unable to put off to sea;[4] the pestilence at Surat slaying three-fourths of the English settlement; and the refugees at Lagundy withering away

[1] Orders by the President and Council at Surat, April 29, 1633. *Calendar of State Papers, ut supra*, No. 434.

[2] *Idem.* No. 283, July 11, 1632.

[3] MS. Court Book, No. 17, p. 113*a*, July 11, 1640.

[4] *Ante*, p. 93.

like infected sheep.[1] The average mortality was, indeed, appalling, and during five years, for which the results can be worked out, one-fourth of the Company's factors in the East (men in the prime of life) perished.[2] They dine to the sound of soft music, a physician wrote of the English at Surat, yet 'I reckon they walk but in charnel houses.'[3] 1600 to 1660

The Company chose its servants for home and abroad by election at the Court of Committees, and marked its sense of the trust reposed in the higher grades by grave ceremonial. For a President at Surat they required 'a person so qualified that he may be an honour to Christianity and to this nation in those parts,' also 'able and knowing in managing of affairs.' 'Every gentleman present' at the Court, therefore, 'was desired to lay his hand on his heart and consult with himself where such a man may be found.'[4] The President thus chosen in 1658 for Surat[5] declared himself reluctant to accept the burden, but eventually yielded, and sailed with 150*l.* for his outfit, and all the pomp of a farewell dinner.

The money salaries in the factories seem to

[1] *Ante*, p. 60 and vol. i. p. 424.

[2] Forty-eight out of 190 in 1630–1634. *Calendar of State Papers*, East Indies, 1630–1634, p. xvi.

[3] *A New Account of East India and Persia*, by John Fryer, M.D., p. 68, London, 1698. Fryer deals with the period from 1672 to 1681, when the English had to some extent learned to accommodate their dress, dwellings, and diet to Indian conditions. His reason for the mortality is 'the climate being extremely unhealthy.'

[4] MS. Court Book, No. 24, pp. 25, 25*a*, January 1658.

[5] Mr. Nathaniel Wyche. MS. Court Book, No. 24, pp. 26*a*, 49.

1600 to 1660 have been lower than those of the India House officials at home.[1] Such comparisons, however, are attended with difficulty, as the duties were not identical, although the positions of the high officials at Surat, who directed the whole of the Company's trade in the East, were not less onerous and responsible than those at the India House. But they were usually held by younger men. It was not till a later period that the necessity became recognised of granting a higher scale of pay for Indian than for home service.

By the arrangements made under Cromwell's charter, a total sum of 1,110*l.* was sanctioned for a mercantile staff of sixteen persons at the controlling Presidency of Surat; of 200*l.* for establishments of six persons at each of the subordinate agencies, Madras and Bantam; and of 100*l.* for a staff of four persons at minor factories,[2] as in Bengal. But these sums were exclusive of lodging and free board at the common table of the factory; indeed, the diet and sumptuary allowances to the

[1] For example, in 1658, the chief accountant at the India House received 220*l.*, and the chief accountant at Surat, 150*l.*; the cashier at the India House, 150*l.*, and the 'General Purser' at Surat, 100*l.*; the 'Writer of Letters' at the India House and Keeper of the Calicoe Warehouse, 150*l.*, and the Warehouse Keeper at Surat, 70*l.*

[2] MS. Court Book, No. 24, pp. 24, 24*a*. The list for Surat drawn up on the 7th January, 1658, was as follows: A President, 500*l.*; an Accomptant, 150*l.*; a General Purser, 100*l.*; a Warehouse Keeper, 70*l.*; (these four were of the Council); a Secretary, 40*l.*, five Factors at 30*l.* each, 150*l.*; five 'Young Men for Writers' at 20*l.* each, 100*l.* Total, 1,110*l.*, besides a surgeon and a chaplain, 100*l.* MS. Court Book, *ut supra*, p. 39. A chaplain sometimes received a stipend of only 50*l.* and 10*l.* with which to buy books, but his salary varied from time to time.

President exceeded his whole salary.[1] The three senior members next to the President, who constituted the Council, might live outside the factory, and in that case they had house and table allowances of their own. 1600 to 1660

The money salaries formed, however, but a part of the emoluments of the Company's servants in the East. From the commencement it followed the Portuguese precedent,[2] and supplemented their wages by granting them an interest in the trade, and in certain cases a share in the general profits.[3] The Company tried in this way to limit its servants to adventures of known amount, and from the first it compelled them to give security to abstain from private trade.[4]

[1] Salary 500*l*. Diet allowance of 20*l*. per head for twelve juniors in the factory, 240*l*.; sumptuary allowance, 260*l*; total allowances, 600*l*. MS. Court Book, No. 24, p. 23.

[2] *Ante*, vol. i. p. 175.

[3] Thus, in 1600 a captain was to have 100*l*. as wages, with a credit of 200*l*. for an adventure on his own account, and a reward rising from 500*l*. to 2,000*l*., according as the voyage yielded a profit of two to five times the capital outlay. The factors and supercargoes received their remuneration in like manner, partly in cash, and partly in the right to an adventure to the amount of twice their money wages—from the factors of the first class, who received 100*l*. in cash, and 200*l*. as an adventure, down to those of the fourth class, who received 20*l*. in cash, and 40*l*. as an adventure. Court Minutes of October 8 and November 6 to 22, 1600. Stevens' *Dawn of Trade in the East Indies*, pp. 37, 81; Bruce, i. 129, 131.

[4] Court Minutes, 1600. Private trade, except under license from the Company, was forbidden by both the Charters of Elizabeth and James I. See, also, index to vol. i. of this History ('Trade, private'), and the indices to the *First Letter Book of the East India Company*, Birdwood and Foster. *Letters Received from its Servants in the East*, vol. ii., and the *Calendar of State Papers* (East India Series), for innumerable references to private trading by the Company's servants.

1600 to 1660 The Company's servants were thus early taught to have an eye to other sources than their salaries for their gains. They gradually improved upon their teachers, and came to regard their pay as a mere retainer, while they looked to private trade for their real remuneration. As long as the Company
1600–1612 confined its operations to Separate Voyages, each with its own mercantile staff which, for the most part, went out and returned in the ships, such private trading would be kept within bounds. A deputation of Directors from time to time boarded the homeward Indiamen off Dover or in the Downs, and took an inventory of the cargo before any of it could be surreptitiously landed.[1] Any excessive amount of private freight with difficulty escaped detection, although the Company was not too strict to mark the perquisites of servants who brought home large profits to itself.

When, however, the system of Separate Voyages
1613–1660 gave place in 1612 to Joint-Stock series of voyages, each series extending over several years, private trading took a firmer root. The successive joint-stock groups of adventurers had interests of their own not altogether identical with, and in course of time divergent from, those of the permanent Company. Some of them were by no means anxious that the Directors should board their ships or make out lists of their contents. Denunciations against secret trading, which were heard from the very

[1] A deputation of this sort went to Dover as late as 1643. MS. Court Book, No. 19, p. 2*a*. Dover was always a suspected place for shooting cargo, as in the case of Lord Denbigh, *ante*, p. 32.

first voyage in 1600, became louder as they grew 1600 to 1660
less effectual. The old days when the Company could secure honesty by making doublets without pockets for its spice-porters were over.[1] It determined to regulate a practice which it could not prevent, and drew up a long list of commodities[2] which its servants might export or import on their own account, within fixed measurements of cargo space. The Company concentrated its efforts not against private trading, but against excessive private trading.

Private trade by the cubic foot proved, however, as difficult to control as the old unlicensed dealings. The Directors appealed for help to the Crown, and Charles I., ever gracious in granting favours which cost him nothing, repeatedly denounced secret trading by the Company's servants.
His proclamation of 1632 increased the allowance 1632
of licensed freight to the various grades, but made any excess of it a Star Chamber offence, gave the Company the right of search and arrest, and commanded all public officers to aid it in enforcing these wide powers.[3] The increasing importance

[1] *Ante*, vol. i. p. 279.

[2] These exports included, among other articles, English drapery, woollens, silk stockings, garters, ribbons, hats, shoes, pewter, iron, looking-glasses, saffron, and 'aqua vitæ, and all other strong waters.' The chief imports licensed for private trade by the Company's servants were pepper, sugar, ginger, preserved nutmegs, drugs of all sorts, the more common precious stones, carpets, damasks, taffetas, and porcelain. The inferior grades were allowed freight for one chest of these commodities, not to exceed four feet long by one and a half feet in depth and width. Captains, factors, masters, pursers, and mates were allowed two chests apiece.

[3] Proclamation dated Whitehall, February 19, 1632, *Calendar of State Papers*, East Indies,

of the joint-stock groups, as distinguished from the permanent Company, threw new difficulties in the way. Before long the Company and the Star Chamber itself were struggling for existence, and had small leisure for trade delinquents.

1600 to 1630 While the Company thus found it hard to check secret freight in its own homeward-bound ships, the private trading of its servants in the East passed beyond control. The few Englishmen left behind in 1601 to collect pepper and cloves for the next cargo had grown by 1630 into a permanent staff about one hundred and forty strong.[1] Appointed by the Company, and technically its servants, their actual dealings were with successive groups of adventurers who sometimes fell out with each other and with the Directors at home. Each successive 'joint-stock,' or group of adventurers, practically took over the permanent staff, ships, factories, and forts of its predecessors. The establishments in India found themselves servants of many masters; masters with conflicting interests, and changing every few years. If each new group of adventurers got its consignments sold quickly, and found a good return cargo in readiness, it did not ask how the Indian factors employed their leisure between the annual arrival of the fleets.

A time came, moreover, when new joint-stocks could not be raised at home, and annual fleets

1630–34, No. 263. The proclamation raised the allowance to four chests of the previous size to commanders, captains, and factors; three chests to masters; and two chests to pursers, masters' mates, boatswains, carpenters, gunners, and stewards.

[1] *Calendar of State Papers*, East Indies, 1630–1634, p. xvi.

ceased to arrive in the East. The Indian factors, thus left to their own resources, struck out a port-to-port trade for themselves. The Company kept over twenty vessels[1] in the Eastern seas to distribute the goods brought from Europe, and to collect cargoes in the Archipelago or the Indian roadsteads. This coasting trade, chiefly carried on by barter, required local knowledge, yielded high profits, and amid the encroachments of the King and the confusion which followed his downfall, it passed into the hands of the Company's servants.[2] For a time, indeed, no one else was forthcoming to carry it on, save perhaps Courten's captains who proved willing accomplices. In vain the Directors at home imposed fines of increasing severity[3] on its servants for clandestine traffic, and denounced them as caterpillars who 'devour the Company's fruits.'[4] Rebuke and punishment proved alike powerless; its servants paid the fines, and went on with their private trade.

1620 to 1630

1636–40

In 1640 a shareholder declared that 'the Company do send shipps and trade to no purpose, in regard that one-fourth part thereof is for other men's profit.'[5] The local compact of 1635 between Surat and Goa gave new opportunities for secret trade with the Portuguese; and the Dutch servants in the East, whatever the public relations between

1640

[1] *Ante*, pp. 60, 61.

[2] Exactly what had happened in the Portuguese settlements. *Ante*, vol. i. pp. 175–6.

[3] For example, MS. Court Books, No. 15, p. 176*a*, 1634 (400*l.*); No. 20, p. 147*a*, 1648 (500*l.*); No. 21, p. 98, 1652 (800*l.*).

[4] *Calendar of State Papers*, East Indies, 1630–34, No. 230.

[5] MS. Court Book, No. 17, p. 165.

1640 to 1645 Holland and England, were always happy to do private business with the English factors for their mutual benefit. Nor did these abuses fail to find connivance at home. Any official at the India House might hope to be elected to a post in the East, and some were not too eager to abolish the surreptitious traffic which would form the chief source of their emoluments. The Directors themselves were called to declare on oath that they had no complicity in the matter.[1]

1645 to 1656 A further development took place when, amid the distresses of the Civil War and for a time under the Commonwealth, the India trade became practically open to the nation. The generality clamoured in the Company's courts at home for the liberty of individual trading, on the ground that the Company had not the capital wherewith to send out more ships.[2] The servants in India quietly assumed the privilege. They became, in fact, commission agents, and the successive groups of adventurers or managers of Particular Voyages paid a percentage for selling their consignments and collecting return cargoes.[3] Indeed, the United Joint Stock projected in the second year of the Commonwealth resolved to admit the factors in the East as partners in their adventure.[4]

It has been needful to explain, with some fulness, the origin of the private trade of the Com-

[1] MS. Court Book, No. 19, p. 138; March 14, 1645.

[2] *Ante*, p. 120.

[3] The percentage was paid at home to the Company or the several Joint Stocks.

[4] MS. Court Book, No. 20, p. 240, February 1650.

pany's servants in the East, in order to understand the dimensions which it afterwards attained, and the success with which it defied control. For more than a century and a half it formed the bitter cry of the English Directors, as it formed the standing complaint of the Portuguese kings and of the Dutch Company. In the case of the three nationalities, the system inevitably arose from the position of their servants in the East—men with small salaries, and encouraged from the first to regard their salaries as but part of their gains. All that can be said is that the English factors availed themselves of their opportunities to a not greater excess than the Dutch, and with a moderation unknown to the Portuguese. 1600 to 1660

There is no English counterpart of the Portuguese commodore of two royal ships, who lost one by overloading it with a double cargo, while he freighted the other with his own goods; or of squadrons on guard deserting their station in order to trade; or of the coasting voyage which yielded 2,450*l.* to the captain and 78*l.* to the king.[1] From the founding of the Company by Elizabeth to the death of Cromwell I find only two large fortunes brought home from the East. But the case of Methwold, enriched by private trade, yet courted by the Directors on his return, and afterwards elected Deputy-Governor, formed an example which neither

[1] *Ante*, vol. i. pp. 176–178. For the abuses of private trade by the Portuguese officials in India, and the vain attempts of the Government to repress them, see also pp. 174, 175, 178–182 of the same volume.

1600 to 1660 persistent rebukes nor intermittent fines could deter his fellow-factors from trying to imitate. If the authorities at home went against them, local European feeling in India was strong in their support. At Bantam the factors arrested and
1631 imprisoned the Company's agent for trying to put down their private trade.[1]

Besides the shore establishments in India, the Company had always a large body of servants afloat. As Madras, Bombay, and Calcutta emerged only after a series of tentative settlements along the coast, so the magnificent East Indiaman of the eighteenth century was the result of many experiments in shipping tried during the seventeenth. The
1600 to 1609 Company started in 1600 by buying four vessels secondhand, and continued to purchase old craft down to 1609.[2] But it found vessels constructed for short European voyages unsuited to the armed
1607 trade of the East, and in 1607 it resolved to build ships of its own.[3] Till then it had only required repairing docks, which it borrowed from the Admiralty.[4] It now leased a great dock of its own

[1] *Calendar of State Papers*, East Indies, 1630–1634, Nos. 247, 255, 1631.

[2] The first four vessels aggregated 1,400 tons, and their crews 280 men. *Ante*, vol. i. 277. The prices paid on the second-hand system from 1600 to 1609 may be judged from the following. In 1600 the *Mare Scurge* (afterwards the *Dragon* or *Red Dragon*), a strong privateer of 600 tons, 8,700*l.*; the *Susan*, a trader of 240 tons, 1,600*l.*; the *Guift*, a victualler of 130 tons, to be cast off at sea at the discretion of the commander, 300*l.* In 1607–8 the *Union*, 400 tons, 1,250*l.*; in 1609 the *Bonaventure* (afterwards the *Expedition*), 2,200*l.*, with 329*l.* for repairs. *India Office List of Marine Records*; Mr. Registrar Danvers' Introduction, pp. v, vi.

[3] Court Minutes of 21st August, 1607.

[4] *Idem*, 25th September, 1600.

at Deptford,[1] and on the 30th December, 1609 the King came down in state to launch the Company's first two ships.[2] The system of building its own ships continued for twenty years, encouraged by the royal bounty of five shillings a ton.[3] 1609 to 1629

It was this new class of vessels, strongly constructed for war or trade, that broke the Portuguese power in the Asiatic seas, and enabled the English Company, with its insignificant fleets, to struggle, ship for ship, with the Dutch. But it cost more money[4] than the second-hand system, and involved a large payment for dead stock afloat from each fresh group of subscribers. When, after King Charles' desertion in the Amboyna troubles, capital for new adventures could not be raised, the Company began to feel the building of its own ships a heavy burden. Under the old second-hand system it had sometimes reserved an option of returning a ship to its vendor at half-price after the voyage.[5]

[1] Court Minutes, 5th September, 1607.

[2] They were the *Trades Increase*, 1,100 tons, and the pinnace, *Peppercorn*. *Ante*, vol. i. pp. 288, 289.

[3] Granted by Henry VIII.; revived by Elizabeth, and continued by James I., on all English-built vessels of 100 tons and upwards. In 1614 the Company received 921*l*. 5*s*. as bounty for the *Trades Increase*, *Peppercorn*, *Clove*, *Thomas*, *James*, *Hosiander*, and 491*l*. 10*s*. as bounty for the *New Year's Gift*, *Hope* and *Expectation*. Court Minutes, 15th March and 8th June, 1614.

[4] To build a ship of 600 to 700 tons cost the Company 5,000*l*. to 6,000*l*. *Calendar of State Papers*, East Indies, 1630–1634, No. 560, April 1634. The *Mare Scurge*, or *Dragon*, a strong warship of 600 tons, had been bought second-hand for 3,700*l*.

[5] Thus the *Susan* was bought from Mr. Alderman Bannyng for 1,600*l*., on condition that he would re-purchase it for 800*l*.

1629 to 1657 In 1629 it tried to extend this principle, and to supersede the building of its ships by a system of hiring. But at first it found no one willing to let ships for the India voyage, even although it offered up to 45*l.* a ton of freight. Gradually, however, shipowners came forward. Before the close of Charles I.'s reign an ample supply of freight to India could be hired on fair terms, and the Company was trying to sell its shipbuilding docks.[1]

On the reconstitution of the Company under
1657 Cromwell's Charter in 1657, it continued the system of hiring freight, supplemented by a new plan of getting ships built for its service, although not at its own cost. The hiring led to abuses, as it was not conducted by open tender, but left to a small committee chosen from the body of Directors, among whom were shipowners who avowedly let their own ships to the Company. The new system of getting ships built for it, on condition of giving them preferential employment, developed into the permanent basis of the Company's marine. It commenced in 1657 with 'three good able three-decked ships of 450 to 500 tons,'[2] to be specially constructed for the Company's needs on the promise of their regular employment at the rates of freight

on its return from India, if the Company desired.

[1] In 1642 the freight paid for a voyage to Bantam had fallen to 25*l.* per ton, and in 1645 to 20*l.* Towards the close of the Commonwealth the freight to Surat and back ranged from 18*l.* to 22*l.* In 1645 the Company had under consideration a proposal to sell its Blackwall docks, and in 1652 the docks were in possession of Mr. Henry Johnson on a 21 years' lease at a rent of 200*l.* *per annum.* *India Office List of Marine Records*, p. viii.

[2] Marine Records, Miscellaneous, No. 1. *Idem*, p. x.

from time to time current. Under this system a privileged body of shipowners grew up who created and maintained a noble fleet for the Company. 1657

It is difficult to present a continuous computation of the Company's trade under Charles I. and the Commonwealth. Many documents have disappeared, and the secrecy enjoined in respect to accounts renders it doubtful whether a complete record ever existed.[1] That secrecy was imposed not alone on the staff of the Company at home and abroad, but also on all servants of the successive groups of subscribers with whose capital the trading was actually done. Each successive group had to make its profits out of its own venture, and then to get rid of its 'remaines' or fixed capital in India to its successor. It objected to disclose facts which might be useful to other adventurers, and detrimental to itself. The managing body of the Company—that is, the Governor and Committee of Twenty-four as constituted by the charters—saw that fair play was done between the successive groups of subscribers, but the accounts came before it in strict confidence, and although it declared the results it refused to divulge the details. We even find the generality much aggrieved because the Book of Orders, or bye-laws of the Company, was withheld from it; nor were any financial dis-

[1] Bruce, who compiled his *Annals* from the papers existing for each year in the India House at the beginning of this century, furnishes valuable data for individual years, but fails to yield anything like a consecutive account. My own attempt at a presentment makes use of his materials, and supplements them by a re-examination of the manuscript records in the India Office.

1600 to 1660 closures made to members until the final balance was struck.[1]

Any leakage of information to the outside public was jealously guarded against. The first attempt at an East India trade-corporation[2] under Edward VI. had been officially styled 'the Mystery and Company of the Merchant Adventurers,' and the Company of Elizabeth preserved the traditional secrecy of the mediæval guild. With regard to its successes or its failures it maintained an equal silence; and resented public congratulation only less than public censure. The poet under the first Stuarts combined the functions of the political pamphleteer and the company promoter. Prince Rupert's Madagascar scheme had been sung by Davenant,[3] and the first public suggestion of the offer of the crown to Cromwell is said to have occurred in Waller's verse.[4] A needy bard thought he might earn something by an ode on the safe arrival of
1649 seven of the Company's ships. The General Court, after deliberation, paid him 3*l.* for his lines, but desired him 'neither to print them, nor proceed any further in making verses upon any occasion which may concern the Company.'[5]

Apart from this tradition of secrecy, it is doubtful whether the Company itself possessed a

[1] MS. Court Book, No. 15, p. 215.

[2] Formed December 18, 1551. *Ante*, vol. i. 199.

[3] *Ante*, p. 32. Davenant's *Works*, p. 205, ed. 1673.

[4] On the capture of the Spanish vessels, 1656. *Poems*, p. 198, ed. 1711.

[5] September 5, 1649. The versifier was Francis Lenton, 'Queenes Poet' and frequenter of the Fleece Tavern, then fallen on evil days. MS. Court Book, No. 20, p. 194*a*.

complete and continuous statement of accounts. 1600 to 1660
Its book-keeping was still of the mediæval type; laboriously exact for a private merchant, sufficing for a trade-guild, but inadequate to the Company's development of the old Regulated system into rudimentary forms of the modern Joint Stock. The cent. per cent. profits of the separate voyages were reduced to a very moderate interest, if calculated over the many years required to wind up their accounts.[1] The Third Joint Stock, subscribed in 1631, was still struggling with new financial combinations in 1642,[2] and we have seen it demanding a share in the Dutch compensation twelve years later.

Indeed the factors in the East frequently complained that they were unable to keep separate the liabilities of the successive groups of subscribers. A ship arrived with such confused accounts that the Directors, after three or four days' dispute, still differed as to whom the cargo belonged; while as to the great debt of 100,000*l.* in India, who 'owes it no man can tell.'[3] The science of audit which has grown with the growth of the Joint Stock system had not yet emerged, and the chartered accountant—the financial conscience of Limited Liability—was then unknown.

The preceding volume set forth the Company's early trade by Separate Voyages from 1600 to 1612, and by the First and the Second Joint Stocks, each

[1] *Ante*, vol. i. pp. 280, 292.

[2] MS. Court Book, No. 18, p. 111*a*.

[3] *Calendar of State Papers*, East Indies, 1630–1634, No. 610, where a good example of intricacy, even in the 'particular' Persian voyages, will be found.

1613 intended for four years, from 1613 to 1620.[1] The Second Joint Stock should have been dissolved in 1621, but the Dutch aggressions which culminated in Amboyna made men hesitate to subscribe to a new Indian venture, and the Second Joint Stock
to 1627 group continued to trade till 1627. Its power of raising loans enabled it to send forth thirty-six ships from 1621 to 1628.[2]

Large profits[3] were realised on individual voyages. But when the last hopes of support from the King against the Dutch flickered out, money could no longer be borrowed on the common seal,
1628 and in 1628 the Governor and Directors had to pledge their private credit in order to obtain cargoes.[4] They tried to restore confidence by drawing up a statement which showed a balance of half a million sterling,[5] yet only thirty members came forward with a subscription,[6] just sufficient for a separate Persian voyage.

[1] *Ante*, vol. i. pp. 277–305, 306–308, 364–5.

[2] More strictly from the season 1621–22 to the season 1627–28, besides 4 pinnaces. I have compiled the total from the yearly shipments given in Bruce's *Annals*, i. pp. 225–278.

[3] The bullion and merchandise exported from 25th March, 1620 to 25th March, 1624 was 264,516*l.*, and the return cargoes realised 1,255,444*l.* Macpherson, p. 111.

[4] In June 1622 the debt was 150,000*l.*, chiefly at 9 per cent.; in August 1624, 200,000*l.*; in June 1628, 230,000*l.*; in March 1629, 300,000*l.* *Calendar of State Papers*, East Indies, 1622–1624, Nos. 107, 573; *Idem*, 1625–1629, Nos. 663, 805, &c.

[5] June 1628. The Quick Stock in India was taken at 250,000*l.*, estimated to produce 600,000*l.*, or 700,000*l.* in Europe, and to leave 500,000*l.* available for distribution. *Calendar of State Papers*, East Indies, 1625–1629, No. 665.

[6] 40,000*l.* December 1628. *Idem*, No. 771. Subsequently two other 'particular' Persian voyages were subscribed for, but a proposal for a fourth in May 1631 only elicited 11,000*l.*, and

At length, in 1631, a new group of subscribers 1631
formed themselves into the Third Joint Stock, with a capital of 420,700*l.*[1] Another project for a North-West Passage exploration had caught the public fancy—a passage declared to be as feasible as that from Dover to Calais[2]—and an expedition had started round the Arctic circle with letters from the East India Company to its factors in Java. The Third Joint Stock ran a course similar to its predecessor—large gains on individual cargoes, heavy losses from the Dutch, and an inability to get itself wound up and to finally distribute its profits. In addition, it had to struggle against Courten's Association. Yet, in spite of having to reduce salaries, inasmuch as its business 'grew every day less and less,'[3] the Third Joint Stock forms a landmark in the advance of English commerce in the East.

Its servants, or those of the Company through whom it acted, made the English the ascendent trading nation on the Indian coast. The Hollanders had long complained of our liberality and of the presents by which we won the native authorities to our side. They now realised that our system of business was really better suited than theirs to the settled order of the Mughal Empire. The Dutch Directors at home pointed

was dropped. The 'Continuation' of the Second Joint Stock expired at Christmas 1627, and an attempt to raise a new general subscription in January 1628 failed. *Idem*, No. 386. Macpherson, p. 111.

[1] Bruce, i. 306.

[2] Sir Thomas Button to Secretary of State Lord Dorchester. *Calendar of State Papers*, 1630–1634, No. 6.

[3] *Idem*, No. 589.

1631 out that we carried larger cargoes in fewer vessels, and that we had not to maintain in India the costly fortifications which ate up the profits of their trade in the Archipelago. The Dutch factors in the East contrasted the initiative and freedom of action allowed to the English agents, who bought or sold at each turn of the market, with the Dutch method of 'having to wait for orders from the Governor-General' in Java.[1] While our servants thus outstripped the Dutch within the Mughal Empire, they established, as we have seen, free commerce outside it with the Portuguese.

The 420,700*l.* subscribed for the Third Joint Stock in 1631 were soon absorbed in taking over the 'remaines' of the Second, or in ships, factories, and ventures of its own. Again the process of
1638 borrowing began, and by 1638 the Company declared that 800,000*l.* had already been laid out, while still further sums were required, but could not be raised owing to the infringements on its Charter by the Crown.[2] No redress being forthcoming from the King, the Company tried in
1640 1640 to raise a new subscription under the title of the Fourth Joint Stock, but without success.[3] So the Third Joint Stock, whose shares fell to 60 per cent., drifted on to the welter of the Civil War.

[1] August 1631. MS. Series of Dutch Records in the India Office.

[2] Answer of the Governor, &c., of the East India Company to a Declaration exhibited to His Majesty, 1638. Bruce, i. 347.

[3] Issued 28th January, 1640, but only 22,500*l.* subscribed; the Governor in vain rebuked the generality for their slackness on April 17.

The various devices by which the Company kept its head above the sea of troubles have been already related.[1] A detailed account of that period of confusion, with its Joint Stocks, Particular or General Voyages, Assada Merchants, Merchant Adventurers, and Interlopers, would weary the reader without advancing my narrative. I embody the material facts in a footnote which endeavours to present, for the first time, a continuous view of the Company's trade from its commencement in 1600 to the close of the Commonwealth in 1660.[2] 1641 to 1657

[1] Chapter vii. *The Company under the Commonwealth*, p. 103 *et seq.*

[2] CHRONOLOGICAL SURVEY OF THE COMPANY'S TRADE 1600–1660.

In Six Periods.

FIRST PERIOD.—Separate Voyages 1600–1612.

1600–1612. *The Nine Separate Voyages*, employing 26 ships, with an aggregate capital of 466,179*l.* *Ante*, vol. i. p. 291.

SECOND PERIOD.—*First and Second Joint Stocks*, 1613–1627.

1613–1616. *First Joint Stock*, 29 ships, aggregate capital 429,000*l.* *Ante*, vol. i. p. 307.

1617–1620. *Second Joint Stock*, 25 ships, aggregate capital 1,629,040*l.* (sometimes given in round numbers as 1,600,000*l.*). *Ante*, vol. i. p. 364 and *note*.

1621–1627. *Continuation of Second Joint Stock*, 36 ships, trading partly on the original capital of the Second Joint Stock and partly on borrowed money. *Ante*, pp. 173–4.

Christmas, 1627. *The Second Joint Stock expires.*

January 1628. Failure of proposed new stock (*ante*, p. 18), and, as a substitute, the formation of separate Persian Voyages (p. 174, *note* 6).

THIRD PERIOD.—*Interlude of the Three Separate Persian Voyages*, 1628–1631. The capital of the First Voyage was 40,000*l.* The total number of ships sent out in the three seasons 1628–9. 1629–30, 1630–1, was fifteen, of which eleven were sent to Persia. In May 1631, a subscription was opened for a Fourth Persian Voyage, but only 11,000*l.* being subscribed it was dropped.

FOURTH PERIOD.—1631 till after 1642. *Third Joint Stock.* Original subscription, 420,700*l.* *Ante*, pp. 174–6. The date of the final dissolution of the Third Joint Stock cannot be fixed. I take

The essential point is: How did the Company maintain its authority over this kaleidoscopic series

1642 as the terminal year, because in December 1642 the first meeting of adventurers in the Fourth Joint Stock took place. (MS. Court Book, No. 18, p. 133.)

The Persian Voyages (1st, 2nd, and 3rd) were kept separate till 1634, when their 'remaines' were taken over by the Third Joint Stock at a valuation. (*Cal. State Papers*, East Indies, 1630–34, No. 609.) It was this Third Joint Stock that had to fight the long battle with Courten's Association. *Ante*, pp. 33–45.

FIFTH PERIOD.—Confusion of Joint Stocks and Particular Voyages.

1641. *First 'Particular' or 'General' Voyage. Ante*, p. 106. Nominal capital 120,000*l.* (MS. Court Book, No. 18, p. 8*a*), but apparently only 80,450*l.* subscribed. This 'Particular' Voyage conducted its actual trading by means of the servants of the Third Joint Stock, paying it one per cent. for the use of its establishments at home, and six per cent. for the services of its factors and factories in the East. (MS. Court Book, No. 18, p. 20*a.*)

1642 (October). *Failure of proposal* to unite First General Voyage and Third Joint Stock. (MS. Court Book, No. 18, p. 111*a.*)

1642 (December). *First Meeting of Adventurers of the Fourth Joint Stock.* (MS. Court Book, No. 18, p. 133.) The Preamble had been issued in January 1640, but without practical result, as in April only 22,500*l.* had been subscribed; by 1643 the subscriptions amounted to 105,000*l.*

1647. *Second 'Particular' or 'General' Voyage.* The Company in doubt whether to have a new Joint Stock or a New Voyage. (MS. Court Book, No. 20, pp. 45, 58.) Decided to form the 'Second General Voyage' owing to the Lords having rejected the Ordinance for Trade. *Ante*, p. 106. Second General Voyage allows Fourth Joint Stock the same commission for the use of its servants and establishments that the First Particular Voyage had allowed the Third Joint Stock. (MS. Court Book, No. 22, p. 18*a.*)

1649 (January). Resolution to send out no more adventures either upon Stock or Voyage after April 30, 1649. *Ante*, p. 115.

1649 (September). Proposed voyage for five years' continuance with a stock of 400,000*l.* (MS. Court Book, No. 20, p. 201.) It fails owing to the opposition of the Assada Merchants.

1650 (January 31). *The United Joint Stock.* Formed, under a resolution of the House of Commons, by the union of the Company and the Assada Merchants. *Ante*, pp. 115–119. To continue

of makeshifts? Its continuous existence was secured by the yearly appointment of the officials named in its charter, but by what means did those officials exercise a continuous control over the successive Joint Stocks and Particular Voyages, each with a separate capital and interests of its own? At first sight every Joint Stock or Particular Voyage appears to be a distinct group under a separate board of management. But a closer scrutiny discloses a constant element on all the boards. The Governor, Deputy-Governor, and Treasurer of the Company, are invariably members of them, and their remaining members were drawn in whole or in part from the Committee of Twenty-four who formed the chartered governing body of the corporation.[1] 1641 to 1657

till 1653. (MS. Court Book, No. 20, p. 236.) By March 1650, the subscription amounted to 191,700*l.* The United Joint Stock bought 'the remaines' in India both of the Fourth Joint Stock and Second General Voyage for 20,000*l.* The Company's trade almost at a standstill. (MS. Court Book, No. 21, p. 58.) The MS. Court Books tend to minimise the opposition, but it is evident that a body of Merchant Adventurers, made up in part of dissentient members of the old Courten's or Assada Association, were trading on a large scale independently of the Governing Body of the East India Company.

1653–57. *Five years of practically Open Trade.* *Ante*, pp. 118–120.

SIXTH PERIOD, 1657–1660.—*The permanent Joint Stock*, under Cromwell's charter of 1657. *Ante*, pp. 131–137. Capital £739,782, of which only 369,891*l.* were called up.

[1] Thus the First, Second, Third, and Fourth Joint Stocks were managed by the Governor, Deputy, Treasurer, and the Committee of Twenty-four; that is, by the permanent officials of the Company: the First Persian Voyage (1628) by the same, 'with the addition of eight of the chief of the new adventurers;' the First Particular or General Voyage (1641) by a special committee of

1657 The higher permanent officials of the Company thus acted as a unifying influence on the shifting groups which actually subscribed the capital, and their presence was rigorously insisted on at the meetings of the separate adventurers.[1] The boards of different Joint Stocks or Particular Voyages sat in the forenoon and afternoon of the same day. They recorded their minutes in distinct books. But the lists of the members present prove that they consisted to a large extent of the same men. Thus the apparently hopeless confusion from 1650 onwards, when no fewer than five[2] distinct 'courts' or committees of management existed, simplifies itself. Their meetings never clash; the Governor, Deputy, or Treasurer attends each in turn at different hours, and exercises in all the initiative and control of the business. Sometimes, indeed, the Governor, without rising from his chair, merely asks certain members to withdraw or others to come in, and thus a Committee of the Second General Voyage is transformed into a meeting of the Fourth Joint Stock.

eight, in conjunction with the Company's Committee of Twenty-four (MS. Court Book, No. 18, p. 20*a*); the Second Particular or General Voyage (1647) by a committee of sixteen (MS. Court Book, No. 22, p. 1); and the United Joint Stock (1650) by a committee of thirteen, in part made up of, and acting in conjunction with, the Governor, Deputy, Treasurer, and Committee of Twenty-four. (MS. Court Book, No. 23, p. 1*a*, &c.)

[1] As by the subscribers to the Second General Voyage, 1647, MS. Court Book, No. 22, p. 2.

[2] Namely (1) 'The Court of Committees' of the Company, *i.e.* the Twenty-four; (2) The Third Joint Stock at rare intervals; (3) 'The Court of Committee of the Fourth Joint Stock,' and of (4) The Second General Voyage; (5) The United Joint Stock.

Not only, however, did the governing bodies of 1600-1657
the successive Joint Stocks and Particular or General Voyages consist to a large extent of the same men, but the capital for the different adventures was in part found by the same subscribers. In some cases, indeed, one Joint Stock or Particular Voyage took a share in another,[1] or partially merged into it. A corporate as well as an individual unity of interest was thus created. But conflicting claims frequently threatened to overpower the influences which made for cohesion. It speaks highly for the honesty of purpose and business capacity of the Englishmen of that century that they managed to make such a system work during fifty-seven years. There is throughout these records a daily sense of the Great Taskmaster's eye. The piety of the counting-house may to a later age seem out of place. Yet, as the Indian custom of beginning each morning's entries by inscribing the name of his deity at the top of the page has a very real meaning to the Hindu, so the religious openings and endings of the Company's letters had a true significance to the writers.[2] We may smile, but they did not, at the quaint conjunction in the rule of conduct which the Directors laid down for their servants in the East, to aim in all things 'at the Glory of God and the Interests of their Employers.'[3]

[1] For example, the United Joint Stock of 1650 appointed a committee to purchase a 5,000*l.* adventure in the New Joint Stock of 1657. MS. Court Book, No. 23, p. 316. 16 March, 1658.

[2] For printed examples see *The First Letter Book of the East India Company*, Birdwood and Foster, pp. 40, 42, 295, 306, &c. 1893.

[3] MS. Letter Book, No. 3, p. 502.

CHAPTER VII

THE COMPANY UNDER THE RESTORATION

1660—1688

1660 THE wave of loyalty which in 1660 swept across the nation touched high-water mark in the Courts of the East India Company. It flooded out the republican element from the committees, and left the 'generality' a royalist corporation. Their address of welcome to the restored monarch was accompanied by a present of plate worth 3,000*l*., followed by one of 1,000*l*. in value to his brother the Duke of York. These compliments formed the precursors of a long series of loans to His Majesty amounting to 170,000*l*. during sixteen years;[1] and of not less magnificent gifts, including an unsolicited vote of ten thousand

[1] I have compiled the following loans to the King from the MS. Court Books from 1662 to the treaty of Nimeguen in 1678, and there may have been others. (1) June 1662, 10,000*l*. (2) April 1666, 50,000*l*. on the request of the King, and to enable him to pay off his seamen, on the royal assurance that it should not be used as a precedent. (3) July 1667, another 20,000*l*.) to help His Majesty in the Dutch war. (4) August 1676, 40,000*l*. (5) January 1678, 20,000*l*. (6) October 1678, 30,000*l*. Total, at least 170,000*l*. to 1678; beyond which date my figures do not go. The King faithfully repaid these loans. MS. Court Books, Nos. 24, 25, 30, 31 (p. 45): many entries.

guineas to the King, together with a like sum to His Royal Highness.[1] 1660 to 1685

A new spirit of devotion also animates the Company's secret records. When Charles I. did it the unexampled honour of sending the Lords of his Council to explain away his acts,[2] the Directors listened with civil mistrust. If Charles II. requested a loan they voted it 'all standing bare.' Even when he touched their most sensitive point, by intervening in the election of their officers, they could still describe him as 'the sun who influenced all their actions,' and without whose beams 'they must wither and decay.'[3] Nor was this altogether the language of hypocrisy or of servile adulation. It expressed their feeling, which during twenty-five years of close relations with Charles II. grew into a fixed belief, that whatever happened the King was and would always be the Company's friend.

If his levity or fleeting resentment brought him to the edge of a quarrel, he knew how at the last moment to draw back with an air of gracious compliance. Thus in 1676 he wrote to the Company not to elect certain persons who 'have

[1] MS. Court Book, No. 32, p. 164. October 5, 1681, voted unasked, 10,000 guineas to the King. Macaulay mentions a similar sum to the Duke of York. (*Works*, iii. 473. Ed. 1866.) The MS. records frequently refer to presents to the King and enforce on the factors in India the duty of sending home curiosities, birds and beasts. On one occasion the Court ordered one male and two female black dwarfs for the notorious Renée Louise de Kerouaille, Duchess of Portsmouth. MS. Letter Books, No. 5, p. 275; No. 7, pp. 142, 447, &c.

[2] In 1628. *Ante*, vol. i. p. 414.

[3] MS. Court Books, No. 25, p. 71*a*, and No. 30, pp. 1, 2.

1660 to 1685 behaved very ill towards His Majesty,' and enforced his command by summoning the Governor to Whitehall. Then finding his position untenable, Charles invented a courteous excuse for cancelling his letter, and finally healed all wounds by conferring a baronetcy on the object of his recent displeasure.[1] 'There is nothing' wrote the Directors in the later years of his long reign 'that we can modestly ask for our Company in India which His Majesty will not readily be pleased to grant us.'[2]

The Company was bound to the King not by sentiment alone. Its energies, paralysed under Charles I. and pent up during the Commonwealth, had received fresh life from the charter which formed one of Cromwell's last great acts. Under the Restoration the Company developed at home from a series of groups of adventurers into a continuous corporation with a united and permanent capital. Abroad, its establishment grew from factories into settlements no longer exclusively made up of its own servants, but comprising also outside populations, for whose government it had to seek new powers. Instead of constantly running for help to the Privy Council, as in the time of Elizabeth,[3] the Company now went to the King. Between 1661 and 1683 Charles II. granted

[1] MS. Court Book, No. 29, p. 245 ff.; No. 30, p. 1 ff. April 1676. The two persons whose election Charles II. desired to prevent were Josia Child and Thomas Papillon; and the knowledge of his wish, even after he had withdrawn his interference, prevented their election that year. Two years later (1678) Charles II. made Josia Child a baronet.

[2] MS. Letter Book, No. 6, p. 519. 1682.

[3] *Ante*, vol. i. p. 257.

to it no fewer than five charters of prime importance, which occupy fifty per cent. more space in the Company's printed series than the charters from 1600 to 1660.[1] 1660 to 1685

It depended upon the Crown to uphold its trade monopoly amid the rising clamour of the nation, to secure its new possessions by diplomacy with the Portuguese, and to protect them by arms against the Dutch. It had also to lean on the King for an altogether new kind of support, in quelling the mutinies of its own servants, and in controlling the population, Indian and European, which grew up under the shelter of its forts. Charles II. found the Company a trading body; he left it a nascent territorial power, with the right of coinage, the command of fortresses and of English and Indian troops, the authority to form alliances and to make peace or war, the jurisdiction over subjects, and other attributes of a delegated sovereignty.

This staunch and consistent friendship of Charles II. involves no reversal of the verdict of history as to his general character. For if the Company leaned on the King, the King looked to the Company for support in the policy which lay nearest his heart. Throughout his reign England

[1] Namely from p. 54 to p. 124; the charters of Elizabeth and James I. run from p. 3 to p. 53. *Charters granted to the East India Company.* India Office Library, printed quarto. Besides these printed charters there were during both periods numerous Letters Patent authorising the export of treasure, and other acts of trade or of local jurisdiction. The Minor Letters Patent issued by Charles II. not printed in the quarto, although entered in the schedule, were thirteen in number.

1660 to 1685 had to choose between Versailles and The Hague. The nation gravitated at first slowly, then with an overwhelming conviction, towards Holland: the King bound himself by ties of increasing stringency to France. In the long conflict between the royal policy and the popular will, Charles II. found in the East India Company his one unfailing ally.

It stood as the representative not only of its own historical feud with Holland in the East, of the memories of Amboyna, and of Cromwell's avenging war, but also of the international rivalry which embittered the whole sea-commerce of the two Protestant Powers. In the early years of the Restoration this hatred to the Dutch was a dominant feeling alike in the City and at the Court, among the landed gentry weary of Puritan rule, and in the Church, with its claims to a Catholic continuity which it denied to the reformed sects of Holland. Dryden's coarse travesty of Amboyna, although addressed to the passions of the vulgar, was inspired by the deliberate hate which the Royal entourage and the leaders of English foreign commerce bore to the Dutch.[1] Swift came from a

[1] For the trade-hatred see the passage quoted from the *Tragedy of Amboyna*. *Ante*, vol. i. pp. 427–429. The English aristocratic and religious contempt of Holland is embodied in Beaumont's speech: 'Not being gentlemen, you have stolen the arms of the best families of Europe; and wanting a name you made bold with the first of the Divine attributes; and call'd yourselves the High and Mighty, though let me tell you that besides the Blasphemy the title is ridiculous, for High is no more proper for the Netherlands than Mighty is for seven little rascally provinces, no bigger in all than a shire in England.' Act II. Scene I. Dryden's *Works*, v. 38 (Scott and Saintsbury's Edition).

different class. In Sir William Temple's household he had breathed the very atmosphere of the Triple Alliance, and he fawned neither on merchant princes nor on Kings. Yet Swift's clerical disdain for the Dutch religion is as corrosive sublimate to the laureate's venal invective. When Gulliver, passing for a Dutchman in Japan, refused to trample on the crucifix, the Emperor declared that he was the first of that nation who had shown any scruple, and 'began to doubt whether I was a real Hollander or not; but rather suspected I must be a Christian.'[1] 1660 to 1685

For a time, indeed, there were two well-marked currents of popular feeling alike in England and Holland. At The Hague De Witt and the oligarchy sought a French alliance, while the Prince of Orange's party looked towards England. Political necessity made the English and Dutch allies in Europe; trade rivalry made them enemies in Asia. As England welcomed the help of Holland in 1669 against France in the Low Countries, so in 1672 England welcomed the help of France against Holland on the Madras coast. Even Sir William Temple debated whether England or France would gain most by the ruin of Holland.[2] 'Us they distrust,' the French Ambassador wrote of the English in 1672, 'Spain they despise, Holland they hate.'

The English people did not turn decisively to

[1] *Gulliver's Travels.* A Voyage to Laputa. Chapter xi.

[2] Essay on *The Constitution and Interests of the Empire, Sweden, Denmark, &c. Works,* vol. ii. pp. 227–8. 4 vols. 1757.

1660 to 1685 the Dutch till they found the King bartering their birthright for a French pension and threatening their religion with a Catholic reaction engineered by Louis Quatorze. But the East India Company remained bound, alike by the traditions of the past and by the needs of the present, to its old hostility to the Hollanders. Its interests, like those of the King, diverged from the growing sentiment of the country. For this divergence it paid in the end a heavy price. But meanwhile it served as a rallying centre for the antipathy to Holland, with which maritime and commercial England, as distinguished from the strongly Protestant masses, was imbued. Charles II. and James II. could deny no favour to a corporation which formed the strongest support of the French policy of the Crown against the Dutch proclivities of the nation.

April 1661 In 1661 the King issued a new charter to the Company,[1] ignoring that of Cromwell, but confirming and extending those of Elizabeth and James I. It follows closely the language of the original instruments of 1600 and 1609; no longer, however, basing its concessions on the old narrow ground of a petition from a specified group of adventurers. It assumes the existence of the Company as a well-tried institution, which had rendered services to England, and had suffered wrongs from the foreign enemy.

The new governing body was composed of men distinguished by the royal favour. In the Charter of Elizabeth neither the Governor nor a single one

[1] Dated the 3rd April, 1661. The original is preserved in the India Office.

of the Twenty-four Directors is designated even as 1661
'gentleman.'[1] In that of James I. the Governor alone is a knight, and the Twenty-four are still plain citizens without any recognised style.[2] The Charter of Charles II. designates not only the Governor, but eleven of the Twenty-four as knights, one as esquire and eleven as gentlemen, while the twenty-fourth was a peer of the realm.[3] The extended trade of the Company is recognised by increasing the license for the export of bullion from 30,000*l.* to 50,000*l.* on any single voyage.[4] Wide powers are given for the control of the Company's factories; for jurisdiction over English subjects, whether its own servants or otherwise, in the East; for the erection of fortifications; for the export of munitions of war, duty free; and for the transport of 'such number of men' as the Company may find needful for garrisons.

But even before this renewal of its general charter, the King had pledged himself to the Company in its conflict with Holland. The last transaction of the Directors with Cromwell was a petition against the Dutch,[5] the short rule of his son was harassed by similar demands, and the first Dec. 1660
charter granted by Charles II. arose out of Dutch grievances.[6] In the following summer, 1661,

[1] India Office Library Quarto of Charters, p. 7.

[2] *Idem*, p. 35.

[3] George Lord Berkeley, *Idem*, p. 57.

[4] *Idem*, pp. 18, 45, 67.

[5] *Ante*, p. 141.

[6] Letters patent empowering the Company to take and possess the Island of Pularoon form the first of Charles the Second's 'Charters' in the list appended to the India Office Library Quarto (App. p. 9). It is there dated

1661 Charles entered into like obligations to Portugal receiving Bombay as part of the Infanta Catherine's dowry, and engaging to maintain the Portuguese possessions against Holland. Bombay was granted not merely as a wedding gift, but for the express purpose of enabling the English King to defend the Portuguese settlements in India from the Dutch.[1]

1662 Next year, 1662, the Royal interest in the Eastern trade was further strengthened by a charter to the Duke of York to form an African Company, which should take over the factories of the East India Company on the Guinea coast.[2] The Dutch aggressions went on as before, intercepting our commerce and blockading the approaches to the Malabar ports and Southern Islands.[3] But the King was now owner, through his wife, of a territory on the Indian seaboard; his brother was head of the African Company: and the pecuniary interests as well as the French leanings of the Royal family were decisively arrayed against Holland. Charles's sale of Dunkirk and other moves in the game of European politics aroused indignation at The Hague. Yet it was a dispute about the Duke of York's African factories that led to an actual breach, and the Eastern trade

11 January, 1660, perhaps by a clerical error for December 1660, the date of the 'Commission' in Bruce's *Annals*, i. p. 555, footnote; or possibly it is the old style date for a subsequent instrument granted in January 1661 [N.S.].

1 Treaty of Whitehall, 23rd June, 1661; article 11, and the secret article to the treaty.

2 Agreement between the London East India Company and the Royal African Company, dated 16 October, 1662, cf. *ante*, pp. 115, 140.

3 Bruce, vol. ii. pp. 136, 148.

figures in English text books,[1] alike under the Restoration and the Commonwealth, as a *casus belli* to the two Protestant Powers. 1665

For the Dutch war of 1665 to 1667, the Commons 'voted sums unexampled in our history,'[2] but it ended in Europe with the Hollanders burning the dockyards at Chatham, and with a French pension to Charles. In India it might have cost us our chief possessions but for the stern order imposed by the Mughal Emperor. Beyond the limits of his rule, the Dutch made themselves masters of Calicut and Cochin, and reasserted their possession of Pularoon. Indeed, just before the war, our President at Surat had feared that the English were about to undergo the same fate in India which they had suffered in the Spice Islands, and be driven out by the Hollanders. Yet although a Dutch squadron hovered off Swally, it did not dare to land troops under the Mughal cannon, and the Company's agents could write that the war only affected them by increasing the risks at sea.[3] At its close,[4] in 1667, the Treaty of Breda finally relinquished Pularoon together with other tropical settlements to the Dutch, and secured New 1665 to 1667 1667

[1] For example in the *History of England* by Dr. Bright, Master of University College, Oxford. 'The war arose from very trifling circumstances. A dispute had arisen between the African colonies of England and Holland,' &c. Vol. ii. p. 735, Ed. 1887. Cawston and Keane's *Early Chartered Companies*, pp. 231–2.

[2] Macaulay, *Works*, i. 150, Ed. 1866.

[3] Bruce, vol. ii. pp. 172, 173.

[4] War declared, February 1665. Treaty of Breda, 31st July, 1667. Besides Pularoon, the island of Damm was made over to the Dutch in the Banda Sea, and Surinam in Guiana.

York, whose destiny was then unguessed, to the English.

Charles had by this time grown weary of his connection with the East. His brother the Duke of York's African venture[1] fared so badly that it surrendered back its charter to the Crown, although His Royal Highness soon reconstructed the Company on a larger capital. The Queen's dowry of Bombay had brought nothing but trouble
1662 to His Majesty. In 1662 he sent out a fleet of five ships of war under the Earl of Marlborough to take possession, together with a land force of about 500 officers and men. But the Portuguese governor refused to deliver up his charge and a local dispute arose as to whether the cession signified Bombay island alone, or included its adjacent dependencies of Thana and Salsette.[2] The troops, eaten up by scurvy, were not allowed to disembark; and after placing the Company in peril of the Mughal resentment by a temporary landing at Swally,[3] the Earl of Marlborough put them on an uninhabited isle and sailed for England.

This rock of Anjidiva, about twelve leagues

[1] Its history is briefly sketched in Cawston and Keane's *Early Chartered Companies*, pp. 231, 232, Ed. 1896. The Duke of York's next African Company was incorporated in 1672, and maintained its monopoly of the Guinea trade till the Declaration of Right in 1689.

[2] Pepys gives expression to the popular English feeling; 'The Portugalls have choused us it seems in the island of Bombay.' Diary, 15th May, 1663. Ed. 1893.

[3] Sir George Oxenden, the President at Surat, had good reason to know that the Mughal Government would not for a moment tolerate the presence of foreign troops within its territories.

south of Goa, became the grave of the little army. 1663 to 1665
The General, Sir Abraham Shipman, in vain offered to make over the rights of the Crown to the Company's President at Surat, and after seeing his men waste away from hunger and disease, himself died broken-hearted in 1664. His secretary Cooke assumed the command, and, to save the remnant, renounced the dependencies of Bombay to the Portuguese Viceroy at Goa, on condition that the perishing band might be allowed possession of Bombay island itself.[1] In
February 1665 the gaunt and fever-stricken 1665
survivors landed at Bombay,[2] having buried their leader together with all their commissioned officers save one, and mustering only 97 out of the 400 privates who sailed from England in 1662.[3]

Charles II.'s diplomacy at Lisbon proved of none effect. The diplomatists who had framed the marriage treaty knew little of Indian geography, and the term 'Island and Port of Bombay' might or might not include Salsette, which was separated by a narrow tidal channel, at

[1] Convention with the Viceroy of Goa, Nov. 1664.

[2] The Instrument of Delivery, dated 18 February, 1665, and the onerous conditions attached to it, are printed in Sir James Campbell's *Materials towards a Statistical Account of the Town and Island of Bombay*. Vol. i. pp. 15-21. Government Press, Bombay, 1893. This admirable collection supplies for the first time an authentic narrative of the early history of the settlement from the official records.

[3] Muster taken at Bombay by Mr. Gary, a member of the Surat Council, on the 22nd February, 1665. Besides Secretary Cooke, of the comissioned officers only one ensign survived with four sergeants and six corporals. The force, consisting of four companies, each 100 strong, besides officers, had left England in February and March 1662.

one part barely 125 yards wide. As a matter of fact Salsette with its fort or 'Thana' remained Portuguese till the Marathas captured it in 1739. The English in turn took it from the Marathas in 1774, and it finally passed to the East India Company by the Maratha treaty of Salbai in 1782.

1666 But although Charles would not push his remonstrances with Portugal to an actual quarrel, he promptly disavowed the local surrender of his rights to the Goa Viceroy, and in 1666 despatched Sir Gervase Lucas to supersede Cooke as Governor of Bombay. Sir Gervase[1] died in
1667 the following year, and the King found himself burdened with a possession which made heavy demands on his purse, yielded no return, and threatened to involve him in disputes with the Company at Surat, the Portuguese at Goa, the Maratha armies inland, and the outlying provinces of the Mughal Empire itself. Six months after the death of Lucas, Charles made up his mind to get rid of his Indian acquisition, and declared to the East India Company that he gave it the first chance, 'albeit there were some, both foreigners and others, desirous to have it.'[2]

The Company had long fixed an eye on Bombay. Its position, half-way down the Indian seaboard, pointed it out as a naval rendezvous and place of arms, which might control the Dutch and Portuguese settlements further south, and dominate the whole port-to-port trade of Western

[1] Arrived at Bombay 5 Nov., 1666; died 21st May, 1667.

[2] MS. Court Book, No. 26, p. 65*a*, Nov. 22, 1667.

India. At the same time it lay beyond the effective authority of the Mughal, and could therefore be fortified without offending the Imperial Court. In 1626, the Company had joined with the Dutch, under Van Speult of Amboyna infamy, in seizing Bombay, but could not retain possession.[1] After Methwold's convention with Goa in 1635, it came to be regarded as the best site on the coast; the Surat Council built ships at the neighbouring creek of Bassein; and in 1652–3 recommended that both Bombay and Bassein should be bought from the Portuguese.[2] But as Charles vaunted the merits of a place of which he was tired,[3] so the Company now depreciated the value of a place which it had long wanted. The Directors cautiously answered that, if freed from all past outlay, they would ease His Majesty 'of that great burden and expense which the keeping of it hath hitherto been to the Crown. Though they plainly foresee the vast charges the Company will be put unto by this undertaking: and withal assured their Lordships that if the Portugals had offered them

1667

1667-8

[1] The ship's journals are given in Sir George Birdwood's *Report on the Old Records of the India Office*, pp. 214–5, footnote, Ed. 1891; and the localities are identified in Mr. J. Douglas' *Bombay and Western India*, vol. i. 37, 40.

[2] Bruce's *Annals*, i. 334, 366, 472.

[3] In March 1667, the Lord Chamberlain stated that the King had 8,000 subjects in Bombay, and derived a revenue of 900*l.* a year from it. MS. Court Book, No. 25, p. 142*a*. From a statement prepared by Mr. Gary in the same year, the whole revenues of Bombay with the surrounding villages amounted to 6,490*l.*; while Sir Abraham Shipman had estimated the cost of the garrison alone at 7,371*l.* exclusive of artificers and contingencies. James Campbell's *Materials*, i. 23, 24.

this island before His Majesty was possessed thereof, the Company would not have accepted it.'[1]

1668 Charles was by that time resolved to get rid of his unlucky possession on any terms, and in March 1668 Bombay, together with all its stores and munitions of war, passed as a thing of nought from the Crown to the Company, at a quit-rent of 10*l*. a year.[2] Even Baldæus, the shrewd Dutch historian of the times, spoke slightingly of Bombay as a place of little trade.[3] His Majesty's representative handed it over with military honours to the Company on the 23rd September, 1668. The President at Surat became also Governor and Commander-in-Chief of Bombay, but was to continue to reside at Surat and administer the new acquisition by a Deputy Governor. The Company resolved to strengthen the place so as 'to resist a potent enemy by sea and land,' and at the same time sent its factors the Act for Rebuilding London after the great fire,[4] to show them how to lay out the town 'uniform.' The King's troops on the spot re-enlisted as its garrison. For its colonisation twenty single women of sober lives were to be

[1] MS. Court Book, No. 26, p. 65*a*.

[2] Letters Patent dated 27 March, 1668, printed in full (but with again a clerical error of 1669 for 1668) in the India Office Library Quarto of Charters, pp. 80–95. To be holden 'as of the Manor of East Greenwich, in the County of Kent, in free and common soccage,' at a rent of ten pounds, to be paid 'in gold on the 30th day of September, yearly, for ever.'

[3] *Naauwkeurige Beschryvinge van Malabar en Choromandel*. . . . Philippus Baldæus. Amsterdam 1672, p. 70.

[4] MS. Court Book, No. 26, p. 182*a*.

shipped, for whom the Company provided victuals 1668
for the first year, and 'one suit of wearing apparel,'[1] on the condition that they should only marry Protestants. Under the Restoration the factories in India tend to become settlements, to which English women are encouraged to emigrate,[2] and in which Englishmen, not of the Company's service, are allowed under certain terms to reside.[3]

By 1671 the Surat President had come to 1671
speak of Bombay as a 'colony.'[4] Englishmen were tempted to settle and breed 'hogs and ducks.'[5] Indian artificers were attracted by assured pay 'for the first year or two;' and 'handicraftsmen of all other nations' were to be invited 'with their families, provided they be of the reformed religion.'[6] The native merchants at Surat refused, however, to migrate unless under a guarantee direct from the Company in England, whose ordinances are 'always of force,' while the Surat 'President and Council are mutable and do

[1] *Idem.* Contrast this with the Company's old policy. *Ante*, vol. i. p. 356.

[2] MS. Letter Book 4, p. 235. MS. Court Book, No. 26, p. 177*a*.

[3] The conditions of such residence, just after the Restoration, and their relaxation in 1670, are recorded in the Company's MS. Letter Book, No. 3, pp. 98, 124, 138 (1662). 'But for those English that shall come and live under your jurisdiction, and shall not endeavour to undermine our trade . . . let such be permitted to live peaceably and quietly without disturbance or discouragement.' Also in Letter Book, No. 4, p. 381. Letter to Bantam, 4 Oct., 1670: 'We, for the advantage of our nation, do permit several English to trade up and down in India, where it may not interfere with our trade.' Vide *post*, p. 281.

[4] Letter to the Court of Committees dated 10 January, 1671. Printed, Campbell's *Materials*, vol. i. pp. 39, 40.

[5] Campbell's *Materials*, vol. i. p. 32.

[6] *Idem*, i. p. 42.

1671 often alter what their predecessors have granted."[1] They shrank from the risks of a weakly fortified outpost in the debateable ground between the armies of the Mughal and the Maratha. The mortality among the English, ill-fed and miserably housed amid the tidal marshes, was appalling. 'Three years was the average duration of European life;' of every 500 who came to live in the island 400 were buried there;[2] and a new and terrible disease, the Chinese death[3] or cholera morbus, killed with excruciating pains in twenty-four hours in spite of an equally excruciating treatment with red-hot irons.[4] Even [Sir] John Child, who shrank from nothing, refused the appointment of Second in Council at Bombay, in terror of the climate.[5]

The misery was aggravated from the first by dissensions between the officers of the Crown and the Company within the settlement, and before long by a foreign enemy from without. In 1671 Charles II. replaced the conciliatory Temple at The Hague by Sir George Downing, who had

[1] Petition of the Surat Mahajan or Chief Council of the Banias, January 1671. Campbell's *Materials*, vol. i. p. 46.

[2] Chaplain Anderson's *English in Western India*, chiefly from the Surat Records, pp. 131–2. Ed. 1856.

[3] Mordexim (Bluteau), Mordechine (Ovington), Mort-de-Chine corrupted into Mort-de-Chien. Cholera, like the bubonic plague, followed the old trade route from China to Bombay.

[4] 'Take an iron ring about an inch and a half in diametre, and thick in proportion. Then heating it red hot in the fire, extend the patient on the back, and apply the ring to his navel.' Manuchi's 'infallible remedy,' quoted by Chaplain Anderson, p. 133.

[5] Letter from the President and Council of Surat to the Factors at Rajapur: 16 Nov., 1676.

already urged the Company to make extravagant demands on the Dutch.[1] In the following year 1672
the King justified his second war with Holland (February 1672), partly on the wrongs of the East India Company. He tried to form a confederate fleet with France and Portugal which should humble Holland alike on the African and the Indian coasts.[2] The hard fighting in the East fell, however, to the French, although the Dutch for a time threatened our sea-line between Surat and Bombay. The Company's homeward-bound ships in the Bay of Bengal were also caught by a superior Dutch squadron, and lost three of their number after an honourable engagement which English patriotism has recounted in somewhat florid terms.[3] Six thousand troops were said to be assigned to the defence of Bombay;[4] the Dutch took St. Helena, which was speedily recaptured by four English men-of-war;[5] and on the restoration of peace in February 1674 the two 1674
nations appointed commissioners to settle disputes in the East Indies.[6]

The Company's possessions on the Indian coast

[1] *Works of Sir William Temple*, vol. i. p. 463. Ed. 1757.

[2] The original documents are cited by Bruce, vol. ii. p. 22 footnote.

[3] *A New Account of East India and Persia*, by John Fryer, M.D., 1698, p. 45. But see Bruce's more sober narrative from the records, *Annals*, ii. p. 345, 22nd August, 1673.

[4] *The East India Trade, a most Profitable Trade to the Kingdom*, p. 20. 1677.

[5] MS. Letter Book, No. 5, p. 63. Cf. *A Relation of the Retaking of St. Helena* . . . 1673.

[6] Treaty of Westminster between England and Holland, 17th February, 1674; and Marine Treaty with Holland, 11th December, 1674.

rendered necessary an assured line of communication with England. The Cape of Good Hope had been seized by Holland in 1652, and for nearly a century and a half it remained a Dutch colony. Since the return voyage of Captain Lancaster in 1603, however, the London Company had regarded St. Helena as a possible midway house. The first English ambassador to India visited it,[1] but the Dutch took possession of it in 1645, and colonised it for seven years until they withdrew their settlers
1652 to the Cape. In 1652 the English Company's servants occupied the vacant isle, yet so feebly that the Dutch retook it during each of Charles II.'s wars with Holland.[2] The series of captures and recaptures ended with St. Helena being finally seized by the King's ships under Captain Munden
1673 in 1673, and by His Majesty granting it for ever to the East India Company. A Royal Charter empowered the Company to fortify, plant, and colonise the island, to export thither munitions of war free of duty, to carry forth from the Realm recruits for its garrison, to make laws for its government, to exercise criminal jurisdiction, and to put down mutiny or rebellion by martial law.[3]

[1] Letter from Sir Thomas Roe dated 29th August, 1619, *Factory Record Miscellaneous*, i. Mr. George McCall Theal's *History of South Africa* (1888) should be consulted for the early history of the Cape.

[2] In 1665 and 1673. India Office Folio of Factory Records, p. xxiv. 1897.

[3] Charter of the 16th December in the 25th year of Charles II.—1673. India Office Library Quarto of Charters, pp. 96–107, where the date is accidentally given as 1674. The island was to be held like Bombay on the tenure of free and common soccage, but without any quit rent. Charles II. had previously confirmed the rights

All subjects born in St. Helena were to be deemed 1673
natural-born subjects of England, and the island was attached technically, like Bombay, to the Manor of East Greenwich in the County of Kent. It became the 'Sea Inn'[1] of the Eastern trade, the Company flying the Union flag on this side of St. Helena and its own for the rest of the voyage to India.

From the Bay of Bengal to St. Helena in mid Atlantic the Company began to find its servants wielding an armed authority, which it did not know how to control. Its hasty conversion to royalty at home still left the leaven of the Republic in its settlements abroad. Evelyn relates how the General Court under Cromwell's Charter had been the scene of a religious commotion, raised by the straiter brethren, who scrupled to take the prescribed oath.[2] The Indian factories were split into hostile camps of Puritans appointed under the Commonwealth, and Royalists sent out since the Restoration. Meanwhile the old permanent chiefs in London, three of whom had covered a period of forty-six years, gave place to a stream of new men, to Governors who could not be re-elected beyond a second year.[3] At the very moment when the

of the Company in Saint Helena in 1661, but its recapture by the King's forces from the Dutch voided that grant.

[1] *A View of St. Helena*, the Harleian Miscellany, viii. 332 (1746).

[2] 26 November, 1657. *Diary of John Evelyn*, p. 254. Reprint, 1870.

[3] List of Governors of the Company from Cromwell's Charter in 1657 to the Revolution of 1688. William Cockayne, 1657: he had been Governor since 1643. Maurice Thomson, 1658. Thomas

1657 extended powers of its servants in the East demanded a firm control in England, the changes at home weakened the governing body.

The signal of revolt came from Bombay, where Cooke, the discredited chief of the King's forces, headed a faction against the Company's representatives in 1666.[1] A more serious struggle was
1666 at the same time going on in Madras. In the first fervours of the Restoration the Company had sent out an ardent Royalist, Sir Edward Winter, as Governor of Madras. He found the factory just emerged from a siege, and a prey to the Indian dynastic wars which were chronic in the Carnatic. A local chief told him with a sneer that he need not hope for redress till 'the English horns and

Andrew, 1659. Andrew Riccard, 1660, re-elected 1661. Sir Thomas Chamberlain, 1662, re-elected 1663. Sir William Thomson, 1664, re-elected 1665. Sir Andrew Riccard, 1666, re-elected 1667. Sir William Thomson, 1668, re-elected 1669. Sir Andrew Riccard, 1670, re-elected 1671. Sir John Banks, 1672, re-elected 1673. Nathaniel Herne, 1674, re-elected 1675. Sir William Thomson, 1676, re-elected 1677. Sir Nathaniel Herne, 1678, re-elected 1679. Sir William Thomson, 1680. Sir Josia Child, 1681, re-elected 1682. Sir John Banks, 1683. Sir Joseph Ashe, 1684, re-elected 1685. Sir Josia Child, 1686, re-elected 1687. Sir Benjamin Bathurst, 1688, re-elected 1689. This list is derived from an India Office document in the handwriting of Mr. C. C. Prinsep, corrected from the India Office MSS. The members of the Committee of Twenty-four, or Court of Directors, were constantly, and in some cases continuously, re-elected.

[1] Besides the insurrections to be mentioned in the text, there were many occasions on which 'ye 3d article ot ye Hon'ble Company's lawes for ye preservation of ye peace and suppressing of mutiny, sedition, and rebellion' had to be enforced. *E.g.* Surat letter to Bombay, dated 16th May, 1672. *Selections from State Papers, Bombay, Home Series*, edited by Mr. G. W. Forrest, vol. i. p. 64. Bombay Government Press, 4to. 1887. A very valuable series.

teeth grew.'[1] Sir Edward took him at his word and projected a costly scheme of fortifications and reprisals, which speedily procured his supersession from home in 1665.

His successor, George Foxcroft,[2] appointed 1665
when the reaction which followed the Restoration had damped the loyalty of the Directors, at once put himself at the head of the Puritan faction in the settlement, and indulged in republican discussions which to the King's party sounded nothing short of treason. Sir Edward Winter, who had been reduced to second in Council, called out the soldiers, mortally wounded one of the opposite leaders, and threw the newly arrived Governor, Foxcroft, together with his son and another of his chief supporters, into prison.[3] Winter, in letters to Charles II. and the Archbishop of Canterbury, declared that loyalty to the Crown had alone induced him to seize the authority.

The affrighted Directors hurried out a Commissioner armed with joint powers from the King and the Company, commanding the release of the Governor, and offering pardon to those mutineers who would return to their duty. But Sir Edward Winter, relying on the goodwill of the royal general at Bombay, brushed aside these instructions as forgeries, and kept the lawful governor, Foxcroft, in confinement for three years.[4] It was not till 1665 to 1668

[1] *Madras in the Olden Time*, by J. Talboys Wheeler, vol. i. p. 34. Madras 1861. 3 vols.

[2] Reached Madras, June 1665.

[3] September 16, 1665, according to Yule, *Hedges' Diary*, vol. ii. pp. 277, 280. September 14th according to Bruce, *Annals*, ii. p. 180.

[4] Released August 22, 1668.

1668 1668, when the Company despatched five armed ships with orders to blockade Madras if needful, that a feeble compromise could be arrived at, by which Foxcroft was restored to the governorship for twelve months, and Winter allowed to remain for a like period in India to wind up his affairs.[1]

In Bombay, with its larger garrison and outside population, rebellion assumed a bolder front. In
1674 1674 a mutiny of the garrison, for a month's pay and their discharge on the expiry of their three years' service, was only quelled by the execution of the ringleader, while two others were condemned to death, and the commander of the forces was deported to England.[2] Nine years later a more resolute soldier seized on the government and held it for a year in defiance of the Company. Richard Keigwin, an officer of the Royal Navy, had led the landing party which retook St. Helena from the Dutch in 1673, and was appointed governor of that island. After a chequered career in the Company's service, during which he won a brilliant victory over the Maratha fleet, he was reinstated as commander of the troops at Bombay, with the rank of Third in Council, in 1681.[3] Fryer, who witnessed the Bombay mutiny in 1674, had observed that the Company's Government, with its subtlety for gain, 'quadrates not with a British

[1] The story is pieced together from Sir Henry Yule's Edition of the *Diary of William Hedges*, vol. ii. pp. 186, 199, 277–281. Ed. 1888. Winter's official narrative of the proceedings, together with the principal other documents, are printed by Yule at p. 277 ff.

[2] Bruce, quoting the original documents, *Annals*, ii. 367–8.

[3] Chaplain Anderson's *English in Western India*, p. 221.

militia.'[1] Its niggardly dealings disaffected the garrison, and in 1683 Keigwin, with grievances also of his own, imprisoned the head of the civil government,[2] boarded a Company's ship in the harbour and landed 50,000 rupees for his military chest.

Keigwin, elected Governor by the popular vote, issued a proclamation in the King's name, citing the 'intolerable extortions, oppressions, and unjust impositions' of the Company, and accusing its servants of 'not maintaining the honour due to His Majesty's Crown,' and of 'making His Majesty's laws . . . subject to their depraved wills.'[3] He wrote long letters to the King and the Duke of York justifying his action,[4] and invented a sort of national seal bearing the Union flag with a patriotic inscription.[5] The brave sailor had a somewhat confused idea of a political manifesto, and to the misdeeds of the Company's servants as 'dishonourers of their King,' he added the crimes of Sabbath-breaking and witchcraft. But he gave a colour of legality to his government by declaring it under the immediate authority of the Crown, and he ruled with moderation. From the Marathas he obtained leave to plant factories in South-Western India, exemption from duties on the eastern coast, and compensation of 4,000*l.* for depredations. His

[1] *A New Account of East India*, 1672–1681, pp. 64–5. 1698.

[2] Mr. Ward, Deputy Governor for the President at Surat.

[3] India Office MS. Records; O.C. (*i.e.* Original Correspondence) 5026.

[4] An abstract of his letter to the King is preserved in the Bodleian Library. Rawlinson MSS. A. 257.

[5] 'Vexillum Reg. Mag. Brit. concordia et unitas.'

1683 reforms in the taxation of Bombay were retained after the suppression of his revolt, and by encouraging 'interlopers' he extended the local trade.

For a time, indeed, he harboured the ambition of subverting the Company's whole rule in Western India with his devoted Bombay garrison of 150 English and 200 Indian soldiers. On the 1st
1684 January, 1684, he called on the Council at Surat to arrest the President, Sir John Child. The rebellion, however, did not spread effectively beyond Bombay. Child, as President at Surat and Governor of Bombay, made fruitless efforts to treat with the mutineers, who laughed at his proffered forgiveness, and proclaimed themselves the true servants of the King.[1] But Charles II. on hearing of the revolt, ordered Keigwin under the sign-manual to surrender the fort, sent out a ship of war, and appointed Child admiral and captain-general of the Company's forces on land and sea. The rebel
Nov. 1684 leader yielded to His Majesty's command, in spite of the popular shouts of 'no Governor but Keigwin;'[2] and the mutiny ended in a full pardon and a public dinner, with twenty-one guns to the health of the King, a due number for the Queen and each member of the royal family, and fifteen for the Company.[3] Keigwin afterwards received the command of a frigate in the royal navy, and fell gallantly leading the assault at St. Christopher's on June 21, 1690.

[1] India Office MSS. O.C. 5038, 5080, 5098.

[2] *Diary of William Hedges*, ii. 169. He surrendered the fort to Vice-Admiral Sir Thomas Grantham, November 1684.

[3] *Idem*, pp. 170, 178: to the great disgust of the Surat Council, p. 182.

Charles II. might have easily aggravated the Company's difficulties with its servants abroad. For in each case the mutineers posed as faithful servants of His Majesty, and they alleged grievances against a corporation which, with only a delegated authority from the Crown, had proved disloyal (as they maintained) to its trust. But Charles II. was really a more straightforward man than his father, and instead of seeking his profit in cabals against the Company, he preferred frankly to borrow money from it. Public opinion in England, however, again approached a crisis in which the support of the King entailed the disfavour of the Commons. The Company was rudely awakened to this fact by a mutiny nearer home.

As it invited settlers to its newly acquired territory at Bombay, so also it determined to colonise St. Helena. After an experiment under Cromwell's Charter of 1657, Captain Stringer was appointed Governor in 1660, with orders to divide 1660
the island into 150 little estates, and to allot one to any man who would go out as a settler.[1] Each planter was to pay a yearly quit-rent of fruits and vegetables;[2] while a representative body was created in the form of a Council of Six, to

[1] India Office MS. Letter Book, No. 2, December 1660. Fifteen parts were retained by the Company, and five were assigned to Captain Stringer for his trouble. Bruce (*Annals*, ii. 233) puts Captain Stringer's appointment in 1669, but this refers to his second commission. Cf. Souchu de Rennefort's *Histoire des Indes Orientales*, for a visit to Governor Stringer in 1666: pp. 193-202. Ed. 1688.

[2] 'One bunch of Plantons, one pint of Bonavist pease, one pound of potatoes, and one pound of Cassava bread.' India Office MS. Letter Book, Dec. 1660.

1660 to 1673 which the Governor nominated two members and the planters four. But the Company kept the settlers under strict control, compelling them to go forth to their fields on the ringing of a bell at sunrise, to return for dinner at eleven, and to resume work by the bell at one o'clock.

Under the enlarged Charter for St. Helena in 1673 to 1684 1673, the Company reorganised this simple constitution on a semi-feudal basis. Every owner of twenty acres had to furnish a soldier for garrison duty[1]—an obligation afterwards commuted for forty shillings a year. The records of the island exist from 1673 and disclose the cruelties of a small alien community who, like the early Portuguese in India, had to conceal their sense of weakness by the pitiless use of force. The cultivation was conducted by slave labour under terror of the lash. 'Blacks' were burned at the stake for sorcery or alleged attempts at murder, the evidence being always extorted by flogging, while a planter who scourged a slave-boy to death got off with a fine of forty shillings.[2]

All this misery was then common to Christian colonisation in the tropics, and might have been crushed down into silence and the grave if it had been inflicted on the blacks alone. But the local Government, strong in the new charter of 1673,

[1] Letters from the Company to the Governor and Council of St. Helena, dated 24th March and 14th April, 1680: and 1st and 15th August and 9th October. 1683. Cited. Bruce, ii. 441, 509.

[2] *Extracts from the St. Helena Records*, edited by H. R. Janisch, pp. 36, 53, 75; St. Helena 1885.

pressed on the planters with a severity which drove them to revolt. The punishment of the lash was meted out to white men and women. In 1683 two runaway apprentices who had broken into a house were sentenced 'to have the tip of the right ear cut off, and forehead branded with R [Rogue], a pair of pot-hooks to be rivetted about their necks, and to be flogged several times; viz. 21 lashes on Friday, 21 on Monday, and on Thursday 6 in town, 6 on the top of the hill, 6 at half-way tree, 6 on the hill beyond, and 6 more on arriving at home.' [1] On another occasion a planter was accused of a crime and acquitted, but ordered to be flogged before discharge, apparently for putting the Court to the trouble of trying him.[2]

1673 to 1684

It was not, however, till the Company's government at St. Helena alienated the military as well as the planters that armed resistance became possible. Three insurrections took place, in two of which the rebels deposed and imprisoned or sent home the Governor, while in the third they forced the Governor, 'being a weak man,' to 'sign and doe whatever they pleased.' [3] The fourth had more serious consequences. In 1684, 1684
the year after the apprentices had had the flesh flogged off their backs, a mob of sixty soldiers and planters marched to the castle and, displaying the King's flag, demanded the release of a comrade

[1] *Extracts from the St. Helena Records*, p. 18.

[2] *Idem*, pp. 49, 50.

[3] Report to the King by a Secret Committee of the East India Company, 15 August, 1684. Hedges' *Diary*, ii. 357.

1684 who had been imprisoned for reporting certain disloyal words of the Governor about His Majesty. The Governor replied by his guns, killing or wounding seventeen on the spot, and stamping out the mutiny with death sentences and executions. A planter's wife was ordered to have twenty-one lashes, suffer imprisonment, and be ducked three times at the crane, for saying that the sufferers were murdered men.[1]

The punishments did not exceed the custom of the times, nor can they compare with the barbarities after Monmouth's rebellion, and the sentence of Alice Lisle, in the very next year. Yet they might have sufficed. But during 1684 combinations of soldiers and settlers had defied the Company in arms both at St. Helena and Bombay. The Directors, thoroughly aroused, resolved to make an example; and as the King's favour placed the Bombay arch-rebel Keigwin beyond their reach, they singled out St. Helena for vengeance.

1685 In the meanwhile Charles II. died, the rising in the West took place, and the Company found James II. in a mood not less cruel than its own. While Judge Jeffreys was making his Bloody Circuit, Sir John Weybourne[2] received a Royal commission which amounted to sentence of death on the planters of St. Helena. Nineteen, some of whom had played but a passive part in the rising,

[1] *Extracts from the St. Helena Records*, pp. 28, 42, 43. St. Helena 1885.

[2] He arrived at St. Helena November 1685.

were condemned to execution, five were hanged, 1685
and the others were respited only after long suspense. When their wives begged for mercy, Weybourne replied ''Twas not in his power, for they were judged and condemned before he came out of England.'[1] But another power, besides that of the Stuarts, had arisen in the Realm. On the petition of four 'mournful daughters' of one of the victims, the House of Commons severely censured the proceedings and excluded certain of the St. Helena butchers from the great Act of Indemnity in 1689.[2]

If the rapid development of the Company under the Restoration gave birth to forces in its distant settlements which the transitory Governors in London could with difficulty control, those forces contained in themselves their own remedy. For they were the outcome not of weakness, but of a yet undisciplined strength. We have seen how the Surat factors, left to their own resources amid the troubles of the Civil War and Commonwealth, maintained the trade of England in the East. So now a new generation of the Company's servants in India supplemented the feebleness of the governing body at home by a vigour of their own. They found themselves compelled to learn the art of ruling, and they learned it. Surat directed the whole affairs of the Company in the East,[3] and to

[1] *Extracts from the St. Helena Records*, p. 43.

[2] Bodleian Library Pamphlets. Fol. θ. 658. 76. House of Commons Journal, 8 June, 1689. The motion was only carried, however, by 159 to 138 votes.

[3] The destruction of the Portuguese Diu in 1670 by the Maskat Arabs, concentrated the Egypto-

the Presidents of Surat was now transferred the long tenure of office which during the first half of the century characterised the three great governors at home. While eleven Presidents of Surat had succeeded each other between 1613 and 1661, three strong men practically ruled at Surat from 1662 to 1690, and each of them vacated his office only on his death.[1] The work of these three men, the makers of Bombay, summarises the progress of the Company in Western India under the Restoration.

Sir George Oxenden, third son of an honorable family settled in Kent since the reign of Henry II., rose in the Company's service under the Commonwealth, was knighted at the Restoration, and ap-
1662 to 1669 pointed President of Surat in 1662.[2] He arrived when Sivaji was beginning to nibble at the southern
1664 frontier of the Mughal Empire, and in 1664 gallantly withstood the Maratha army at Surat, after the Mughal Governor had shut himself up

Indian trade at Surat, and its importance as the 'Gate of Mecca' was increased by the bigotry of Aurangzeb. Surat was temporarily reduced to an agency of the Company 1678; but reinstated as a presidency three years later, and remained the headquarters of the Company in India until their transfer to Bombay in 1687.

[1] The whole number was four, namely: Sir John Oxenden, 1662–1669; Gerald Aungier (Angier), 1669–1677; Mr. Rolt, who was somewhat of the nature of a stopgap, 1677–1682 Sir John Child, 1682–1690. *Gujarat, Surat and Broach*, vol. ii. p. 101. Government Central Press, Bombay 1877.

[2] For the spelling of his name, and the careers of his brother Christopher and other members of his family in India, see Yule's *Hedges' Diary*, vol. ii. pp. 223, 241, 250, 303. He was born 1620, the son of Sir James Oxenden of Dene, county Kent, and had a large and distinguished Indian connection, including Sir Streynsham Master.

in his castle behind old guns obtained from the wreck of a Dutch ship.[1] The Marathas in thousands surrounded the English house, but Oxenden drove them off by a sally, denounced Sivaji as 'a perfideous rebel' to the Mughal Empire when he offered a separate peace, and held his own till the enemy departed, after destroying all the town except a quarter of a mile round our factory.[2] The Emperor Aurangzeb rewarded his gallantry with a robe of honour and a partial exemption to the English from customs duties. The Company sent Oxenden a gold medal, with a Latin inscription declaring that the Preserver is not less than the Conqueror, and a handsome donation for himself,[3] his Council and subordinates. He faced with equal courage the threatened assault of the Dutch during the war of 1665–1667, bore with tact and resolution the humours of the King's first governors of Bombay, and took over that island on behalf of the Company in 1668.[4] Next year Oxenden visited Bombay, drew up a code of

1662 to 1669

1664

1668

[1] Baldæus (*ante*, p. 196), chap. i. p. 3. Amsterdam, ed. 1672.

[2] Letter from the Surat Council to the Company, dated January 28, 1664. Printed in *Selections from State Papers Bombay, Home Series*, edited by G. W. Forrest, vol. i. pp. 24-26. Bombay Government Press 1887.

[3] '£200 in gold.' Hedges' *Diary*, vol. ii. p. 302. The inscription was *Non minor est virtus quam quærere parta tueri*—reproduced on the medal given to Sir Streynsham Master for his defence of the factory at Surat against the Marathas in 1670.

[4] By deputy, as his own relations with the royal officers had been strained. The King's representatives since 1662 had been successively Admiral the Earl of Marlborough, General Sir Abraham Shipman, Mr. Cooke, Sir Gervase Lucas, and Mr. Gary, who made over the island in 1668, and afterwards became a member of the Surat Council and Judge in Bombay.

1669 rules for its administration, and died at Surat. There he rests, with his brother Christopher, under an imposing domed mausoleum forty feet high, '*Anglorum in Indiâ, Persiâ, Arabiâ, Præses.*'[1]

1669 to 1677 His successor Gerald Aungier, a brother of the Earl of Longford,[2] was the true founder of Bombay. He saw it threatened from the inland by the Marathas, from the south coast by the Malabar pirates, from the sea by the Dutch, and cut off from the mainland by the Portuguese who retained the adjacent island of Salsette and established a customs-line in the narrow channel between Bombay and the shore. Now in Western India, as from the first on the Madras coast, the Company's servants had to provide for a settlement beyond the limits of the Mughal Empire and of the protection which it impartially afforded to all. The force of circumstances compelled them to adopt the same policy of armed defence.

Aungier at once resolved to make Bombay a place of safety for shipping and trade. The Court of Directors had ordered its fortification, yet they had refused the aid of skilled officers, in as much as 'we know that it is natural to engineers to contrive curiosities that are very expensive.'[3]

[1] For this interesting burial-ground see *Gujarat, Surat and Broach*, ii. 322–326. The Dutch, rivals even in the house of death, resolved to outvie Sir George Oxenden's tomb by a still huger mausoleum with a double cupola to their chief, Baron van Reede, who was buried at Surat in 1691.

[2] Of the first creation. Report of the Secret Committee of the Company to the King, 15 August, 1684. His name appears as Aungier, Augier, Angier.

[3] MS. Letter Book, No. 5, p. 103, March 13, 1674.

But Aungier, with such help as he could get, 1669 to 1677
pushed on the works, lined the shore with Martello towers[1] against the Malabar pirates, and completed the main fortress with heavy ordnance and sixty light field-pieces. In due time skilled engineers were obtained from home. At Bombay he compelled all owners of land to serve as a militia, excepting the Brahman and Banya castes who commuted their military service for a money payment. This force, which in 1677 mustered 600 men, was officered by the English gentlemen of the factory, and stiffened by 400 regular infantry, chiefly Europeans or of semi-European descent,[2] and forty troopers, each of whom could, in case of need, take up a foot-soldier behind him. Many of the Europeans were Germans, enlisted because less given to drunkenness than the riff-raff which the Company's crimps swept up from the prison-yards and slums of London. A more regular force of three companies of Englishmen and two of Rajputs was projected. The chief military officer received, in 1676, a seat in Council, and although the case was not to form a precedent, it became one.

Aungier's arrangements for defence were made
none too soon. In 1670, he had shown both 1670
courage and discretion during a second attack of the Maratha Sivaji at Surat, in which he saved

[1] Commenced, however, soon after the acquisition of the island.

[2] 'Topasses,' or hat-wearers, applied to the dark-skinned Portuguese half-castes. The numbers of the force varied, but those given above refer to Aungier's period of office, 1669-1677.

1670 the Company's goods while one of his Council[1] won the thanks of the Directors and a gold medal from home. But Aungier soon gave up the pomp and luxury of Surat, with his elegant sea-side residence at Swally Marine, for the hard life of the
1672–75 new settlement. During three years[2] he toiled on amid the pestiferous swamps, putrid fish-curing grounds, and burning red rocks of Bombay, not then as now clothed with trees and gardens. In 1673, his work was brought to a sudden test by the attempt of a Dutch fleet to surprise the island.

1673 The enemy is said to have numbered 6,000 men, but Aungier, 'with the calmness of a philosopher and the courage of a centurion,' to use Orme's words, made a display of force far above the reality—300 European and 400 topasses or half-caste troops, the native militia of 500 men under English officers, and 300 Bhundaris armed with clubs.[3] The Dutch Admiral, Van Goen, was too far off to judge either of the weapons or of the discipline of this motley array, but he saw the muzzles of the heavy cannon on the fort, the line

[1] Sir Streynsham Master, who bore the brunt of the danger, while Aungier removed the Company's goods for safety from Surat to Swally. The letter from the President and Council of Surat to the Company, dated Swally Marine, 20 Nov., 1670, gives a full account of the transaction, and is printed by Yule, Hedges' *Diary*, ii. 226–229. The Court Minutes of 10th Dec., 1673, record the delivery of the medal.

[2] 1672–1675. Forrest's *Selections from State Papers Bombay, Home Series*, vol. i. Introd. pp. xv–xvii.

[3] The Bhundaris or clubmen long formed the bodyguard of the Governor of Bombay, and to the end of the Company's rule carried a Union flag and blew a large trumpet before the High Sheriff at the opening of quarter sessions.

of Martello towers, and three English armed 1673
vessels (the largest carrying thirty guns) in the harbour, with five French ships lying by to help them. So he put out to sea and left Aungier to complete his defences.

But with Gerald Aungier defence meant only an instrument of trade. The native Governor at Surat, dreading the loss of revenue that would result from the transfer of English commerce to Bombay, which lay beyond the customs-line of the Mughal Empire, had forbidden Aungier to leave Surat except on payment of a great sum. Aungier replied that he was 'a free merchant and no slave or prisoner,' and set off in spite of a threatening demonstration of 2,000 horse and foot; for which the Governor, being like most Mughal officers a gentleman, was afterwards ashamed.[1] The chief English import into India was bullion, so a mint was set up at Bombay to turn it into the more profitable form of current coins, a proceeding confirmed by a Charter from Charles II.[2]
The honest weight of these coins (stamped with 1676
Persian characters until the Mughal took offence at such a use of the imperial script) won general

[1] Letter to the Company dated Surat, 23rd April, 1672. *Selections from State Papers Bombay, Home Series*, vol. i. pp. 60, 61.

[2] Court of Directors' instructions for a mint at Bombay, issued 1670; Letters Patent obtained 5th Oct. of the 28th year Charles II., 1676, not 1677 as in the India Office Library Quarto of Charters, p. 108. In 1697 the value of the rupee minted at Surat or Bombay was fixed at 2*s.* 6*d.*; of the xeraphin minted at Bombay at 1*s.* 8*d.*; of the Persian Shahi for trade at Karwar, 4*s.*; and of the pagoda for Calicut, at 9*s.*

acceptance in Western India and gave a new impulse to the Company's trade.

1674 The reform of the revenue system of Bombay was more directly the act of Aungier. Under the Portuguese, the people had been compelled to pay one-fourth of the produce of their land. Aungier convened 'a general assembly of the chief representatives of the said people,' and in 1674, with their consent commuted this burden for a fixed sum of 1,666*l.*,[1] leaving to the cultivators any profits from their increased industry, subject only to military service in the case of those who had held from the Crown of Portugal. To promote manufactures, cotton was served out from the Company's stores; while the Banyas or capitalist class were encouraged to settle by a formal agreement securing their quarter from the intrusion of any Christian or Musalman, and forbidding the slaughter of animals within it. All castes were protected in the celebration of their own religious ceremonies; and as a striking contrast to the Portuguese cruelties of forced labour, no native was to be compelled to carry burdens against his will.[2]

Aungier closely studied the religion of the Hindus,[3] and he was the first Englishman who discerned the political uses to which their caste system might be put. In 1672, he proposed to the

[1] Twenty thousand xeraphins. For this remarkable convention and representative assembly, see the original documents printed for the first time in Forrest's *Selections from State Papers Bombay*, *Home Series*, ii. 383–387.

[2] Surat Letter to Bombay, 22 March, 1677.

[3] Hedges' *Diary*, ii. p. 316.

Court of Directors that societies or fellowships 1672
should be formed among the native merchants—which really meant that the old Hindu trade guilds should receive official recognition. He desired that the various races and castes within the Company's jurisdiction should be represented by elected chiefs or 'consuls,' to act as magistrates in petty cases. His proposals received some years later the sanction from home.[1]

As the natives gained confidence and flocked 1675
to Bombay, its insanitary condition became terrible. In 1675 Aungier submitted to the Directors a scheme for draining the tidal swamps, left dry and foul under the blazing sun half the day, and after several surveys the tardy consent of the Court was obtained.[2] He also projected an English hospital with a regular resident surgeon; a modest building for seventy patients, to cost 400*l.* for erection and 100*l.* for annual expenses—but the forerunner of those noble institutions for medical relief which now cover the length and breadth of the Indian Empire. 'The lamentable loss of your men,' he urged, 'doth call on us for a speedy erecting of the fabric,' so until it could be built, he turned the law-court into an infirmary: and to his arrangements a marked decrease of the mortality in the following year was ascribed.[3]

[1] India Office MSS., O. C. 3614; MS. Letter Books, No. 6, p. 406, No. 7, pp. 219, 507, &c.

[2] Surat Letters, dated 11th and 17th January, 1675; finally sanctioned by the Court of Directors, February 1684.

[3] Surat Letters, dated 18th December, 1675, and 17th January, 1676; Bombay Letter, dated 24th January, 1677.

For the spiritual needs of his countrymen Aungier eagerly took up a scheme of his predecessor, Oxenden, and planned the first Protestant church in Bombay. Till then, service had been conducted in a room in the Fort. The President headed a subscription for an edifice to contain a
1675 thousand people, the Company's servants aiding 'freely and conscientiously,' 'some offering one year's wage, some half a year's, and the least a quarter.' He begged the Directors to make good the balance, and meanwhile set three chaplains of Surat and Bombay to buy bricks, facing stones and timber, pending the sanction from home.[1]

While thus careful for the bodies and souls of the settlers, Aungier enforced a strict control over them. Under the authority of the Company, he established three courts of justice in Bombay; a tribunal for small causes in which one of the factors sat with native assessors, a Court of Appeal presided over by the Deputy Governor and Members of Council, and a court-martial consisting of the Deputy Governor with three military officers. Each court was to meet once a week, but trial by jury, although discussed, was
1676 not deemed practicable. Nor did Aungier favour 'the vexatious suites and contrivances layed by

[1] Surat Letter to the Court, dated 17th January, 1676, cited in Chaplain Anderson's *English in Western India*, p. 140, 1856. I am not sure that I have been able to discriminate exactly between Oxenden's and Aungier's share in this transaction. The long unsigned letter, in Sir Streynsham Master's handwriting, dated Bombay, 18th January, 1672, and printed by Yule in Hedges' *Diary*, ii. pp 305–318, gives a graphic account of the spiritual state of the Company's settlements.

common barristors to disturb the quiet of good 1676
people.'[1] A regular police force was provided, together with a gaol built in the Bazaar, so that the prisoners might, according to the old English custom, beg from passers-by. His stern repression of the mutiny of 1674 furnishes the first example of a Company's officer inflicting the extreme powers of martial law in India.[2]

The most imminent dangers to Bombay came from the pirates of the Malabar seaboard and from the Marathas on the mainland. The Malabar pirates held a chain of precipitous strongholds and difficult creeks, from near Bombay to Cape Comorin, and it was a confederacy of one of their chiefs[3] with Albuquerque which had captured Goa for the Portuguese. Their fleets scoured the coast-route, in squadrons of twenty ships apiece at a distance of five miles apart, so that once a merchant craft came in sight, they could close in on her and render escape impossible—a strategy commented on by Marco Polo. More cruel still were their forays on shore, plundering and burning hamlets and killing the inhabitants or carrying them off as slaves.

They soon learned to keep clear of the guns of the Company's ships, and the line of Martello towers put a stop to their descents on Bombay Island. Yet they cut off the native coasters—craft

[1] Meaning, of course, *barrators*. Aungier to the Council at Bombay, 8th February, 1676. Forrest's *Selections from State Papers Bombay, Home Series*, i. p. 81.

[2] Bruce's *Annals*, ii. p. 368.

[3] The famous Timoja, *ante*, vol. i. p. 152.

1677 which scuttled from port to port like frightened rabbits from one burrow to another; and as late as 1677 they seized an Englishman in a Portuguese vessel, and, on ransom being refused, tied him to a tree and lanced him to death.[1] Aungier did what he could against these pests, by a cruiser stationed at Bombay, light 'frigates' built in the neighbouring creeks, and the grabs of Surat with their oars and sails and two to six small guns. But, although he cleared the approaches to the new English settlement, the pirate power was not broken till Clive captured its stronghold in 1756.

In the Marathas, Aungier found an enemy more formidable, yet under a responsible head with whom it was possible to deal. Their leader, Sivaji, did not forget Oxenden's resistance at Surat in 1662, or Aungier's skilful tactics during the second Maratha attack in 1670. Sivaji found he could strangle the landward trade of Bombay, and cut off even its supply of firewood, while the English factories further south lay absolutely at his mercy. But, a brave man himself, he preferred to have other brave men as his friends rather than his enemies in his struggle with the Mughal Empire. So he gave the English a lesson in 1673 by plundering one of their outlying factories,[2] and

[1] Anderson's *English in Western India*, pp. 178–9. These West-coast pirates, called Sanganians or Sindanians, were known to Arrian.

[2] Hubli, in Dharwar District, afterwards the centre of the cotton trade in the Southern Maratha country.

then received with an open mind their petition for indemnity and alliance.

His fleet, although consisting of three vessels and eighty-five 'frigates' or oared galleys, could not encounter the heavily armed ships of the Company. He saw quite clearly that Bombay might become a thorn in his side, as a port of entry for the Mughal troops, unless he kept on good terms with its owners. Accordingly in 1674, 1674
when the Deputy Governor of Bombay attended his installation on the Maratha throne, a treaty was entered into by which Sivaji agreed that the English should establish factories along the southern coast, pay a moderate import tax of 2½ per cent., and recoup themselves for his depredations by leave to purchase goods under their market value for three years, and a temporary exemption from customs duties.[1]

The Mughal generals had watched this trafficking with the Maratha enemy, yet found themselves powerless to interfere from the mainland. But besides the Malabar pirates and the Maratha fleet, there was a third naval force on the Bombay littoral. Arabs, or Arabian converts, from Abyssinia had long been settled on the Malabar coast, and their language has given many nautical terms, to India.[2] Under the title of Siddis, a corruption of the Arabic Sayyid, lord, whence also The Çid[3]

[1] Signed 6th April, 1674. I summarise from Fryer, Grant Duff, and Chaplain Anderson.

[2] For example, the Surat 'Grab' was the Arab *ghoráb*, Marathi *guráb*, a galley.

[3] And the 'seedy boy' of the P. & O. steamers to this day. A

of Spanish romance, they supplied the mercenary fleets of the southern Musalman kings, and afterwards of the Mughals. They naturally looked with disfavour on the rise of a new naval power to the northward between them and the Mughal
1672 Empire. In 1672, they demanded leave from us to land at Bombay, and ravage the Maratha districts on the mainland. Aungier refused, but they returned after inflicting a defeat on the Marathas further down the coast, enforced our hospitality, and burned several houses at Bombay.

Aungier now found himself between the fleet of the Mughal Empire at sea and the Maratha armies on shore. If he refused the Siddi the use of Bombay harbour, the Mughal Emperor might make reprisals on our factory at Surat in the North. If he showed the Siddi too much friendship, Sivaji would assuredly burn our factories in the South. Year after year the Mughal fleet insisted on 'wintering' at Bombay—that is to say, on passing the tempestuous monsoon months from
1674 June to October within the harbour. In 1674, Aungier stipulated that the Siddi sailors should land with no other weapon than their swords, and that not more than 300 of them should remain on shore at one time. Yet, in spite of his precautions, frequent affrays, Musalman insults to Brahmans, and kidnapping from the Maratha mainland took place. Each October the Siddi's

Siddi when asked what was meant by the term, replied a Habshi, being the Indian form of our word Abyssinian. *Life of Sir Thomas Munro*, G. R. Gleig, 1831, i. p. 287.

fleet put out again to sea to ravage the Maratha coast, and so Bombay had another respite for nine months. Aungier behaved with a courage and tact which carried the settlement through the most perilous years of this crisis, but the Siddi long continued to enforce hospitality at Bombay.[1] 1672 to 1677

Even these troublesome guests contributed, in Aungier's skilful hands, towards the aggrandisement of the new settlement. For Bombay became recognised as the best naval station on the Indian coast, alike for the Mughal fleet and for native merchantmen; a harbour of refuge from the Maratha 'frigates' and the Malabar pirates, in which, if the peace was sometimes broken, person and property were on the whole secure. The Armenians, most cautious of oriental traders, followed in the train of the Banyas or Hindu capitalists of Surat.[2] Within a few years the population multiplied from 10,000 to 60,000; the revenue increased threefold, and the Company resolved that one half its shipping from London should load direct for Bombay, without touching at Swally Roads.[3]

[1] Orme's *Fragments*, Bruce's *Annals*, Fryer's *New Account of East India and Persia*, Grant Duff's *History of the Marathas*, Anderson's *English in Western India*, and Sir James Campbell's *Materials* (Bombay, 1893).

[2] The original documents are summarised in Campbell's Official Materials for the History of Bombay, vol. i. pp. 46, 56–59, Bombay Government Press, 1893, and many of them printed in Forrest's *Selections from State Papers Bombay, Home Series*, vol. i. Government Press, 1887.

[3] Anderson's *English in Western India*, pp. 141, 142. Bombay Island, as received from the Portuguese in 1664, was sixteen square miles in area, with an estimated revenue of 2,823*l.* a year and 10,000 inhabitants. Aungier left the revenue at 9,254*l.*; but it had risen considerably before he assumed office.

1671 Aungier proposed indeed to the Court of Directors, as early as 1671, to make Bombay their head-quarters in India, and the permanent seat of their President,[1] a proposal not carried out till long after he had passed away. This was but one of many rebuffs which his zeal received from home. In January 1678, we learn that he had ceased to 'please the Committee and others,' who 'say he is making up his bundle' for himself.[2] But by that time the worn-out President had laid down 'his bundle' for ever. He died as he had lived
1677 in harness, at Surat on the 30th of June, 1677. 'Multiplicity of words may multiply the sense of our loss, but cannot depict his greatness,' wrote the Bombay Council.[3] 'He found,' wrote an impartial eye-witness, 'a disaffected and incongruous Council, he has now knit them into a bond of at least seeming friendship.'[4]

Aungier discerned that the same dangers which beset Madras beyond the Mughal sphere of protection in Eastern India now threatened Bombay from the breaking-up of the Mughal frontier on the Western coast. He urged the Company, in

[1] The Surat Council to the Company, dated 3rd February, 1671. Forrest's *Selections from State Papers Bombay, Home Series*, vol. i. p. 50.

[2] Private Letter, dated 12th January, 1678. Printed in Yule's *Hedges' Diary*, ii. pp. 245-6.

[3] Surat Letter to Bombay, 30th June, 1677; Bombay Letter to Surat, 11th July, 1677.

[4] *A New Account of East India and Persia*, by John Fryer, M.D., p. 66. 1698. Hamilton, who as an interloper had seldom a good word for the Company's servants, records half a century later that 'the name of Mr. Aungier is much revered by the ancient people of Surat and Bombay.' Captain Alexander Hamilton's *New Account of the East Indies*, 2 vols. 1727, vol. i. pp. 186–7.

its dealings with the native powers, to cease its 1677 'paper protests and threatenings,' for 'the times now require you to manage your general commerce with your sword in your hands.'[1] He recommended the employment of privateers, showed a brave front to the rival native fleets, and ordered his sea-captains 'to personate a more rough and bold appearance.' 'I persuade myself,' he wrote to the Company, 'that God hath greater blessings to bestow on you,' for its power in India, as compared with its European rivals, had 'a more sure lasting foundation than any other nation whatsoever.'[2] His courage for a moment warmed even the Court of Directors, who, in 1677, sent him discretionary powers to secure his position by the employment of armed ships.[3] But before the arrival of the despatch Aungier was dead.

Of his successor, Mr. Rolt,[4] little need be 1677 to 1682 written. A commonplace official, called from the agency in Persia, Rolt never understood the political situation in India, and only felt himself squeezed in a helpless way between the Mughals and the Marathas. If the Marathas seized a Portuguese position near Bombay, the Mughals replied by landing a force at Bombay itself. Bombay became not only the naval station coveted by both their fleets, but also a port of entry for the Imperial troops. The Marathas made reprisals on

[1] India Office MSS. Original Correspondence 4258. Letter of 22 January, 1677.

[2] *Idem*, 3929.

[3] Bruce's *Annals*, ii. p. 405.

[4] President of Surat and Governor of Bombay, 1677–1682. Mr. Henry Oxenden was Deputy Governor of Bombay.

1677 to 1682 our isolated settlements further down the coast, compelled us to abandon the factory at Rajapur,[1] and in October 1679, seized the island of Khaneri in Bombay harbour. The Siddi, or Mughal admiral, rejoined by occupying the adjacent island of Haneri. The English waters became the battle-ground of the two navies, and for several years Bombay lay at the mercy of both. The Directors at home forbad the use of force, and the Bombay Council had to submit by humiliating engagements to the occupation of the islands by the rival native Powers.[2] The Directors in their despondency retrenched the military establishment, and it seemed as if Bombay might at any moment be lost to the English.

1682 But the greatness of the danger awoke a new spirit in the Company. In 1682, two remarkable brothers obtained an ascendency in its counsels—Sir Josia Child at home and (Sir) John Child in India. Of Sir Josia it must here suffice to say that, having served on the Council of Twenty-four since 1674, he was elected Governor of the Company in 1681.[3] John Child had been sent as a little boy to his uncle, the chief of the factory at Rajapur, and grew to manhood within the Maratha

[1] Bruce's *Annals*, ii. p. 428. 1678–9.

[2] *Idem*, ii. pp. 442, 447, 457, &c. The islands appear as 'Hendry-Kendry' in the records.

[3] The tenures of office of the two brothers synchronise as follows. Sir John Child, President of Surat and Governor of Bombay, 1682 to 1690. Sir Josia Child, Governor of the Company at home, 1681 and 1682, 1686 and 1687; Deputy Governor 1688 and 1689, and during the intervening years a ruling power in the Committee of Twenty-four. India Office MSS.

sphere on the south-western coast. He thus 1682
learned the strength of the new Hindu confederacy, and realised that its object was not mere frontier ravaging, but a determined attack on the southern provinces of the Mughal Empire. The time of anarchy which he had foreseen as a youth had now arrived; and in 1682 he found himself appointed chief of the Company's affairs at Surat and Bombay, with a brother, even abler and more resolute than himself, dominant in the Court of Directors at home.

'What has your sword done? Who ever felt your power?' the natives asked with a sneer; 'we see the Dutch outdo you: the Portugals have behaved themselves like men. You can scarce keep Bombaim, which you got, as we know, not by your valour, but compact.'[1] To similar taunts the President at Madras had replied sixteen years before by a project of armed defence, the cost of which terrified the Court of Directors and procured his prompt supersession. But John Child had now the support of his brother, the Governor of the Company, and of the growing conviction, both at home and in India, that if we were to come safe out of the Mughal-Maratha struggle we must meet force by force.

The brothers had, however, to encounter a frightened faction which dreaded that military expenditure would diminish their dividends, and urged that even the presence of the two hostile fleets in Bombay harbour, with their forces

[1] Fryer, Letter VII., dated 25th January, 1681, p. 415. Ed. 1698.

to feed and to clothe, increased the trade of the settlement. 'I know Child at home scatters the guineas there,' wrote a dismissed servant of the Company in India, 'as the other Child does the rupees here, and both to one purpose.'[1] John Child fell upon such malcontents with a heavy hand, and resolved that, if he could not extort respect from the native Powers, he would at least make the English in India learn they had got a master. Private traders or 'interlopers' he marched through the streets with irons on their necks,[2] and his harshness to the widow of one of Keigwin's mutineers stamps him as a vindictive man. But Mughal and Maratha alike began to feel a new strength in the Company.

At first the situation seemed well nigh desperate. In 1682, Bantam, the Company's headquarters in the Far East, where we had found a resting place after Amboyna, was finally captured by the Dutch, and the English factory laid in ruins. The Court of Directors accordingly determined still further to concentrate upon India, and to consider Bombay

1683 to 1684 as 'an independent settlement, and the seat of the power and trade of the English in the East Indies.'[3] But Bombay harbour lay open to the Mughal and

[1] 1684. Hedges' *Diary*, ii. p. 115.

[2] Hamilton's *New Account of the East Indies*, i. p. 221. Hamilton was himself an interloper, and records alike the sufferings of his class, and their calumnies against the Company's servants. John Child's severity to interlopers marked him out for invective, and Hamilton's volumes, written in this spirit, have hitherto supplied the materials for the perverted history of the period.

[3] 1683–4. Bruce's *Annals*, ii. pp. 492, 498, citing the original letters of November 1683, and April 1684.

Maratha fleets, while Keigwin's usurpation[1] proclaimed the Company's weakness on shore. 1683 to 1684

Yet the situation at Surat was even more untenable. The town had twice been taken by the Marathas; and their armies, with the prestige conferred by having a rebel son[2] of the Emperor in their camp, kept Southern India in a state of chronic invasion and alarm. By 1683 the anarchy had reached a height which compelled Aurangzeb to put himself at the head of the array of the Empire. He quitted for ever his splendid Court in Northern India, and during the next quarter of a century ran the course of profitless victories and exhausting defeats amid which his reign dragged to a disastrous close. His war expenditure had already reduced him to financial straits, and shortly before Child became President, the English at Surat only purchased exemption from the imperial exactions by a heavy bribe to the local governor.[3]

The first act in the Decline of the Mughal Empire was in fact begun, and the Company soon learned that, alike in Eastern and Western India, safety could only be found under the guns of its ships. We shall see how in Bengal its search for a coast settlement ended in the founding of Calcutta. In Western India it led, during exactly the same years, to the withdrawal of its headquarters from Surat to Bombay. The Court of

[1] *Ante*, pp. 205-6.

[2] Prince Akbar, 1680-1681: whether most of a traitor to his father or to the Marathas remains doubtful.

[3] Bruce, quoting the original despatch. *Annals*, ii. p. 456. 1680-81.

1684 Directors, rudely awakened to the danger, abandoned their policy of retrenchment, and in 1684 issued orders for the effective defence of Bombay by troops, fortifications, and armed vessels to be stationed in the harbour.[1] Their aversion to military outlay and their resolve to remain peaceful merchants remained as strong as ever. But, they wrote, 'though our business is only trade and security, not conquest which the Dutch have aimed at, we dare not trade boldly, nor leave great stocks' 'where we have not the security of a fort.'[2]

Surat, separated from the sea by fourteen miles of an unnavigable river, dominated by the Mughal who would not allow of foreign garrisons, yet could not secure it from the Marathas, had become obviously unsafe. Only after various half-hearted orders and many misgivings, however, did the Court of Directors make up its mind to the decisive
1686 step. But in 1686 Sir Josia Child was again elected Governor of the Company; and in 1687 Bombay became the chief seat of the English in India, under his brother Sir John, who had received a baronetcy in 1685 and was in fact, if not in name, the first Governor-General of the English Settlements.[3]

[1] The original documents are printed in whole or part in Sir James Campbell's *Materials for the History of Bombay*, i. pp. 85 ff. and Forrest's *Selections from State Papers Bombay*.

[2] Letter from the Court dated 2nd July, 1684.

[3] Bruce repeatedly styles him Governor-General. *Annals*, ii. pp. 568, 585, 587. Governor and General would be officially correct; the title of Governor-General being first authoritatively given to Warren Hastings by Lord North's Act of 1773. This question is dis-

In South-Western India the presence of the Emperor at the head of the Grand Army still gave a show of that Mughal protection which was soon to become an august legend. In South-Eastern India it was not a question of a crumbling frontier, but of a collapsed empire. The Hindu suzerainty of the South had gone down on the field of Talikot in 1565, and during the seventeenth century its **17th cent.** fragments were being as fiercely fought over as the dismembered Mughal dominions were to be fought for in the eighteenth. Not only the native princes but the European nations were grappling for the possession of the Madras coast. The French occupation of St. Thomé, on the outskirt of our settlement,[1] proved, notwithstanding the Anglo-French alliance in Europe, a thorn in our side; and every morning the offing was anxiously scanned in terror of the arrival of a great Dutch fleet. Sir Edward Winter's proposals for armed defence had only led to his recall, and in 1674 'our enemies **1674** being at sea and land within less than musket shot,' [2] the Council contemplated the abandonment of Madras. They adopted, however, the alternative

cussed in Sir George Birdwood's *Report on the Old Records of the India Office*, pp. 228-9 footnote. Ed. 1891.

[1] Now an integral part of Madras city.

[2] *Extracts from the Government Records in Fort St. George*, p. 28. Madras Government Press, 1871; Consultation of 2nd February, 1674. I gratefully thank the Madras Government for the series of these Extracts (3 vols.), for its *Press Lists* or Calendars from 1670 to 1754 (17 vols.), for its *Diary and Consultation Book* from 1681, admirably edited by Mr. A. T. Pringle (5 vols.), and for other unpublished materials—altogether a magnificent contribution to the history of the English in India.

1674 of strengthening their 'low, slight, tottering walls.[1]'

In 1677 a more terrible enemy than the local
1677 princes or rival European Powers threatened Madras. The Maratha leader, Sivaji, swept across Southern India with an army of sixty thousand men, and seized the fortress[2] of the ruined Vijayanagar Empire which commanded the coast. He contented himself at first by ordering the English to send him talismans and antidotes against poison, but next year Madras was only saved from plunder by his reverses in Mysore. Our President, Sir Streynsham Master,[3] who had saved the Company's goods during the Maratha pillage of Surat,[4] strengthened the Madras fort, and took advantage of the lull to inaugurate
1678 domestic reforms. In 1678 he set up a high Court of Judicature; the President and Council to sit twice a week in the Fort Chapel, and 'the trial to be by Jury.'[5] On the following Easter Monday he laid the foundations of St. Mary's Church, 'to

[1] *Consultation* of 2nd February, 1674, p. 29, *ut supra*. Mr. Talboys Wheeler, *Madras*, i. 78. also summarises the records.

[2] Gingi, 82 miles south-west from Madras.

[3] Presidents of Madras, 1662–1709: Sir Edward Winter, 1662–1665; Foxcroft, 1665–1670, but imprisoned from September 1665 to August 1668, during Winter's rebellion and usurpation; Sir William Langhorne, 1670–1677; Sir Streynsham Master, 1677–1681; William Gifford, 1681–1687; Elihu Yale, 1687–1692; Nathaniel Higginson, 1692–1698; Thomas Pitt, 1698–1709. For Sir Streynsham Master's career see Hedges' *Diary*, vol. ii. pp. 12, 13, 47, 48, 200, especially 221 to 259, 304 ff.

[4] In 1670. *Ante*, pp. 215-6.

[5] *Consultation* of the 18th March, 1678. When not otherwise stated, all Madras documents are quoted from the official series enumerated *ante*, p. 233, footnote 2.

be built with the voluntary contributions of the English in these parts.'[1] At the same time he introduced stringent laws against Roman Catholics, punishing priests who attempted the conversion of Protestants by expulsion from the settlement, and compelling all children of Anglo-Portuguese marriages to be brought up in the Reformed Faith.[2] Such religious rigour contrasts with the toleration shown by the Council at Bombay, who had to adjust their Anglican zeal to the needs of a large Catholic population. 1678

These measures were rudely interrupted by a 1681
neighbouring chief[3] who blockaded the settlement and reduced it to the verge of starvation. The Directors at home, vexed by the cost of defending the city against the Marathas, and still trusting to farmans rather than to forts, superseded Sir Streynsham Master in 1681. Two years later the 1683
arrival of Aurangzeb with his Grand Army in Southern India quelled for a time the ambitions of the local princes. His conquest of Golconda, the great State inland from the south-eastern seaboard, was celebrated by the English Council at Madras in 1687 by a salute of 15 guns.[4]

Again the internal development of the little colony was resumed. In 1683, a bank with a capital of 100,000*l.* to be raised locally by the

[1] *Consultation* of 1st April, 1678.

[2] *Extracts* from the Government Records, 1670–1677, pp. 72, 73; 1679–1681, pp. 13, 14, &c.

[3] The Lingapa or Naik of Punamallu, thirteen miles west of Madras. *Consultations* for 1681, 4th series, p. 12, &c.

[4] October 1687.

1683 Council at 6 per cent. was set on foot.[1] Sir John Child, the presiding genius of the Company in India, lamented the defenceless state of Madras, but meanwhile counselled conciliation. 'What I shall do if you quarrel with the Mogull, I cannot see,' he wrote to the Madras Council on the last day of
1684 1684. Yet 'daily affronts, great indignities and often slightings' have made him 'even passionately desirous of showing some force, having used all fair means' in vain. He saw that, if we were to keep our heads above the growing anarchy, we must be prepared to face the Emperor himself, for 'righting with him and his subjects the honour of our king and country that now lies a bleeding.' Child sets forth the dangers of such a war, but shows how our ships might inflict great loss on the pilgrim fleets. He has already got so far as to begin a paragraph with the words 'When we quarrell [with] the Mogull.'[2]

The Madras Council carefully avoided any cause of offence and went on with the improve-
1688 ment of its civil administration. In 1688 it established, under orders from Sir Josia Child in London, a regular system of municipal government, with a Mayor and twelve Aldermen who were to wear scarlet robes, and sixty to one hundred burgesses or town councillors in black

[1] *Diary and Consultation Book*, 21st June, 1683, 1st Series, vol. ii. p. 48.

[2] Letter from John Child to the President of the Coast of Coromandel &c., and Governor of Fort St. George and Council, dated 31st December, 1684, printed at pp. 31–35 of the Madras *Diary and Consultation Book*, 1st Series, vol. iv.

(afterwards changed to white) silk gowns. The 1688
Mayor and certain Aldermen were to act as Justices of the Peace; and of this body of thirteen not more than three should be English, three Portuguese, and seven Musalmans or Hindus. Sir Josia Child avowedly based this corporation upon a Dutch model, and desired that it should be really representative. The people, he wrote, will more willingly pay 'five shillings towards the public good, being taxed by themselves, than sixpence imposed by our despotical power—notwithstanding they shall submit to [it] when we see cause.'[1]

On September 29, 1688, the Madras Corporation, thus constituted, assembled to hear the Company's charter read out, and 'marched in their several robes, with the Maces before the
Mayor, to the Town Hall.'[2] Six months later their 1689
municipal deliberations were rudely interrupted by the arrival of the northern servants of the Company, who had taken to their ships and fled in a body from the Ganges.[3]

The catastrophe, obviously inevitable in Southern India, had come with an unexpected thunderclap from Bengal. That fertile province, one of the most lucrative and most remote of the Mughal dominions, formed a favourite provision

[1] Despatch from the Court of Directors to Madras, dated 28th September, 1687. First printed (I believe) in Mr. Talboys Wheeler's *Madras*, i. 194-204. Madras 1861.

[2] The Proceedings are printed by Mr. Talboys Wheeler, i. pp. 205-6.

[3] Madras *Consultations*. 7th March, 1689.

1650 for a son or a foster-brother of the Emperor. In 1650, the English had obtained a license for free trade in it from Sultan Shuja, son of the Emperor Shah Jahan and Viceroy of Bengal, in return for medical services and an outlay of 3,000 rupees.[1] This document having been lost on its way to Madras, the Viceroy issued a fresh grant exempting
1656 the English from duties or demands of any sort on 'goods imported or exported either by land or by water.'[2] A few years later Sultan Shuja perished in the fratricidal struggle for the throne, but the grant of free trade was continued in return for a yearly payment[3] of 3,000 rupees. In 1664,
1664 Shaista Khan, the son and grandson of Grand Viziers and brother of the lovely Empress who lies beneath the Taj, became Viceroy of Bengal, and hastened to wring a fortune out of the province.

The English seem to have suffered neither more nor less than other infidels under his rapacious rule. He solemnly confirmed, for a consideration, all their previous privileges.[4] Then, callous to his
1672 plighted word, he seized their saltpetre boats, stopped their trade till they paid blackmail, compelled them to supply soldiers for his distant wars, and subjected them to the same duties and

[1] *Ante*, pp. 98, 99.

[2] Nishan granted by the Sultan Shuja to the English in Bengal, 1656. Printed as Appendix II. to Stewart's *History of Bengal*, chiefly from native sources. Calcutta. Ed. 1847.

[3] Peshkash: Stewart's *History of Bengal*, p. 181.

[4] This grant, dated 1672, is printed as Appendix III. to Stewart's *History*. It gave the Company's goods the right to 'pass customs free, without any let, impediment or demands whatsoever.'

exactions as the Hindus.[1] At length in 1677 the 1677
President of Madras had to warn him that unless these oppressions ceased the Company would entirely withdraw from Bengal.[2]

In the same year Shaista Khan resigned his office. A lull intervened, during which the English repurchased exemption from dues for a payment of 21,000 rupees to one of his successors.[3] But in
1679 Shaista Khan returned to Bengal, and the 1679
English, in dread of his exactions, obtained at a great cost a farman from the Emperor himself, which, while maintaining the usual dues at Surat,
exempted the English from customs 'at all other 1680
places.'[4] The smoke of the 300 guns with which their ships in the Hugli saluted this document had scarcely cleared away, when the Viceroy taught them the worthlessness of so distant a protector.

The Directors, realising the capabilities of the Gangetic trade, and confiding in the Emperor's farman, declared the Bengal factories independent
of Madras in 1681,[5] and twenty European soldiers 1681
were sent thence as a guard of honour for the new agent at Húgli town. The Viceroy, however, forbade the purchase of any saltpetre, threw the

[1] Stewart, p. 190, quoting Blake's and Clavel's Reports, dated October 1668 and December 1676.

[2] *Idem*, Letter from the Governor of Madras to Shaista Khan, dated 7 May, 1677.

[3] *Idem*, p. 191.

[4] Farman of the Emperor Aurangzeb, 1680, printed as Appendix V. to Stewart's *History*.

[5] William Hedges, whose *Diary* forms the nucleus of Sir Henry Yule's three volumes, was appointed the first 'Agent and Governor of all affairs and Factories in the Bay of Bengal.' Nov. 1681. *Diary*, ii. p. 17.

1681 to 1685 factor[1] engaged on that duty into prison, and alleging some obscurity in the Emperor's farman, imposed a $3\frac{1}{2}$ per cent. duty on all the Company's goods.[2] The rate of duty mattered little; for the levying of any charge whatever enabled his officers to extort unlimited blackmail. He knew he had the English in his power, and he resolved to make them feel it. Their European rivals had wisely built their factories somewhat lower down the river, but the English, trusting to the repeated grants for which they had liberally paid, were settled in the Mughal garrison-town of Húgli itself.
1685 In 1685, our agent, perceiving the danger of the situation, asked leave to fortify a landing place for his goods near the mouth of the Húgli, which was infested by river pirates and buccaneering interlopers.[3]

This request the Viceroy sternly refused, and represented it to the Emperor as an act of insolent defiance. The Company's ships had to sail without obtaining cargoes, while its inland trade was left to the mercy of the local military commanders, one of whom threw his troops round our factory at Kasimbazar.[4] The English had now, in the words of a historian who has worked from the native sources, 'either to relinquish the trade to

[1] Mr. Peacock at Patna.

[2] Stewart's *History*, p. 196.

[3] *Idem.*

[4] The original records of this period are examined in Sir Henry Yule's edition of Hedges' *Diary*, vol. ii. and more recently by Mr. C. R. Wilson in vol. i. of his *Early Annals of the English in Bengal, being the Bengal Public Consultations for the first half of the Eighteenth Century*, a work of great value, and planned on a magnificent scale.

Bengal entirely; or, by having recourse to arms, to effect by force what they could not obtain by entreaty."[1]

With great reluctance the Court of Directors adopted the latter course. On the 14th of January, 1686, they gave their solemn adhesion to the conclusion which had been forced on their servants in the East; namely, that since the native governors have taken to 'trampling upon us, and extorting what they please of our estate from us, by the besieging of our Factorys and stopping of our boats upon the Ganges, they will never forbare doing so till we have made them as sensible of our Power, as we have of our Truth and Justice.' Then follow the epoch-making words, 'and we after many Deliberations are firmly of the same Opinion, and resolve with God's blessing to pursue it.'[2] 1686

This resolve, wrung from the Company by the necessity of self-preservation, was opposed to its most cherished traditions. Sir Thomas Roe had clearly defined its policy in 1616, and the whole history of the Company in India had been one long effort to maintain the principles then laid down. 'A war and traffic are incompatible,' he wrote.[3]

[1] Stewart, p. 196. Calcutta. Ed. 1847.

[2] Letter from the Secret Committee, consisting of Sir Joseph Ash (the Governor of the Company), Sir Josia Child (Deputy Governor), Sir Benjamin Bathurst and Mr. Joseph Herne, to the Agent and Governor in Bengal, Hedges' *Diary*, ii. p. 51.

[3] Letter from Sir Thomas Roe to the East India Company, dated 24 November, 1616, printed in part by Purchas, i. 589, and in full by Mr. William Foster, *Embassy of Sir Thomas Roe*, vol. ii. 342–352. Ed. 1899. I modernise the spelling.

(1616) 'By my consent you shall no way engage yourselves but at sea, where you are like to gain as often as to lose. It is the beggaring of the Portugal, notwithstanding his many rich residences and territories that he keeps soldiers that spend it, yet his garrisons are mean. He never profited by the Indies, since he defended them. Observe this well. It hath been also the error of the Dutch, who seek Plantation here by the sword. They turn a wonderful stock, they prowl in all places, they possess some of the best; yet their dead payes [payments] consume all the gain. Let this be received as a rule that if you will profit, seek it at Sea, and in quiet trade; for without controversy, it is an error to affect garrisons and land-wars in India.'

1616 to 1686 The advice was sound with regard to the only part of India of which Roe had knowledge, and practically the only part with which the Company was then concerned, to wit, the provinces under the firm sway of the Mughal Empire. He counselled the Company to establish their trade upon grants direct from the Emperor, and not to rely on the provincial governors whose 'ordinary farmans are not worth a half-penny.'[1] So resolutely did the Directors cling to these maxims that they applied them to their settlements on the south-eastern coast far beyond the limits of the Mughal Empire, forbade fortifications, grudged every rupee laid out on their defence, and actually
1645 brought to trial one of their servants 'to answer

[1] Mr. Foster's *Embassy of Sir Thomas Roe*, vol. i. p. xliii.

the charge of the building of Fort St. George'[1] 1645
[*i.e.* Madras]. Bitter experience taught them that a 'fenceless factory' was there a mere spoil for dynastic claimants and predatory chiefs, yet they censured or superseded one President after another for spending too much on the walls.

When the acquisition of Bombay carried the Company beyond the sphere of Mughal protection 1668 to 1686
on the western coast also, it shrank in like manner from accepting the fact that it must protect itself, or not be protected at all.[2] For the fortifications which its servants knew to be indispensable if Bombay were to be retained, the Court of Directors at first refused engineer officers, and it afterwards allowed two hostile native fleets to occupy the harbour rather than risk a conflict with either.

If at length it was compelled in Bengal to abandon the Roe doctrine of unarmed traffic, it was because it found itself there exposed to a combination of dangers elsewhere unknown. The Viceroy of Bengal, a great officer of the Empire,[3]

[1] *Ante*, p. 81.

[2] In 1673 the Directors, steadfast to the Roe doctrine, reiterated their orders not to come to any conflict with the native Powers because we are 'under their protection.' MS. Letter Book, No. 5, p. 69.

[3] In order to understand the absolute authority of this magnate, alike in oppressing the English, in chastising their resistance, and in contemptuous indifference to their proceedings after their punishment, it is needful to bear in mind the all-powerful family which he represented. Shaista Khan, Viceroy of Bengal (or more strictly Nawáb = Deputy or Vice-gerent) was the grandson of Itmad-ud-daula (*d.* 1622), grand-vizier to the Emperor Jahangir; and son of Asaf Khan (*d.* 1641), grand-vizier to the two emperors, Jahangir and Shah Jahan. He

1668 to 1686 could wield the authority of the Emperor, yet was too distant for effective imperial control. The Afghan army of Bengal had in earlier years hurled back the Mughal invasion, and for a time driven the new dynasty out of India. Tardily conquered by Akbar, Bengal with Orissa long formed the arena of rebellions and of fratricidal struggles by Imperial princes. Aurangzeb for a time enforced a strict check. But Aurangzeb was now far off in Southern India, face to face with the vast combination before which his power was eventually to waste away. The Bengal Viceroy could oppress the infidels without fear, and he did so without mercy.[1]

himself became, on his father's death, grand-vizier to Shah Jahan. His aunt was the famous Empress Nur Jahan, who ruled Jahangir; his sister was the beautiful Empress Mumtaz Mahal who bore to Shah Jahan his fourteen children, and now lies with him in the Taj at Agra; one of his nieces married the Emperor Aurangzeb; another of his nieces married Sultan Murad Baksh (son of the Emperor Shah Jahan), who disputed the throne with Aurangzeb and for a time seemed to have got possession of it. Shaista Khan's career shows what such a connection meant at the Mughal Court. Born about 1608, he became successively governor of Berar; grand-vizier to the Emperor; viceroy of Gujarat; generalissimo of the Golconda war, under the nominal leadership of an imperial prince; viceroy of the Deccan; and viceroy of Bengal. He held the last high office, with a short break, for a quarter of a century, and was endeared to the Emperor Aurangzeb by wounds received in his service, and by a yet closer bond—the betrayal to him of Dara Shikoh, the brother of Aurangzeb and rival claimant for the throne. Shaista Khan died in 1694, in his 93rd lunar year, or, as we should say, aged 86,

[1] In 1686 our Bengal factories drew up a long list of their losses and claims for compensation, amounting to Rs.6,625,000, say, 700,000*l*. Some of the items are obviously thrown in to swell the account, but they include monies 'forced from our merchants,' or 'plundered out of factories,' or 'extorted in presents,' with claims for

In 1677 we have seen the Madras Council warn 1677
him that unless his extortions ceased the Company
must withdraw from Bengal. In 1680 the English
tried in vain to restrain him by a farman from the
Emperor direct. Under Aurangzeb's father such a 1680
farman would have been implicitly obeyed: but
now, wrote Mr. Charnock, the governors make
'small accompt thereof.'[1] In 1682, our Chief Agent 1682
in Bengal journeyed to the Viceregal Court at
Dacca and humbly remonstrated against the
'general stop of our trade'—still in vain.[2] In
1685 the Húgli Council, feeling their position so 1685
high up the river to be unsafe, fruitlessly begged
leave to quit it for a landing-place further down.
For the first time in its history, the Company found itself under a Mughal oppressor whom the Emperor's farman failed to control, and whom its petitions and presents were powerless to appease. The Roe doctrine of 'quiet trade' had obviously ceased to apply to Bengal: as it had never really applied to Madras or Bombay, nor indeed anywhere outside the provinces in which the Imperial authority could secure Imperial protection.

The renunciation of that doctrine in January
1686 was the only course left to the Company. 1686
History, which loves to spare our memories by labelling great changes in policy with a single name, has ascribed this fresh departure to the brothers Child. The brothers Child did indeed

'demolishing,' 'plundering,' 'besieging,' and 'burning.' The Húgli Council to the General and Council at Surat, 9th Dec., 1686.

[1] Hedges' *Diary*, ii. 46, &c.

[2] *Idem*, i. 33–37.

1686 discern more clearly than their contemporaries that the coming anarchy in India created a new necessity for self-defence. Yet thirteen months had not passed since John Child wrote to the Madras Council 'what I shall do if you quarrel with the Mogull, I cannot see'[1]; while Sir Josia Child had compelled the Bombay Council to submit to the occupation of the harbour by hostile fleets, and forbidden it to strike a blow. 'Although we have formerly wrote you that we will have no war for Hendry-Kendry,' runs one of his first despatches after election to the Governorship of the Company
(1681) in 1681, 'yet all war is so contrary to our constitution as well as our interest, that we cannot too often inculcate to you our aversion thereunto.'[2] In the second year of his governorship Sir Josia Child repeated the injunction in even stronger
(1684) terms. Yet by 1684, the Court of Directors (no longer under his governorship) had got so far as to declare that 'though our business is only trade and security, not conquest,' 'yet we dare not trade boldly or leave great stocks where we have not the security of a fort.'[3] In 1685 they ordered the Black Town of Madras to be walled in and fortified at the expense of the inhabitants, 'whether it displease or please them or anybody else.'[4] They also

[1] *Ante*, p. 236.

[2] Letter from the Court of Directors to the Bombay Council dated 22nd April, 1681; again enforced by despatch of May 1682. Quoted, Anderson's *English in Western India*, p. 175, ed. 1856. Sir Josia Child was elected Governor of the Company on the 12th April, and sworn in on the same day. MS. Court Book.

[3] *Ante*, p. 232.

[4] MS. Letter Book, No. 7, p. 446. Letter of 16th March, 1685.

desired a defensible position in Bengal where 'our 1685
great ships may lie within command of the guns of our fort.'[1] Sir Josia Child again became Governor in April 1686, but the solemn renunciation of the Roe doctrine of unarmed traffic was resolved on in January under the governorship of Sir Joseph Ash.

As a matter of fact the Company possessed 1686
neither the information nor the officers for the effective prosecution of a war in India. It easily obtained the royal sanction for an armament, as James II. was a large shareholder; indeed His Majesty's India stock proved one of his most valuable assets at St. Germains three years later.[2] The expedition consisted of six companies of infantry and ten ships of twelve to seventy guns (some of them mere tenders), under Captain Nicholson with the title of admiral until he reached the Ganges, when the Agent in Bengal was to act both as admiral and commander-in-chief. The troops sailed with only lieutenants, as the colonel, lieut.-colonel, major and captains were to be supplied from the factory gentlemen. On the west coast of India the squadron was to cut off the native shipping and declare war on the Mughal Emperor. On the east coast, after obtaining, if possible, 400 additional soldiers at Madras, it was to bring away the Company's servants from Bengal, lay hold of all Mughal ships at sea, capture and fortify Chittagong at the north-east extremity of the bay,

[1] MS. Letter Book, No. 7, p. 260. Letter of 5th March, 1684.

[2] James II. sold 7,000*l.* E.I.C. stock on 16th January, 1689, a few weeks after his arrival in France. Historical MSS. Commission Report, 10, app. iv., p. 330.

establish there a mint, then advance up the Ganges to the Viceroy's capital at Dacca, and extort from him a treaty by force of arms. It was also to take vengeance on the King of Siam, by seizing his vessels for wrongs done to the Company; and it was to give tardy effect to the Marriage Treaty of 1661 by driving out the Portuguese from the dependencies of Bombay.[1]

Of this vast programme, conceived in ludicrous ignorance of the geographical distances and with astounding disregard of the opposing forces, not a single item was carried out. Misfortunes and miscalculations dogged the expedition. At length in the autumn of 1686 two ships and their light-armed tenders entered the Húgli river with 308 soldiers,[2] to make war on an Empire which had at that moment an army of at least 100,000[3] men in the field. The Viceroy of Bengal alone could lead out 40,000 troops, and the Garrison of the single town of Húgli numbered 3,300. An attempt at a pilot service for the river was begun in 1668,[4] but the twenty miles below Húgli town proved almost impassable by large ships, and the 308 English soldiers had to be sent up in small craft.

[1] The original documents are cited in Bruce's *Annals*, ii. p. 561. Sir Henry Yule in Hedges' *Diary*, ii. 52, gives the names of only nine vessels, including tenders or 'frigates.'

[2] Wilson's *Early Annals of the English in Bengal*, pp. 94–96. Each ship had a tender or 'frigate' built for speed and carrying 12 guns.

[3] Dr. J. F. Gemelli Careri, an eye-witness, states that in 1695 Aurangzeb had in his own camp at Galgala 100,000 foot and 60,000 horse; and estimates his total army at 300,000 horse and 400,000 foot, probably including many camp-followers. Churchill's *Collection of Voyages*, 1742, vol. iv. pp. 221, 235. On p. 225, 1,000,000 seems to be a misprint for 100,000.

[4] Hedges' *Diary*, iii. p. 199.

The Chief of the Bengal Council was a man typical alike of the good and the evil in the Company's servants at that time. Job Charnock went out to India in 1655 or 1656, apparently not in the Company's service, but soon obtained a five years' engagement in it.[1] He appears in the first roll of the new Company formed under Cromwell's Charter as Fourth Member of Council at Kasimbazar with a salary of 20*l*. in January 1658.[2] In 1664 he only agreed to remain in India on condition of being appointed Chief of the Council at Patna, in which office[3] he continued until 1680, with his salary raised to 40*l*. and finally to 60*l*. In that inland station he witnessed the beginning of the anarchy amid which the Mughal Empire was to perish: 'the whole Kingdome,' to quote his reports, 'lying in a very miserable feeble condition, the great ones plundering and robbing the feebler,' and the Emperor's order sunk to 'as small vallue as an ordinary Governour's.'[4] He himself, according to Orme, 'personally received the most ignominious treatment, having, not long before, been imprisoned and scourged by the Nabob.'[5] 'Throughout the Imperial dominions,' wrote the native historian of Aurangzeb's reign, 'no fear and (1655 to 1686)

[1] Hedges' *Diary*, ii. p. 45.

[2] MS. Court Book, 12th and 18th January, 1658.

[3] Hedges' *Diary*, ii. 45, 46. Wilson, p. 92.

[4] Job Charnock to the Húgli Council, 6 July, 1678. Hedges' *Diary*, ii. 46.

[5] *A History of the Military Transactions of the British Nation in Indostan*, by Robert Orme, *sub anno* 1685, vol. ii. p. 12. Ed. 1778.

(1655 to 1686) dread of punishment remained in the hearts' of the provincial grandees.[1]

Charnock married a Hindu girl, according to tradition a young Brahman widow whom he rescued from her husband's funeral pyre, and he adopted native customs. The bribery of Court officials seemed to him the normal method of getting business done,[2] and after many wedded years he is said to have commemorated the death of his wife by the annual sacrifice of a cock to her manes.[3] Such a sacrifice is repugnant to orthodox Hinduism: but the young widow would become an out-caste by her marriage to Charnock, and like other out-caste women she probably joined one of the local sects which mitigated the harshness of the caste system. The chief of these sects at Patna was that of the Five Saints of Behar, among whose rites was the sacrifice of a cock.[4] Hamilton's story that Charnock became a convert to paganism is an 'interloper's' calumny. Charnock brought up his family as Christians,[5] and died himself 'in the hope of a blessed resurrection on the coming of Christ the Judge;' as his tomb in St. John's Churchyard, Calcutta, attests to this day.

[1] The Muntakhabu-l Lubád of Kháfi Khán: Sir Henry Elliot's *History of India*, vol. vii. p. 248.

[2] Job Charnock to the Húgli Council, 28th October, 1678.

[3] I have discussed this tradition in my *Thackerays in India*, p. 35, 1897.

[4] *Journal of the Asiatic Society of Bengal*, vol. lxiii. part iii. 1894.

[5] His mausoleum contains inscriptions to his eldest daughter Maria [died 1697], married Sir Charles Eyre, afterwards the first 'Governor' of Bengal, and to his youngest daughter, wife of Jonathan White of the Bengal Council (*post*, p. 270).

Having refused a transfer to the superior Council of Madras,[1] Charnock naturally expected, on Bengal being raised to an independent establishment in 1681, that he would be appointed its head. He stood high in the favour of the Court of Directors as 'our old and good servant Mr. Job Charnock,' no 'prowler for himself beyond what was just and modest.'[2] 'They would rather dismiss the whole of their other Agents than that Mr. Charnock should not be chief of Kasimbazar.'[3] But local 'animosities' ran strong against him, and he saw the headship of the Bengal Council at Húgli given twice in succession to other men.[4] 1681

[1] Letter from the Patna Council, dated 28 October, 1678.

[2] Letter from the Court of Directors, dated 5 January, 1681.

[3] Court Letter to Madras, quoted by Bruce, *Annals*, ii. 450. One of the reasons alleged by the Court for the dismissal of Sir Streynsham Master was his harsh treatment of Charnock, although Master's outlay on fortifications at Madras formed, perhaps, his major offence. Hedges' *Diary*, ii. pp. 246-7.

[4] The chiefs of Bengal, with their various titles, from the establishment of the factory at Húgli by a deputation from Masulipatam, were as follows: Agents at Húgli; James Bridgeman, 1650-1657; George Gawton, 1657-1658; Jonathan Trevisa, 1658-1662.

In 1661-1662, the Bengal establishment was formally made subordinate to Fort St. George (Madras), and under the control of the Presidents of Madras the following agents governed Bengal with the title of 'Chief of the factories in the Bay,' residing as before at Húgli; William Blake, 1662-1668; Shem Bridges, 1668-1669; Henry Powell, 1669-1670; Walter Clavell, 1670-1677 (during his period of office Streynsham Master, President of Madras, reorganizes the Bengal factories, 1676); Matthias Vincent, 1677-1682 (Streynsham Master again visits and reorganizes the Bengal factories, 1679).

In 1681 the Bengal establishment was separated from Fort St, George, and William Hedges (actual commission dated 24 November, 1681) was appointed 'Agent and Governor of the factories in Bengal.' But on his dismissal in 1684, Bengal was again made subordinate to Madras. In 1684 (August to

1681 With some soothing words from the Directors,[1] Charnock had in 1681 to content himself with the subordinate post of Chief of the Kasimbazar Factory, close to the great city of Murshidabad, and about two days' journey up the river from Húgli town. The native middle-men, aware of the Viceroy's hostility to the English, harassed the factory by law-suits, and Charnock refused to pay the sums awarded by, as he maintained, an unjust and a venal judge. On the death of our chief Agent at Húgli in August 1685, he succeeded to that office; but the local general surrounded Kasimbazar with troops, and it was not till April 1686 that Charnock escaped through the military cordon and reached Húgli.[2]

1686 He found the factory threatened on all sides. While the Viceroy in his distant capital at Dacca, listened politely to our petitions and gave us fair words, his Highness at the same time ordered an

October) William Gifford, President of Madras, came up to act in Bengal. The following were 'Agents and Chiefs of the Bay,' subservient to the Presidents of Madras:—John Beard, the elder, 1684–1685; Job Charnock, who removed the headquarters of the English from Húgli to Calcutta, 1686–1693; Francis Ellis, 1693–1694; Charles Eyre (later Sir Charles), 1694–1699; John Beard, the younger, 1699. Bengal was now finally separated from Madras and Sir Charles Eyre (commission dated December 20, 1699) was sent out as 'President of Bengal and Governor of Fort William.'

It should be borne in mind that, as to these dates, authorities sometimes differ according as they take the actual date of the commission or that of assuming office. In the above list, except where expressly stated to the contrary, the latter mode has been adopted.

[1] Letter from the Court dated 18 November, 1681.

[2] The details are given in the MS. Kasimbazar Consultations, which unfortunately break off in November, 1685. Hedges' *Diary*, ii. 53.

overwhelming body of troops to Húgli. The 1686
pompous declaration of war against the Mughal Empire which the Court of Directors designed, had not then reached the Dacca Court, and probably never did. But the Viceroy knew that some increase had been made to our little garrison at Húgli, so he 'surrounded the factory[1]' with 'two or three hundred horse and three or four thousand foot.'[2] The local Governor, now ready for a rupture, insolently denied the English all the necessaries for trade, and forbade them to purchase victuals in the bazar, or to send their soldiers thither for supplies.[3]

On the 28th October, 1686 the explosion took Oct. 1686
place. Three of our garrison who went out to buy their morning food, were set upon by the native soldiery, and the news reached the factory that two of them, 'desperately cut and wounded,' were 'lying dying in the highway.' Charnock hurried forth a company 'to bring in their bodies dead or alive, but to offer violence to no man, except they were assaulted.'[4] A general fight ensued, which ended in the English beating off the native troops, inflicting severe reprisals, and returning victorious to their factory, which Charnock tried to strengthen by ordering up some light-armed vessels to lie off the town. But he knew that a position separated by a hundred miles of a scarcely navigable river

[1] Orme, *History*, vol. ii. p. 12, ed. 1861.

[2] Letter from the Húgli Council to Sir John Child and the Council at Surat, dated 24 Nov., 1686.

[3] *Idem*, par. 8.

[4] *Idem*, par. 9.

1686 from the Company's larger ships on the sea-board could not be maintained. His garrison, even with the reinforcement from England, did 'not number 400 fighting men.'[1] He doubtless remembered also, that in that same month of October, fifty-four years previously, the Mughals had utterly destroyed the Portuguese settlement at Húgli, enslaved or circumcised its male survivors, and sent its fairest maidens to the harems of the Imperial Court.[2] After fruitless negotiations, he
Dec. 20 1686 put the Company's goods and servants on board his light vessels and dropped down the Húgli river twenty-seven miles to the site of the modern Calcutta.

The place was well chosen for making a stand against a land-force. At a reach of the river, then about seventy miles from the sea and accessible at high tide to heavily armed ships, the stream had scooped for itself a long deep pool—now Calcutta harbour. It was early known to the Portuguese, whose galliasses from 1530 onwards anchored there, and transferred cargo to country boats, so as to avoid the shallows upwards to Húgli town. On the arrival of the Goa fleet each year, a bazar of mat huts sprang into existence on the west bank[3] of the pool. On the departure of the heavy Portuguese vessels, after transhipping cargo, the mat huts were burned down, and the west bank

[1] Charnock to the Madras Council, printed in Hedges' *Diary*, ii. 57.

[2] Stewart's *History of Bengal*, p. 158. Calcutta, Ed. 1847.

[3] At Betor, now adjoining Sibpur, opposite to Calcutta, but a little further down the river. Wilson's *Early Annals of the English in Bengal*, p. 133.

relapsed into solitude until the return of the Goa 1686
fleet next season. But three hamlets,[1] the chief of which was known as Sutanati Hát, literally 'Cotton Thread Mart,' grew up on the eastern bank for the sale of country-made yarns and cloths.

It seemed as if nature had determined that the spot should be one of anchorage only, and no abiding place for man. From the west bank stretched a country ravaged by great rivers during a third of the year, and open during the other two-thirds to the banditti of Orissa and Southern Bengal. The eastern bank appeared even more unfit for human habitation. For although well raised above the river, it sloped down behind into a swampy jungle, with only a narrow strip, then about a mile in breadth, between the stream and the fens. Inland from this strip spread a vast agglomeration of brackish lagoons, now known within their curtailed limits as the Salt Water Lakes—a deadly region, long given up to malaria and the crocodile. By creeks through the strip of higher ground, the fœtid ooze from the swamps swayed backwards and forwards with the rise and fall of the tide.

This drowned land had been formed by the silting up of an old historic channel of the Ganges, which diverged eastwards from what is now the

[1] Namely, Sutanati, Kalikata (= Calcutta) and Govindpur. See map. Several families of modern Calcutta, Baisakhs and Sets, claim descent from the original trade-settlers at Sutanati, probably during the Portuguese period, 16th century.

1686 Húgli, a few miles below Sutanati. Although nothing remains to mark its course save a line of green hollows, an occasional pond, and a little piece of a canal, the peasantry still speak of it as the 'Original Ganges' or 'Old Ganges,'[1] through which the holy Mother-river reached the sea before her waters were diverted into the present Húgli. On its banks stood a famous shrine of Hindu antiquity, Kálí-ghát, now on the outskirts of Calcutta, and whence the town derived its name.[2] The path of pilgrimage to this sacred spot lay through a dense jungle along the narrow strip between the modern Húgli and the swamps. That forest path has become the most fashionable street[3] of the City of Palaces, while a series of crumbling little temples and burning-ghats for the dead dot the route of the ancient vanished river.

Before the year 1686 the 'Old Ganges' had dwindled into a line of shallow ponds. Its silted-up channel could no longer draw off the mass of waters from the brackish fens which, thus shut off from their old exit to the sea, spread over a hundred square miles, and rendered the Húgli bank unassailable by troops from the east.

[1] The Adi-Ganga, literally 'The First Ganges;' or Buda-Ganga, 'The Old Ganges.' For an account of ancient Calcutta see my *Imperial Gazetteer of India*, vol. iii. p. 247, &c. Ed. 1885.

[2] Through the Musalman official form Kalikata, mentioned in Todar Mall's rent-roll of the Mughal Empire (circ. 1582) and preserved in the Aín-i-Akbari. See my *Statistical Account of Bengal*, i. 364. Kalikata appears in the *Aín* as a 'mahal' or small revenue division—that is, the area round Kálíghát, probably including the hamlets of Sutanati and Govindpur.

[3] Chowringhi.

Charnock perceived that a European Power which 1686 dared the unhealthiness of the place, and whose ships could command the river approaches on the north, south and west, would, whatever it might suffer from nature, be safe from the attack of man.

On December 20, 1686 [1] he made the venture. The local Governor at Húgli had received a sharp lesson from the skirmish in October and Charnock could report that 'our coming off was very Peaceable.' During January 1687 he erected some 1687 hovels on the river bank at Sutanati, even hoped for permission to build a factory, and got the length of signing twelve articles [2] with the Viceroy's agent, which confirmed the previous grants of trade to the English, customs free. But in February, the swamps having shrunk to their cold weather dimensions, the Viceroy put an end to parleys by sending an army to crush the new settlement. 'The country all up in arms round us, and without any hope of peace,' wrote Charnock, the English had again to take to their ships, and seek refuge seventy miles further down the river, where, amid the tidal flats and creeks of Hijili, its waters merge into the sea.[3] On their way they destroyed the

[1] The date is given in his first surviving letter from 'Chuttanuttea,' dated 31 December, 1686, to Sir John Child and the Surat Council: printed in Hedges' *Diary*, ii. 59.

[2] Dated 11th January, 1687, and printed in full in Hedges' *Diary*, ii. 60-61.

[3] Arrived at Hijili 27th February, 1687. Charnock's Report to Sir John Child, dated 10th September, 1687. This, and other contemporary documents, are printed in Hedges' *Diary*, ii. 60-71; but see also Wilson's *Early Annals of the English in Bengal*, pp. 102-111, based thereon and in part on my *Statistical Account of Bengal*, vol. iii.

1687 imperial salt-stores and some riverside forts, while the Company's ships made a diversion by sacking and burning Balasor.[1] As a sequel to the latter exploit one of our long-boats fell into the enemy's hands with its crew of sixteen men—of whom three were executed and their heads stuck up in Húgli town.[2]

A high dyke, like the rampart round a Roman encampment, now encircles Hijili and defends it from inundation. It was then an island swamp, separated by channels from the mainland, and but half rescued from the sea; 'having a great store of wild hogs, deer, wild buffaloes and tigers,' very fertile at places above the water level, yet so unhealthy that it had passed into a native proverb.[3] In 'that Direful Place,' as Charnock calls it, he and his hunted four hundred seized a little fort, a mere shell surrounded by a thin wall now nearly submerged by the river, but with their ships in front, and creeks all round. The Viceroy's army of 12,000 men closed in behind, cut off supplies, pounded the garrison with cannon across a too narrow creek, and forced our ships from their
May 1687 anchorage. On May 28, 1687, the besiegers were only driven out of the trenches by desperate fighting.

[1] The small forts were at Thana, a little below Calcutta on the other or western side of the river. For the ransack of Balasor, see Charnock's Report to Sir John Child, 10th September, 1687.

[2] Wilson's *Early Annals of the English in Bengal*, p. 107.

[3] 'It is one thing to go to Hijili, but quite another to come back alive': an analogue of *Facilis descensus Averni—sed revocare gradum . . . hic labor est.*

Our starving men could do no more. In the 1687
three months Charnock had buried two hundred soldiers, another hundred lay sick or wounded, only one hundred remained able to bear arms, many of them tottering invalids, almost all emaciated with fever and ague. Of forty officers, only himself, one lieutenant and four sergeants were alive and fit for duty. His principal ship sprang another great leak, not one of the others was half-manned, and the end seemed to have come, when a vessel carrying the English colours hove in sight with seventy fresh men on board. By an audacious stratagem, Charnock magnified his reinforcement into a new army, and displayed a delusive show of strength with banners, trumpets, drums and loud huzzas. The Mughal general, completely deceived, held back, and on June 4 sent a flag of truce.

Charnock, who had been the soul of the defence, June 1687
now obtained an honourable capitulation. The general agreed to procure the Viceroy's acceptance of the twelve articles of January,[1] and on June 11, Charnock marched out the remnant of his men, gaunt and ragged, yet with drums beating and colours flying. He did not, however, dare to return to Calcutta; but sought an intermediate refuge for three months at Ulubaria, sixteen miles below it, within gunshot of his ships, and again protected by creeks or channels on the inland. After a scolding from the Viceroy, he obtained a contemptuous permission

[1] Agreement dated 8th June, 1687, and counterpart dated 9th June, printed in Hedges' *Diary*, ii. 70.

1687 to stay where he was or to re-settle in Húgli town.[1] But to re-settle at Húgli town was to put himself again under the paw of the panther; while to stay on at Ulubaria was to cut himself off from the inland trade. So in September 1687, Charnock crept further up the river, and anchored for the second time in the pool which now forms the port of Calcutta.

Sept. 1687 Here he again opened 'negociations' for leave to build a factory, and meanwhile hutted the remnant of his troops on the high eastern bank. For a year he laboured at the double task of buying a permit from the Viceroy, and erecting a 1687–8 factory in anticipation of it. Charnock had now spent thirty-four hard years in Bengal, and was an old man as the age of Englishmen then reckoned in India. But the rugged veteran seems to have been quite unconscious that he was doing anything heroic. His Honourable Masters, indeed, so far from thanking him, marvelled at the 'insensible patience' and 'sheepish' submission of their Bengal servants.[2] As for Charnock's magnificent defence of Hijili, 'it was not your wit

[1] Parwana from the Nawab Shaista Khan, dated Dacca 21st July, 1687. It begins thus: 'Consider Yourselfe what manner of Evill has been enacted by you, and those rash fights made with the King's forces and with myself, and fired 3,000 Canon Shott, and plundered and took prizes the Shippes of Moors, and afflicted God's people. If the matter should fully in every particular be made known to the King [Aurangzeb], the Offense in noe wise would be forgiven'—but an aged and merciful viceroy will not exact punishment. This is the sort of document which English historians have hitherto called 'treaties'! Hedges' *Diary*, ii. 70, 71.

[2] Letters from the Court of Directors dated 12 August, 1685 and 12 December, 1687.

or contrivance, but God Almighty's good Providence which hath always graciously superintended the affairs of this Company,' to which he owed his deliverance. Their grand plan of campaign, with six companies of infantry against the Mughal Empire, had miscarried, and Charnock must bear the blame. 'If you had immediately according to the King our Sovereign's orders and our own, proceeded directly for Chittagong, while our forces were strong and vigorous, the Mogull would have consented to our holding and keeping that place in amity with him.' [1] 1687-8

As a matter of fact, it was due to accidental causes that the English were not swept off the face of Bengal. The Emperor engrossed by his great wars in Southern India scarcely deigned to notice the petty tumult on the Húgli, except by calling for a map [2] of that scarcely known region.

The Viceroy of Bengal, then in his eighty-fifth lunar year, had betaken himself to the round of devotions amid which a pious Musalman prepares for death,[3] and thought he had sufficiently punished the traders by driving them out of their miserable refuge at Hijili.

Charnock thus got a respite of a year. He had tried four places on the river: Húgli town, 100 miles from the sea and beyond the protection of his ships: Ulubaria, literally 'the Abode of Owls,'

[1] Letter of the Court of Directors, dated 27th August, 1687.

[2] Letter from the Patna Factory to Sir John Child, 25th June, 1687. Hedges' *Diary*, ii. 63, 64.

[3] He retired from the Viceroyalty of Bengal in 1689, and died in 1694, in his 93rd lunar year.

1687–8 about half way down, where there was no trade: the fever creeks of Hijili near its mouth; and, twice over, the long pool at Sutanati and its high eastern bank protected by swamps to landward. With infinite labour and endurance of misery through the hot weather and drenching rains of 1688, he there threw up a rough shelter for his ague-stricken followers and began some poor
Sept. 1688 defensive works. To him arrived on September 20, 1688, Captain Heath with another reproachful despatch from the Directors, and orders to put the whole survivors on board ship and to sail for the conquest of Chittagong.

Charnock pleaded hard for his rising settlement. The despatch grudgingly allowed that if he had already fortified some suitable place, their servants might stay there, 'since we can't now help it.'[1] With the aid of this argument Charnock managed to avert the catastrophe for some weeks. But Heath, a 'capricious and futile feather-brained'[2] sea-captain, had not the eye of genius with which Charnock, and Clive after him, discerned the strength of the high eastern bank of the Calcutta pool, alike for commerce and for war.
Nov. 1688 On the 8th November, 1688, after much wrangling and several sudden changes of mind, the impetuous sailor ordered Charnock and the rest of the Company's servants on board, leaving the

[1] Letter of Court of Directors to the President and Council of Fort St. George, dated London, 25th January, 1688.

[2] Sir Henry Yule's words; Hedges' *Diary*, ii. 76. The contemporary documents for Heath's expedition and its results then follow: pp. 77–87.

inland factors, and even our agents[1] at the 1688-9
Viceroy's Court, to imprisonment in irons.

He had but a hazy notion whither he was going. His Honourable Masters distinctly told him to capture Chittagong. But their despatch[2] from London shows that they fancied he would find that place somewhere 'up the great Ganges'! As a matter of fact it lay on a little river far to the east on the wild frontier between Bengal and Arakan, and, although once an emporium of sea-board commerce, was cut off from the inland Gangetic trade. Heath began his adventures by sacking and burning Balasor,[3] a short distance south of the Húgli estuary, but failed to bring off the Company's factors, who were 'bound with fetters'[4] for his misdeeds. After again abandoning an envoy at the local governor's Court, he sailed for Chittagong with a miscellaneous flotilla of some fifteen vessels, large and small, and about 300 soldiers, of whom over 150 were half-castes or 'Portuguese.' But on his arrival at Chittagong[5]

[1] Messrs. Eyre and Braddyll.

[2] Printed in Hedges' *Diary*, ii. 78. I suggest that the mistake of the Directors arose from the circumstance that their geography, derived by slow filtration from the Portuguese, was a century old. The Portuguese, *circ.* 1530, had found the two chief seaports of Bengal at Sátgáon (just above the later Húgli town) which commanded the Gangetic trade, and at Chittagong, the emporium of the Burmese and sea-board commerce. The Sátgáon creek had silted up before the English arrived at Húgli, and Chittagong, after becoming a pirate nest of the Portuguese and Arakanese, had lost the remnants of its mercantile importance under the land-loving Mughals.

[3] 28th November to 4th December, 1688.

[4] Minute by the Bengal Council at Madras, 22 March, 1689.

[5] About the 18th of January, 1689.

1688-9 he found the place defended by ten thousand men, and after a month of distracted councils of war, hollow negotiations with the native governor, and vain offers of service to the King of Arakan, he once more abandoned an unfortunate English envoy, and gave up the enterprise. His crowded human cargoes had been dying of scurvy, and on 17th Feb-
Feb. 1689 ruary, 1689 he resolved to seek refuge for his vagrant fleet at Madras; giving, in his own words, 'orders for every ship to make the best of her way.'[1]

At Madras Charnock ate his heart out for fifteen weary months. The experiment of making Bengal an independent presidency in 1681 had, after a miserable experience, been abandoned in 1684, and the Húgli Council replaced under Madras. Charnock was therefore in the position of a subordinate agent who, having lost all the property entrusted to him, fled with his whole establishment for refuge to the head settlement. But the indefatigable Nestor set to work to patch up the ruin which Heath and his Honourable Masters had wrought in Bengal. Aurangzeb did not take the distant scuffles with traders too seriously.[2] Indeed during the very autumn of 1687, when Charnock stole back with his remnant from Hijili to Calcutta, the superior Council of

[1] Captain William Heath's *Short Account* to the President and Council at Fort St. George, dated 16 August, 1688.

[2] Even Mountstuart Elphinstone in his full and careful account of these years (1686–1690) makes no mention of the English war, although he relates at some length our capture of a pilgrim ship in 1693. In Book XI. he merely refers to the war to state that Khafi Khan, the contemporary historian, 'takes no notice of it.'

Madras was celebrating the Emperor's conquest of Golconda by salvoes of cannon. 1689-90

When, however, Sir John Child threatened to withdraw our trade from Surat, and began to cut off Mughal ships and to endanger the route to Mecca, the piety not less than the fiscal interests of Aurangzeb drew his attention to the Company's proceedings. The local officers of his Majesty sufficiently punished its audacity, drove its servants out of Bengal, seized its factories at Surat, Masulipatam and Vizagapatam, threw many of its agents into irons, and attacked Bombay with the Siddi fleet. But although insignificant on land, the English were formidable at sea, and the ocean path of pilgrimage must not be troubled. In December 1689 Sir John Child, having sought aid from the French and Dutch in vain,[1] recognised the hopelessness of the struggle, and solicited peace,[2] which the Emperor granted, although on hard terms.

His Majesty's farman of the 27th February, 1690 sets forth that 'all the English having made a most humble submissive petition that the ill crimes they have done may be pardoned,' and promised to pay a fine of Rs. 150,000 (say 17,000*l.*), to restore all plundered goods, 'and behave themselves for the future no more in such a shameful manner,' the Emperor accepts their submission and grants them a new license for trade, on condition that 'Mr. Child, who did the disgrace, be Feb. 1690

[1] Bruce's *Annals*, ii. 604.

[2] He despatched Messrs. Weldon and Novarro to the Imperial camp. *Idem*, ii. 637.

1690 turned out and expelled.'[1] But by this time Sir John Child was beyond expulsion or disgrace. He had died at Bombay in the midst of his troubles, on the 4th of February, 1690.[2]

A copy[3] of the general pardon was in due time forwarded to the Viceroy of Bengal, who sent a permit to the English to return from Madras. Charnock perceived, however, that no general pardon would cover the particular Bengal grievance, and he refused to return till he obtained a specific promise from the Viceroy that we should have a free trade, unhampered by local exactions, in return for the old payment of Rs. 3,000 a year. The polite Persian[4] who had succeeded to the government of that province, was glad to be able to mark the first year of his rule by setting free[5] the English factors whom Heath had abandoned to captivity and chains. Having received his Highness' guarantee Charnock and his refugees at Madras made their way through the monsoon tempests of 1690 to the Húgli river.

Aug. 1690 At length on Sunday, August 24, 1690, at noon, the weather-beaten band anchored, for the third time, in the long pool of Calcutta. With a poor

[1] The translation as given by Stewart, App. VII. to the *History of Bengal*, is identical, saving one word, with that given by Bruce's *Annals*, ii. 639, 640.

[2] Hedges' *Diary*, ii. 156.

[3] Parwana, dated 23 April, 1690. Given in App. VI. to Stewart's *History of Bengal*.

[4] The Nawab Ibrahim Khan: son of the famous Ali Mardan Khan, a Persian refugee (1637), who had risen to the most exalted position in the Mughal Empire. Ibrahim Khan had himself held the governorships of Kashmir, Lahore, Behar and other high posts, before reaching the Viceroyalty of Bengal.

[5] July 1690. Stewart's *History of Bengal*, p. 205. Calcutta Ed. 1847.

guard of thirty soldiers all told, they scrambled 1690
up the steep mud bank which was thenceforward, without a break, to grow into the British capital of India. They 'found the place in a deplorable condition, nothing being left for our present accommodation, and the rain falling day and night.' If Charnock had thought of his own ease he would have sailed on to Húgli town, and settled there under the protection of the new and friendly Viceroy. This great officer kept his promise, and issued orders explicitly exempting the English trade from customs duties, on the old payment of Rs. 3,000 a year.[2] Charnock's own fellow-servants, huddled together on the malarious river bank, almost mutinied for a return to their houses and gardens in Húgli town. But the old man knew that the Company's goods could never be safe so far beyond the guns of its sea-going ships. He had had enough of 'fenceless factories,' and he resolved to create for his masters a stronghold which should be a surer guarantee than any farman, even if he perished in the attempt. He perished: but not until, by two more years of endurance, he had founded Calcutta.

They were two miserable years. The buildings 1690-1
which he set up with so much labour and peril in 1688 had been burned. Three ruined earth hovels alone remained on the high river bank, and the

[1] Diary and Consultation Book of the Bengal Council, dated August 24, 1690.

[2] Two parwanas of 1690-91, the final one dated 10th February, 1691. App. VIII. and IX. to Stewart's *History of Bengal.*

1690-1 wretched band had to live 'in boats' during the most unhealthy season of the year.[1] Through the pitiless monsoon months of 1690 Charnock struggled on, erecting such shelter as he could 'with mud walls and thatched till we can get ground whereon to build a factory.'[2] In the scorching summer of 1691, we still find him and his desponding followers dwelling in 'only tents, hutts and boats.'[3] It is no wonder that the weaker brethren continued to clamour for their 'profitable easy old habitations' in Húgli town. Nor is it surprising that Charnock sent home 'an incomplete cargo' that year; for which the superior Council, amid the comfort and plenty of Madras, soundly rated him.

1691-2 Yet Calcutta grew. Its deep pool attracted the trade from the Dutch and French settlements higher up the river, and the Indian merchants and Armenians began to flock to a place where they felt safe. But the fever-haunted swamps which stretched behind the river bank exacted a terrible price for its prosperity. 'Death overshadowed every living soul.'[4] The name of Calcutta was identified by our mariners with Golgotha—the place of skulls. Within a decade after Charnock finally landed on the deserted river bank in 1690, it had become a busy mart with 1,200 English inhabitants, of whom 460 were buried between

[1] Bengal Consultations, 24th August, 1690.

[2] *Idem*, 28th August, 1690.

[3] The President and Council of Madras to the Court of Directors, 25th May, 1691.

[4] Wilson's *Early Annals of the English in Bengal*, p. 208.

the months of August and January in one year.[1] The miseries of the fever-stricken band throughout 1690 and 1691 are not to be told in words.

By the middle of 1692 they had made firm 1692
their footing. Indeed the official records complain that Charnock secured a larger investment in that year than he had funds to pay for. The battle was won, but Charnock was not to reap the victory. His last months were embittered by a subordinate[2] who taunted him with the new East India Company about to be formed in England, and of which he and not Charnock would be the chief in Bengal.[3] A terror of getting enmeshed in the distant law-court of Madras paralysed his action and haunted his bedimmed brain. The shadows of the coming night settled heavily on the worn-out man. He grew moody and savage. The government slipped from him into unworthy hands. His closing days
were unlovely and unloved. On January 10th, Jan. 1693
1693 they buried him in a grim enclosure, destined in the next century to become the site of the Old Cathedral of Calcutta.

What little the English world knew of him 1693
was for long made up of stories of his last morose days, told by interlopers[4] who hated him, and by a jealous superior[5] and a commonplace successor

[1] Hamilton's *East Indies*, ii. 7, 8.

[2] Mr. Braddyll, whom Heath abandoned to captivity, and who naturally looked on Charnock as an accomplice in the act of desertion.

[3] Sir John Goldsborough's unfinished letter, *circ.* October 1693. Hedges' *Diary*, ii. 92.

[4] *e.g.* Hamilton's *New Account of the East Indies*.

[5] Elihu Yale, President of the Council at Madras. The Madras Council refused to sign Yale's carping despatches, and Yale was

1693 who did not in the least discern what he had achieved. Even Orme, a usually careful historian, misled by the Old Style date on Charnock's tomb, gives a wrong year for his death—an error followed by all writers during two centuries.[1] Charnock stands forth in the manuscript records as a block of rough-hewn British manhood. Not a beautiful person: for the founders of England's greatness in the East were not such as wear soft raiment and dwell in kings' houses: but a man who had a great and hard task to do and who did it—did it with small thought of self, and with a courage which no danger could daunt nor any difficulties turn aside. It was his lot to found, unthanked, a capital. He rests under his time-stained mausoleum—a wearied exile 'who after long travel in a strange country hath returned to his eternal home.'[2] Perhaps his truest epitaph is a chance

contemptuously rebuked by the Court of Directors' letter to Madras, 3rd January, 1694.

[1] Till pointed out by Sir Henry Yule. Hedges' *Diary*, vol. ii. p. 88 (Ed. 1888).

[2] The whole inscription runs thus: *D.O.M. Iobus Charnock Armiger—Anglus et nup. in hoc —Regno Bengalensi dignissim. Anglorum—Agens mortalitatis suae exuvias—sub hoc marmore deposuit ut—in spe beatae resurrectionis ad—Christi judicis adventum obdormirent—Qui postquam in solo non—suo pene-grinatus esset diu—Reversus est domum suae eternitatis decimo die Januarii* 1692—*Pariter jacet—Maria Jobi primogenita, Caroli Eyre Anglorum—Hicci Praefecti conjux charissima—Quae obiit* 19 *die Februarii A.D.* 1696-97.

An adjoining tablet records in pathetic words the death of his youngest daughter (aged 21), who married Jonathan White, of the Bengal Council. *Siste parumper Christiane Lector—Vel quis es tandem et mecum defle—Duram sexus muliebris sortem—Qui per elapsa tot annorum milia—Culpam prim. Aevae luit Parentis—Et luet usque dum eternum stabit—In dolore paries filios.*

line in a despatch from the Directors a year after his death—'always a faithfull Man to the Company.'

The grand plan of campaign which the 1690
Directors had projected in 1686, and which ended with the humble submission of their Surat Council to Aurangzeb in 1690,[1] left behind four permanent results. The first was a settled conviction that a land-war against the Mughal Empire lay beyond their strength. The second was the knowledge that, as Sir Josia Child foretold,[2] our sea-power could in the end secure terms for us, by blockading the customs-ports and threatening the pilgrim route to Mecca. In the third place the Company made up its mind, once and for all, that it could no longer trust to 'fenceless factories' either within the Empire or outside it. The fourth result of the war was Calcutta—a result due to the stubborn resolution of Job Charnock—and acquiesced in by the Directors 'since we can't now help it.' Charnock thus stands out not only as the founder of the British capital in India, but as the type of the

Charnock's inscription was probably written by 'the merchant parson' Evans; one of his fellow-refugees to Madras. Chaplain Evans returned to England with a great fortune (*circ.* 1698), became Bishop of Bangor, was preferred to the Bishopric of Meath, quarrelled violently with Dean Swift, and died in 1724. A fine epitaph in Dublin commemorates his virtues and twenty years of apostolic labour in India! The Directors' more realistic summing up of Charnock as 'always a faithful Man to the Company' occurs in their letter to the Madras Council, dated 3rd January, 1694.

[1] *Ante*, p. 265.

[2] The Directors indeed exaggerated the effects of the stoppage of trade by the war when they supposed that it 'caused insurrections and an universal lamentation and cry' of '*Peace with the English* or We must all starve.' Court Letter to the Bengal Council, dated 27th August, 1688.

1690 new policy that farmans must be upheld by force, and that a fort is better than an ambassador.

That policy was developed, however, into its final form by a less rugged intelligence than his. Sir Josia Child discerned that if the Company were to abandon the Roe doctrine of peaceful traffic for armed trade, it must supplement the profits of commerce by taxation in its settlements. He had to face an opposition which vehemently, and quite truly, asserted that stone-walls did not pay. Yet, amid the growing anarchy in India, forts had become a necessity of trade, and he resolved that they should also defray their expenses. He impressed on the Company that the new demands made on it for self-defence could only be met by a territorial revenue, and that its old system must be re-formed upon the Dutch model.

1684 to 1690 From 1684 onwards, we accordingly find in the records a new-born admiration for the 'wisdom' of the Hollanders in combining taxation with trade.[1]
1685 In 1685 the Court of Directors wish to render 'the English nation as formidable as the Dutch or any other Europe nation are, or ever were, in India;' and they dwell on the 'political skill of making all fortified places repay their full charge and expenses' from land-revenues, as the natives 'do live easier under our government than under any government in Asia.'[2] We have seen a representative municipality set up, at Madras, under Sir Josia Child's orders, to facilitate the levying of taxation. In

[1] MS. Letter Book, No. 7, p. 260, 5th March, 1684.

[2] *Idem*, pp. 160, 449–50, 31st May and 26th August, 1685.

1687 the Directors look 'in a most especiall 1687 manner' to the Madras Council to 'establish such a Politie of civill and military power, and create and secure such a large Revenue as may bee the foundation of a large, well-grounded, sure ENGLISH DOMINION IN INDIA FOR ALL TIME TO COME.'[1] Yet they add, 'we would have you do no wrong or violence to any in amity with us. . . . JUST AND STOUT is the motto we hope to deserve and 1688 wear.'[2]

The final declaration of this policy took place 1689 in the following year—a declaration usually misrepresented as an abrupt departure from peaceful trade to territorial aggrandisement, but which we now see to have been gradually forced upon the Company from 1684 onwards by necessities similar to those which compelled Aurangzeb, in 1683, to quit for ever his magnificent capital, and to head the array of the Mughal Empire. 'The increase of our revenue is no less the subject of our care, and must always be yours, as much as our trade,' the Court of Directors wrote to the Bombay Council in 1689. ''Tis that must maintain our force, when twenty accidents may interrupt our trade. 'Tis that must make us a nation in India. Without that, we are but as a great number of Interlopers, united by His Majesty's Royal Charter, fit only to trade where no body of power thinks it their interest to prevent us. And upon this account it is that the wise Dutch, in all their general advices which we

[1] Letter to Fort St. George, dated 12 December, 1687.

[2] *Idem*, dated 27 August, 1688.

1690 have seen, write ten paragraphs concerning their government, their civil and military policy, warfare, and the increase of their revenue for one paragraph they write concerning trade. And the last, viz. revenue, is the soul and life of all the rest. Without that they could not subsist, notwithstanding they have the Spice Islands, Japan and most of the Pepper Trade entirely to themselves.'[1]

Thus after nearly a century of stubborn adherence to its own methods, the Company found itself compelled to abandon them for a system which it had always viewed with aversion. The change resulted from no increased liking for the Dutch. It was forced upon the English by the same train of events which turned Aurangzeb into a wandering soldier for the last twenty-four years of his life, with no Court save his camp, and which on his death broke up the Mughal Empire.

[1] Despatch of the Court of Directors to 'Our Generall of India and our President and Councill of India residing at Bombay;' dated 11 September, 1689. Letter Book, No. 9, India Office MSS.

CHAPTER VIII

THE COMPANY AND PARLIAMENT

1688–1698

There had thus grown up within the realm a body standing apart from the nation, yet wielding in India the national powers of coining money, levying taxes, building forts, maintaining troops, and making war or peace. That such a body should continue exempt from Parliamentary control must depend either on the absence of public envy, or on the popularity of the Sovereign by whose prerogative it was maintained. Under Charles I. the profits of the India trade had proved too uncertain to excite the jealousy of the Commons: under Charles II. the royal authority sufficed to protect it from their interference. But the kingly prerogative received its death-wound during James II.'s assault on the liberties of his people, and the Revolution brought the Company face to face with Parliament.

In the last chapter we had to advance some years beyond the English epoch of 1688 in order to 1688
carry the narrative of the Indian settlements to a point of natural pause. In the present chapter, if we are clearly to understand how and why Parliament intervened, we must glance back at

certain home-aspects of the Company under the Restoration.

The continuity of capital and permanent union
1657 of interests initiated under Cromwell's charter of 1657,[1] secured steady returns unknown in the days of Particular Voyages and successive Joint Stocks. But Charles I.'s cabals and Courten's Association were still fresh in men's minds, nor did the City at first feel sure that Charles II. would keep faith with the Company. Several years elapsed, moreover, before the profits of the new corporation began to
1661 come in.[2] In 1661 its stock stood at 6 to 8 per cent. discount,[3] and about 1665 during the Dutch war the 100*l.* share only fetched 70*l.*[4] But the appraisement of assets, provided for at the end of the seven years from the subscription of 1657, disclosed their actual value at one-third more than the original
1669 outlay,[5] and in 1669 the market price of 100*l.* stock was 130*l.*[6] A similar appraisement, after the first septennial one, was to be made every three years.[7]

These periodical audits mark a new departure from the method of secret book-keeping followed by

[1] *Ante*, pp. 133–137.

[2] MS. Letter Book, No. 3, p. 123, March 1662. The 'Letter Books' here quoted are preserved in the India Office Archives.

[3] MS. Letter Book, No. 2, unpaged.

[4] *The East India Trade a most profitable Trade to the Kingdom*, 1677, p. 17. India Office Pamphlets.

[5] *Idem*, p. 17. According to Macpherson, p. 126, the figures stood thus: Company's gross assets, 661,441*l.*; its debts at 165,807*l.*; and its net assets at 495,634*l.* to represent the original subscription of 369,891*l.* The original members were offered leave to withdraw their capital, but no one did so.

[6] MS. Letter Book, No. 4, p. 277.

[7] *Mercurius Politicus*, October 22–29, 1657.

the Company down to Cromwell's charter of 1657. They were originally designed to allow members to withdraw their capital at its real value, but they also enabled outsiders to judge of the profits of the business, and acted as an advertisement. They formed the forerunners of the published accounts upon which the modern system of joint stock rests, and rendered the shares a marketable security on the basis of ascertained returns. The East India Company thus anticipated one of the most substantial benefits now enjoyed by corporations under the Public Companies' Acts. It was the first English corporation which combined the modern advantages of a continuous joint stock and a periodical audit of a semi-public character, with a monopoly inherited from mediæval commerce. It thus became the favourite investment under the Restoration, and its stock sprang up to unprecedented rates.

In 1677 the price of 100*l.* stock had risen to 1677
245*l.*,[1] and in 1681 to 280*l.*[2] In January 1682, 1682
besides a dividend of fifty per cent., a bonus of one hundred per cent. was credited to the shareholders,[3] who practically received back their whole

[1] *The East India Trade a most profitable Trade to the Kingdom*, 1677, p. 17.

[2] *A Treatise wherein is demonstrated that the East India Trade is the most national of all Foreign Trades*, by φιλόπατρις (sometimes identified as Sir Josia Child), 1681, p. 11.

[3] Chandler's *History and Proceedings of the House of Commons*, iii. pp. 85, 86, ed. 1742. The words of the Report of the Parliamentary Commission are: 'That at a general court, November 2, 1681, a call was made for the residue of the adventurers' subscriptions at 100 per cent. at two equal payments.' [It will be remembered that only one-half the subscribed capital was called up in 1658.] 'That, January 18, 1681, the said call was revoked and a dividend of 150 per cent. was ordered, viz.,

capital of 369,891*l.* subscribed in 1658, and yet retained a share worth more than double their original subscription. Evelyn mentions that in December 1682, he sold for 750*l.* to the Royal Society his India stock purchased for 250*l.* in 1657; being a gain of two hundred per cent.[1]
1683 The high-water mark was reached in 1683 when 100*l.* of stock sold for 360*l.*, and even changed hands at 500*l.*[2]

The transactions of the Company were on a
1675 scale that seemed to justify these rates. In 1675 its exports amounted to 430,000*l.*, which brought back Eastern produce exceeding 860,000*l.* in value; besides the 'licensed' private trade of its ship-owners, servants, and others, reckoned as high as 150,000*l.* of exports and 300,000*l.* of imports; or a total return of, say, 1,160,000*l.* for 580,000*l.* sent
1684 out.[3] In 1684 no less than 1,800,000*l.* worth of produce was said to have been disposed of at three of its recent sales, and the Company was accused of devouring 'above half the trade of the nation.'[4]
1657 to 1691 The dividends paid during the twenty-four years from its reconstruction in 1657 to 1691 aggregated

100 per cent. to double their stock, and 50 per cent. in money.'

[1] Evelyn's *Diary*, December 18, 1682.

[2] Anderson's *History of Commerce*, ii. 564.

[3] *A Treatise concerning the East India Trade being a most profitable Trade for the Kingdom*, 1680, reprinted 1696, pp. 7, 8. The exact figures are: Company's exports, 320,000*l.* in bullion, and 110,000*l.* in merchandise; imports, 860,000*l.*; 'licensed' exports 80,000*l.* to 100,000*l.* in bullion; 40,000*l.* to 50,000*l.* in goods; imports, 250,000*l.* to 300,000*l.*

[4] According to Pollexfen and Sir George Treby in the Sandys case. Howell's *State Trials*, x. 431, 404.

840½ per cent.[1] of the subscribed capital, or nearly 25 per cent. per annum. The profits during the nine years from 1676 to 1685 amounted to 963,639*l.*[2] These profits were made, however, not by trading on the original subscription alone, but with the help of borrowed capital which the Company raised at low rates. In 1681 it employed in this way 550,000*l.* on which it had reduced the interest from six to three per cent. without causing the lenders to call back their money.[3]

1676 to 1685

Such were the gains of a continuous Indian trade conducted on the Roe doctrine of peaceful traffic. But in 1683 the growing disorders in India compelled Aurangzeb to take the field in person. For the Company, it ceased thenceforward to be a question of a few forts outside the limits of the Imperial protection, as at Madras and Bombay, and became one of self-defence alike within the provinces of the Empire and beyond them. The garrison charges ate into the profits of the trade, and the war with the Mughal authorities was said to have cost the Company 400,000*l.* in cash besides the loss of a million to the shareholders and the Crown from the interruption of the trade.[4] Nor did Sir Josia Child's scheme for defraying the outlay

1683

[1] Report of the Parliamentary Committee, June 13, 1698. Chandler's *History and Proceedings of the House of Commons*, vol. iii. p. 86. The percentage is calculated on 369,891*l.* actually paid up in 1657–8.

[2] Anderson's *History of Commerce*, ii. 574.

[3] *Idem*, ii. 557.

[4] *A Brief Account of the Great Oppressions and Injuries which the Managers of the East India Company have acted on the Lives, Liberties and Estates of their fellow-subjects* [no date]. Bodleian Library pamphlets. Fol. θ, 658 (24).

on defence by means of a territorial revenue bear immediate fruit. Political causes at home contributed to shake the Company's credit, and in spite of high dividends being still declared (without careful calculation,[1] if not out of capital) the market value of the Company's stock declined. The 100*l.* share which was said to have fetched 500*l.* in 1683
1692 only sold for 190*l.* in 1692.

Meanwhile the Company's profits had awakened the jealousy of the outside commercial world. That a body of monopolists should be able to return their whole capital to the shareholders in 1682, and that their stock should still sell at 360 to 500 per cent. in the following year, seemed a fraud upon the nation. Hundreds of private
1665 merchants had been ruined by the Plague of 1665 and the Great Fire of 1666, but the Company passed through these calamities almost unscathed. When driven out of London by the pestilence, the Directors held their meetings at pleasant country houses,[2] while a courageous sub-committee of five carried on the Company's business in town, and those subordinate officials who remained were handsomely rewarded for their risks.[3] Nor were

[1] Report of the Parliamentary Committee, *ut supra*, 13th June, 1698.

[2] As at Mr. Peter Vandeputt's mansion, at Clapton: his 'lady' receiving a present of 20*l.* value for the trouble to which she was thus put. MS. Court Book, No. 25, pp. 20, 20*a*, 31*a*, 51*a*, &c.

[3] *Idem*, pp. 13*a*, 33. The India Office records curiously exhibit the plague from the pious trader's point of view: the Lord having resolved 'to manifest his sore displeasure against the inhabitants of our sinful provoking nation by visiting them with the Plague of Pestilence.' MS. Letter Book, No. 3, p. 498, &c.

they less fortunate in the Great Fire of 1666, 1666
as, to use their own words, 'in this sad calamity God was pleased to be very favourable to the Company's interest, having preserved most of our goods, excepting some saltpetre, and our Pepper at the Exchange cellar.' [1]

During the first part of Charles II.'s reign, his support and the interest of his brother the Duke of York in the African trade,[2] stemmed the rising opposition to the Company's monopoly. The Company itself also recognised the necessity of broadening its basis. A demand arose within its own body for a return to the Regulated system under which individual members or groups might send out ventures on their separate account. This would have amounted to the subversion of its new constitution framed under Cromwell's charter and continued under that of Charles II. But the governing body eased off the opposition by timely concessions. It granted liberty to all English subjects below the age of forty to take up their abode in its Indian settlements, and to trade practically with the whole world, so long as they refrained from the prohibited commodities to and from Europe.[3] It allowed its time-expired servants to remain in India, which meant to continue the private business which they had established for themselves while in its employ—a privilege which

[1] MS. Letter Book, No. 4, p. 39.

[2] *Ante*, p. 197.

[3] MS. Letter Book, No. 5, p. 181, 5th March, 1675, for Bombay. MS. Letter Book, No. 3, p. 98, 20th February, 1662, for Madras, &c.

its dismissed officials also assumed.[1] It allowed its captains and seamen a fair allowance of personal freight; and as public opinion pressed more heavily, it authorised a system of Permission Ships for private adventurers under its license and control.[2]

These concessions stand out in contrast to the Company's old instructions 'to seize and send home' all Englishmen not in its service. They mark that transition of factories into settlements which forms a distinctive feature of its history
1675 under the Restoration. In 1675 the Directors could truly affirm that 'for the advantage of our nation' they had given up to all His Majesty's subjects not only the port-to-port trade of India northwards of the equator, but 'also to any countries southwards thereof in any commodity whatsoever,' provided they did not trade in the prohibited articles with Europe.[3] This liberal policy, not less than Charles' personal support, explains the comparative acquiescence of the nation in the Company's monopoly during the first part of his reign.

But, as the profits of the Company grew more dazzling, such indulgences failed to satisfy either

[1] See, among many examples, those of John Petit and George Bowcher: India Office MS. Records, O.C. 5053; and of Hedges himself, and Douglas. Hedges' *Diary*, ii. 124.

[2] Collection of Pamphlets Bodleian Library, Fol. *θ*, 658 (24). In January 1689, twelve Permission Ships, carrying 254 guns, were at sea. *A Supplement*, 1689, *to a former Treatise concerning the East India trade.* India Office Tracts, vol. 485.

[3] Many references, *e.g.* MS. Letter Books, No. 4, p. 381 (1670), and No. 5, pp. 181, 226 (1675).

its servants abroad or the public at home. In 1676 1676
the Madras Council protested against the 'impracticable and destructive condition of registering' imposed upon their private trade. 'Your servants who have gone through the heat and burden of the day for you (refraining from your own rich enclosures of the out and home trade) desire no more but the common and uncorrupted liberty' of the port-to-port trade in the East. Compulsory registration left them 'only like those fowl we send a fishing with a string about their necks to make them disgorge as fast as they set foot ashore.'[1]

The surprising meekness with which the Directors replied to these taunts is due to the fact that they differed among themselves as to the advantages or disadvantages of a more open trade.[2] In
1681 their disputes culminated in an attempt to 1681
wind up the Company. The two able men, Thomas Papillon and Sir Josia Child, who had for years controlled its policy, then arrayed their forces on opposite sides. Thomas Papillon[3] served as a
Director with certain breaks from 1663 to 1682,[4] 1663 to 1682
and had represented the Company in the Dutch negotiations. He was by conviction a free-trader

[1] Sir William Langhorn and the Madras Council to the Company, July–November, 1676. MS. Records, O.C. 4215.

[2] 'We shall always be willing to receive advice from our servants when it is offered in such manner as becomes both us and them; but expostulations and criminations and reproaches are not to be borne with, especially when our designs tend to their advantage as well as ours; and this shall serve for answer to all the paragraphs of your letter of this kind.' MS. Letter Book, No. 5, p. 492, 1677.

[3] Born 1623; died 1702.

[4] MS. Court Books.

as regards the internal commerce of the realm, and he retained a republican spirit which stirred him to oppose arbitrary power by means of the law courts and in Parliament.

Josia Child[1] had acted as victualler to the Navy under the Commonwealth, and continued his connection with the Admiralty in official capacities after the Restoration, his name being frequently coupled with that of Papillon in the State Papers.[2] He was chosen a Director of the East
1674 to 1699 India Company in 1674 and annually re-elected to the governing body with the exception of one year until his death in 1699. The exceptional year was
1676 1676, when an intimation of the King's displeasure with both Child and Papillon (apparently arising out of a Government contract) secured their exclusion. From that date Josia Child turned his eyes towards royal favour, and was made a baronet in 1678; while Papillon grew more stoutly inde-
1678 pendent, and opposed in Parliament the bill of 1679 for prohibiting the importation of Irish cattle into England.

A similar divergence had taken place among the other Directors,[3] many of whom were, like Papillon, Whigs elected when the glow of Restoration loyalty had passed off. It was to these men that Josia, as a friend of Papillon, owed his first election in 1674; and it was from them that he found

[1] Born 1630; died 1699.

[2] E.g. *Calendar of State Papers*, Domestic, 1671–2, pp. 285, 464, 514; 1672, pp. 53, 297, 355, &c.

[3] It should be remembered that, for the sake of brevity, I speak of the 'Twenty-four Committees,' or Members of the Committee of Twenty-four, as Directors.

himself severed six years later, not by his courtly leanings alone, but by deeper differences as to the conduct of the Company's affairs. Papillon believed that the demand for an open trade must be met by reconstituting the Company on a broader basis; Child hoped that, with the King's support, the Company would maintain its monopoly against all opposition within and without. By 1680 his commanding personality, great wealth, and rare talents for business had placed him at the head of a following not less powerful than that of his former friends.

In 1681 the opposing forces met: the strict 1681
monopolists, headed by Sir Josia Child, newly elected governor of the Company; the reformers by Papillon its Deputy-Governor. On November 11 a petition to the King was brought forward by Child's influence, praying for a royal proclamation against Interlopers. Papillon moved that a clause be inserted, by which the Company offered, after three years' notice, to wind up the Joint Stock of 1657, and in the meantime to open to the public a subscription-book for a new Joint Stock in which outsiders might freely take part.[1] Child's party opposed the amendment as designed 'to do us a mischief,' and it was lost. Papillon and his adherents were thrown out of office at the next annual election (1682); while Sir Josia Child 'forsook all his old friends that first introduced him

[1] *Memoirs of Thomas Papillon, of London, Merchant,* by A. F. W. Papillon, pp. 80-83. Ed. 1887. The three years' notice was to run from 10th April, 1682.

with great difficulty into the Committee,'[1] and allied himself to 'the great ministers and chief men at Court,' with whom his lavish presents enabled him to do 'what he pleased.'[2] In 1683 he married one of his daughters to the Marquess of Worcester, eldest son of the Duke of Beaufort, with a dowry of 50,000*l.*[3] Luttrell mentions a rumour that another daughter, with a portion of 40,000*l.*, was engaged to the Duke of Richmond in 1692;[4] while his son, Sir Richard Child, was ennobled in the following century as Viscount Castlemaine and Earl of Tylney. He himself had bought Wanstead Park (now one of the great pleasure grounds of London[5]) in 1673, the year before he became a Director of the East India Company, and he poured out his quickly won wealth, reckoned at 200,000*l.*, 'in planting walnut trees about his seat and making fish-ponds many miles in circuit.'[6] But neither the amassing of a fortune nor the spending of it could engross his active mind. Sir Josia Child stands as a foremost figure among the economic writers of the Restoration, the champion of restriction alike as to the rate of interest at home and the India trade.[7]

[1] *Some Remarks upon the Present State of the East India Company's Affairs*, 1690.

[2] *Idem.*

[3] Evelyn's *Diary*, 16 March, 1683.

[4] Narcissus Luttrell's *Brief Historical Relation of State Affairs*, 4th October, 1692, vol. ii. p. 583. Ed. 1857.

[5] Purchased by the Corporation of London, who conveyed it to the Epping Forest Committee in trust for the public. Inaugurated as a People's Park, August 1882. Edward Walford's *Greater London*, part x. p. 479.

[6] Evelyn's *Diary*, 16th March, 1683.

[7] His early pamphlet, written

Papillon and others of his party, finding they had no chance of re-election to the governing body, sold out their stock, and a blow struck at them as Exclusionists through the law courts cowed further resistance within the Company. In
February 1684 Sir Samuel Barnardiston, one of 1684
Papillon's chief friends, was haled before Judge Jeffreys, as being of a 'factious, seditious, and disaffected temper,' was sentenced to a fine of 10,000*l.*, and, in default, lay in prison until 1688.[1] In November 1684 the stroke fell on Papillon himself, against whom a subservient jury awarded damages for an outrageous sum, also of 10,000*l.*[2] To avoid ruin Papillon mortgaged his estates and fled to Utrecht. Sir Josia Child, having thus stricken down his opponents at home, while his brother marched Interlopers in chains through the Indian bazaars, now applied the policy of Thorough to the Company with a vigour worthy of Strafford himself.

Papillon's defeat in 1681 convinced the com- 1681
mercial world that reform could not be expected from within the Company. But Child, unlike Strafford, had no Star Chamber at his back, and the outsiders resolved to break down the India monopoly by every constitutional engine which

in 1665, developed, through four editions during his life-time, into *The New Discourse of Trade*, and was frequently re-issued and translated after his death in 1699. He urged the reduction of interest by statute, from 6 to 4 per cent. He has been also identified with φιλόπατρις, the author of *A Treatise wherein is demonstrated that the East India Trade is the most national of all Foreign Trades*, 1681.

[1] Howell's *State Trials*, vol. ix. (1816), 1334–1371.

[2] *Idem*, vol. x. 319–372.

money and legal skill could set at work. Their first effort took the form of a petition to the King. The Levant or Turkey Merchants, a corporation more ancient and for long more profitable to the realm than the East India Company itself, urged that the countries on both sides of the Red Sea were subject to the Ottoman Sultan, within whose dominions they had full liberty to trade. They therefore asked leave to send their ships to that sea by the most convenient route, namely, the Cape of Good Hope. This practically involved a new enterprise for converting the old caravan trade with the Asiatic dependencies of the Porte
1682 into a seaborne commerce. In April 1682 the arguments, or the influence of the East India Company, secured the rejection of the project by His Majesty in Council, and the East India Directors boasted that the matter had been laid for ever at rest, as 'a thing in itself frivolous and serving only to amuse idle and ignorant people, not Princes nor Councils of State.'[2]

The outside merchants, now hopeless of concessions from the Company or of a hearing by the King, had recourse to the law courts. In August
1683 1683 Charles II. issued Letters Patent to render the Company's powers still more effectual, and authorised it to set up Admiralty tribunals of its own nominees, wherewith to confiscate the ships and goods of its rivals.[3] Nothing remained but

[1] Bruce's *Annals*, ii. 476, or for a more instructive account, Macpherson, 137-8.

[2] MS. Letter Book, No. 6, pp. 519, 527, 529.

[3] India Office Library Quarto of Charters, pp. 116-124.

to deny the right of the Crown to grant such authority, and the case of Thomas Sandys, an Interloper, was used to raise the whole question of the royal prerogative to create a monopoly of the India trade. This great trial was fought out during more than a year [1] before the Lord Chief Justice Jeffreys by the ablest lawyers of the age —three of whom became in turn Lord Chief Justice of England.[2] Nor was there any attempt to disguise the magnitude of the two interests at stake: on the one hand, the King's Prerogative; on the other, a commerce acknowledged to be 'the greatest that ever England knew,' and magnified into 'one quarter part of the trade of the whole world.' [3]

So brilliant a bar could scarcely refrain from a little histrionic sword-play. Several of the more showy passes have, indeed, an air of unreality to the modern critic. But the trial will always be memorable in English history as a record of the arguments by which the leading lawyers of the Restoration sought, in all seriousness, to uphold

[1] Trial began Michaelmas Term, 35 Car. II. (1683), Howell's *State Trials*, x. 371: Judgment delivered, Hilary Term, 1685: *idem*, x. 515, 519–554.

[2] Namely Holt, counsel for the plaintiff Company, and Sir George Treby and Henry Pollexfen, counsel for the defendant Sandys. The Attorney-General (Sir Robert Sawyer), Mr. Solicitor-General Finch (afterwards Earl of Nottingham), and Mr. Williams also argued the case at length.

[3] Pollexfen's speech. I have chiefly followed the proceedings as given in Howell's *State Trials*, vol. x. (1811), 371–554; and in *The Argument of the Lord Chief Justice . . . concerning the Great Case of Monopolies between the East India Company, Plaintiff, and Thomas Sandys, Defendant*, London, 1689. But I have also examined the pamphlets and MSS. in the Bodleian Library.

the Royal Prerogative of foreign trade. Holt opened with the following propositions. No subject of England can trade with infidels, except by license from the King; for, as Coke said in Calvin's case, infidels are '*perpetui inimici*,' or standing enemies of the realm.[1] Foreign trade depends on compacts of the Sovereign with foreign princes, and English subjects have therefore a right to foreign trade not *ad libitum* or without control, but subject to the King's restraining power.[2] The King in the exercise of his power hath restrained the Indian trade by granting it to the plaintiff Company. Nor does the grant come within the prohibited monopolies. For a monopoly, by its legal definition, is a grant whereby persons 'are sought to be restrained of any freedom or liberty that they had before, or hindered in their lawful trade.' But the defendant Interloper never had any freedom of the India trade. Moreover, Elizabeth's charter to the East India Company was given at the very time that the Parliament was attacking unlawful monopolies. No objection was made to the grant either then or during the agitation against monopolies under her successor; and, indeed, it comes within the proviso of the Act of 21 James I. that the prohibition against monopolies shall not ex-

[1] Holt quotes in support of this doctrine, Grotius *De Bello et Pace*, i. 2, c. 15, par. 11. Howell's *State Trials*, x. 375.

[2] Holt quotes in support of this proposition, Magna Carta cap. 30, Selden's *Mare Clausum*, and several precedents, including that of 29 Car. I., prohibiting the import of French merchandise. Howell's *State Trials*, x. 376–379.

tend to companies erected for the maintenance or ordering of any trade or merchandise.[1]

Sir George Treby replied for the defendant Interloper by pleading the statute of Edward III. 'that the sea be open to all manner of merchants,' and argued that, although the King had a right to create the East India Company, he exceeded his prerogative in restraining his other subjects from the trade. He denounced as a 'conceit, absurd, monkish, fantastical and fanatical,' the doctrine that there could be no traffic with infidels except by permission of the King; and he showed that Turks and Jews might trade with Christians and maintain actions at law. To the argument that, as foreign trade depends on royal treaties, and may therefore be restrained and controlled by the Crown, he answered that no one can pretend the King had made leagues with Indian princes allowing one part of his subjects to trade thither and excluding the rest. Sir George Treby denied that the proviso of the Monopoly Act (21 James I.) applied to the Company, for it only continued in force such privileged corporations as were then in being, while the plaintiff Company owed its existence to the charter of Charles II.[2]

Pollexfen argued for those who specially objected to the joint-stock character of the Company, and

[1] Howell's *State Trials*, x. 379–381. For this and other saving clauses of 21 & 22 Jac. i. cap. iii. see pp. 276–7 of Mr. G. W. Prothero's *Select Statutes*, &c., Clarendon Press, 1894.

[2] Howell's *State Trials*, x. 385-404. This argument is based on the assumption that the East India Company was not a continuous corporation dating from Elizabeth's charter.

he contrasts it in scathing terms with the Regulated system of the Turkey fellowship. The latter, he says not too accurately, admitted every man, and each creditor or debtor knew the person with whom he dealt. 'But this invisible East India Merchant,' this 'invisible body subsisting only in *intelligentia legis*, a body politic without soul or conscience,' engrosses the whole trade for a handful of monopolists, who at one time are so powerful that 'scarce any man would contend with them; so invisible at another time, as a dun could scarce find them.' A Regulated company, he allowed, might come within the proviso of 21 James I., but how could a joint-stock corporation like the East India Company pretend that it was a body erected for the maintenance and enlargement of commerce, when it shut out all but its own members from the trade? [1]

It is not needful to follow the other speakers. Lord Jeffreys declared it 'a case of great weight and consequence, perhaps as ever any case that has come into Westminster Hall,' and suggested that it should be argued again in the next Michaelmas term. With brutal cynicism he observed that he knew the defendant's counsel would not object to this, 'but whether your client will or no, I cannot well tell nor do not much care.' [2] During the further hearing few fresh points emerged, except that Sir William Williams (who had been Speaker of the House of Commons and who, until his submission to James II., stood conspicuous among

[1] Howell's *State Trials*, x. 429–436. [2] *Idem*, x. 454–6.

the Whig lawyers) urged that the question was really one to be determined by Parliament.

Jeffreys delivered a lengthy judgment[1] in which he practically adopted Holt's arguments, and held the East India Company's charter to be a lawful exercise of the King's prerogative. He further declared that the Company's exclusive privileges were not an illegal monopoly, and that they came within the provision of the Monopoly Act of 21 James I. He saw that the defendant's counsel by admitting the lawfulness of the grants to Regulated companies, like the Turkey corporation, had undermined their own case; and that the difference between the Regulated and the Joint Stock methods of doing business did not affect the King's prerogative to issue an exclusive charter.

The judgment is disfigured by fulsome eulogies of the Sovereign, by sneers at the suggestion that the case required the consideration of Parliament, and by invectives against the defendant—who 'by his interloping has been the first subject that within this kingdom, for near an hundred years last past, hath in Westminster Hall publicly opposed himself against the King's undoubted prerogative in the grant now before us.'[2] 'The interlopers against the King's prerogative in this particular,' he declares, 'and the horrid conspirators against the King's life in this last hellish conspiracy, first

[1] *The Argument of the Lord Chief Justice . . . concerning the Great Case of Monopolies between the East India Company, Plaintiff, and Thomas Sandys, Defendant.* London, 1689. Also Howell's *State Trials*, vol. x.

[2] *The Argument of the Lord Chief Justice*, &c., p. 4.

appeared in Westminster Hall about the same time.'[1] But the judgment, notwithstanding its servility and insolence, was a sound one from the historical point of view. The East India Company's monopoly had been granted or confirmed as a lawful exercise of the prerogative by Elizabeth, by James I., by Charles I., and by Charles II. In the two great attacks on monopolies by Parliament it had not been arraigned; and indeed during the period when Parliament was itself the ruling power the House of Commons had re-affirmed the necessity of an exclusive charter for the conduct of the Indian trade.[2]

Sir Josia Child, now supreme in the Company, secure of the King, and armed by the Lord Chief Justice's decision, urged his policy of Thorough
1685 with whip and spur. In 1685 he resolved to prosecute no fewer than forty-eight Interlopers.[3] The latter without hope from the Crown or the courts, betook themselves to forcible resistance; interloping degenerated into piracy; and from the Interlopers, and the attempts to suppress them, sprang melodramatic corsairs of the Kidd and Avery type.[4] Indeed the transition of an illegal

[1] *The Argument of the Lord Chief Justice*, &c. Ed. 1689, p. 29. Jeffreys had himself conducted the trial of Algernon Sidney for the 'hellish conspiracy' or Rye House Plot of 1683.

[2] 1646. *Ante*, p. 42.

[3] Bruce's *Annals*, ii. 551.

[4] For references to Avery (Avory or Every) and Kidd, see Sir Henry Yule's *Hedges' Diary*; and for notices of them the *Dictionary of National Biography*, vol. ii. p. 275; vol. xxxi. p. 93. A recollection of Avory perhaps suggested the name of Amory in *Pendennis*; Kidd, the boy's own buccaneer, was a sequel to piratical interloping rather than a product of it.

armed trade into buccaneering was easy, and it went on apace after the overthrow of the party of concession within the Company in 1681.

A single example must suffice. The manuscripts 1683
of 1683 record the iniquities of John Hand, master of the *Bristol*, who cleared his ship at the customs house as bound for Lisbon and Brazil, and sailed with papers that defied the vigilance of the East India Company.[1] On reaching the Madeiras, Hand called his crew together, and told them that they were bound for the East Indies. Some of the sailors were sorely troubled, but none dared say a word, the captain 'being a mighty passionate man.' During his voyage, if the natives whom he seized hesitated to act as pilots, he confronted them with a block and a carpenter's axe. On one occasion the mate, being ordered to rummage a ship which Hand had boarded, ventured on the civil remonstrance, 'Captain, you must consider what you do.' Whereupon the captain 'kicked him off the quarter-deck and several others for the same reason.' At Sumatra he fired on a Dutch vessel, and his piracies only ended with his death when landing a party to plunder and burn a town of the 'Black Dogs.'[2]

Hand was the type of the ruffian Interloper, who gradually gave up the pretence of trade. Before the end of the century Madagascar had become a pirate haunt, where reprobates like Kidd plundered the shipping along the African coast; while others, like Avery, with his headquarters at Perim, levied

[1] The following narrative is taken from MS. Records O.C. 5035 in the India Office.

[2] *Idem.*

blackmail on all craft entering or leaving the Red Sea. But besides the ruffian type of Interloper, who tended to turn buccaneer, there was a much larger class who simply traded to India in defiance of the law. The outside merchants of London and Bristol found them abundant capital. Their cargoes, intended for India, could be shipped under papers for Brazil, and bartered, at an immense profit, in the port-to-port trade of the East. After selling their vessel for more than her value, they might remit their fortune through the Dutch Company, or take the risk of doubling it by themselves bringing it home in the form of diamonds and pearls. Or they could carry on a continuous business by fitting out ships at Cadiz and trading between India and the European continent.[1] Nor were the Company's servants in the East altogether averse to the 'free captain' who generously furnished freight for their private commerce without the restraints of registration. While, therefore, the Directors fulminated against Interlopers from London, and Presidents and Councils in India officially looked at them askance, friendly drinking-bouts with the intruders took place at the mouth of the Húgli, and on the Coromandel coast. Captain Alley on one occasion defiantly dined on board a Company's ship with 'great mirth and jollity' amid salvoes of guns all the afternoon.[2] In 1684 a sturdy King's partizan like Keigwin openly made use of the Interlopers to extend the trade of Bombay.[3]

[1] As Captain Alley did on more than one lucrative voyage. Hedges' *Diary*, ii. 101.

[2] Hedges' *Diary*, i. 137–8.

[3] *Ante*, pp. 205–6. Still more striking was the respect of Sir

One plain-spoken captain declared that 'if he did not like the Company's employment this voyage, he would turn Interloper the next.'[1]

A safe and profitable business in Interloping was thus established on an enormous scale. For besides the support of the outside mercantile community in London, and the connivance of the Company's servants in India,[2] the Interlopers found friends among the native princes. When a factor got dismissed he set up as an adventurer on his own account.[3] The Bengal Viceroy proved as willing to 'doe the Interlopers' Business'[4] for a consideration as he was to allow the Company to do its own. On the Madras coast the unlicensed traders made a determined struggle to establish shore settlements which should compete with those of the Company.[5] Four sites had been selected[6] by them, and the Fort St. George records disclose the long war of bribery and intrigue which ended in the Company's servants securing the native authorities to their side.

Thomas Grantham (sent out by the King and Company to suppress Keigwin) towards interlopers. Hedges' *Diary*, April 29, 1685, i. 201.

[1] Hedges' *Diary*, May 24, 1683, i. 90.

[2] The Directors had frequently to threaten their servants in India with penalties for 'assistance or countenance' to Interlopers; e.g. Letter to Surat, March 19, 1680, enclosing a mandate from Charles II. to the same effect; Court Book, September 24, 1680, &c.

[3] As in the case of Allen Catchpole, for which Sir Henry Yule gives the original documents in Hedges' *Diary*, ii. 110-112. For other examples see footnote, *ante*, p. 282.

[4] Beard's letter, cited Hedges' *Diary*, ii. 111.

[5] Among them Alley, Aubeny, and John Smith. *Consultation Book of Fort St. George for* 1683, 1st series, vol. ii. pp. ix-xvi, &c. Government Press, Madras, 1884.

[6] *Idem*, p. 12.

The typical Interloper of the trading as distinguished from the corsair class was Thomas Pitt, father of the Earl of Londonderry, and grandfather of the great Earl of Chatham. His story has been pieced together from the manuscript archives,[1] and it bridges over the interval between Jeffreys' condemnation of the Interlopers under the charter of the King and their triumph under the sanction of Parliament. Thomas Pitt settled at Balasor as
1674 an Interloper in 1674, and during the next seven years did a lucrative trade on the Bay of Bengal and as far as the Persian Gulf, in spite of repeated commands from the Court of Directors to arrest
1681 and deport him to England.[2] In 1681 he took a trip home, and notwithstanding a writ *ne exeat regno* obtained against him by the Company, he boldly returned to India next year in an interloping vessel laden with chests of money for a venture on a larger scale. He purchased the protection of the native governor, and traded in a strongly-armed sloop;[3] parading his trumpeters and red-coated guards on shore before the very walls of the Húgli factory.[4]

In vain the Company's servants appealed to the Bengal Viceroy; they could easily procure an

[1] *Documentary Contributions to a Biography of Thomas Pitt, Interloper, Governor of Fort St. George, and Progenitor of an Illustrious Family*, by Sir Henry Yule, K.C.S.I., in vol. iii. of his Hedges' *Diary*, pp. 1–166.

[2] For example, letters from the Court to the Húgli Council, dated 24th December, 1675, 19th December, 1676, 12th December, 1677, in which the audacious Interloper appears as Pitts or Pytts.

[3] Commanded by his confederate Captain Dorrel or Dorrill, for whom see Hedges' *Diary*, ii. 123–125, iii. p. 2, &c.

[4] Hedges' *Diary*, iii. p. 11.

'order' against the intruder; but a higher bribe from Pitt as easily prevented its execution. Returning home with a fortune in 1683, he was arrested at the suit of the Company, bound over in recognisances of 40,000*l.*, and after four years' litigation was condemned in 1687, as an Interloper, to a penalty of 1,000*l.*, afterwards reduced to 400*l.* In 1689 he entered Parliament, and soon secured a permanent seat by buying the manor of Stratford, together with the pocket borough of Old Sarum, from the Earl of Salisbury. He now took his place among the political opponents of monopoly, and made another interloping expedition to Balasor in 1693, without even vacating his seat in the Commons. By that time, as we shall see, the Company was struggling for existence alike in Parliament and in the City. In 1694 it came to 1694
terms with the Interlopers, and in 1697 appointed[1] Pitt to be President of the Council at Madras. During eleven years he governed vigorously, alike in the Company's interests and in his own; and returned to England in 1709 with immense wealth,[2] 1709
including the Pitt Diamond, which he sold for 130,000*l.* to the Regent of France.[3]

Meanwhile a war of pamphlets prepared the nation for a change in the constitution of the

[1] 26th November, 1697; commission dated 5th January, 1698: Pitt arrived at Madras 7th July, 1698; laid down his office, 17th September, 1709.

[2] For an abstract of his will see Hedges' *Diary*, iii. 163–166.

[3] In 1717. The diamond became one of the most famous of the jewels of the French Crown, was valued at 481,000*l.* in 1791, and 'remains the finest diamond in the world.' Sir Henry Yule traces its history from contemporary sources in vol. iii. of Hedges' *Diary*, pp. 125–147.

Company. As the subscription of 1657 had never been wound up, it was alleged that no opportunity had been given to outsiders to join the Company, and that the whole stock was practically held by sixty to eighty members.[1] Even of these a large proportion were mere dummies; fourteen shareholders engrossed a third of the stock,[2] while one alone, Sir Josia Child, possessed eighty votes. A cabal of ten or twelve men had 'the absolute management of the whole trade.'[3] The Company replied that in reality the shareholders numbered 556, while no adventurer had sixty votes.[4] But one fact clearly emerged—that the actual power had fallen into the hands of a small and exclusive clique.

Even what we should now regard as merits in the Company's finance, were then loudly reproached against it. Pollexfen complained to the House of Commons that the Company, instead of raising new stock and thus admitting fresh subscribers,

[1] *Britannia Languens* (1680): *Early English Tracts on Commerce*, 1856, p. 341. Bodleian Library. But for an alleged opening for new subscribers in 1664, see Macpherson's *European Commerce with India*, p. 126.

[2] *Some Remarks upon the Present State of the East India Company's Affairs*, 1690.

[3] *The Allegations of the Turkey Company and others against the East India Company*, 1681. Bodleian Library.

[4] *A Treatise wherein is demonstrated that the East India Trade is the most national of all Foreign Trades*, by Φιλόπατρις (Sir Josia Child ?), 1681, p. 15. *The East India Company's Answer to the Allegations of the Turkey Company*, 1681. The discrepancy between the statements of the opponents of the Company and its advocates may be in part explained by the wholesale manufacture of faggot-shareholders. The Turkey Company was said to have then had only 600 members against the East India Company's 556.

supplemented its capital by over 600,000*l.* borrowed at 4 or 5 per cent., which enabled it to pay dividends of 90 per cent. on its shares. The Cromwellian origin and the Stuart protection of the continuous stock of 1657 alike came in for denunciation; as a stock 'founded and planted in a direct opposition to the native Liberty of the subject; cultivated, cherished, and influenced by the hand of tyranny and arbitrary power; watered with the tears, groans, and estates of the subjects of England; and . . . grown up to an unbounded despotic power.'[1]

Such denunciations may sound to us both foolish and false. But as the mediæval dogma against exporting money from the realm died hard under the first two Stuarts,[2] so the mediæval system of Regulated companies served as a stalking-horse against the India Joint Stock under the last two. All the trade guilds and most of the commercial corporations of England still remained on the Regulated basis, according to which each member of a fellowship might do business on his own account.[3] The East India trade had thus to struggle against two of the strongest traditions of seventeenth-century commerce. It was founded in defiance of the principle that to export money impoverished the nation; it was developed in defiance of the opinion that the true model for corporate commerce was a Regulated company.

[1] *Reasons humbly offered against grafting or splicing, and for dissolving this Present East India Company*, 1690.

[2] *Ante*, pp. 19, 20, 25.

[3] *Ante*, vol. i. 254-256, 258-265, 275.

The mercantile morality of the time was also arrayed against it. For as the India stock became a freely saleable commodity,[1] a system of speculative dealing in it arose which outraged the notions of sober trade. Sir Josia Child, 'that original of stock-jobbing,'[2] was accused of manipulating the share-market by setting afloat rumours of losses at sea. He certainly practised to perfection some of the least creditable devices of the modern Stock Exchange. One set of his brokers would 'look sour, shake their heads, suggest bad news from India,' and let it leak out that they had orders from Sir Josia to dispose of a large parcel of shares for what they would fetch. In a few hours Change Alley swarmed with sellers, and buyers disappeared. Prices fell sharply, and another set of Josia's brokers 'with privacy and caution' began to purchase. Thus, writes a pamphleteer, 'by selling 10,000*l.* stock at four or five per cent. loss, he would buy 100,000*l.* at ten or twelve per cent. under price; and in a few weeks by just the contrary method set them all a buying, and then sell them their own stock again at ten or twelve per cent. profit.'[3]

Very vehement, also, was the opposition of the silk, linen, and wool manufacturers of England to the Indian cottons and art fabrics. They lamented the 'vain and immodest affectation' of foreign

[1] *Ante*, p. 277.

[2] *The Anatomy of Exchange-Alley*, by a Jobber. 1719, p. 13.

[3] *Idem, ut supra*, pp. 14–15. For other pamphlets on the subject see *The Villany of Stock Jobbers Detected* (1701), and *The Freeholders' Plea against Stock-jobbing Elections of Parliament Men* (1701); both pamphlets are attributed in the Bodleian Catalogue to Defoe.

cloths, and demanded severe restrictions on the importation of silks and 'painted calicoes.' Their denunciations against Indian commodities, including even coffee, which they described as serving 'neither for nourishment nor debauchery,' went to swell the general clamour against the Company.[1]

To that clamour Child turned a deaf ear. James II., himself a keen company promoter, and a large holder of India stock, issued in 1686 a 1686
fresh charter[2] to the Company, which incorporated all the most stringent provisions in the Letters Patent of his predecessors. His Majesty 'being fully satisfied' of the necessity of 'one General Joint Stock, and that a loose and general trade would be the ruin of the whole,' granted to the East India Company the amplest jurisdiction, civil and military, including law-martial, the right of coining Indian money in its settlements, and of employing troops and fleets alike against native princes and European Interlopers. The royal admirals and officers of justice were commanded to aid in the enforcement of these powers on land and on sea. In 1687, Sir Josia Child triumphantly 1687
contrasted the Company's former position as 'mere trading merchants,' with its new dignities 'since

[1] For the pamphlet literature see *Prince Butler's Tale Representing the State of the Wool Case* (1699); *Britannia Languens* (1680); *A True Relation of the Rise and Progress of the East India Company, showing how their manufactures have been, are, and will be prejudicial to the manufactures of England.* No date (*circ.* 1700). Bodleian Library.

[2] Dated 12th April, 1686. India Office Library Quarto of Charters, pp. 125–140.

His Majesty has been pleased by his Royal Charters . . . to form us into the condition of a Sovereign State in India.'[1] Two years later, James II. from his asylum in France had sold out his India stock;[2] Jeffreys had drunk himself to death in the Tower,[3] and the Commons were about to resolve in favour of a new East India Company.

The Parliamentary struggle which followed is worked with consummate art into Macaulay's history of the Revolution. We see the East India Company now whirled in the eddies of fierce political currents, now carried steadily forwards by the constitutional movements of the time.[4] My humbler task is to show how, from the clamour and confused trade notions of the seventeenth century was evolved the great corporation which won India for England in the eighteenth, and which ruled India for England until the middle of the nineteenth. Yet if the narrative loses in broad and striking effects, it may perhaps gain something in clearness. We shall at any rate find that the national settlement of the India trade depended only in its momentary accidents on Whig or Tory majorities, and was determined by deeper causes than the absence of county members who had gone to see a tiger baited by dogs.[5]

Only once under the Restoration had Parlia-

[1] MS. Letter Book, No. 8, p. 419. Letter of the 28th September, 1687, written during Sir Josia Child's second Governorship of the Company.

[2] January 16, 1689. *Ante*, p. 303.

[3] April 18, 1689.

[4] Lord Macaulay's *Works*, vols. iii. and iv. Ed. 1866.

[5] As according to Evelyn's *Diary*, March 5, 1699.

ment seriously intervened in the India trade. Soon after the accession of Charles II., an Interloper[1] appealed to the King and House of Lords against the seizure of his ship by the Company. The Directors denied the jurisdiction of the Peers and complained to the Commons, who held that the Lords could not take cognisance of a question of property in the first instance. The Upper House gave damages of 5,000*l.* against the Company, while the Lower one resolved that whosoever should presume to execute their Lordships' decree should be deemed a betrayer of the rights and liberties of the Commons of England, and be guilty of a breach of privilege. Years of violent altercation ensued, until the King in 1670 persuaded both 1670
Houses to erase the proceedings from their Journals. Thenceforward to the fall of the Stuarts in 1688, the Company heard little of either Lords or Commons, save Jeffreys' taunts at the suggestion that the India trade required the consideration of Parliament.

On the Revolution, that suggestion speedily became an accomplished fact. The clamour against the Company forced itself on the ears of the Convention Parliament, which turned for a moment from the settlement of the nation to listen

[1] Thomas Skinner, a London merchant, who arrived in India in 1658, and established himself in the small island of Barella, which he bought from the King of Jambi in Sumatra. The Company, in virtue of the powers given it by Cromwell's charter of 1657, confiscated the island, together with Skinner's vessel and goods. After various delays the Lords in 1666 ordered the case to be tried before the House.

to the four 'mournful daughters' of St. Helena, and do justice against the licensed assassins.[1] The struggle between the monopolists and the Interlopers was now transferred from the law-courts to the Commons; both parties were heard, and on
1690 January 16, 1690, a committee of the House reported 'the best way to manage the East India trade is to have it in a new Company and a new Joint Stock, and this to be established by Act of Parliament; but the present Company to continue the trade, exclusive of all others, either Interlopers or Permission Ships, until it is established.[2] The Interlopers promptly subscribed 180,000*l.* to give effect to the Resolution, but before decisive steps could be taken, King William dissolved Parliament.[3]

The Interlopers had learned, however, the strength of corporate action, and they now formed themselves into an association for the furtherance of their common cause. Many great merchants of London and Bristol joined them; the Skinners' Company lent them its cedar-panelled parlour and
1691 stately hall; and in 1691 they were ready for a trial of strength with the old Company. From this date the term Interlopers cannot in fairness be applied to the opponents of the East India monopoly. There were in reality two rival bodies, the old Company doing business on the strength of a Stuart charter in Leadenhall Street; and the

[1] 8th June, 1689. *Ante*, p. 211.

[2] Letter from the Court of Directors to Bombay, 31st January, 1690. Bruce, iii. 82.

[3] Prorogued 27th January, 1690; and immediately afterwards dissolved.

new society, unrecognised by law, but strongly organised and meeting regularly at Skinners' Hall in Dowgate. The once friends and subsequent enemies, Papillon and Child, renewed the conflict, interrupted in 1682—a conflict now only to end, after eight more years of bitter strife, with Sir Josia's death. In 1699 Papillon re-entered Parliament, while over the old Company Child[1] still ruled supreme.

In May 1691 it was announced that the war 1691
with the Mughal Empire had ended prosperously for the Company with a grant of even 'greater advantages than before.'[2] But the ignominious terms of the Farman leaked out, and both the Company and the Dowgate Association again brought their claims before the Commons. The old Company, uneasy about its Stuart Charter, was not averse to a Parliamentary settlement; its opponents also sought a Parliamentary grant, but
in favour of a new Corporation. In October 1691 Oct. 1691
the House resolved that the trade with the East Indies was beneficial to the nation, and that it could be best carried on by a Joint Stock Company possessed of exclusive privileges.[3] The question now narrowed itself as to which of the rivals should form the said Company. After vehement debates[4] Resolutions were passed increasing the

[1] Governor in 1686 and 1687; Deputy-Governor in 1688 and 1689; and thereafter a Director or 'Committee' until his death in 1699.

[2] *London Gazette*, May 7-11, 1691.

[3] *Journals of the House of Commons*, 29th October, 1691.

[4] Nov. and Dec., 1691.

capital of the old Company to $1\frac{1}{2}$ million sterling, and limiting the share of any single proprietor to 5,000*l*. This plan would have retained the old Company, but remodelled it on a basis broad enough to incorporate the Dowgate Association. But Child and his friends refused any compromise, and a bill founded on the Resolutions, after being read twice, could get no further. In Feb. 1692 February 1692 the Commons, having thus failed through Child's obstinacy to arrive at a settlement, presented an address to the King, praying him to dissolve the old Company and to issue a Charter to a new one on such terms as His Majesty might see fit.[1]

So far Sir Josia Child had been outmatched in Parliament. Papillon and his friends, whom Child drove out of the Company in 1682, were for the most part Whigs; Sir Josia started with the support of the Tories. But the Whig House of Commons which carried the country through the Revolution, and the Tory House elected during the reaction that followed it, had alike decided in favour of a new Company. Child did not however despair; for the venue was now transferred from Parliament, in whose management he was a novice, to the Court, in whose corruption he was a practised hand. King William might look with disdain on the gratifications which had smoothed the way for charters from James and Charles, but Child believed, not without reason, that the royal entourage would prove amenable

[1] *Journals of the House of Commons*, February 4 and 6, 1692.

under the House of Orange as under the Stuarts.[1] 'I believe in my conscience,' he wrote after Parliament had referred the settlement of the question to the King, 'there will be no change of the Company while I live, or, if any, no other than like the change of the moon . . . the same good old Company again, which will serve none of the ends of our furious brain-sick adversaries.'[2] July 1692

But before Child could set his secret machinery in motion the King took up the business in consultation with the Privy Council, and in November 1692 His Majesty communicated the results to Parliament. Nov. 1692 With dignified sincerity he expressed his desire to meet the views of the Commons, but the Judges had advised him that the old Company could not be dissolved without three years' notice, and it stood firmly on its rights. He therefore fell back on the compromise adopted by the House twelve months before, and proposed that the capital of the old Company, valued at 740,000*l.*,[3] should be raised by a fresh subscription to $1\frac{1}{2}$ or 2 millions sterling, and that the new subscribers should be incorporated with the present members under a charter for twenty-one years.[4]

[1] 'All who could help or hurt at Court,' says Macaulay in a striking passage on Child's dealings with the Whitehall of the Restoration, 'ministers, mistresses, priests, were kept in good humour by presents of shawls and silks, birds' nests, and attar of roses, bulses of diamonds, and bags of guineas.' *Works*, iii. 473 (1866), citing '*Pierce*' *Butler's Tale* by a slip of the pen for *Prince Butler's Tale.*

[2] July 1692, Rawlinson MSS. A. 303, fol. 301, Bodleian Library.

[3] By the Privy Council, but at over 1,500,000*l.* by the Company itself. For purposes of taxation it was taken by the Act of Parliament in the same year at 744,000*l.* 4 & 5 Gul. et Mar. c. 15.

[4] Macpherson's *European Com-*

But Child again doggedly opposed any compro-
Feb. 1693 mise, and in February 1693 the Commons prayed the King by an address of the whole House to dissolve the East India Company after three years' notice. William graciously promised to consider their wishes, and next month left England for the French campaign.[1]

Child now found his opportunity. He had already bribed discreetly; during 1693 he poured out 80,468*l.* in corrupting the Ministers and Court.[2] On the very day after William's departure for the war the Company, by an act of negligence so extraordinary as to suggest design, committed a default that vitiated its grant. In the late session Parliament had laid a tax on the capital of the three great Joint Stock Companies,[3] the first instalment to be paid on March 25 on pain of forfeiting their charters. The East India Company delayed payment a little beyond the due date, and incurred the penalty. But Sir Josia Child, now sure of the Ministers, used the default to secure a new royal charter before Parliament should reassemble. The Dowgate Association,

merce with India, pp. 146–147, 1812.

[1] March 24, 1693.

[2] Besides the statements of enemies we have the following abstract drawn up by the clerks of the India House for private reference, but called for by the Commons' Committee in 1695: Secret Service Moneys, 1688, 1,284*l.*; 1689, 2,096*l.*; 1690, 3,056*l.*; 1691, 11,372*l.*; 1692, 4,659*l.*; 1693 (the year of the new charter), 80,468*l.*; 1694, 4,075*l.* *An Exact Collection of the Debates and Proceedings in Parliament in* 1694 *and* 1695, *upon the Enquiry into the late Briberies and Corrupt Practices*, p. 6, 1695.

[3] The Royal African, the Hudson's Bay, and the East India Company, 4 & 5 Gul. et Mar. c. 15.

driven to extremities, raised the old question as to the King's prerogative before the Privy Council. But the Privy Council was presided over by Caermarthen, and Caermarthen had received several thousand pounds from Child. The King, face to face with the armies of Louis Quatorze, had little leisure for trade wrangles at home, and in October 1693 a new charter issued to the East India Company.[1] It condoned the default, and confirmed the Company in all rights or privileges conveyed by the Stuart charters, subject to certain regulations to be framed by His Majesty. These regulations re-established the Company for twenty-one years, but provided for a new subscription of 744,000*l.* to be added to the Company's capital, and restricted any member from holding more than 10,000*l.* of stock or having over ten votes.[2]

Oct. 1693

They somewhat modified the compromise pro-

[1] Charter of William and Mary, dated October 7, 1693, India Office Library Quarto, pp. 141–151. It names Sir Thomas Cooke, a submissive creature of Child, and whose son was married to Child's daughter in 1691, as Governor: while Sir Josia stands third in the committee of twenty-four, after the names of the Earl of Berkley and the Lord Mayor of London. The original charter is preserved in the India Office, which has an almost complete collection of the Company's charters and Letters Patent from 1661.

[2] Letters Patent, dated November 11, 1693. Among the minor provisions were the following: the freedom of the Company to purchasers not otherwise entitled to it was fixed at 5*l.* The qualifications for a Governor or Deputy-Governor was 4,000*l.* stock; for a 'Committee' or Director, 1,000*l.*; and no holder of less than 1,000*l.* could vote in the General Courts. Permission ships and 'licensed' trade were forbidden under penalty of forfeiting the charter; the Company was annually to export English merchandise to the value of 100,000*l.*; and to supply the King with 500 tons of saltpetre at 38*l.* 10s. per ton in time of peace, and 45*l.* in time of war. India Office Library Quarto of Charters, pp. 153–168.

posed by the Commons in December 1692, and adopted by the Privy Council in 1693, for retaining the old Company, but opening it to the outside world by a new subscription which should double its capital. The House of Commons felt itself overreached, bribery was suspected, and an incident occurred which fanned its resentment into a flame. The company procured an order from the Privy Council to detain the ship *Redbridge*, with papers made out for Alicant, but with India as her real Oct. 1693 or suspected destination.[1] Child had lately written with confident audacity to India that the time was come to make an end of interloping,[2] and relying on the venal Ministers, he now resolved to stop it at its source in the Thames.

The City seethed with excitement, and the Commons appointed a Committee of the whole House with Papillon (Child's old antagonist) as chairman, to consider the petitions which came in from both sides.[3] The chief owner[4] of the cargo boldly stated in his evidence that 'he did not think it any sin to trade to the East Indies, and would trade thither till there was an Act of Parliament

[1] October 21, 1693.

[2] April 24, 1693, Rawlinson MSS. A. 303, fol. 267. According to a perhaps exaggerated story of Hamilton (*New Account of the East Indies*, vol. i. p. 232, ed. 1727) Child instructed the Company's judge at Bombay that his orders must be carried out, and that the laws of England were only a heap of nonsense put together by ignorant country gentlemen who could not make laws even for the good government of their own families, much less for foreign commerce.

[3] *Journals of the House of Commons*, January 6, 1694.

[4] Gilbert Heathcote, afterwards Knight and Baronet and Lord Mayor of London.

to the contrary.'[1] On the 8th January, 1694, the Jan. 1694
committee reported that the detention of the ship was illegal, and on the 19th the House resolved 'that all the subjects of England have equal right to trade to the East Indies unless prohibited by Act of Parliament.'[2]

Child's subtleties had thus resulted in a blow not only to the Company but to the royal prerogative. The nation, however, was too deeply immersed in the Flanders campaign, the Triennial Bill, and Fenwick's conspiracy, to allow of a trade dispute being magnified into a quarrel with the Crown. The House of Commons having declared the India trade open to the nation, William enlarged his recent charter so as, *inter alia*, to revoke the provisions against licensed trade, and the matter
was allowed to drop.[3] In 1695, Parliament 1695

[1] *Journals of the House of Commons*, January 8, 1694.

[2] *Idem*, January 19, 1694.

[3] By Letters Patent, dated September 28, 1694, he empowered the Company to allow its captains and sea officers to engage in a regulated traffic with the East, and he endeavoured to strengthen the popular element in its constitution. For example, he authorised any six members to require a General Court to be called after eight days' notice, and all private committees were to be chosen by the General Court and not the directors. A blow was aimed at Child's bribery by the provision that no payment should be made except on a statement of the person who was to receive it, and the purposes for which it was incurred, unless by a vote of the General Court. The bye-laws framed under Cromwell's charter of 1657, providing that no Governor or Deputy-Governor should continue in office for more than two years together, and that eight new members should be elected annually to the Committee of Twenty-four, were now incorporated in the charter. If the charter did not prove profitable to the realm, it might be revoked on three years' notice. All the directors, or Committee of Twenty-four, had to be elected afresh each year; but since Cromwell's charter only sixteen of the twenty-four

inquired into the bribery which Child had practised; but Sir Josia screened himself behind his creature and connection by marriage, Sir Thomas Cooke, M.P., who was committed to the Tower by the Commons, and 'bemoaned himself weeping' at the bar of the Lords.[1]

1695 In the same year Scotland made a second attempt to strike into the India trade. We have seen how the patent granted by James I. to a Scottish company, in 1617, was speedily recalled under pressure from its English rival.[2] An Act of the Scottish Parliament now incorporated 'The Company of Scotland trading to Africa and the Indies,'[3] under a pledge of special protection from King William, who hoped it might prove a salve for the massacre of Glencoe. But the Scottish

could be re-elected. The system was worked so as to retain desirable men always on the Committee, and to pass a flow of new men on trial through it. For example, Sir Samuel Barnardiston was re-elected every year from 1661 to 1682, except in 1668 and 1669, when he was Deputy-Governor. The cases of Papillon and Sir Josia Child have been mentioned on page 284. The Committee thus combined the advantages of continuity of tradition and of fresh blood. Of the twenty-four elected in 1670, two had already served for twelve years, eleven had served for over seven years, while only eight members had less than four years previous experience, and only two were elected for the first time. MS. Court Books, for whose examination in regard to this point I thank Mr. W. Foster.

[1] *An Exact Collection of the Debates, &c.*, pp. 18–20, 1695: *A Brief Historical Relation of State Affairs from September* 1678 *to April* 1714, by Narcissus Luttrell, ii. 192, ed. 1857.

[2] *Ante*, pp. 365–366, vol. i.

[3] June 26, 1695. The prime mover in the scheme was William Paterson (1658–1719), founder of the Bank of England. The proceedings of the Scottish Company, so far as they bear on the English East India Company, are summarised in Macpherson's *History of European Commerce with India*, pp. 149–153.

Company, after spending its resources on the Darien colonisation scheme, fell a victim to foreign intrigues, and its shareholders only received a tardy compensation on the union of the two kingdoms. The English East India Company, however, affected to regard its rivalry as serious, and in 1696 again pressed for a Parliamentary sanction 1696
for its own trade.[1]

It became evident that the existing state of things, with the India trade confined by royal charter to an exclusive company, yet declared free to the nation by the House of Commons, could not continue. The East was practically open to all who would take the risks, arising out of the conflict of authorities. Soon, however, the English manufacturer's dread of Indian imports rose to a frenzy. In 1697 mobs of three thousand weavers assembled to attack Child's mansion, assaulted the East India House and nearly got possession of the Company's treasure.[2] The Dowgate Association and the Company now arrayed their forces for a final struggle. In 1698, the Company offered a loan of 700,000*l.* at 4 per cent. to the State for the confirmation of its charter by Act of Parliament; a tender which the Dowgate Association promptly outbid by offering two millions sterling at 8 per cent. The Chancellor of the Exchequer was

[1] It failed to obtain it, because Parliament had authorised the Government to raise two and a half millions sterling, and was apprehensive lest a settlement of the India trade would divert subscriptions from the public loan.

[2] Narcissus Luttrell, *ut supra*, iv. 200; Macpherson, p. 153. The mobs were dispersed by the militia and the 'press-gang.'

June 1698 in straits for the larger sum, and in June 1698 the Commons passed a Bill[1] for the creation of a new East India Company. It was violently opposed in the Lords, but eventually passed without alteration as a Supply Bill, in spite of a protest[2] signed by twenty-one peers.

This auction of the India trade by Parliament merely gave a constitutional recognition to a practice which had long been in force. The ruling power in England had always recognised that an exclusive grant of the India trade possessed a distinct money value which in some form or other must be paid. As Charles I. could not obtain cash from the Company, he sought his profit in a clandestine association with more generous financial friends, Sir Paul Pindar and Sir William Courten.[3] The Long Parliament and Cromwell openly compelled the Company to lend large sums for the public service,[4] although the legend that 500,000*l.* was asked for the charter of 1657 is a grotesque exaggeration.[5] Charles II. and James II.

[1] By 115 to 78 votes June 25, 1698, *Journals of the House of Commons*, whose dates differ slightly from those in Macaulay and others. By its title the Act was a money bill, with a rider for the settlement of Indian affairs: namely, 'An Act for raising a sum, not exceeding two millions, upon a fund for payment of annuities after the rate of eight *per centum per annum*, and for settling a trade to the East Indies.'

[2] On the second reading in the Upper House it was only carried by 65 to 48 votes, although *nem. con.* on the third reading as a Supply Bill. It will be remembered that in 1646, during the Long Parliament, the lords rejected the 'Ordinance for the Trade' which the Commons had passed as a charter to the East India Company, *ante*, p. 42.

[3] *Ante*, pp. 28, 30, 33–41.

[4] *Ante*, p. 112.

[5] It depends on a piece of gossip in a letter from Percy Church to Secretary Nicholas, dated Paris, March $\frac{5}{15}$, 1658,

simply took from the Company as much as it would give, and the courtiers loyally followed their Majesties' example.[1] In 1698 Parliament, when 1698
placing the monopoly on a statutory basis, recognised that compensation should be taken for the curtailment of the general liberty of trade, and inaugurated the system of loans from the Company for the benefit of the nation—a system destined to extensive developments.

The Act of 1698[2] skilfully avoided a conflict with the Crown. It did not grant a charter, but it created a corporation to whom the King was to grant charters. It provided that a subscription for a loan of two millions sterling to the State should be opened, and that each subscriber should be privileged to trade with India on a capital of the same amount as he had paid into the public loan. Any person, Englishman or Foreigner, or any corporation or company (except the Bank of England) might subscribe. The contributors were constituted in a body corporate under the title of the General Society,[3] and the interest on their two millions was secured by an assignment on the

giving among other reasons for Cromwell's dissolving Parliament the inability of the East India Company to pay that sum. *Calendar of State Papers, Domestic*, 1657–8, p. 314. The whole subscription called up under the charter of 1657 was only 369,891*l*.

[1] *Ante*, p. 182.

[2] 9 & 10 Gul. III. c. 44. As the Act is fully recited, and for practical purposes incorporated in the Royal charters immediately founded upon it, a very brief account of it must suffice.

[3] In full, 'The General Society intituled to the advantages given by an Act of Parliament for advancing a sum not exceeding two millions, for the service of the Crown of England.'

duties from salt, stamped parchment, vellum, and paper. To this General Society was secured the exclusive trade to India, saving the rights of the old Company, which would expire after three years' notice, and such private ships as had set forth on the strength of the Resolution of the House of Commons in 1694.[1] While each subscriber might trade separately on his own account, the Act provided that any number of them might unite to trade on their combined capital, and His Majesty was empowered to incorporate by charter such members into a joint-stock company. The Act was to hold good for ever, or until repayment by the State of the two millions on three years' notice after the 29th September, 1711.

July 1698 The Act received the Royal Assent on July 5, 1698; the subscription books were laid open at Mercers' Hall on Thursday, the 14th,[2] and by Saturday, the 16th, more than the two millions were promised. The King contributed 10,000*l.*, the Lords of the Treasury 5,000*l.* a piece, prominent Interlopers 35,000*l.* and 10,000*l.*, but the list is chiefly made up of ordinary investors,[3] many of

[1] 19th January, 1694, *ante*, p. 313. Such ships must have cleared from England before the 1st July, 1698, in order to have the advantage of this saving clause. The three years' notice to the old Company was to expire on 29th September, 1701.

[2] At eight o'clock, says the *London Gazette* for July 11–14, 1698.

[3] Names long famous in the Company's employment, and some of them still surviving in the Indian services of the Crown, occur in the list, including that of Woollaston (Wollaston); a name entitled to the gratitude of the author of this book for never-failing help in regard to the India Office records.

them women, and some of them quakers.[1] The fear lest the Dutch Company would take advantage of the clause admitting foreigners, and so secure a controlling voice in the new society, proved groundless. Dutch names, like the unmistakeable one of Dirk Vander Stegen, appear in the list, but not in greater numbers than might be expected from the connection of the King and the City with Holland. But what the Dutch Company failed to do the old English Company by a bold financial stroke accomplished. It subscribed, through its treasurer, 315,000*l.*, and thus in addition to its chartered status, it became by far the largest contributor, and the dominant partner in the General Society constituted by the Act of Parliament.[2]

The rapidity with which the two millions were forthcoming shows how firmly the India trade had now taken hold of the national imagination. Country subscribers who, like the Bristol merchants, deferred making up their minds for even a day or two after the Royal Assent on July 5, found themselves too late, and offers of many hundreds of thousands of pounds arrived after the subscription books were closed. This, too, just after the losses of a long war, during which no fewer than 4,200 British merchant vessels fell into

[1] The original subscription books with the autographs of the subscribers in a beautiful state of preservation are in the India Office. At the end of each day the list was signed and sealed by the King's Commissioners. By the evening of the 14th over 600,000*l.* had been subscribed.

[2] The entry in the subscription books is simply 'I, John Du Bois doe subscribe for 315,000*l.*'

the hands of the enemy.[1] 'The despatch of so great a work in less than three days' time,' writes a contemporary, who estimates that four millions sterling might have been easily raised, 'after the nation had borne so chargeable a war for so many years surprised and amazed all the world.'[2]

The great majority of the subscribers, including most of the Dowgate Association, realised the dangers of separate trading to India on the Regulated system, and applied to the King, under the alternative provision of the Act, to be incorporated Sept. 1698 into a joint-stock company. On September 5, 1698, William granted a full and complete charter to them under the name of 'The English Company trading to the East Indies.'[3] The grant sets forth, with an elaboration of detail which fills sixty-five quarto pages, the whole basis and constitution of the East India trade. The King acknowledges the new powers claimed by the Commons yet saves the ancient rights of the Crown, by issuing his charter in pursuance of the Act of Parliament 'and by virtue of our Prerogative Royal.' It is technically addressed to the whole General Society, but it practically incorporates such members of them as choose to trade on a joint-stock. The system of

[1] Macpherson, *European Commerce with India*, p. 153. The peace of Ryswick had been concluded only in the previous autumn.

[2] *A Collection of the Parliamentary Debates of England from the year* 1668, iii. 115. See also for this episode *A Short History of the Last Parliament*, 1699, pp. 60, 61; and Narcissus Luttrell under date July 16, 1698, iv. 403.

[3] India Office Library Quarto of Charters, pp. 188–242. From this title, the new association was known as the 'English Company,' while the old was henceforward styled the 'London Company.'

management by a Committee of Twenty-four is borrowed from the old Company, but the members of the committees receive for the first time in this charter their historical name of Directors.[1] All merchandise was still to be sold at auction 'by inch of candle;'[2] five hundred tons of saltpetre were to be yearly supplied to the Crown at cost price; the account books were to lie open at certain times to be viewed by the generality; and the old tendency for control to be engrossed by a clique was guarded against by empowering any nine members (with a share of 500*l.* a piece) to demand a General Court of the Company. Various philanthropic provisions also appear for the first time. Quakers were allowed to make a solemn affirmation instead of an oath; a minister and a schoolmaster were to be maintained at St. Helena; and a chaplain on every ship of 500 tons burden and at each garrison or superior factory in the East. All ministers stationed in India 'shall be obliged to learn within one year after their arrival the Portuguese language, and shall apply themselves to learn the native language of the country where they shall reside, the better to enable them to instruct the Gentoos that shall be the servants or slaves of the same Company, or of their agents, in the Protestant Religion.'[3] The charter was to endure

[1] Among the first twenty-four Directors named in the charter we find sturdy interlopers like Gilbert Heathcote and dismissed servants of the old Company like Streynsham Master.

[2] India Office Library Quarto of Charters, p. 217.

[3] *Idem*, p. 221.

for ever, subject to the proviso of redemption after 1711 in the Act of Parliament.

This memorable charter of 1698, which in breadth of view and benevolence of intention forms a worthy memorial of the joint effort of Parliament and the Crown, failed in one respect. It attempted too much; for it endeavoured to combine the old Regulated Company in which each member might do business on his own account with the Joint Stock Company in which the members merged their individuality in a corporate management, with whom alone rested the right to trade.[1] But if it thus tried to combine the Regulated and the Joint Stock systems, it did so with a clear prevision of the difficulties of the attempt. The Turkey Company had proved that a Regulated Company could be successfully worked by means of consuls and ambassadors to the Governments in whose territories the individual
1698 members traded. The Act of 1698, and William's charter to the new East India Company founded thereon, provided therefore that a duty of five per cent. on all Indian imports should be applied to the maintenance of ambassadors, to be accredited by the King on the nomination of the Company to the Indian Courts. It was hoped that as consuls and ministers plenipotentiary protected the individual traders of the Turkey Regulated Company

[1] It must be remembered that public opinion still supported the Regulated system, and found representatives alike in the old Company, the Dowgate Association, and the miscellaneous subscribers to the General Society. William's charter was a compromise made to suit the prejudices as well as the facts of his time.

in the Levant, so consuls and ministers would protect individual traders of the new East India Company at Bombay, Madras, and Calcutta. It was forgotten that our fleets could speak to the Mediterranean Powers if they refused to listen to our ambassadors, while the Indian potentates were beyond the reach of our armies and fleets.

NOTE.

These were the last words written by Sir William Hunter. They were penned only a few days before he died. It has been thought best to leave this chapter unfinished, exactly as it stood at the time of his death. As explained in the Introduction, the materials which he left have been utilised to add a concluding chapter, bringing down the history to the final amalgamation of the two Companies.

CHAPTER IX

STRIFE AND UNION OF THE COMPANIES

1698–1708

ON the same day that gentlemen and merchants thronged through the doors of Mercers' Hall to enrol their names in the subscription books of the General Society, the King sent to the Court of Directors in Leadenhall Street formal notice under his sign manual that their privileges would terminate at the end of three years' time.[1]

The Old, or London Company at first reeled under the blow, which they felt to be 'the greatest hardship that had been done to any subject.'[2] Their stock fell with unprecedented rapidity to a fraction over 33, while throughout August and September it never rose above 42¾ per cent.[3] But in

[1] Rawlinson MSS., A. 303, fol. 161, Bodleian Library. Copy of the King's mandate, dated 14 July, 1698. The three years were to count from the next quarter-day, 29 September, 1698, to 29 September, 1701; *ante*, p. 318, footnote 1.

[2] Letter of the Directors to Bombay, 25 April, 1700. India Office MSS. Letter Book, No. 10.

[3] These figures are derived from a very valuable record, the weekly price list of East India Stock, 1692–1705, tabulated from John Houghton's *Collections*, and printed in Thorold Rogers' *History of Agriculture and Prices*, vol. vi. pp. 721–725. On a reference to this work it will be noticed that in the list for 1698 a double set of figures is given from July to October. This may possibly be due to a printer's error, but in any case a comparison with Narcissus Luttrell's *Brief Historical Rela-*

spite of the ominous prospect the Directors resolutely braced themselves to face the storm. If to the outside world their position seemed well-nigh hopeless, they knew their cause was not yet lost. Indeed, the more they considered the facts, the less reason they saw for despondency. After all, the New Company would be a more tangible foe to grapple with than the 'nibbling interlopers.'[1] Superficial observers might see in the King's action the extinction of one Company and the erection of another, but the reality was very different. The Old Company had still their 'charter for three years inviolable,' and their 'Utensils, viz. Houses, Forts and Factories . . . abroad and at home ready fitted.' There was not one word in the act or charter as to any sale or conveyance of these to the New Company. Further, as a Corporation subscribing to the General Society they had the right to trade even after 1701 for 315,000*l.*, 'which keeps the way open to all our Propriety and Possessions in India.'[2] To the cynical mind it might seem as though Parliament had but paralysed the Old Company with a grievous wound,

tion, vol. iv. pp. 405–417, proves the lower numbers to be the correct ones. Bruce, the apologist of the Old Company, ignores this extraordinary decline, and rather implies that it was the New Company's stock which fell (*Annals*, iii. pp. 259, 291), but his figures are derived from the Old Company's Letters, and must be accepted with reservations. From Luttrell's impartial testimony it is clear that the New Company's stock from July to the end of the year only varied from 100 to 96 per cent., while as late as December the Old Company's still stood at 42.

[1] Despatch of the Court to Bengal, 26 August, 1698. India Office MSS. Letter Book, No. 10.

[2] Letter to Madras, 26 August, 1698. *Idem.*

and brought into the world another that was crippled from its birth.

In truth, when the Government granted the New, or English Company its charter, it adopted a characteristically English method of evading a difficulty. To give the exclusive trade in the East to one association, and at the same time to retain in existence another exercising rival powers, was not theoretically an ideal expedient, and yet it was perhaps the best practical solution of a complicated problem. No doubt, since the Old Company firmly refused to widen its basis from within, the logical and consistent course was to give it the legal three years' notice and allow the New Company to begin trading at the expiration of that period. But what guarantee had Parliament or the King that the new association could at once step into the vacuum caused by the withdrawal of its opponents? The Old Company would have little inducement to smooth the path for those who were to come after, and in the allotted three years might so effectually wind up its affairs as to endanger the continuity of the English connection with India. To launch the New Company upon the troubled waters and await the issue, may well have seemed to the statesmen of that day the only feasible plan, in the hope that the rival associations would realise the suicidal nature of the inevitable struggle, and be forced to some form of mutual compromise. In fact, the idea of ultimate amalgamation was imminent from the very first. Even the Directors of Leadenhall Street, with all their sturdy independence, looked forward to it as the natural end. But they had no intention of coming in at once. In the event of an immediate union, their rivals, as yet untried by disasters and basking in the beams of popular favour, would necessarily obtain an overwhelming influence. They determined to use all the advantages their position gave them to exact the most favourable terms. Time at least was on their side. The New Company had yet to learn the elements of traffic with the East, 'and we may presume,' wrote the Directors of the Old Company with fine scorn, 'we are a little better stocked with experience, having surmounted a great many difficulties and losses in late and former times.' Before long, no doubt, the New Company's stock would fall in value, 'and by that time it is probable we may both be weary of fighting and giving the world occasion to laugh at our folly, and may then shake hands and be friends, when they have smarted as much as they have made us for several years past.'[1]

They did not deceive themselves as to the perilous nature of the struggle; two Companies, they wrote, could no more exist side by side in India than 'two kings at the same time regnant in

[1] Letter to Madras, 26 Aug., 1698. India Office MSS. Letter Book, No. 10. It must be remembered that from 1698, for a time at least, four classes of merchants were legalised to trade to the East —(1) the New Company; (2) the Old Company, till 1701; (3) those subscribers to the General Society who had held aloof from the Joint Stock of the New Company, and whose capital amounted to about 22,000*l.*; (4) much less important, a few separate traders who had sent out ships to India prior to 1 July, 1698, and who were allowed to complete the voyage, *Ante*, p. 318, footnote.

the same kingdom:' and again, in more homely phrase, they compared themselves and their rivals to two earthen vessels which must break if knocked together, or to two buckets in a well, one of which must perforce descend as the other ascended. But they had everything to gain and nothing to lose from a conflict. They were buoyed up at least by the courage of despair: 'When things are at the worst they must mend;' 'we think ourselves upon the ground already, so can't have a great fall.'[1]

There is a proud pathos in their stern determination not to submit, 'our joints are too stiff to yield to our juniors, we are veteran soldiers in this warfare.' They wrote to their servants in the East in terms of high courage, 'we have showed our faces to fortune formerly when all the world stood aghast at our losses and expected we should have given up the ghost, yet then we called in fresh money and went on with a resolution unknown to any other than this Company. . . . Take pattern from us and show all around you that such blustering storms are so far from tearing us up, that it only a little shakes the roots, and makes them thereby take the better hold, and we grow the firmer and flourish the faster.'[2]

In the meantime the New Company's Directors were holding their first meetings. At the out-

[1] Letters of the Court to Bengal 26 August, to Madras 28 October, 1698, and to Bombay 17 March, 1699. India Office MSS. Letter Book No. 10.

[2] *Idem.* Letters to Bengal 26 August, 1698, and to Persia 2 August, 1699.

set they were confronted with the task of raising money for the trade. It must not be forgotten that the two millions was paid over to Government, and besides interest at 8 per cent. procured for the subscribers only the right to trade to India annually to the amount of their subscriptions. The interest due to all holders of stock in the General Society was, in the case of the English East India Company, to be paid over to the association as a corporate body and to be used as trading capital. On the New Company's capital of 1,662,000*l.*,[1] the interest would be only 132,960*l.* It was necessary to supplement this sum, and fresh money had therefore to be raised by *ad valorem* levies on the original subscriptions.[2] But as the majority of the subscribers had already invested as much as they could possibly afford, further sums were only wrung from them with extreme difficulty, and it soon became apparent that for the first few years the exports of the New Company were not likely to equal those of their rivals. To make the discrepancy still more marked, the Old Company by a special effort had raised new capital to the amount of 400,000*l.*

Hence within a few months of its establishment the Court of the New Company was already beginning to think of a Coalition, 'a new-fashioned word now in vogue in all public places,' wrote the Directors of the Old Company, 'by which we think

[1] *Vide post*, p. 379, footnote.

[2] *E.g.*, 15 September, 1698, a call of 20 per cent. was made, and in August, 1699, another of 15 per cent.

they mean our stock should be joined to theirs.'[1] Nov. 1698 In November 1698, Thomas Papillon, in the 'laudable employment of mediator,' made tentative proposals to the authorities of Leadenhall Street, and Feb. 1699 in February 1699, the General Court of the New Company passed a formal resolution in favour of an agreement 'upon safe, just, and reasonable terms.'[2]

But at present the Old Company shunned entertaining any such proposals. They had other work on hand. For some time certain qualms had beset them as to the security of their position after 1701. It is true the Act of 1698 allowed individuals or corporations subscribing to the General Society who had elected to hold aloof from the joint stock of the New Company to trade annually to the amount of their subscriptions. But the adventurers of the Old Company were in a peculiar position. The King's notice terminated their existence as the 'London Company of Merchants trading to the East Indies.' Would it also dissolve them as a corporation subscribing to the General Society—would they be allowed to transfer to themselves as a corporate body the sum of 315,000*l.*, which, in the Subscription Books, still stood in the name of John Du Bois,[3]

[1] India Office MSS. Letter Book, No. 10. Despatch of the Court to Madras, 28 October, 1698.

[2] *Idem.* Letter of the Old Company to Bombay, 17 March, 1699. Also MS. Court Book, No. 37A, p. 170, Court Minutes of the New Company for 2 February, 1699.

[3] India Office MSS. Letter Book, No. 11, Letter of the New Company to Sir Edward Littleton, 12 April, 1700.

and to make up which 1,200 subscribers had contributed?[1]

They hoped to remove this ambiguity by Act of Parliament, and on February 24 presented a petition praying to be continued a corporation after September 29, 1701. It was at this very time, when their business was still impending before the Commons, that the New Company came forward with proposals for a union. The Directors of Leadenhall Street were in a sad quandary. If they agreed prematurely to a coalition, and their petition was accepted, they would reap little benefit from their success; if they definitely rejected all overtures and the petition failed, they would have thrown away a valuable opportunity. They had recourse to subterfuge and evasion. When the New Company's emissaries appeared in Leadenhall Street they were told that the Court was not sitting, though they came on the advertised Court days. When they asked to see the Secretary, he begged to be excused on the plea of indisposition. Once it came to their knowledge that, as they were seen approaching, he hurriedly left the India House.[2] By these somewhat ignoble devices the Old Company staved off their rivals till Parliament had come to a decision. A few more days decided their fate. On March 3, a Bill was brought in embodying the clauses of the petition, but was rejected six days later on the second reading

Feb. 1699

March 1699

[1] See the Company's petition to Parliament, printed in the *Journals of the House of Commons*, 24 February, 1699.

[2] Court Minutes of the New Company, 24 February and 7 March, 1699. Court Book, No. 37 A, India Office MSS.

by a narrow majority of ten—a defeat in all probability due to the fact that the Company, not content with being continued a corporation, claimed to be also exempted from the 5 per cent. import duty levied on all subscribers to the General Society for the support of an Ambassador in the East.[1]

The Directors tried to make light of their repulse. They averred it was only a 'loss of some time, but not of our cause or hopes,' and attributed it to an unlucky accident which kept some of their supporters away from the House.[2] Yet it is, perhaps, significant that they no longer turned a deaf ear to the New Company's proposals, but entered into negotiations for an agreement within a fortnight of their defeat in the Commons. Each Company chose seven representatives who were to meet together and discuss the terms of union, and each also elected a grand committee to whom the smaller body of seven were to make their reports and to be responsible.[3]

It is unnecessary to follow in detail the fluctuations of the conference which dragged on its tedious course from March 22 to December 20, and proved absolutely abortive. After months of diplomatic wrangling on minor issues the New Company presented an ultimatum that the Old Company should take up so much more of the

March–Dec. 1699

[1] *Journals of the House of Commons*, 24th, 27th February, 3rd and 9th March, 1699. The votes were 149 to 139.

[2] Letter of the Old Company to Bombay, 6 April, 1699. India Office MSS. Letter Book, No. 10.

[3] The Old Company chose a Grand Committee of fifty-two; the New, one of forty-eight, *i.e.*, the twenty-four Directors *plus* twenty-four Adventurers with at least 2,000*l.* stock.

fund as would make their subscription up to one million sterling, a demand which the latter firmly refused to entertain.[1]

In the beginning of the next year the Old Company won a great triumph. They again petitioned the Commons to be continued a corporation, and prudently dropped the invidious claim to immunity from the five per cent. duty on imports. A Bill was speedily drafted on the lines of the petition and on February 12 passed the third reading unopposed. Feb. 1700 The friends of the New Company only injured their own cause by moving an amendment definitely obliging their opponents to pay the ambassadorial tax. On challenging a division they were defeated, and the House thus seemed to record its tacit admission of the Old Company's claim to be exempt.[2]

It must not be supposed that this bill made void the King's formal notice of dissolution. Theoretically, the days of the Old Company's full plenitude of power were numbered. The Act merely enabled them to trade on an annual capital of 315,000*l.*, till the final repayment of the loan of two millions by the State.[3] But practically, the margin allowed was so ample that, together

[1] The negotiations may be followed in full detail in the Rawlinson MSS., A. 302, fol. 167, *seq.* Bodleian Library.

[2] *Journals of the House of Commons*, 19, 24, 27 January, 1, 6, 8, 9, and 12 February, 1700.

[3] The Company, however, was allowed to retain and trade under its old name—a concession of no small advantage when the Act came to be announced in the East; since it gave the factors plausible grounds for their boast that their masters were confirmed in all their former privileges. The text of the Act, which was a private bill, is given in the Rawlinson MSS., A. 303, fol. 113.

with the possession of their revenues and forts in the East, it made the nominal curtailment of their privileges of little moment. The Directors triumphantly proclaimed that the Act gave them all they ever desired. The bill had passed the Commons. Two weeks later it was agreed to by the Lords, but the Royal assent had not yet dwindled to a mere formality, and the Company spared no pains to make its victory complete. It was the custom of the day for those interested in the passing of any particular measure personally to solicit the Royal favour. Accordingly on February 29, 'at twelve o'clock in the forenoon' an elaborate cavalcade started from the doors of the India House to wait upon the King at Kensington, consisting of 'my Lord Mayor, ten or twelve of the Aldermen, the Sheriff and about a hundred men of the adventurers, in above sixty of their own coaches.'[1] His Majesty received them graciously, but hinted his preference for an amalgamation, and at another interview a few weeks later greeted them with the words, 'Gentlemen, you know my mind already, I am for a union.'[2] The Directors replied they would do their best to come to some agreement if only their bill were made law, and on the Dissolution
April 1700 of Parliament, April 11, the words were pronounced which the Company so ardently desired to hear, 'Le Roy le veult.'

[1] Bruce (*Annals*, iii. 293) gives the date as 8 March, an error for 29 February, as is certain from the letter of the Old Company to Madras, 6 March, 1700. India Office MSS. Letter Book, No. 10, and Narcissus Luttrell's *Brief Historical Relation*, vol. iv. p. 618.

[2] Luttrell, vol. iv. p. 624, March 16.

The great object thus attained, the Company recked little of their vague promise to the King. The letters to the East are tinged with a new strain of exultant hope: 'Now we are established by Act of Parliament . . . It secures our foundation . . . We shall exert ourselves with a new vigour. . . . We can now call our estate our own.' Whereas immediately before the passing of the bill their stock was quoted at 70 per cent., on April 13th it stood at 149. No wonder the Company felt new pulsations of strength, 'We are neither winding up our bottom, lessening our trade, resigning our forts, deserting our faithful servants, letting fall our courts of justice, or any other ways giving up our cause.'[1] The event in a corresponding measure was a heavy blow to the New Company. Their stock fell five per cent. in three days on the mere presentation of the petition, and they began to despair of a union altogether; 'it will put them and us,' they wrote, 'at a greater distance, and we see now no likelihood of an agreement with them.'[2]

For nine months the question of a union remained in abeyance, and there succeeded an outward lull in the strife of the two Companies at home. Before resuming the narrative of those further events which led ultimately to a settlement, we must turn our eyes to that distant arena

[1] Letters of the Old Company to Madras, 12 April and 18 June, 1700. India Office MSS. Letter Book, No. 10. Narcissus Luttrell, *ut supra*, vol. iv. pp. 610, 633; cf. Houghton's figures, Thorold Rogers' *History of Agriculture and Prices*, vol. vi., p. 722.

[2] Narcissus Luttrell, *ut supra*, vol. iv. p. 605; Letter of the New Company to Sir Edward Littleton, 12 April, 1700. India Office MSS. Letter Book, No. 11.

of the East, where another phase of the same struggle was working itself out to a more or less independent issue.

With the exception of the famous embassy to the Great Mogul, which will be dealt with later, the New Company made few innovations in the attempt to establish themselves in India. Like the Old Company, they determined to set up three Presidencies, and they fixed them, moreover, where their rivals were already settled. This brought the inevitable conflict at once to a head. The struggle resolved itself into a threefold duel between the Presidents of each Company in Bengal, Bombay, and Madras, and the issue largely depended upon the personal qualities of the combatants. The New Company had been singularly ill advised in choosing its representatives. All three Presidents were dismissed servants of the Old Company, they had shown themselves faithless to their former employers, they proved either faithless or incapable in the service of their new masters.

Something may profitably be said of the legal aspect of the question. The New Company's agents were given the rank of 'King's Consul,' and this led them to claim authority not only over their own factors but over all the English living in India, including the servants of the Old Company. The latter resisted, and have therefore been charged with defying the authority of the State.[1]

[1] *E.g.* by Anderson, *English in Western India*. This writer takes throughout the most unfavourable view of the Old Com-

But they claimed, and with considerable reason, that the act could only mean they should be subject to the Consular power after the year 1701. Till then they were permitted to retain their full privileges—privileges which included absolute sovereignty within the walls of their own settlements and the exercise of the highest judicial and administrative functions. It was a sufficient breach of public faith that the New Company were allowed to begin trading before the legal three years had elapsed; it would be monstrous if they were also permitted to interfere with the Old Company's right of self-government. After September 1701, the Old Company's servants would no doubt pass under the jurisdiction of the Consuls, but at present both they and the Directors laughed at such 'strange bugbear powers.'[1] Thomas Pitt put the case in a nutshell when he wrote to the New Company's President, 'You may lock up your Consul's commission till my masters' time is expired.'[2]

Unfortunately the New Company's agents were not minded to follow this excellent advice. Rather they flourished the commissions in their opponents' faces. Indeed whatever may have been the theoretical rights of the matter, there can be no two opinions as to the tactless

pany's servants; but a careful examination of the MS. Records on both sides certainly bears out the later view of Sir Henry Yule and Mr. C. R. Wilson, that the New Company's agents were the less capable and the more dishonest.

[1] Letter of the Old Company to Persia, Aug. 21st, 1700. India Office MSS. Letter Book, No. 10.

[2] Hedges' *Diary*, vol. iii. p. 49.

folly of their general conduct. Their obvious policy was quietly to establish trading relations with the Native Powers and avoid all collisions with men whose tenure of power would terminate so soon. But they courted resistance. They could never cease proclaiming that they came 'on Parliamentary sanction, the greatest authority our nation affords.'[1] They clamoured for flags to be lowered on their approach, they ordered the servants of the Old Company to attend their factories and hear the commissions publicly read,[2] they even promised patronage and 'protection' if a due submission were shown. Such arrogant assumption of superiority by men who came out branded with the stigma of dismissal from their former service and who had neither 'forces, power, nor interest in the country'[3] was more than the representatives of the Old Company could endure. It galled them to the quick and they hastened to show their resentment. Even the Directors of the New Company acknowledged that their servants had given needless provocation and counselled greater restraint.[4] It proved all in vain; the Consuls were too infatuated to listen.

[1] Letter of Sir Edward Littleton to John Beard, 29 July, 1699. Rawlinson MSS., A. 302.

[2] Hedges' *Diary*, vol. iii. p. 44.

[3] *Idem*, p. 48.

[4] Letter of the New Company to Sir Nicholas Waite, 7 April, 1700. 'We fear a violent contest upon that occasion' (*i.e.* the Consular powers) 'without it may not produce any advantage to us; for the Old Company have even by our Act the liberty of trade until 29 September, 1701, and their agents as we are told would have shown their respects to our President and Council becoming Englishmen had their expostulatory

On the western coast of India, Sir John Gayer, a man of no genius but honest and conscientious, was in charge of the Old Company's affairs. Originally a sea-captain, he had been appointed Governor of Bombay and 'General of India' in April 1693, and had held staunchly to his post in the face of many difficulties. In this western Presidency the English first began to feel the shock of the dissolution of the Mughal Empire. As the grip of the central authority relaxed, the forces of disorder started into existence. The daring depredations of the pirates that harried the Bombay coast had made the English seem in the native eyes 'as despicable as the Portuguese, and as odious as the Jews in Spain.'[1] Bombay was in fact just entering upon the darkest period of her fortunes. With every advantage in point of situation and harbourage, she was out-distanced in the race for supremacy by Calcutta, and for a considerable time by Madras. For the next sixty years the Presidency was hard pressed by Maratha hordes on land and the corsair fleets on the seaboard. The cloud of desultory and ceaseless warfare never lifted till Clive finally swept the pirates from their fastnesses. Then only did Bombay really recover her position and compete again for empire with her sister cities.[2]

letters for not pulling down the flag been prudently answered' (*post*, p. 341), 'and themselves desired to accompany the President, but instead thereof without consulting the Governments that [the flag] was pulled down [and] hoisted again by their authority, by which we lost ground.' India Office MSS. Letter Book, No. 11.

[1] Letter from Surat, 17 April, 1699. India Office MSS. Miscellaneous Factory Records, No. 5.

[2] For the extraordinary position obtained by the pirates in the next twenty years see a rare

Worn out by his long and arduous period of
1699 office, Sir John Gayer, in 1699, prayed the Court to accept his resignation. But he was destined to endure another ten weary years before the release came. Interlopers brought the first tidings of the New Company's establishment. From them the Mughal Governor of Surat learnt a distorted story: that news having been received in England of the Old Company's misdoings the King had summoned a 'council of justice'[1] and settled a new company, 'who are good persons of quality and very honourable,' the Old Company had then been dissolved and 'cast off as an abominable branch of the people' and an ambassador with men-of-war was coming to seize their servants and inflict on them 'condign punishment.'[2]

The news was followed in a few months by the arrival of Sir Nicholas Waite, the New Company's President, who touched at Bombay January 11th,
Jan. 1700 1700, and reached Surat eight days later. Though showing occasional glimpses of a greater measure of political insight than was possessed by most of the New Company's servants, Waite was of an insolent and overbearing disposition and had a fatal genius for misplaced energy which in the end caused his new masters bitterly to rue the day of his appointment. There was probably a strain of insanity in his composition, for some of

and interesting book, Clement Downing's *History of the Indian Wars*, 1737.

[1] Probably a confused reference to the Lords Justices.

[2] India Office MSS.: O.C. 6633, and Letter Book No. 10. Letter of the Old Company to Calcutta, 5 Jan., 1700.

his letters are so turgid and incoherent as to be absolutely unintelligible. Such a man was hardly likely to realise Sir John Gayer's courteous aspiration, that God would raise him up 'to act for His glory, and the good of our nation.'[1]

At Surat Sir Nicholas Waite haughtily ordered Colt, the Old Company's President, to lower the St. George's flag that floated over the factory. The latter was prepared to give the new-comer a civil welcome, but this high-handed treatment stung him into resistance and he refused to obey. The Mughal Governor of Surat supported him, declaring that the 'Farman' of the English King was of no value unless admitted by order of the Emperor. With strange infatuation Waite despatched a small body of men and forcibly hauled down the flag. Against this gross violation of the Emperor's neutral territory the Mughal Governor protested by sending a body of his own troops to replace it.

'Sir Nicholas Waite sticks at nothing to blacken us,'[2] wrote the despairing servants of the Old Company, and indeed there seemed no end to the follies which his restless intriguing brain prompted him to commit. The distinction between the two Companies was a Western subtlety not likely to be appreciated by Eastern minds. Sir John Gayer had early pointed out to his rival that, however much their general interests were opposed, it would simply be equivalent to political suicide for the one

[1] Letter of Sir John Gayer to Sir Nicholas Waite, 16 Jan., 1700. Rawlinson MSS., A. 302.

[2] Letter from Surat, 28 Dec., 1700. Misc. Factory Records, No. 5. India Office MSS.

Company to embroil the other with the native Powers.[1] Such a policy was certain to recoil on the head of its initiator. But no counsels of prudence could restrain Sir Nicholas. He wrote to the Emperor accusing the Old Company of being 'thieves and confederates with the pirates'—a proceeding which certainly brought about the ruin of the Old Company's establishment in Western India, but also as we shall see did more than anything else to wreck the embassy of Sir William Norris.

Feb. 1701 Aurangzeb, who had long chafed at the losses inflicted on his sea-borne trade, and already suspected the English of complicity with the marauders, seized eagerly on the opportunity thus afforded him. Orders were despatched from the Imperial camp that the Old Company's servants should be seized and their goods confiscated. Sir John Gayer and his wife had just left Bombay for Surat, to compose if possible the differences between Colt and Sir Nicholas Waite. At Swally they were arrested by Mughal officers, carried to Surat, and there with Colt and other servants of the Old Company kept in more or less rigorous imprisonment for years.[2] Release was only offered them at the price of extortionate ransoms which they could not pay. At one time it seemed to the captives that more than their liberty was in jeopardy, and the covert threats of the Mughal Governor wrung from Sir John Gayer

[1] Letter to Sir Nicholas Waite, 16 January, 1700. Rawlinson MSS., A. 302.

[2] G. W. Forrest, *Selections from State Papers, Bombay*, Home Series, vol. i, p. 227, February 1701.

a despairing defiance, 'If the King's orders are to kill us, let him come and do it quickly, we will sell our lives as dear as we can.'

In the Bay of Bengal the struggle lay between Sir Edward Littleton and John Beard. The former had been expelled the Old Company's service for corrupt dealing in 1682. His name appears on the first board of Directors of the New Company, and next year he was knighted and sent out to be President in Bengal with three other dismissed servants of the Old Company on his staff. A thoroughly unscrupulous and self-seeking man, Littleton forfeited the esteem of his new masters even before he left England by persistently ignoring their strict orders as to the time of sailing. Provoked by his continued disobedience and irrelevant excuses, they lost patience and revoked his commission. But the offender had highly placed connections. His kinsman the Speaker, Sir Thomas Littleton, and Robert Harley, at this time rapidly coming to the front as an able and subtle debater in the Commons, interceded for him.[1] He was re-appointed and reached the Bengal coast in
July 1699. His rival John Beard had risen by sheer 1699
merit to be Governor of Fort William through every grade of the Old Company's service. A man of sterling honesty and a shrewd mother-wit, he proved fully capable of safeguarding his masters' interests.

From Balasore, Littleton despatched letters

[1] Court Book No. 37*a*, pp. 174, 175. India Office MSS. Edward Harley, Robert's younger brother, himself waited upon the Court to hear their decision.

to Calcutta which are typical of the claims put forward by the New Company's agents.[1] He announced that all territorial sovereignty and political authority had passed from the Old Company, 'nothing more remaining to you of that nature than what properly belongs to Masters or Heads of families, being purely oeconomical.'[2] While intimating that he expected Beard to provide him with small boats and pilots, he haughtily ordered him to suspend all applications to the Great Mogul in the future and to forbear issuing passes for native goods. He concluded with a scarcely veiled threat, 'nor will our hands wax weaker but stronger daily.'

Such letters serve to show how bitter must have been the disillusionment in store for the servants of the New Company. The Parliament of England had indeed given them the sanction of its great authority, but it by no means followed, as they fondly supposed, that the Powers in the East would receive them as the accredited representatives of British commerce. As soon as they touched the Indian littoral they sank to the position of mere parvenus who had to carve out

[1] India Office MSS.: O.C. 6633; and Rawlinson MSS., A. 302. Bodleian Library. Letters dated 28 and 29 July, 1699.

[2] Letter dated Aug. 28, 1699. In a second letter bearing the same date Littleton, whose orthography was not unimpeachable, repeated this warning in the form 'the authority of your employers is only Oecumenical.' With grave sarcasm Beard replied (6 Oct.), 'You say in your letter that our Masters are Oecumenical, a hard word, we find it comes from Oecumenicus, Mr. Adam Littleton says it signifies universal or general, but you mistake in words as in other matters and believe you meant Oeconomical, derived from Oeconomicus, the order and government of a house.' Rawlinson MSS., A. 302.

for themselves a niche in the fabric of the Mughal Empire. At home the Old Company might seem but the remnant of an unpopular monopoly rooted in the patronage and favours of Stuart Kings. In India it was a well-defined part of the body politic recognised by Imperial authority and exercising functions legalised by special Imperial rescripts and decrees. The New Company's servants confidently expected to step at once into the position of their long established rivals and from that starting point to proceed to fresh privileges and wider powers. 'We come upon as old and good a footing as yourselves and all our predecessors,' wrote Sir Edward Littleton, 'upon the ancient amity and friendship the original agreement and contract between the two crowns obtained amplified or ratified about four score years since by his Excellency Sir Thomas Roe . . . of which all Farmans etc. since procured to this day are but declarative or the natural issue thereof.'[1] Littleton and his colleagues forgot that this view of the matter might not commend itself to the Native Powers; they denied the continuity of the trade when it was a question of taking over the Old Company's debts, they affirmed it when it was a question of stepping into their privileges.

John Beard answered these grandiloquent 1699
manifestoes with laconic brevity. He professed himself quite satisfied with his masters' authority and ignored Littleton's requests for assistance. In reply to more violent letters he contented himself

[1] Letter to John Beard, 28 Aug. Rawlinson MSS., A. 302.

with fixing a proclamation on the gates of Calcutta, enjoining all Englishmen under the protection of the Old Company to refuse obedience to any orders of President Littleton, and went quietly about his business as before.

Littleton was furious. The proclamation was a direct denial of his consular rank. He complained of it in a letter to the Duke of Shrewsbury as a 'pestilent paper . . . of very traitorous import,' and warned Beard that he was guilty of high treason; 'to provoke princes is dangerous, they have long and strong hands, can reach far and punish severely.'[1] But Beard was quite unmoved. The memory of Winter and Keigwin had taught men to laugh at charges of treason made in India, which were apt to be sadly whittled away ere they could be presented at the bar of English tribunals.

1700 The President of the New Company soon found himself in difficulties. Two of his council sickened and died. The ranks of his military guard were thinned by death and desertion. One by one the brilliant hopes with which he had arrived in India vanished into thin air. He, the King's Consul and President for a Company established by Parliamentary sanction, after months of effort could obtain no better terms for trading than had been granted to common Interlopers.[2] John Beard pushed his advantage with cruel irony. On the arrival of Sir William Norris in India, Littleton

[1] India Office MSS.: O.C. 6814. Rawlinson MSS., A. 302.

[2] Bruce, *Annals*, vol. iii. p. 415.

wrote to demand copies of all the Farmans and privileges the English had ever obtained in Bengal, that the Ambassador might know the better what privileges to claim. Beard refused on the plea that he must first obtain the consent of his superior the Governor of Fort St. George. His masters, he said, had obtained these privileges 'with great fatigue and large expense.' 'Part you knew,' he continues bitterly, 'in the time you had the happiness to raise a fortune by their service, and may guess at the cost of the others by what you have expended of your new masters' stock in getting a dustuck . . . for this year's business.' [1]

On the Coromandel coast the New Company appointed John Pitt President of their affairs, with residence and head-quarters at Masulipatam. Well intentioned, but of an excitable temperament and utterly destitute of political insight, he proved no match for his relative the 'Great President,' Thomas Pitt, Governor of Madras. The latter's brusque and original personality concealed qualities that stamped him as one of the ablest Englishmen hitherto sent to India, and at the conclusion of his career the Old Company bore willing testimony to his great services in their cause. 'Your active genius and hearty espousing our interest,' they wrote, 'has been the mainspring that has set all the other wheels in motion . . . during the struggle and competition with the New Company.' [2]

[1] Letters of Littleton, 1 Feb., and Beard, 6 Feb., 1700. Rawlinson MSS., A. 302.

[2] Letter of the Court to Thomas Pitt, 12 Feb., 1706. India Office MSS. Letter Book, No. 10.

1699 Arriving on the coast in July 1699, John Pitt refused to salute the Union Flag, flying over the Old Company's factory, 'believing the privilege of wearing it in their forts ceased by virtue of the late Act.' On the other hand he required that the same flag should be lowered as a compliment to himself. Thomas Pitt replied that by the new Act the Old Company retained its full rights till 1701, and that if the new President chose to offer the first salute, it would be returned 'according to custom and good manners.'[1]

At this moderate answer John Pitt flared out and sent back an insulting message in which he attributed the Governor's conduct 'in part to the heat of the country which has altered your temper.' It was a false move, and from this time Thomas Pitt showed him no mercy. He forbade any Englishmen in the Old Company's service 'to obey or regard any summons . . . from Mr. John Pitt or any one else under the pretence of his being a President for the New Company or a Consul.' Privately he wrote and advised a progressive course of study in Æsop's fables, warned him that if he had occasion to pass by Fort St. George he must behave himself very civilly, 'with no drums, flags nor trumpets within our bounds, for there shall be but one Governor whilst I am here,' and concluded with the contemptuous words: 'When the Moors have banged you and stripped you of what you have, upon your submission and begging pardon for what you have done, I may chance to protect

[1] O.C. 6687, 6688. India Office MSS.

you.'[1] The unfortunate agent of the New Company, morbidly self-conscious of his dignity, was goaded into desperation by such treatment. But he only floundered more deeply into the morass, and his subsequent conduct of affairs was one long series of disastrous failures.

In the record of the New Company's vicissitudes, the most important incident remains to be related. Reference has already been made to the provision of the Act of 1698, which sanctioned the despatch of an ambassador to the East.[2] In the war of contemporary pamphleteers that heralded the birth of the New Company, opponents of the old régime clamoured for the maintenance of an Embassy at the Imperial Court as an alternative to the possession of 'forts' or 'cautionary towns,'[3] and, in spite of Sir Josia Child's warning that the plan was impossible in countries where His Majesty 'hath no alliance nor can have any by reason of their distance or barbarity,'[4] the idea had become a main pillar in the trade policy of the New Company. Within a few days of their first meeting the Court proceeded to choose an ambassador. Four names were submitted to the adventurers, and though an influential party intrigued on behalf of a peer of the realm, Lord Howard of Escrick, the choice of the majority fell upon a member of the Lower House, William Norris, M.P. for Liverpool.[5] He was created a

[1] Hedges' *Diary*, vol. iii. pp. 43, 44, 46-49.

[2] *Ante*, p. 322.

[3] Somer's *Tracts*, vol. viii. ed. 1812, p. 469. Charles Davenant, *Works*, 5 vols. ed. 1771, vol. ii. p. 130.

[4] *A Discourse about Trade*, 1690, pp. 80, 81.

[5] Court Book, 37*a*, under date 4 October, 1698, India Office MSS. Narcissus Luttrell, *Brief Historical Relation*, vol. iv. p. 438.

baronet by Letters Patent,[1] and his salary, to be paid by the Company, was fixed first at 1,500*l.*, and finally at 2,000*l.* He was to be accompanied by a secretary—his own brother, Dr. Edward Norris, a chaplain, a surgeon, seven 'musicians,' and a large retinue of personal attendants, some of whom were to be clad in gorgeous liveries of scarlet cloth, trimmed with gold and silver lace.[2]

The Old Company watched these preparations with feelings of grave apprehension, and at one time determined to send an emissary of their own to India as a counteracting influence. For this purpose they selected Dr. Charles Davenant, M.P. for Great Bedwin, eldest son of that Sir William Davenant who as Court poet had sung the praises of princely interlopers in the disastrous days of Charles I.[3] An eminent controversialist on political and commercial subjects, Davenant, in his defence of the Old Company had stumbled on economic doctrines which seem to foreshadow the conclusions of a later age, and had proclaimed in notable and prophetic words that whatever country obtained 'the full and undisputed possession' of the India trade would 'give law to all the commercial world.'[4] It was intended that he should establish a Court of Admiralty and advise the Company's agents on their conduct

[1] Chetham Society's Publications, vol. ix. p. 40. Norris writes to his brother that the Lords Justices 'were pleased to say my character as the King's ambassador extraordinary required it.'

[2] Court Book, 37*a*, pp. 38, 57, 59, 80. India Office MSS. Narcissus Luttrell, vol. iv. p. 451.

[3] *Ante*, pp. 32, 33.

[4] *Works*, ed. 1771, vol. i. p. 94.

towards the Ambassador and the Consuls.[1] But in the end the Directors decided that his mission was unnecessary and resolved to rely on the unaided efforts of their servants.

The Embassy made an unfortunate beginning.[2] It was left to the ambassador's discretion to select a port of disembarkation. John Pitt, who coveted the distinction of entertaining the King's representative in his own presidency, strongly urged him to land at Masulipatam, and in an evil hour Norris listened to his advice. He disembarked September 25, 1699, hailing as a happy omen for his success that it was upon the same day of the month that Sir Thomas Roe had landed at Surat eighty-four years before.[3] Sept. 1699

The Emperor was at this time encamped at the head of the Mughal armies in the heart of the Maratha country, so that the selection of Masulipatam as a starting point for the expedition was a piece of fatuous folly thoroughly characteristic of the 'crack-brained' President of the New Company. More astonishing is the fact that it took Sir

[1] The gossip of the time said that Davenant was to receive as a reward 10,000*l.*, and as much more when he returned. Luttrell, vol. iv. p. 637. Davenant himself discusses the question of his mission. *Works*, vol. ii. pp. 159–161.

[2] The chief authority for the Embassy is Norris' Letter Book, which is preserved in the India Office, and forms vols. 19 and 20 of the collection known as Miscellaneous Factory Records. The Bodleian Library possesses the Diary of Sir William Norris from 12 September, 1699 to 23 April, 1701. Rawlinson MSS., C. 912, 913.

[3] Letter of Norris to Court of Directors, 11 March, 1700, Miscellaneous Factory Records, No. 19, p. 67. India Office. The actual date of Roe's landing seems to have been September 26; see Mr. William Foster's *Embassy of Sir T. Roe*, vol. i. p. 46.

William Norris several months to realise that a journey of nine hundred miles across the troubled scene of the Deccan seething with civil strife and commotion was an impossibility. His sanguine mind anticipated a sort of triumphal progress, 'We shall march like a small army,' he wrote . . . believe I shall set out in a greater state and equipage than ever any European ambassador yet appeared in India.' He fondly believed that even the machinations of the Old Company's servants who were 'fully resolved . . . to sacrifice the nation's honour and the trade itself to their own malice and revenge . . . would vanish like clouds before the sun when I come to make my appearance.'[1]

For months he remained at Masulipatam at the cost of a ruinous drain on the Company's exchequer, resolutely refusing to sacrifice one iota of the full pageantry which he considered due to his rank. Gradually, however, it dawned upon him that John Pitt was utterly unable to fulfil his oft-renewed and specious promises of an escort and supplies. Letters from Sir Nicholas Waite, who urged him to come to Surat, and commented upon the President's conduct in no measured terms, finally drew away the veil from his eyes.

Aug. 1700 For want of a ship he was unable to embark till August 23, having thus wasted nearly a year without advancing a step towards the attainment of his object. Ill luck still dogged him. The

[1] Letter to James Vernon, Secretary of State, 11 March, 1700, Miscellanous Factory Records, No. 19, pp. 56-61.

voyage which was usually reckoned to take six weeks, through contrary winds lasted three months and a half, and he only landed at Swally Dec. 10. Dec. 1700
At Surat, with his incorrigible love of display, he squandered 1,800 gold mohurs in bribes to the Mughal Governor and his officials, to procure the honour of a public entry into the town.

Preparations for the expedition were now rapidly pushed forward, and on January 26, 1701, Jan. 1701
Norris started from Surat with a train of sixty Europeans and three hundred natives bearing many curious and costly presents, with an especial gift of twelve brass cannon, which the Directors fondly hoped 'would sound loud in the Emperor's ears, and prevail with him to grant whatever you shall have occasion to ask.'[1]

The route to be followed lay south-east of Surat, for the Emperor was engaged in the siege of a Maratha stronghold known as Panalla Fort, half-way between Kolapur and Bijapur. A journey of thirty-eight days along terribly rough roads brought the ambassador to Brampore, the modern Burhanpuri, four hundred and seventy miles from his starting point. At this town Asad Khan, the Grand Vizier of the Empire, lay encamped. Norris sued for an audience, but stipulated that he should be allowed to come with his drums beating and trumpets playing. This condition was refused by the haughty minister of Aurangzeb, and Norris in dudgeon declined the conference, thus wantonly

[1] Letter of the Court of Directors to Norris, 4 April 1699, Misc. Factory Records, No 19, p. 45.

incurring the enmity of the one person who might April 1701 have made the embassy a success. He reached Panalla[1] on April 4th. On the 28th an audience was granted and the embassy was marshalled in an elaborate procession which Norris has described with complacent exactness.[2] The etiquette of Aurangzeb's punctilious Court was so far relaxed out of compliment to the English that they were allowed 'to salute the Emperor after the same manner we would do our own king.'[3]

The aged Emperor received them graciously, and Farmans for the three Presidencies were readily promised. But Sir William Norris was destined to learn by bitter experience what delays and evasions could be created by the intriguing and venal satellites of an Oriental Court. The fluent promises remained unfulfilled. Aurangzeb amidst the clouds of rebellion and civil strife, the secret whispers of remorse, and the ever-gnawing sense of ultimate failure that darkened the end of his long life, had little thought to spare for the representatives of those Western traders whose settlements fringed the coasts of his vast dominions. In one respect only they seemed to touch the vital interests of the Empire. On them had been laid the duty of patrolling the ocean highway followed by Mughal vessels that crept with their living freights of pilgrims to the sacred shrine of Mecca. Imperial posts from the western seaports were ever bringing tidings that this duty was but ill fulfilled.

[1] Misc. Factory Records, No. 20, p. 34.

[2] *Idem*, p. 61 *seq.*

[3] Letter to Sir Nicholas Waite, 29 April, 1701. *Idem*, p. 69.

And here once again appeared the baleful influence of Sir Nicholas Waite's meddlesome interference. Long before the embassy appeared he had sent despatches to the Emperor requesting privileges for the Presidency of Surat, and offering to guarantee in return the suppression of piracy on the Indian seas. This proposal now returned to Aurangzeb's recollection. After weeks of tedious negotiation and chicanery his demands were crystallised into an ultimatum. Farmans should be granted for all three Presidencies, but only on condition that Sir Nicholas Waite's unauthorised offer was carried into effect.

To this Sir William Norris would not, and indeed could not, agree. The question was complicated by an already existing arrangement of a semi-international character. The English, French, and Dutch settled in Surat had been compelled to sign a security bond for payment of the losses the Emperor's subjects might sustain from piratical depredations. A regular division of Eastern water-ways had been made between the three European nations. The Dutch were responsible for the protection of the coast from Surat to the Red Sea, the French for the Persian Gulf, and the English for the 'Southern Indian Seas,' by which was understood the waters that washed the Bengal and Coromandel coasts.[1] To have acceded to the Emperor's demand was equivalent to placing the whole burden on the Company's shoulders. The Dutch especially, wrote Norris, would have had

[1] Misc. Factory Records, No. 19, p. 97.

great reason to rejoice 'to have had such a thorn pulled out of their foot and stuck into ours.'[1] Had the ambassador been ever so willing to accept the condition, it was out of his power to do so. Sir Nicholas had not only compromised his colleague by his unauthorised offer to Aurangzeb, but was also mainly responsible for the fact that it could not be carried into effect. He had been escorted to India by four men-of-war which were to be employed in an attack on the pirates, but he had quarrelled with the commodore, and the officers of the fleet suspended all operations.[2]

In vain Norris offered a large bribe, a lac of rupees, if the Emperor would forego the impossible condition. He found his position being gradually undermined at the Court. Native Agents in the pay of the Old Company were busily intriguing against him. The Emperor professed to doubt, perhaps he really did doubt, which was the authorised Company. Imperial letters were sent to Seid Sedula, 'an holy priest at Surat,' asking for a report on the question. The rapidly dwindling resources of the Presidency were thus still further drained, for the priest let it be known that a sum of ten thousand rupees to be paid to himself was the price of a report favourable to the New Company.[3]

Matters now came to a crisis. To a final

[1] Misc. Factory Records, No. 20, p. 639.

[2] Bruce, *Annals*, vol. iii. pp. 264, 336, 337, 370. This fleet achieved nothing. Sir John Gayer afterwards reported in a private letter to the Court that three of the vessels were sent home with cargoes of goods to the account of Sir Nicholas Waite, while the fourth went down in a storm in the distant China seas.

[3] Misc. Factory Records, No. 20, p. 283. India Office MSS.

appeal the Emperor sent the curt message that unless he would accept the condition of the 'Seas' he 'knew the same way back to England that he came.'[1] The insult was more than the mortified ambassador could brook. He struck his tent and started homewards without waiting to take a personal leave of the Emperor. Messenger after messenger followed him from the Court calling upon him to return, and promising that negotiations should be reopened. But Norris was in no mood to be mocked and deluded further, and pressed on his way. Nov. 5, 1701

At Burhanpuri he found his path barred by an army of fifty thousand men, commanded by the Grand Vizier, Asad Khan, who drew a cordon round his little band. It seemed at first as though the Emperor had doomed them to annihilation. The ambassador drew up his handful of men in a hollow square, 'pointing our four guns four several ways,' and stood despairingly at bay. But the enemy made no attempt to attack. After an hour or two they sent a flag of truce with the assurance that they intended him no harm if he would engage not to continue his march for the present.[2] Chafing against the delay, the ambassador saw no course but to yield, and for two months and a half he was detained at Burhanpuri.[3] He gained nothing by his enforced sojourn. The Emperor did indeed send a letter and a sword to be presented to the Nov. 22, 1701, to Feb. 7, 1702

[1] Misc. Factory Records, No. 20, p. 566.

[2] *Idem*, pp. 609–612.

[3] From 22 November, 1701 to 7 February, 1702. *Idem*, pp. 609-667.

King of England, but on the more important question of trade rights, Norris could obtain only a vague and unsatisfactory promise that Farmans should be sent.

March 1702 He reached Surat on March 12. The meanness of his reception, contrasting strongly with his pompous state entry fourteen months before, was eloquently emblematic of his failure.[1] An angry quarrel ensued between the ambassador and Sir Nicholas Waite, to whose interference Norris, with some reason, attributed the disastrous results of his expedition. On the other hand the President accused him of incompetence, of gross extravagance, and of having broken off negotiations so abruptly that in the case of any European Power he 'would have obliged satisfaction to that sovereignty affronted, or engaged both States into breach of friendship, if not a war.'[2] Norris retorted that Waite was none of the 'best qualified judges of what was necessary for the support of the King's honour, especially in such points as concerned his ambassador.'[3] But he had made a serious technical error, which gave his relentless opponent a strong handle against him, for the twelfth article of his instructions forbade him to leave the Imperial Court till the President had given his consent.

In truth, the failure of the embassy was scarcely a matter for surprise. It was due in great part to

[1] Letter from Surat, 1 April, 1702. Misc. Factory Records, No. 5, p. 139. India Office.

[2] Letter of 1 December, 1701. *Idem*, No. 20, p. 595.

[3] *Idem*, p. 629.

the inherent difficulties of the undertaking. Sir William Norris himself was honest and conscientious. He had won a considerable reputation in the House of Commons, but he was never able to adapt himself, as did Sir Thomas Roe, to the utterly different political conditions of an Oriental despotism. With the 'weight of the King's honour and the Company's affairs pressing heavy' upon him, he lacked that pliability of disposition which knows instinctively when to yield and when to insist. He was too jealous of his personal dignity, and had little sense of economy. Even the servants of the Old Company gave him the nickname of 'Sir William Prodigality,'[1] and the cost of the embassy is said to have amounted to 676,880 rupees. His position, moreover, was an extremely anomalous one; though the King's representative, he was dependent on the various Presidencies for supplies of money, and during the whole of his journey he had to keep up a running controversy as to what was, and what was not, sufficient for his needs. In their hard struggle to carry on the trade, the Presidents of the New Company's settlements found it out of their power to satisfy his numerous demands; but the ambassador attributed their failure to want of will, and inveighed bitterly against those 'that posted me away with large promises and full assurances of supplies . . . without mature thought or consideration whether they were able to make their promises or assurances good.'[2]

[1] Letter from Surat, 18 October, 1701. Miscellaneous Factory Records, No. 5, p. 130.

[2] *Idem*, No 20, p. 136.

At a critical moment in the negotiations with the Emperor, a heavy blow fell upon him. In July 1700, when he was still waiting wearily at Masulipatam, he heard with a foreboding of despair the news that the bill to continue the Old Company a corporation was lying before Parliament. 'It absolutely contradicts,' he wrote, 'what I have in charge, and am instructed to acquaint the Great Mogul with, that the Old Company are to determine the 29th September, 1701.' He felt bitterly that Parliament was only too ready to play fast and loose with the India trade: 'really the honour of the nation is so far concerned in this last particular, not to mention a word of public faith and justice, that I cannot but hope and believe such a bill can never pass.'[1] But the dreaded news of its passing reached him at the Imperial Court. The fact was blazoned abroad by the agents of the Old Company. The complicated provisions of the Act were so ambiguous as to cause difficulties of interpretation even in England. The laboured explanations of the baffled ambassador must have seemed to the Mughal officers the shufflings of a detected pretender. It was at least clear that the New Company had no longer a monopoly of Parliamentary support, and that the Old Company was not to be dissolved. Parted from the colleagues whom he might have consulted, and himself in doubt as to the full scope and meaning of the Act, Sir William Norris must have recognised in this

[1] Misc. Factory Records, No. 19. Letter to Sir Edward Littleton, 23 July, 1700.

last stroke of fate the death knell of any yet lingering hope of success.

The only wish of Sir William Norris was now to leave India as soon as possible. He could not even find a passage on any ship belonging to the Company, but was obliged to embark on the 'Scipio,' a vessel belonging to a Separate Trader. Worn out with physical illness and mental anxiety he died at sea October 10th, before reaching St. Helena. The last few weeks of his life were spent in composing with feverish energy an elaborate vindication of his conduct to be laid before the Court of Directors.

May 1702

Oct. 1702

Sir Nicholas Waite and the ambassador might hurl mutual recriminations at each other. The servants of the Old Company as impartial lookers-on did not stop to mete out to each his exact measure of responsibility, but declared roundly that 'never two men with such public characters have done the nation so much dishonour as Sir William and Sir Nicholas.'[1] Indeed, the Mughal Empire still had enough vitality and enough internal coherency to make a breach with the Emperor a serious thing. The hurtful effects of Sir Nicholas Waite's accusations of piracy against the Old Company, coupled with the ambassador's refusal to take the whole burden of protecting the seas upon his masters' shoulders, were felt throughout the length and breadth of India. Imperial proclamations were issued that the goods and persons of the English should be seized.[2] On the Western coast,

[1] Misc. Factory Records, No. 5. Letter from Surat, 18 October, 1701.

[2] The Emperor's rescript was dated 16 November, 1701, eleven

the captivity of the Old Company's servants at Surat was rendered still more stringent. In Bengal the blow fell mainly on the New Company. Their factors were arrested in the defenceless up-country stations, while their rivals, with the greater part of their property, found immunity behind the newly erected ramparts of Fort William. In Southern India the Nawab of the Carnatic marched with a formidable force against Madras and subjected it to a severe three months' siege, memorable for the brilliant defence and intrepid conduct of Thomas Pitt.[1]

Feb. and March 1702

Feb. to May 1702

To such a disastrous state were the fortunes of the English in India reduced in the spring of the year 1702. It is usual to represent both sides in the struggle as equally exhausted. But though sadly shattered the Old Company had weathered the storm. Long experience and permanency of settlement had turned the scale in their favour. In Bengal and on the Coromandel coast they had decidedly carried the day. They had seen the New Company's embassy set forth with grandiose aims and brilliant hopes only to end in failure and discredit. On the Bombay seaboard their fortunes were indeed under a dark cloud, but this was at least as much due to the hostility of the Native Powers as the efforts of their rivals. Had the struggle lasted another year, it seems likely that the servants of the New Company would have been forced to relax their last hold on the Indian littoral.

days after the abrupt departure of Sir William Norris.

[1] The siege lasted from 6 February to 5 May, 1702.

The success of the Old Company was neutralised by the union which was announced in India some months later. To understand how that union was effected we must retrace our steps and resume the narrative of events in England.

The lull in the strife of the two Companies at home[1] was followed by a great upheaval of popular feeling. Parliament, which had stood prorogued from April 11, 1700, was dissolved December 19. April to Dec. 1700
It seemed not unlikely that Peers and Commons might again take into consideration the question of the India trade. Both Companies therefore threw themselves with fervid energy into the turmoil of the elections for the new Parliament which was to assemble at Westminster, February 6, 1701. If we are to credit the statements of contemporaries, this conflict of 'a few merchants' almost overshadowed in the popular imagination the grave question of Europe's impending convulsion in the war of the Spanish Succession. The combatants not only 'miserably divided the Capital City of this nation'[2] and made the election to the office of Lord Mayor a test of each other's strength,[3] but on the wider arena of national politics they threatened to absorb the two great historic divisions of the people. 'Whig and Tory,' writes a pamphleteer of the day, 'and all other parties are

[1] *Ante*, p. 335.

[2] *A Letter to a Member of Parliament*, London, 1701, p. 4. The writer is quoting from John Toland's *Art of Governing by Parties*.

[3] The election for Lord Mayor in October 1700 was memorable for the partisanship displayed by the Companies. Historical MSS. Commission Report 10. Appendix iv. p. 450.

swallowed up by them, not abolished, which were to be wished, but sheltered under these new names.' [1]

Dec. 1700–Jan. 1701 To the rivalry of the Companies was attributed the beginning of corruption at elections 'by private entertainments, public feasts, and bribes,' a custom hitherto 'unknown and believed impossible.' [2] Wire-pullers, it was said, sat in Jonathan's or Garraway's famous coffee-house buying rotten boroughs from needy county magnates. Merchants and shopkeepers posted down from London, and were returned by country constituencies in the interest of the respective Companies. A new term 'Parliament-jobbing' was coined, to designate this degradation of politics by the gamblers of commerce. Moralists contemplated with strong disapproval the stir in the nation. 'An election for Parliament is now in progress,' says one writer, 'but the grand question' about any candidate 'is *not* as it ought to be, Is he a man of sense, of religion, of honesty, and estate? But what Company is he for, the New or the Old?' [3] Men began to fear that in time the disastrous rivalry of the disputants would 'clog the wheels of government' and seriously impair our naval strength. Public business was often at a stand, 'what heats and animosities have been caused by this Division? What distractions in the public councils? Our elections are not free, neither our debates of Parliament.' Better the

[1] *A Letter to a Member of Parliament, ut supra*, p. 5.

[2] *Idem*, p. 5.

[3] *The Freeholders' Plea against Stock-jobbing Elections of Parliament-men*, 1701, pp. 7–10.

abolition of both Companies, and the establishment of an open trade, that the kingdom might be 'once again in peace.'[1]

Contemporaries no doubt viewed the trend of events through a somewhat distorting haze, but unquestionably in the new Parliament the India interest was largely represented. The New Company boasted that seven of their Directors, two of whom were elected for the City of London, had found seats, 'besides several others that are considerable subscribers.'[2]

But William III., with eyes ever rivetted on the war-cloud that was gathering over Europe, had no wish to see a commercial controversy engrossing the time and energies of Parliament, for whom he had other work in prospect. He hoped to have the question settled outside the walls of Westminster Hall. Accordingly through James Vernon, Secretary of State, he reminded the Old Company of their former promise to himself and desired to know what steps had been taken towards a union. The Directors dared not ignore the royal hint. General Court meetings of both Companies were held in December 1700, and January 1701, and seven representatives on each side were again elected to meet in conference. But before any definite issue emerged the Old Company made one last effort to cut away the ground from under their rivals' feet. In April 1701, **Dec. 1700–Jan. 1701** **April 1701**

[1] *Considerations on the East India Trade*, 1701.

[2] Letter of the Directors to Sir William Norris, 13 Feb. 1701. Miscellaneous Factory Records, No. 20, p. 287. India Office MSS.

Parliament appointed a committee to receive proposals for clearing off the National Debt. The Directors of Leadenhall Street promptly offered to pay back within twenty months time the New Company's 1,663,000*l.*, and the Separate Traders 22,000*l.*, which together with their own subscription of 315,000*l.* made up the original 2,000,000*l.*, and take over the whole debt at an annual interest of five per cent.[1] The Old Company cherished the greater hopes of success because on April 14 the Commons had carried to the bar of the Lords articles of impeachment against the most prominent Whig leaders, and amongst them Charles Montague, Earl of Halifax, to whose initiative and support when Chancellor of the Exchequer the New Company largely owed its existence.[2] But though the committee reported in favour of the proposal the House rejected it.

1701–2 Baffled in this their last appeal to the legislature, the Old Company resumed negotiations with their opponents. For nearly a year nothing came of the interminable conferences of the Committees of Seven, despite the mediation of Sir Basil Firebrace, a man of whom little is known, but who probably played an important part in the secret history of his time. An adept at every form

[1] *Journals of the House of Commons.* Rawlinson MSS., A. 302, fol. 372, Bodleian Library. The Company's proposals to Parliament dated 30 April, 1701.

[2] Letter of the Directors to Bombay, 6 May, 1701; Letter Book, No. 10. India Office MSS. 'The great friends of the New Company, and whoformed them and their Act have been lately impeached by Parliament.' For Montague's part in founding the New Company, see *Memoirs of Charles, Earl of Halifax*, 1715, p. 52 *seq.*

of discreditable intrigue, he had stained his hands by the acceptance of secret service money from Charles II. In April, he came forward with proposals for an agreement, and the Directors of the Old Company promised to pay him an immense reward[1] if a settlement were concluded before 29th September, 1701. Why the Court should employ a man of such antecedents, and above all, why they should offer so disproportionate a recompense, remains a mystery. But Sir Basil had been an important go-between for the Company in the bribery and corruption of 1694,[2] and it may perhaps be conjectured that he was again employed as an agent for the distribution of money to influential persons. He failed to bring about an agreement within the specified time and the year drew to a close with the question still unsolved.[3] June 1701

[1] Court Minutes of the Old Company for 23 April and 6 June, 1701. Court Book No. 20. India Office MSS. It was agreed that Sir Basil Firebrace should be allowed to purchase 150,000*l.* of stock at 80*l.* per cent.

[2] *An Exact Collection of the Debates and Proceedings in Parliament in* 1694 *and* 1695 *upon the Enquiry into the late Briberies and Corrupt Practices*, 1695, pp. 25, 30, 31, 33-37.

[3] The Company were not easily quit of Sir Basil Firebrace, and though the union was not completed by the time agreed upon, they had in the end to pay him almost the full amount promised. On 26 September, 1701, he applied for an extension of the time allowed him: this the Court refused, though they promised him vaguely such a recompense as might seem proper. When the union was an accomplished fact, Sir Basil claimed the fulfilment of the original bargain, whereupon the Court informed him that 'the covenants entered into between him and the Company, 6 June, 1701, did determine on 29 September, 1701, and were therefore void.' As a result Firebrace brought a Chancery action against the Company, but in June 1705 the Court compromised the matter by agreeing to pay him 1½ per cent. on the whole stock of the Company. He received a

1702 But in the first few weeks of 1702 it became clear that the union could not be much longer postponed. To this many causes contributed. The King, Parliament, and the Nation were growing utterly weary of the ceaseless strife. Against both Companies alike came flooding up once more the old waves of prejudice and hatred on the crest of which the New Company had been borne to power. Many of those who supported it then had been bitterly disappointed since. A Regulated association was to have taken the place of a Joint-Stock. The old bad monopoly was to be abolished. A new era was to dawn for English manufactures. But these fair promises had proved illusory. A small band of Separate Traders struggling feebly and ineffectually against the two great corporations was all that remained of the regulated basis of the General Society. The market was flooded with Indian goods. For some time past a fierce clamour had been rising among the mercers of Cheapside and the weavers of Spitalfields to whom it seemed that the Companies were 'striving hard which shall ride on the fore horse, but both agreed to drive on to our ruin.'[1] Pamphleteers of the day prophesied that the injury to home manufactures would 'produce empty purses,

first instalment of 2,500*l.* in July 1705, and a further sum of 21,119*l.* in the following month. See the Court Minutes of the Old Company, 26 and 27 September, 1701, 19 June, 3 November, 1702, 12 February, 1703, and for June, July and August 1705. Court Books, 38, 39 and 40. India Office MSS.

[1] *A True Relation of . . . the East India Trade, showing how their manufactures have been, are, and will be prejudicial to the manufactures of England.* No date but circ. 1700.

empty houses, empty towns, a small, poor, weak and slender people.'[1]

Parliament was again and again petitioned to legislate against the importation of Indian silks. In vain had Davenant some years before exposed the economic fallacy of such a policy by arguments that might have been forged in the armoury of Adam Smith. 'Trade,' he wrote, 'is in its nature free, finds its own channel, and best directeth its own course. . . . Governments in relation to it are to take a providential care of the whole, but generally to let second causes work their own way . . . in the main all Traffics whatsoever are beneficial to a country . . . Few laws relating to trade are the mark of a nation that thrives by traffic.'[2] The writer was half a century before his time and his appeals went unheeded. Parliament passed two Acts, which both obtained the Royal assent on the 11th of April, prohibiting the wear of Indian April 1700 wrought silks in England after the 29th September, 1701, and laying heavy dues on their importation.[3] The Directors of the Companies themselves always consistently declared that it was this 'heavy load upon the trade,' together with the glut in the market caused by the competition of two sets of

[1] *An English Winding-sheet for the East India Manufactors*, 1700.

[2] Davenant's *Works*, ed. 1771, vol. i. pp. 98, 99. The anonymous author of *Considerations on the East India Trade*, 1701, also inveighed against these protective tariffs, with remarkable ability. The Tract well repays perusal and won the high praise of Lord Macaulay, who declared it was 'excellent, first-rate. I have seen nothing of that age equal to it.'

[3] Acts 11 and 12 Gul. iii. c. 3 and 10.

sellers of Indian wares, that more than anything else impelled them to a union.[1]

Thus the opposition of the Old Company was gradually beaten down. They had indeed on the whole, as we have seen, prevailed in India, and Thomas Pitt afterwards upbraided them for being over-hasty in concluding the union,[2] but even in the East it was a Pyrrhic triumph, a political rather than a commercial victory, which had burdened their settlements with a heavy load of debt. Their comparative success abroad was counterbalanced by the state of affairs at home, for the truth is that, in spite of all their efforts, they had never quite been able to persuade the nation that their position was as stable as that of their rivals, behind whom seemed always to loom the patronage and support of Parliament. Throughout the period of conflict Old stock always stood lower than New. Even in April 1700, when it went up to 149 on the passing of their Bill, that of their opponents did not fall below 151.[3]

Finally the prospect of the great European

[1] Letter of the New Company, 12 April, 1700, to Sir Edward Littleton, Letter Book No. 11, and of the Old Company, 5 March, 1702, to Bengal, Letter Book No. 10. India Office MSS.

[2] Hedges' *Diary*, vol. iii. p. 103. Thomas Pitt writes to the Court of Directors that if resistance had been continued 'there had not by this been a New Company's man in the land of the living in these parts.' 19 September, 1706.

[3] Luttrell's *Brief Historical Relation*, vol. iv. p. 633. Also Houghton's list, already mentioned (*ante*, p. 633), printed in Thorold Rogers' *History of Agriculture and Prices*, vol. vi. pp. 721–725. From this table the value of the stock of both companies can be compared from 1698–1705. Immediately before the union (Ap. 27, 1702), the Old Company's stock stood at 84½, the New at 129¼.

struggle, daily becoming more and more imminent, forced both Companies to realise the folly of mutual dissensions. Even at this early period the danger from French rivalry was dimly foreseen. For the 'fair mistress' of the India trade the English and the Dutch seemed still the principal rivals, but France wrote Davenant 'stands by subtle, insinuating, and liberal, ready either to court or to force a favour.'[1] Even should she prove impotent in the East, her privateers would prey on the homeward-bound Indian fleets as they beat up the Bay of Biscay or English Channel. Strong convoys would be needed, and the King perhaps might withhold his aid if his wishes were persistently disregarded.

Exactly a week before the declaration of war with France and Spain, the Instrument of Union was ratified by the General Court of both Companies, 27th of April, 1702. By this agreement **April 1702** a court of twenty-four Managers was appointed, of whom twelve were to be elected by each Company. They were to have the real control over the settlements for the future, and to superintend the 'united,' i.e. the active trade, fixing the total amount of annual exports half of which was to be provided by each Company. At the same time the factors of both Companies were to manage the separate stocks sent out before the date of the union and were allowed seven years to clear all debts and wind up their affairs. At the end of that time the London Company was to

[1] Davenant's *Works* (ed. 1771), vol. ii. pp. 187–8.

convey the islands of Bombay and St. Helena to the English Company and resign their charter to the Queen; thenceforward the charter of the English Company was to be considered that of both, and the name of the amalgamated associations was to be 'The United Company of Merchants of England Trading to the East Indies.'

The legal charter of union took the form of an Indenture Tripartite between the Queen and the two Companies, and was dated July 22nd, 1702. The Old Company was to buy 673,000*l.* additional stock in the General Society so as to make their share equal to that of the New Company. The dead stock, i.e. houses, factories and forts of the Old Company, were valued at 330,000*l.* and of their rivals at 70,000*l.*, and the latter were called upon to pay 130,000*l.*, so as to equalise matters. The details of this transaction were settled by another deed bearing the same date, styled the Indenture Quinque-Partite of Conveyance of the Dead-stock of the Two East India Companies.[1]

July 1702

Letters were promptly despatched to the East calling on the servants of both sides to 'consult and act jointly for our future mutual advantage.' But it proved easier to sign legal documents in England than to sheath the sword in India where men had to deal with grim realities. The fierce flames of enmity so assiduously fanned in the past by warlike despatches from home were

[1] For fuller details of these two documents see Bruce, *Annals*, vol. iii. pp. 485-492. The original of the former is preserved in the India Office.

not to be extinguished at the mere word of command. One instance of the past strife reveals the spirit in which it had been waged. When Sir William Norris landed at Surat, in revenge for some fancied insult, he arrested three members of the Old Company's council and handed them over in irons to the Mughal Governor. And when Thomas Pitt heard of it, he penned the ferocious aspiration ''tis pity there was never a Felton amongst them;'[1] thus the one side disregarded the tie of a common nationality, the other appealed to the assassin's knife. Antagonists of this stamp, men who for three years had opposed each other by every weapon legal or illegal that came to hand, were suddenly called upon to act together under the formal sanction of a paper union and to 'bury all that is past in silence and forgetfulness.'[2] It was not perhaps surprising that for some years the wheels of administration refused to run smoothly. There were other difficulties than those engendered by personal feuds and animosities. The form of provisional union adopted was, perhaps unavoidably so, a tissue of complexities—a compromise so clumsy as to be almost unworkable. At home three Courts of Twenty-four were meeting simultaneously, for besides the Court of Managers both Old and New Company continued to elect Directors
till 1708, three sets of despatches were sent to 1702–1708
India, and in every factory three stocks had to be managed and three interests conciliated.

[1] Hedges' *Diary*, vol. iii. p. 61.

[2] Letter of the Old Company to Bengal, 5 March, 1702. Letter Book No. 10. India Office MSS.

The history of the two Companies from 1702 till the final consummation of the union may be very briefly summarised. Both at home and abroad a period of torpor succeeded the storm and stress of the past four years. In the instructions sent to India for the future direction of the trade the Court of Managers recognised the superior merit of the Old Company's representatives. In two out of the three Presidencies they were promoted to the chief place, while in the third the Court avoided giving power to the New Company's President by placing both him and his rival on a dignified shelf and establishing a rotation government. The Consular powers were rescinded ; it was tardily recognised that they ought never to have been granted at all.

On the western coast of India Sir John Gayer was appointed Governor of Bombay, and Sir Nicholas Waite was relegated to the subordinate post of the Presidency of Surat. But circumstances prevented the realisation of the Court's intentions. In the event of Sir John Gayer being still imprisoned, Waite was ordered to act temporarily for him, and in the meantime to spare no pains to effect his release. The unscrupulous President of Surat understood the strength of his position and abused it. So far from announcing to the Mughal Governor that Sir John Gayer was now the chosen Chief for the United Company, he offered him, as it afterwards transpired, a heavy bribe to keep the unfortunate man in confinement. Thus left supreme, for six more years he continued his

carnival of misrule. Appeals from home went disregarded. The New Company's factory passed utterly from under his control and became a byword for disorder. Drunken broils and duels were of daily occurrence. He outraged even the lax public opinion of the community by an incestuous marriage with his niece, and that though his wife was still living in England.[1] The patience of the Court of Managers was at last exhausted, and on the passing of the Act of Parliament to complete the union in 1708 they sent orders for his dismissal; 1708
but before the letters arrived in India his own council had been forced to place him under restraint.[2]

The fact that Sir John Gayer, 'the General of India,' did not obtain his release till 1710 testifies 1710
how low the prestige of the English had sunk since the days of Gerald Aungier. He embarked for April 1711
home, but the vessel on which he sailed was attacked by four French men-of-war west of Cape Comorin, and was forced to surrender after a desperate resistance. Sir John Gayer, who bore himself gallantly in the fight, died of his wounds a prisoner in the hands of the French.[3]

[1] Letters from the Old Company's agents at Surat, 20 April and 10 October, 1702, and 22 October, 1705. Misc. Factory Records, No. 5. India Office.

[2] Mr. G. W. Forrest, working from the Bombay Records, believes that Waite resigned and was not dismissed. *Selections from State Papers Bombay, Home Series*, vol. i. p. xxviii. But it is certain from the India Office MSS. that letters were sent out ordering him to lay down the Government, though he may possibly have resigned before they arrived. His dismissal was dated 20 April, 1708. India Office MSS., Letter Book No. 13.

[3] Letter of the Court to Bombay, 4 April, 1712. India Office MSS. Letter Book No. 14. The engagement was fought 3 April, 1711.

1702 On the coast of Coromandel Thomas Pitt was reappointed Governor of Fort St. George. He had proved himself adamant in the service of his masters and implacable in hostility to their rivals. But when the union was effected he wrote frankly to the New Company quoting a saying of William III. '"'Twas my fate and not my choice that made me your enemy" and since you and my masters are united, it shall be my utmost endeavour to purchase your good opinion and deserve your friendship.'[1] His strong and able rule had been the one bright spot in the general mismanagement of the past few years, and the New Company as a whole assented readily enough to his appointment, though a minority, among whom may be mentioned Gilbert Heathcote, still cherished against him an undying prejudice.[2]

The Court of Managers almost apologised for appointing John Pitt governor of Fort St. David with the reversion of the Presidency of Madras when it should become vacant. It was perhaps well for a peaceful settlement that John Pitt died in May
1703 1703, and left the Governor of Fort St. George supreme on the coast. 'Had he lived,' wrote the latter grimly, 'there would have been strange rotation work between him and me . . . 'twas impossible we could ever be reconciled. . . . I think him the ungratefullest wretch that ever was born. He is dead and there's an end.'[3]

[1] Hedges' *Diary*, vol. iii. p. 79.

[2] Letter of E. Harrison to Thomas Pitt, 25 July, 1707. Historical Manuscripts Commission, 13th Report, Appendix III. vol. i. p. 30.

[3] Hedges' *Diary*, vol. iii. p. 85.

In Bengal the Court of Managers elaborated a singularly complicated system of administration. Sir Edward Littleton and John Beard at the head of their councils were employed in winding up the affairs of the respective Companies, while the business of the United Trade was carried on by a third council composed of the four senior servants of each Company presided over on alternate weeks by Ralph Sheldon and Robert Hedges.

The Rotation Government tided over the period from the provisional to the fully consummated union, and indeed continued for a few years longer, but became notorious throughout India for incom-
petency. John Beard died July 7, 1705, having 1705
earned but scant recognition from the Old Company for his able services rendered to their cause. Sir Edward Littleton for some years continued his career of peculation and mismanagement. After long toleration the Court of Managers finally revoked his commission in January 1705, and
he fell a victim to the climate in October 1707. 1707
Godolphin's award records the fact that at the time of his death he owed the unfortunate Company that trusted him a sum of 80,000 Rs.[1]

It was well for the future reputation of the English name in India that the period of civil dissension and intestine strife fell exactly when it did. Twenty years earlier the Empire of Aurangzeb at the zenith of its power might have seized the opportunity to oust the disputants from their settlements in Hindustan. A few years later the

[1] Hedges' *Diary*, vol. ii. pp. 210-222.

Peace of Utrecht would have given the French leisure to profit by the division in the English camp. Even as it was the natural development and growth of the Presidencies was arrested or thrown back for years.

The time was now ripe for the final union. At home the cumbrous machinery of co-existent Courts of Directors with a superior Court of Managers had not worked smoothly. The latter, realising that the conflict of jarring interests would prove ruinous to the trade, voted in 1707 for an immediate and complete amalgamation, but the 'snake in the grass' was 'jealousy of power.' Each Company feared the other would obtain the preponderating influence. Bitter recriminations and sharp words ensued between the authorities on either side. There seemed a danger that even the partial union of 1702 would be dissolved.[1] But once again the State intervened. The Earl of Godolphin proposed to raise a loan of 1,200,000*l.* for the public service from the United Company, a plan which rendered it necessary that the union should first be effectually carried out. He urged both Companies to heal their differences for the sake of the public good and offered to mediate between them. Further, he plainly hinted that if they still proved recalcitrant there would not be wanting an outside body of private merchants who might play over again the part of the New Company in 1698.

[1] Letter from E. Harrison to Thos. Pitt, July 25, 1707; Hist. MSS. Commission, 13th Report, Appendix IV., vol. i. pp. 28–30.

There was no further delay. An Act of Parliament was rapidly passed through both Houses and received the Royal Assent, March 20, 1708.[1] It ordained that the Company should pay to the Exchequer the sum of 1,200,000*l.*, which, together with the former loan, made up a total of 3,200,000*l.* On this whole amount they were hereafter to receive interest only at the rate of 5 per cent., which produced exactly the same sum as the 8 per cent. on the original 2,000,000*l.* In return, the privileges of the Company were prolonged from three years' notice after September 29, 1711, to three years' notice after March 25, 1726. Both Companies were to submit all matters in dispute to the arbitration of the Earl of Godolphin, and were to bind themselves to accept his award. After the award the Managers of the United Trade were to become the first Board of Directors of the United Company. Among other provisions, the duty of 5 per cent. for the support of ambassadors was rescinded, and the Company were given the right to buy out the Separate Adventurers on three years' notice after 1711.[2] Thus perished the last vestiges of the regulated basis of the General Society.

March 1708

[1] *Journals of the House of Commons*, February 2, 19, 20, 24, and March 13, 17, 20, 1708.

[2] The stock of the Separate Traders amounted to 23,000*l.*, though the Old Company, apparently reckoning the New Company's capital at 1,663,000*l.*, instead of 1,662,000*l.*, which it really was, always estimated it at 22,000*l.* See *ante*, p. 366 and letter of the Court to Bombay, 28 July, 1699. Letter Book No. 10, India Office MSS. But there is a more important discrepancy which seems difficult to explain. In the New Company's charter the amount was estimated at only 7,200*l.*, and even the Act of 1708 always refers to this sum. See Macpherson, *European Commerce with India*, pp. 158, 161, 166.

The famous award was dated and published Sept. 1708 September 29th, 1708. It settled the details of the final amalgamation.

The chief provisions were that, as the debts of the Old Company exceeded their assets in India, they should pay to the United Company the sum of 96,615*l.*, and as the debts of the New Company fell short of their assets, they should receive from the United Company 66,005*l.* The debts of both Companies in England were to be discharged before the 1st of March, 1709.[1]

With the delivery of Godolphin's award an epoch in the history of the British connection with India is closed. Ever since the reign of Charles II., when the Company's sudden rise to an unexampled prosperity exposed it to a storm of envy and hatred, the problem had been to work out in Davenant's words 'a constitution, not defective but sound and wisely ordered, and such a one as may invite the people to venture largely in it.'[2] This had now been achieved. The erection of an antagonistic Company and its amalgamation with the older association had served at least to widen the basis of the Company that sprang from their union. At the same time the principle of a Joint-Stock 'by

[1] For the elaborate provisions of the Award see Bruce, *Annals*, vol. iii. pp. 667–671. The original document is preserved in the India Office. Too much must not be inferred to the prejudice of the Old Company's financial position from their large debts. The directors often complained that they were supposed to be insolvent because they borrowed money, whereas it was their practice to raise capital both in India and England by means of loans rather than by levies from the adventurers.

[2] Davenant's *Works*, vol. ii. p. 126.

which the wealth and strength of many are guided by the care and wisdom of a few,'[1] had been emphatically reaffirmed after a half-hearted and partial return to the regulated system. Even the immense loans to Government, though at first they were felt as a heavy burden, were like grappling irons binding the Company firmly to the rock of State. Henceforward the Government was faced with the prospect of having to find over three millions of money, if it desired to take away the privileges of the trade to the East. From time to time in the future as the formal periods of the Company's rights were extended or renewed, the old cry of opposition was raised, but never again with such volume or potency as in the past. In spite of modifications the constitution of the Company as now established lasted on the same in essentials, to the nineteenth century. The solution so painfully and slowly worked out possessed a durability that might have been lacking in a more facile compromise.

We have now traced the growth of an Elizabethan association of traders through more than a hundred years of manifold vicissitudes, of dearly bought successes, of cruel reverses and of ever-stubborn endeavour. Hated by those outside the pale, cramped and confined by the prejudices of a false political economy, used by sovereigns and statesmen for ends that were not its own, the Company had held on its course, with a dogged tenacity, beating off, neutralising, and absorbing

[1] Davenant's *Works*, vol. ii. p. 136.

opposition till it had won the highest constitutional recognition at home, and laid foundations in India that were destined not to pass away.

A right understanding of the first century of our history in India gives the key to the developments of later years. The success of the Dutch and the French Company was at the beginning far more imposing than our own, for they were cherished and nurtured by the power of the State. But they learnt to rely too exclusively upon that support, and when it was withheld, they fell.

The English Company, on the other hand, was in its inception almost wholly a private enterprise. It had, for the most part, to wrest its privileges from reluctant Kings and indifferent Parliaments, to work out its own salvation in the teeth of opposition and neglect. Later there came a change. In the middle of the eighteenth century, during the French wars the English Company was generously assisted by royal fleets and royal troops —a factor of almost incalculable value in securing the ultimate victory. But the Company profited by that assistance, because in its long, single-handed struggle it had learnt to rely upon itself, and to tide over the periods when the support of the State was either feeble or non-existent.

After the settlement of 1708 there followed thirty-six years of comparative obscurity. The Company rapidly receded from the prominent position in the public eye to which it leapt in 1701. But the time was one of silent inward development, of sound finance, and of commercial prosperity.

The brilliant attack launched by Dupleix and Labourdonnais upon the English settlements in 1746 stung into life a dormant and lethargic, but solid and growing power. At first there was the inevitable recoil before the *élan* and suddenness of the onslaught, but the counterstroke was delivered swiftly and fiercely, directed by the genius of Lawrence and Clive, but poised with all the pent-up strength of energies and resources matured in the quiet period of imperceptible growth. That period was rendered possible by Godolphin's award, which with extraordinary success welded the two Companies into one harmonious whole. It leaves the British in India on the brink of a new era. They had already begun to acquire garrisons, revenues, and territorial possessions. When Charles Eyre in 1697–98 took advantage of a rebellion in Bengal to build Fort William and obtain the rent of the three villages Sutanuti, Calcutta, and Govindpur, and when Thomas Pitt ten years later wrested from the Nawab of the Carnatic the grant of the 'five towns' in the neighbourhood of Madras, they were dimly shadowing forth the policy that conferred vast revenues and provinces upon the nation after the victories of Clive. At present these acquisitions were of small extent and passed almost unnoticed. The problems that involved the Company with Parliament in 1772 and 1781 had not as yet come within the furthest range of political prevision, but England had at least learnt to recognise that the 'business of India' was not 'merely trade, but a constant mixture of Trade and Warfare, Fortification, Military Prudence, and Political Government.' The Factory period was finally closed. Henceforward there was to be no retrograde step. Though they knew it not, and though the goal was far distant, the English in India had definitely entered upon the course which in its latter end was to merge into the overlordship of the peoples of Hindustan from Cape Comorin to the Himalayas.

END OF VOLUME II.

INDEX

A

C

D

E

F

G

H

I

J

K

L

M

N

P

Q

R

S

U

V

W

X

Y

Z

THE EARL OF MAYO.

(*Rulers of India Series.*)

THIRD THOUSAND. ONE VOL. 2*s.* 6*d.*

'A brief but admirable biography.'—TIMES.

'The world is indebted to the author for a fit and attractive record of what was eminently a noble life.'—ACADEMY.

(Oxford and London: The Clarendon Press.)

THE INDIAN EMPIRE:

ITS HISTORY, PEOPLE, AND PRODUCTS.

THIRD AND STANDARD EDITION. WITH MAP. Demy 8vo. 28*s.*

'Never before has the whole subject of Indian history been so adequately and so intelligibly treated.'—PALL MALL GAZETTE.

'A compact body of information arranged and classified on correct principles.' ACADEMY.

'A model of combined lucidity, conciseness, and comprehensiveness.'—ECONOMIST.

(London: Smith, Elder, & Co.)

THE IMPERIAL GAZETTEER OF INDIA.

SECOND EDITION. FOURTEEN VOLS.

(*Out of print.*)

'The publication of the "Imperial Gazetteer of India" marks the completion of the largest national enterprise in statistics which has ever been undertaken. . . . The volumes before us form a complete account of the country, its geography, topography, ethnology, commerce and products. . . . It is one of the grandest works of administrative statistics which have ever been issued by any nation.'—TIMES. (*Two notices.*)

'Dr. Hunter has rendered to the Indian Government and to English people generally the highest service a public servant could achieve.'—ATHENÆUM.

(London: Kegan Paul, Trench, Trübner, & Co., Limited.)

THE INDIAN MUSALMANS.

THIRD EDITION. 10*s.* 6*d.*

(*Out of print.*)

(London: Kegan Paul, Trench, Trübner, & Co., Limited.)

A STATISTICAL ACCOUNT OF BENGAL AND ASSAM.

IN TWENTY-TWO VOLS.

(*Out of print.*)

'Un ensemble d'efforts digne d'une grande nation, et comme aucune autre n'en a fait jusqu'ici de semblable pour son empire colonial.'—REVUE CRITIQUE.

'Twenty volumes of material, collected under the most favourable auspices, are built up under his hands into a vast but accessible storehouse of invaluable facts. Invaluable to the statesman, the administrator, and the historian, they are no less interesting to the general reader. Mr. Hunter undoubtedly has the faculty of making the dry bones of statistics live. But they also contain matter which may be regarded as the fountain of the yet unwritten history of Bengal. They are a guide for administrative action now. They also seem to be the point of a new departure for the future.'—NINETEENTH CENTURY.

(London: Kegan Paul, Trench, Trübner, & Co., Limited.)

FAMINE ASPECTS OF BENGAL DISTRICTS.

SECOND EDITION.

(*Out of print.*)

'One of the boldest efforts yet made by statistical science. . . . In this work he has laid down the basis of a system by which he may fairly claim that scarcity in Bengal has been reduced to an affair of calm administrative calculation.'—DAILY NEWS.

(London: Kegan Paul, Trench, Trübner, & Co., Limited.)

A LIFE OF BRIAN HOUGHTON HODGSON.

BRITISH RESIDENT AT THE COURT OF NEPAL.

14*s.*

'In this life of a great Indian civilian and scholar, Sir William Wilson Hunter has produced a work which might serve as a model for biographies of the kind.'—TIMES.

'A revelation of a remarkable and most interesting personality. A charming book.'
SCOTSMAN.

'Gracefully and tenderly written. . . . The story of Brian Hodgson is not only of interest to the man of affairs, the scholar, and the student of science, but it is a tale which appeals to all who can notice and appreciate genuine human qualities.'—ATHENÆUM.

(London: John Murray.)

A Classified Catalogue

OF WORKS IN

GENERAL LITERATURE

PUBLISHED BY

LONGMANS, GREEN, & CO.

39 PATERNOSTER ROW, LONDON, E.C.

91 AND 93 FIFTH AVENUE, NEW YORK. AND 32 HORNBY ROAD, BOMBAY.

CONTENTS.

INDEX OF AUTHORS AND EDITORS.

INDEX OF AUTHORS AND EDITORS—*continued.*

History, Politics, Polity, Political Memoirs, &c.

Abbott.—*A History of Greece.* By Evelyn Abbott, M.A., LL.D.

Part I.—From the Earliest Times to the Ionian Revolt. Crown 8vo., 10s. 6d.

Part II.—500-445 B.C. Crown 8vo., 10s. 6d.

Part III.—From the Peace of 445 B.C. to the Fall of the Thirty at Athens in 403 B.C. Crown 8vo., 10s. 6d.

Acland and Ransome.—*A Handbook in Outline of the Political History of England to* 1896. Chronologically Arranged. By the Right Hon. A. H. Dyke Acland, and Cyril Ransome, M.A. Crown 8vo., 6s.

Amos.—*Primer of the English Constitution and Government.* For the Use of Colleges, Schools, and Private Students. By Sheldon Amos, M.A. Cr. 8vo., 6s.

Annual Register (The). A Review of Public Events at Home and Abroad, for the year 1899. 8vo., 18s.

Volumes of the *Annual Register* for the years 1863-1898 can still be had. 18s. each.

Arnold.—*Introductory Lectures on Modern History.* By Thomas Arnold, D.D., formerly Head Master of Rugby School. 8vo., 7s. 6d.

Ashbourne.—*Pitt: Some Chapters on His Life and Times.* By the Right Hon. Edward Gibson, Lord Ashbourne, Lord Chancellor of Ireland. With 11 Portraits. 8vo., 21s.

Atkinson.—*Michel de l'Hospital:* being the Lothian Prize Essay for 1899. By C. T. Atkinson, Fellow of Exeter College, Oxford; formerly Demy of Magdalen College. Crown 8vo., 4s. net.

Baden-Powell.—*The Indian Village Community.* Examined with Reference to the Physical, Ethnographic, and Historical Conditions of the Provinces; chiefly on the Basis of the Revenue-Settlement Records and District Manuals. By B. H. Baden-Powell, M.A., C.I.E. With Map. 8vo., 16s.

Bagwell.—*Ireland under the Tudors.* By Richard Bagwell, LL.D. (3 vols.) Vols. I. and II. From the first invasion of the Northmen to the year 1578. 8vo., 32s. Vol. III. 1578-1603. 8vo., 18s.

Besant.—*The History of London.* By Sir Walter Besant. With 74 Illustrations. Crown 8vo., 1s. 9d. Or bound as a School Prize Book, 2s. 6d.

Brassey (Lord).—Papers and Addresses.

Naval and Maritime. 1872-1893. 2 vols. Crown 8vo., 10s.

Brassey (Lord) Papers and Addresses—*continued.*

Mercantile Marine and Navigation, from 1871-1894. Crown 8vo., 5s.

Imperial Federation and Colonisation from 1880-1894. Cr. 8vo., 5s.

Political and Miscellaneous. 1861-1894. Crown 8vo., 5s.

Bright.—*A History of England.* By the Rev. J. Franck Bright, D.D.

Period I. *Mediæval Monarchy:* A.D. 449-1485. Crown 8vo., 4s. 6d.

Period II. *Personal Monarchy.* 1485-1688. Crown 8vo., 5s.

Period III. *Constitutional Monarchy.* 1689-1837. Crown 8vo., 7s. 6d.

Period IV. *The Growth of Democracy.* 1837-1880. Crown 8vo., 6s.

Buckle.—*History of Civilisation in England, France, Spain, and Scotland.* By Henry Thomas Buckle. 3 vols. Crown 8vo., 24s.

Burke.—*A History of Spain, from the Earliest Times to the Death of Ferdinand the Catholic.* By Ulick Ralph Burke, M.A. Edited by Martin A. S. Hume. With 6 Maps. 2 vols. Crown 8vo., 16s. net.

Chesney.—*Indian Polity:* a View of the System of Administration in India. By General Sir George Chesney, K.C.B. With Map showing all the Administrative Divisions of British India. 8vo., 21s.

Churchill (Winston Spencer).

The River War: an Historical Account of the Reconquest of the Soudan. Edited by Colonel F. Rhodes, D.S.O. With 34 Maps and 51 Illustrations, also 7 Portraits. 2 vols. Medium 8vo., 36s.

The Story of the Malakand Field Force, 1897. With 6 Maps and Plans. Crown 8vo., 3s. 6d.

London to Ladysmith viâ Pretoria. With 3 Folding-out Maps and 1 Map and 4 Plans in the Text. Crown 8vo., 6s.

Corbett.—*Drake and the Tudor Navy,* with a History of the Rise of England as a Maritime Power. By Julian S. Corbett. With Portraits, Illustrations and Maps. 2 vols. Crown 8vo., 16s.

Creighton (M., D.D., Lord Bishop of London).

A History of the Papacy from the Great Schism to the Sack of Rome, 1378-1527. 6 vols. Cr. 8vo., 6s. each.

Queen Elizabeth. With Portrait. Crown 8vo., 6s.

History, Politics, Polity, Political Memoirs, &c.—*continued.*

Curzon.—*PERSIA AND THE PERSIAN QUESTION.* By the Right Hon. LORD CURZON OF KEDLESTON. With 9 Maps, 96 Illustrations, Appendices, and an Index. 2 vols. 8vo., 42*s.*

De Tocqueville.—*DEMOCRACY IN AMERICA.* By ALEXIS DE TOCQUEVILLE. Translated by HENRY REEVE, C.B., D.C.L. 2 vols. Crown 8vo., 16*s.*

Dickinson.—*THE DEVELOPMENT OF PARLIAMENT DURING THE NINETEENTH CENTURY.* By G. LOWES DICKINSON, M.A. 8vo., 7*s.* 6*d.*

Froude (JAMES A.).

THE HISTORY OF ENGLAND, from the Fall of Wolsey to the Defeat of the Spanish Armada. 12 vols. Crown 8vo., 3*s.* 6*d.* each.

THE DIVORCE OF CATHERINE OF ARAGON. Crown 8vo., 3*s.* 6*d.*

THE SPANISH STORY OF THE ARMADA, and other Essays. Cr. 8vo., 3*s.* 6*d.*

THE ENGLISH IN IRELAND IN THE EIGHTEENTH CENTURY. 3 vols. Cr. 8vo., 10*s.* 6*d.*

ENGLISH SEAMEN IN THE SIXTEENTH CENTURY. Cr. 8vo., 6*s.*

THE COUNCIL OF TRENT. Crown 8vo., 3*s.* 6*d.*

SHORT STUDIES ON GREAT SUBJECTS. 4 vols. Cr. 8vo., 3*s.* 6*d.* each.

CÆSAR: a Sketch. Cr. 8vo, 3*s.* 6*d.*

Gardiner (SAMUEL RAWSON, D.C.L., LL.D.).

HISTORY OF ENGLAND, from the Accession of James I. to the Outbreak of the Civil War, 1603-1642. 10 vols. Crown 8vo., 6*s.* each.

A HISTORY OF THE GREAT CIVIL WAR, 1642-1649. 4 vols. Cr. 8vo., 6*s.* each.

A HISTORY OF THE COMMONWEALTH AND THE PROTECTORATE. 1649-1660. Vol. I. 1649-1651. With 14 Maps. 8vo., 21*s.* Vol. II. 1651-1654. With 7 Maps. 8vo., 21*s.*

WHAT GUNPOWDER PLOT WAS. With 8 Illustrations. Crown 8vo., 5*s.*

CROMWELL'S PLACE IN HISTORY. Founded on Six Lectures delivered in the University of Oxford. Cr. 8vo., 3*s.* 6*d.*

Gardiner (SAMUEL RAWSON, D.C.L., LL.D.)—*continued.*

THE STUDENT'S HISTORY OF ENGLAND. With 378 Illustrations. Crown 8vo., 12*s.*

Also in Three Volumes, price 4*s.* each.
Vol. I. B.C. 55—A.D. 1509. 173 Illustrations.
Vol. II. 1509-1689. 96 Illustrations.
Vol. III. 1689-1885. 109 Illustrations.

Greville.—*A JOURNAL OF THE REIGNS OF KING GEORGE IV., KING WILLIAM IV., AND QUEEN VICTORIA.* By CHARLES C. F. GREVILLE, formerly Clerk of the Council. 8 vols. Crown 8vo., 3*s.* 6*d.* each.

HARVARD HISTORICAL STUDIES.

THE SUPPRESSION OF THE AFRICAN SLAVE TRADE TO THE UNITED STATES OF AMERICA, 1638-1870. By W. E. B. DU BOIS, Ph.D. 8vo., 7*s.* 6*d.*

THE CONTEST OVER THE RATIFICATON OF THE FEDERAL CONSTITUTION IN MASSACHUSETTS. By S. B. HARDING. A.M. 8vo., 6*s.*

A CRITICAL STUDY OF NULLIFICATION IN SOUTH CAROLINA. By D. F. HOUSTON, A.M. 8vo., 6*s.*

NOMINATIONS FOR ELECTIVE OFFICE IN THE UNITED STATES. By FREDERICK W. DALLINGER, A.M. 8vo., 7*s.* 6*d.*

A BIBLIOGRAPHY OF BRITISH MUNICIPAL HISTORY, INCLUDING GILDS AND PARLIAMENTARY REPRESENTATION. By CHARLES GROSS, Ph.D. 8vo., 12*s.*

THE LIBERTY AND FREE SOIL PARTIES IN THE NORTH WEST. By THEODORE C. SMITH, Ph.D. 8vo, 7*s.* 6*d.*

THE PROVINCIAL GOVERNOR IN THE ENGLISH COLONIES OF NORTH AMERICA. By EVARTS BOUTELL GREENE. 8vo., 7*s.* 6*d.*

THE COUNTY PALATINE OF DURHAM: a Study in Constitutional History. By GAILLARD THOMAS LAPSLEY, Ph.D. 8vo., 10*s.* 6*d.*

*** *Other Volumes are in preparation.*

Hammond.—*A WOMAN'S PART IN A REVOLUTION.* By Mrs. JOHN HAYS HAMMOND. Crown 8vo., 2*s.* 6*d.*

Historic Towns.—Edited by E. A. FREEMAN, D.C.L., and Rev. WILLIAM HUNT, M.A. With Maps and Plans. Crown 8vo., 3*s.* 6*d.* each.

Bristol. By Rev. W. Hunt.
Carlisle. By Mandell Creighton, D.D.
Cinque Ports. By Montagu Burrows.
Colchester. By Rev. E. L. Cutts.
Exeter. By E. A. Freeman.
London. By Rev. W. J. Loftie.
Oxford. By Rev. C. W. Boase.
Winchester. By G. W. Kitchin, D.D.
York. By Rev. James Raine.
New York By Theodore Roosevelt.
Boston (U.S.) By Henry Cabot Lodge.

History, Politics, Polity, Political Memoirs, &c.—*continued.*

Hunter.—*A History of British India.* By Sir William Wilson Hunter, K.C.S.I., M.A., LL.D. Vol. I.—Introductory to the Overthrow of the English in the Spice Archipelago, 1623. With 4 Maps. 8vo., 18*s.*

Joyce (P. W., LL.D.).

A Short History of Ireland, from the Earliest Times to 1603. Crown 8vo., 10*s.* 6*d.*

A Child's History of Ireland. From the Earliest Times to the Death of O'Connell. With specially constructed Map and 160 Illustrations, including Facsimile in full colours of an illuminated page of the Gospel Book of MacDurnan, A.D. 850. Fcp. 8vo., 3*s.* 6*d.*

Kaye and Malleson.—*History of the Indian Mutiny*, 1857-1858. By Sir John W. Kaye and Colonel G. B. Malleson. With Analytical Index and Maps and Plans. 6 vols. Crown 8vo., 3*s.* 6*d.* each.

Kent.—*The English Radicals*: an Historical Sketch. By C. B. Roylance Kent. Crown 8vo., 7*s.* 6*d.*

Lang.—*The Companions of Pickle*: Being a Sequel to 'Pickle the Spy'. By Andrew Lang. With 4 Plates. 8vo., 16*s.*

Lecky (The Rt. Hon. William E. H.)

History of England in the Eighteenth Century.

Library Edition. 8 vols. 8vo. Vols. I. and II., 1700-1760, 36*s.*; Vols. III. and IV., 1760-1784, 36*s.*; Vols. V. and VI., 1784-1793, 36*s.*; Vols. VII. and VIII., 1793-1800, 36*s.*

Cabinet Edition. England. 7 vols. Crown 8vo., 6*s.* each. Ireland. 5 vols. Crown 8vo., 6*s.* each.

History of European Morals from Augustus to Charlemagne. 2 vols. Crown 8vo., 12*s.*

History of the Rise and Influence of the Spirit of Rationalism in Europe. 2 vols. Crown 8vo., 12*s.*

Democracy and Liberty.

Library Edition. 2 vols. 8vo., 36*s.*
Cabinet Edition. 2 vols. Cr. 8vo., 12*s.*

Lowell.—*Governments and Parties in Continental Europe.* By A. Lawrence Lowell. 2 vols. 8vo., 21*s.*

Lytton.—*The History of Lord Lytton's Indian Administration, from* 1876-1880. Compiled from Letters and Official Papers. Edited by Lady Betty Balfour. With Portrait and Map. 8vo., 18*s.*

Macaulay (Lord).

Complete Works.

'Albany' Edition. With 12 Portraits. 12 vols. Large Crown 8vo., 3*s.* 6*d.* each.

'Edinburgh' Edition. 8 vols. 8vo., 6*s.* each.

Cabinet Edition. 16 vols. Post 8vo., £4 16*s.*

History of England from the Accession of James the Second.

Popular Edition. 2 vols. Cr. 8vo., 5*s.*
Student's Edition. 2 vols. Cr. 8vo., 12*s.*
People's Edition. 4 vols. Cr. 8vo., 16*s.*
'Albany' Edition. With 6 Portraits. 6 vols. Large Crown 8vo., 3*s.* 6*d.* each.
Cabinet Edition. 8 vols. Post 8vo., 48*s.*
'Edinburgh' Edition. 4 vols. 8vo., 6*s.* each.
Library Edition. 5 vols. 8vo., £4.

Critical and Historical Essays, with Lays of Ancient Rome, etc., in 1 volume.

Popular Edition. Crown 8vo., 2*s.* 6*d.*
Authorised Edition. Crown 8vo., 2*s.* 6*d.*, or gilt edges, 3*s.* 6*d.*
'Silver Library' Edition. With Portrait and 4 Illustrations to the 'Lays'. Cr. 8vo., 3*s.* 6*d.*

Critical and Historical Essays.

Student's Edition. 1 vol. Cr. 8vo., 6*s.*
People's Edition. 2 vols. Cr. 8vo., 8*s.*
'Trevelyan' Edition. 2 vols. Cr. 8vo., 9*s.*
Cabinet Edition. 4 vols. Post 8vo., 24*s.*
'Edinburgh' Edition. 3 vols. 8vo., 6*s.* each.
Library Edition. 3 vols. 8vo., 36*s.*

Essays, which may be had separately, sewed, 6*d.* each; cloth, 1*s.* each.

Addison and Walpole.	Frederick the Great.
Croker's Boswell's Johnson.	Ranke and Gladstone.
Hallam's Constitutional History.	Lord Bacon.
Warren Hastings.	Lord Clive.
The Earl of Chatham (Two Essays).	Lord Byron, and The Comic Dramatists of the Restoration.

Miscellaneous Writings.

People's Edition. 1 vol. Cr. 8vo., 4*s.* 6*d.*
Library Edition. 2 vols. 8vo., 21*s.*

Miscellaneous Writings, Speeches and Poems.

Popular Edition. Crown 8vo., 2*s.* 6*d.*
Cabinet Edition. 4 vols. Post 8vo., 24*s.*

Selections from the Writings of Lord Macaulay. Edited, with Occasional Notes, by the Right Hon. Sir G. O. Trevelyan, Bart. Crown 8vo., 6*s.*

History, Politics, Polity, Political Memoirs, &c.—*continued.*

Mackinnon.—*The History of Edward the Third.* By James Mackinnon, Ph.D., Lecturer on History in the University of St. Andrews. 8vo., 18s.

May.—*The Constitutional History of England* since the Accession of George III. 1760-1870. By Sir Thomas Erskine May, K.C.B. (Lord Farnborough). 3 vols. Cr. 8vo., 18s.

Merivale (Charles, D.D.).

History of the Romans under the Empire. 8 vols. Crown 8vo., 3s. 6d. each.

The Fall of the Roman Republic: a Short History of the Last Century of the Commonwealth. 12mo., 7s. 6d.

General History of Rome, from the Foundation of the City to the Fall of Augustulus, B.C. 753-A.D. 476. With 5 Maps. Crown 8vo, 7s. 6d.

Montague. — *The Elements of English Constitutional History.* By F. C. Montague, M.A. Crown 8vo., 3s. 6d.

Phillips.—*South African Recollections.* By Florence Phillips (Mrs. Lionel Phillips). With 37 Illustrations from Photographs. 8vo., 7s. 6d.

Powell and Trevelyan. — *The Peasants' Rising and the Lollards:* a Collection of Unpublished Documents, forming an Appendix to 'England in the Age of Wycliffe'. Edited by Edgar Powell and G. M. Trevelyan. 8vo., 6s. net.

Ransome.—*The Rise of Constitutional Government in England.* By Cyril Ransome, M.A. Crown 8vo., 6s.

Seebohm.—*The English Village Community* Examined in its Relations to the Manorial and Tribal Systems, etc. By Frederic Seebohm, LL.D., F.S.A. With 13 Maps and Plates. 8vo., 16s.

Sharpe.—*London and the Kingdom:* a History derived mainly from the Archives at Guildhall in the custody of the Corporation of the City of London. By Reginald R. Sharpe, D.C.L., Records Clerk in the Office of the Town Clerk of the City of London. 3 vols. 8vo. 10s. 6d. each.

Shaw.—*A History of the English Church during the Civil Wars and under the Commonwealth,* 1640-1660. By William A. Shaw, Litt.D. 2 vols. 8vo., 36s.

Smith.—*Carthage and the Carthaginians.* By R. Bosworth Smith, M.A., With Maps, Plans, etc. Cr. 8vo., 3s. 6d.

Statham.—*The History of the Castle, Town and Port of Dover.* By the Rev. S. P. H. Statham. With 4 Plates and 13 Illustrations. Crown 8vo., 10s. 6d.

Stephens. — *A History of the French Revolution.* By H. Morse Stephens. 8vo. Vols. I. and II. 18s. each.

Stubbs.—*History of the University of Dublin,* from its Foundation to the End of the Eighteenth Century. By J. W. Stubbs. 8vo., 12s. 6d.

Sutherland.—*The History of Australia and New Zealand,* from 1606-1890. By Alexander Sutherland, M.A., and George Sutherland, M.A. Crown 8vo., 2s. 6d.

Taylor.—*A Student's Manual of the History of India.* By Colonel Meadows Taylor, C.S.I., etc. Cr. 8vo., 7s. 6d.

Todd. — *Parliamentary Government in the British Colonies.* By Alpheus Todd, LL.D. 8vo., 30s. net.

Trevelyan.—*The American Revolution.* Part I. 1766-1776. By the Rt. Hon. Sir G. O. Trevelyan, Bart. 8vo., 16s.

Trevelyan.—*England in the Age of Wycliffe.* By George Macaulay Trevelyan. 8vo., 15s.

Wakeman and Hassall.—*Essays Introductory to the Study of English Constitutional History.* Edited by Henry Offley Wakeman, M.A., and Arthur Hassall, M.A. Crown 8vo., 6s.

Walpole.—*History of England from the Conclusion of the Great War in 1815 to 1858.* By Sir Spencer Walpole, K.C.B. 6 vols. Cr. 8vo., 6s. each.

Wood-Martin.—*Pagan Ireland: an Archæological Sketch.* A Handbook of Irish Pre-Christian Antiquities. By W. G. Wood-Martin, M.R.I.A. With 512 Illustrations. Crown 8vo., 15s.

Wylie (James Hamilton, M.A.).

History of England under Henry IV. 4 vols. Crown 8vo. Vol. I., 1399-1404, 10s. 6d. Vol. II., 1405-1406, 15s. (*out of print*). Vol. III., 1407-1411, 15s. Vol. IV., 1411-1413, 21s.

The Council of Constance to the Death of John Hus: Being the Ford Lectures delivered in the University of Oxford in Lent Term, 1900. Crown 8vo., 6s. net.

Biography, Personal Memoirs, &c.

Armstrong.—*The Life and Letters of Edmund J. Armstrong.* Edited by G. F. Savage Armstrong. Fcp. 8vo., 7s. 6d.

Bacon.—*The Letters and Life of Francis Bacon, including all his Occasional Works.* Edited by James Spedding. 7 vols. 8vo., £4 4s.

Bagehot.—*Biographical Studies.* By Walter Bagehot. Crown 8vo., 3s. 6d.

Boevey.—'*The Perverse Widow*': being passages from the Life of Catharina, wife of William Boevey, Esq., of Flaxley Abbey, in the County of Gloucester. Compiled by Arthur W. Crawley-Boevey, M.A. With Portraits. 4to., 42s. net.

Carlyle.—*Thomas Carlyle*: A History of his Life. By James Anthony Froude.
1795-1835. 2 vols. Crown 8vo., 7s.
1834-1881. 2 vols. Crown 8vo., 7s.

Cellini.—*Chisel, Pen, and Poignard*; or, Benvenuto Cellini, his Times and his Contemporaries. By the Author of 'The Life of Sir Kenelm Digby,' 'The Life of a Prig,' etc. With 19 Illustrations. Crown 8vo., 5s.

Crozier.—*My Inner Life*: being a Chapter in Personal Evolution and Autobiography. By John Beattie Crozier, Author of 'Civilisation and Progress,' etc. 8vo., 14s.

Dante.—*The Life and Works of Dante Allighieri*: being an Introduction to the Study of the 'Divina Commedia'. By the Rev. J. F. Hogan, D.D., Professor, St. Patrick's College, Maynooth. With Portrait. 8vo., 12s. 6d.

Danton.—*Life of Danton.* By A. H. Beesly. With Portraits of Danton, his Mother, and an Illustration of the Home of his family at Arcis. Crown 8vo., 6s.

Duncan.—*Admiral Duncan.* By The Earl of Camperdown. With 3 Portraits. 8vo., 16s.

Erasmus.—*Life and Letters of Erasmus.* By James Anthony Froude. Crown 8vo., 3s. 6d.

Faraday.—*Faraday as a Discoverer.* By John Tyndall. Crown 8vo, 3s. 6d.

Foreign Courts and Foreign Homes. By A. M. F. Crown 8vo., 6s.

Fox.—*The Early History of Charles James Fox.* By the Right Hon. Sir G. O. Trevelyan, Bart.
Library Edition. 8vo., 18s.
Cheap Edition. Crown 8vo., 3s. 6d.

Halifax.—*The Life and Letters of Sir George Savile, Baronet, First Marquis of Halifax.* By H. C. Foxcroft. 2 vols. 8vo., 36s.

Hamilton.—*Life of Sir William Hamilton.* By R. P. Graves. 8vo. 3 vols. 15s. each. Addendum. 8vo., 6d. sewed.

Havelock.—*Memoirs of Sir Henry Havelock, K.C.B.* By John Clark Marshman. Crown 8vo., 3s. 6d.

Haweis.—*My Musical Life.* By the Rev. H. R. Haweis. With Portrait of Richard Wagner and 3 Illustrations. Crown 8vo., 6s. net.

Hiley.—*Memories of Half a Century.* By the Rev. R. W. Hiley, D.D., Vicar of Wighill, Tadcaster. With Portrait. 8vo., 15s.

Jackson.—*Stonewall Jackson and the American Civil War.* By Lieut.-Col. G. F. R. Henderson. With 2 Portraits and 33 Maps and Plans. 2 vols. 8vo., 42s.

Leslie.—*The Life and Campaigns of Alexander Leslie, First Earl of Leven.* By Charles Sanford Terry, M.A. With Maps and Plans. 8vo., 16s.

Luther.—*Life of Luther.* By Julius Köstlin. With 62 Illustrations and 4 Facsimilies of MSS. Cr. 8vo., 3s. 6d.

Macaulay.—*The Life and Letters of Lord Macaulay.* By the Right Hon. Sir G. O. Trevelyan, Bart.
Popular Edition. 1 vol. Cr. 8vo., 2s. 6d.
Student's Edition 1 vol. Cr. 8vo., 6s.
Cabinet Edition. 2 vols. Post 8vo., 12s.
'Edinburgh' Edition. 2 vols. 8vo., 6s. each
Library Edition. 2 vols. 8vo., 36s.

Marbot.—*The Memoirs of the Baron de Marbot.* Translated from the French. 2 vols. Crown 8vo., 7s.

Max Müller.—*Auld Lang Syne.* By the Right Hon. F. Max Müller. First Series. With Portrait. 8vo, 10s. 6d.
Contents.—Musical Recollections—Literary Recollections—Recollections of Royalties—Beggars.
Second Series. *My Indian Friends.* 8vo, 10s. 6d.

Morris.—*The Life of William Morris.* By J. W. Mackail. With 6 Portraits and 16 Illustrations by E. H. New etc. 2 vols. 8vo., 32s.

Biography, Personal Memoirs, &c.—*continued.*

Palgrave.—*FRANCIS TURNER PALGRAVE:* His Journals, and Memories of his Life. By GWENLLIAN F. PALGRAVE. With Portrait and Illustration. 8vo., 10s. 6d.

Pearson.—*CHARLES HENRY PEARSON, FELLOW OF ORIEL, AND EDUCATION MINISTER IN VICTORIA;* Author of 'National Life and Character'. Memorials by Himself, his Wife, and his Friends. Edited by W. STEBBING, Hon. Fellow of Worcester College, Oxford. With Portrait. 8vo., 14s.

Place.—*THE LIFE OF FRANCIS PLACE,* 1771-1854. By GRAHAM WALLAS, M.A. With 2 Portraits. 8vo., 12s.

Powys.—*PASSAGES FROM THE DIARIES OF MRS. PHILIP LYBBE POWYS,* of Hardwick House, Oxon., 1756-1808. Edited by EMILY J. CLIMENSON, of Shiplake Vicarage, Oxon. With 2 Pedigrees (Lybbe and Powys) and Photogravure Portrait. 8vo., 16s.

Râmakrishna: *HIS LIFE AND SAYINGS.* By the Right Hon. F. MAX MÜLLER. Crown 8vo., 5s.

Reeve.—*MEMOIRS OF THE LIFE AND CORRESPONDENCE OF HENRY REEVE, C.B.,* late Editor of the 'Edinburgh Review,' and Registrar of the Privy Council. By JOHN KNOX LAUGHTON, M.A. With 2 Portraits. 2 vols. 8vo., 28s.

Romanes.—*THE LIFE AND LETTERS OF GEORGE JOHN ROMANES, M.A., LL.D., F.R.S.* Written and Edited by his WIFE. With Portrait and 2 Illustrations. Cr. 8vo., 6s.

Seebohm.—*THE OXFORD REFORMERS—JOHN COLET, ERASMUS, AND THOMAS MORE:* a History of their Fellow-Work. By FREDERIC SEEBOHM. 8vo., 14s.

Shakespeare.—*OUTLINES OF THE LIFE OF SHAKESPEARE.* By J. O. HALLIWELL-PHILLIPPS. With Illustrations and Fac-similes. 2 vols. Royal 8vo., 21s.

Shakespeare's *TRUE LIFE.* By JAMES WALTER With 500 Illustrations by GERALD E. MOIRA. Imp. 8vo., 21s. net.

Stanley (Lady).

THE GIRLHOOD OF MARIA JOSEPHA HOLROYD (Lady Stanley of Alderley). Recorded in Letters of a Hundred Years Ago, from 1776-1796. Edited by J. H. ADEANE. With 6 Portraits. 8vo., 18s.

THE EARLY MARRIED LIFE OF MARIA JOSEPHA, LADY STANLEY, FROM 1796. Edited by J. H. ADEANE. With 10 Portraits and 3 Illustrations. 8vo., 18s.

Turgot—*THE LIFE AND WRITINGS OF TURGOT,* Comptroller-General of France, 1774-1776. Edited for English Readers by W. WALKER STEPHENS. With Portrait. 8vo, 7s. 6d.

Verney.—*MEMOIRS OF THE VERNEY FAMILY.* Compiled from the Letters and Illustrated by the Portraits at Clayden House.

Vols. I. & II., *DURING THE CIVIL WAR.* By FRANCES PARTHENOPE VERNEY. With 38 Portraits, etc. Royal 8vo., 42s.

Vol. III., *DURING THE COMMONWEALTH.* 1650-1660. By MARGARET M. VERNEY. With 10 Portraits, etc. Royal 8vo., 21s.

Vol. IV., *FROM THE RESTORATION TO THE REVOLUTION.* 1660 to 1696. By MARGARET M. VERNEY. With 11 Portraits, etc. Royal 8vo., 21s.

Wellington.—*LIFE OF THE DUKE OF WELLINGTON.* By the Rev. G. R. GLEIG, M.A. Crown 8vo., 3s. 6d.

Travel and Adventure, the Colonies, &c.

Arnold.—*SEAS AND LANDS.* By Sir EDWIN ARNOLD. With 71 Illustrations. Crown 8vo., 3s. 6d.

Ball (JOHN).

THE ALPINE GUIDE. Reconstructed and Revised on behalf of the Alpine Club, by W. A. B. COOLIDGE.

Vol. I., *THE WESTERN ALPS:* the Alpine Region, South of the Rhone Valley, from the Col de Tenda to the Simplon Pass. With 9 New and Revised Maps. Crown 8vo., 12s. net.

HINTS AND NOTES, PRACTICAL AND SCIENTIFIC, FOR TRAVELLERS IN THE ALPS: being a Revision of the General Introduction to the 'Alpine Guide'. Crown 8vo., 3s. net.

Baker (SIR S. W.).

EIGHT YEARS IN CEYLON. With 6 Illustrations. Crown 8vo., 3s. 6d.

THE RIFLE AND THE HOUND IN CEYLON. With 6 Illustrations. Crown 8vo., 3s. 6d.

Bent.—*THE RUINED CITIES OF MASHONALAND:* being a Record of Excavation and Exploration in 1891. By J. THEODORE BENT. With 117 Illustrations. Crown 8vo., 3s. 6d.

Bicknell.—*TRAVEL AND ADVENTURE IN NORTHERN QUEENSLAND.* By ARTHUR C. BICKNELL. With 24 Plates and 22 Illustrations in the Text. 8vo., 15s.

Travel and Adventure, the Colonies, &c.—*continued.*

Brassey.—*VOYAGES AND TRAVELS OF LORD BRASSEY, K.C.B., D.C.L.*, 1862-1894. Arranged and Edited by Captain S. EARDLEY-WILMOT. 2 vols. Cr. 8vo., 10s.

Brassey (THE LATE LADY).

A VOYAGE IN THE 'SUNBEAM'; OUR HOME ON THE OCEAN FOR ELEVEN MONTHS.

Cabinet Edition. With Map and 66 Illustrations. Crown 8vo., 7s. 6d.

'Silver Library' Edition. With 66 Illustrations. Crown 8vo., 3s. 6d.

Popular Edition. With 60 Illustrations. 4to., 6d. sewed, 1s. cloth.

School Edition. With 37 Illustrations. Fcp., 2s. cloth, or 3s. white parchment.

SUNSHINE AND STORM IN THE EAST.

Cabinet Edition. With 2 Maps and 114 Illustrations. Crown 8vo., 7s. 6d.

Popular Edition. With 103 Illustrations. 4to., 6d. sewed, 1s. cloth.

IN THE TRADES, THE TROPICS, AND THE 'ROARING FORTIES'.

Cabinet Edition. With Map and 220 Illustrations. Crown 8vo., 7s. 6d.

Browning.—*A GIRL'S WANDERINGS IN HUNGARY.* By H. ELLEN BROWNING. With Map and 20 Illustrations. Crown 8vo., 3s. 6d.

Froude (JAMES A.).

OCEANA: or England and her Colonies. With 9 Illustrations. Cr. 8vo., 3s. 6d.

THE ENGLISH IN THE WEST INDIES: or, the Bow of Ulysses. With 9 Illustrations. Crown 8vo., 2s. boards, 2s. 6d. cloth.

Howitt.—*VISITS TO REMARKABLE PLACES.* Old Halls, Battle-Fields, Scenes, illustrative of Striking Passages in English History and Poetry. By WILLIAM HOWITT. With 80 Illustrations. Crown 8vo., 3s. 6d.

Knight (E. F.).

THE CRUISE OF THE 'ALERTE': the Narrative of a Search for Treasure on the Desert Island of Trinidad. With 2 Maps and 23 Illustrations. Crown 8vo., 3s. 6d.

WHERE THREE EMPIRES MEET: a Narrative of Recent Travel in Kashmir, Western Tibet, Baltistan, Ladak, Gilgit, and the adjoining Countries. With a Map and 54 Illustrations. Cr. 8vo., 3s. 6d.

THE 'FALCON' ON THE BALTIC: a Voyage from London to Copenhagen in a Three-Tonner. With 10 Full-page Illustrations. Crown 8vo., 3s. 6d.

Lees.—*PEAKS AND PINES*: another Norway Book. By J. A. LEES. With 63 Illustrations and Photographs by the Author. Crown 8vo., 6s.

Lees and Clutterbuck.—B.C. 1887: *A RAMBLE IN BRITISH COLUMBIA.* By J. A. LEES and W. J. CLUTTERBUCK. With Map and 75 Illustrations. Crown 8vo., 3s. 6d.

Macdonald.—*THE GOLD COAST: PAST AND PRESENT.* By GEORGE MACDONALD, Director of Education and H.M. Inspector of Schools for the Gold Coast Colony and the Protectorate. With 32 Illustrations. Crown 8vo., 7s. 6d.

Nansen.—*THE FIRST CROSSING OF GREENLAND.* By FRIDTJOF NANSEN. With 143 Illustrations and a Map. Crown 8vo., 3s. 6d.

Smith.—*CLIMBING IN THE BRITISH ISLES.* By W. P. HASKETT SMITH. With Illustrations by ELLIS CARR, and Numerous Plans.

Part I. *ENGLAND.* 16mo., 3s. 6d.

Part II. *WALES AND IRELAND.* 16mo., 3s. 6d.

Stephen.—*THE PLAY-GROUND OF EUROPE* (The Alps). By LESLIE STEPHEN. With 4 Illustrations. Crown 8vo., 3s. 6d.

Three in Norway. By Two of Them. With a Map and 59 Illustrations. Crown 8vo., 2s. boards, 2s. 6d. cloth.

Tyndall.—(JOHN).

THE GLACIERS OF THE ALPS: being a Narrative of Excursions and Ascents. An Account of the Origin and Phenomena of Glaciers, and an Exposition of the Physical Principles to which they are related. With 61 Illustrations. Crown 8vo., 6s. 6d. net.

HOURS OF EXERCISE IN THE ALPS. With 7 Illustrations. Cr. 8vo., 6s. 6d. net.

Vivian.—*SERVIA*: the Poor Man's Paradise. By HERBERT VIVIAN, M.A., Officer of the Royal Order of Takovo. With Map and Portrait of King Alexander. 8vo., 15s.

Veterinary Medicine, &c.

Steel (JOHN HENRY, F.R.C.V.S., F.Z.S., A.V.D.), late Professor of Veterinary Science and Principal of Bombay Veterinary College.

A TREATISE ON THE DISEASES OF THE DOG; being a Manual of Canine Pathology. Especially adapted for the use of Veterinary Practitioners and Students. With 88 Illustrations. 8vo., 10*s.* 6*d.*

A TREATISE ON THE DISEASES OF THE OX; being a Manual of Bovine Pathology. Especially adapted for the use of Veterinary Practitioners and Students. With 2 Plates and 117 Woodcuts. 8vo., 15*s.*

A TREATISE ON THE DISEASES OF THE SHEEP; being a Manual of Ovine Pathology for the use of Veterinary Practitioners and Students. With Coloured Plate and 99 Woodcuts. 8vo., 12*s.*

OUTLINES OF EQUINE ANATOMY; a Manual for the use of Veterinary Students in the Dissecting Room. Cr. 8vo., 7*s.* 6*d.*

Fitzwygram. — *HORSES AND STABLES.* By Major-General Sir F. FITZWYGRAM, Bart. With 56 pages of Illustrations. 8vo., 2*s.* 6*d.* net.

Schreiner. — *THE ANGORA GOAT* (published under the auspices of the South African Angora Goat Breeders' Association), and a Paper on the Ostrich (reprinted from the *Zoologist* for March, 1897). With 26 Illustrations. By S. C. CRONWRIGHT SCHREINER. 8vo., 10*s.* 6*d.*

'Stonehenge.' — *THE DOG IN HEALTH AND DISEASE.* By 'STONEHENGE'. With 78 Wood Engravings. 8vo., 7*s.* 6*d.*

Youatt (WILLIAM).

THE HORSE. Revised and Enlarged by W. WATSON, M.R.C.V.S. With 52 Wood Engravings. 8vo., 7*s.* 6*d.*

THE DOG. Revised and Enlarged. With 33 Wood Engravings. 8vo., 6*s.*

Sport and Pastime.

THE BADMINTON LIBRARY.

Edited by HIS GRACE THE LATE DUKE OF BEAUFORT, K.G., and A. E. T. WATSON. Complete in 29 Volumes. Crown 8vo., Cloth, Price 10*s.* 6*d.* each Volume.

*** *The Volumes are also issued half-bound in Leather, with gilt top. The price can be had from all Booksellers.*

ARCHERY. By C. J. LONGMAN and Col. H. WALROND. With Contributions by Miss LEGH, Viscount DILLON, etc. With 2 Maps, 23 Plates and 172 Illustrations in the Text. Crown 8vo., 10*s.* 6*d.*

ATHLETICS. By MONTAGUE SHEARMAN. With Chapters on Athletics at School by W. BEACHER THOMAS; Athletic Sports in America by C. H. SHERRILL; a Contribution on Paper-chasing by W. RYE, and an Introduction by Sir RICHARD WEBSTER, Q.C., M.P. With 12 Plates and 37 Illustrations in the Text. Cr. 8vo., 10*s.* 6*d.*

BIG GAME SHOOTING. By CLIVE PHILLIPPS-WOLLEY.

Vol. I. AFRICA AND AMERICA. With Contributions by Sir SAMUEL W. BAKER, W. C. OSWELL, F. C. SELOUS, etc. With 20 Plates and 57 Illustrations in the Text. Crown 8vo., 10*s.* 6*d.*

Vol. II. EUROPE, ASIA, AND THE ARCTIC REGIONS. With Contributions by Lieut.-Colonel R. HEBER PERCY, Major ALGERNON C. HEBER PERCY, etc. With 17 Plates and 56 Illustrations in the Text. Cr. 8vo., 10*s.* 6*d.*

Sport and Pastime—*continued.*

THE BADMINTON LIBRARY—*continued.*

BILLIARDS. By Major W. BROADFOOT, R.E. With Contributions by A. H. BOYD, SYDENHAM DIXON, W. J. FORD, etc. With 11 Plates, 19 Illustrations in the Text, and numerous Diagrams. Cr. 8vo., 10*s.* 6*d.*

COURSING AND FALCONRY. By HARDING COX, CHARLES RICHARDSON, and the Hon. GERALD LASCELLES. With 20 Plates and 55 Illustrations in the Text. Crown 8vo., 10*s.* 6*d.*

CRICKET. By A. G. STEEL and the Hon. R. H. LYTTELTON. With Contributions by ANDREW LANG, W. G. GRACE, F. GALE, etc. With 13 Plates and 52 Illustrations in the Text. Crown 8vo., 10*s.* 6*d.*

CYCLING. By the EARL OF ALBEMARLE and G. LACY HILLIER. With 19 Plates and 44 Illustrations in the Text. Crown 8vo., 10*s.* 6*d.*

DANCING. By Mrs. LILLY GROVE, F.R.G.S. With Contributions by Miss MIDDLETON, The Hon. Mrs. ARMYTAGE, etc. With Musical Examples, and 38 Full-page Plates and 93 Illustrations in the Text. Crown 8vo., 10*s.* 6*d.*

DRIVING. By His Grace the late DUKE of BEAUFORT, K.G. With Contributions by A. E. T. WATSON the EARL OF ONSLOW, etc. With 12 Plates and 54 Illustrations in the Text. Crown 8vo., 10*s.* 6*d.*

FENCING, BOXING, AND WRESTLING. By WALTER H. POLLOCK, F. C. GROVE, C. PREVOST, E. B. MITCHELL, and WALTER ARMSTRONG. With 18 Plates and 24 Illust. in the Text. Cr. 8vo., 10*s.* 6*d.*

FISHING. By H. CHOLMONDELEY-PENNELL.

Vol. I. SALMON AND TROUT. With Contributions by H. R. FRANCIS, Major JOHN P. TRAHERNE, etc. With 9 Plates and numerous Illustrations of Tackle, etc. Crown 8vo., 10*s.* 6*d.*

Vol. II. PIKE AND OTHER COARSE FISH. With Contributions by the MARQUIS OF EXETER, WILLIAM SENIOR, G. CHRISTOPHER DAVIS, etc. With 7 Plates and numerous Illustrations of Tackle, etc. Crown 8vo., 10*s.* 6*d.*

FOOTBALL. By MONTAGUE SHEARMAN, W. J. OAKLEY, G. O. SMITH, FRANK MITCHELL, etc. With 19 Plates and 35 Illustrations in the Text. Cr. 8vo., 10*s.* 6*d.*

GOLF. By HORACE G. HUTCHINSON. With Contributions by the Rt. Hon. A. J. BALFOUR, M.P., Sir WALTER SIMPSON, Bart., ANDREW LANG, etc. With 32 Plates and 57 Illustrations in the Text. Cr. 8vo., 10*s.* 6*d.*

HUNTING. By His Grace the late DUKE OF BEAUFORT, K.G., and MOWBRAY MORRIS. With Contributions by the EARL OF SUFFOLK AND BERKSHIRE, Rev. E. W. L. DAVIES, G. H. LONGMAN, etc. With 5 Plates and 54 Illustrations in the Text. Crown 8vo., 10*s.* 6*d.*

MOUNTAINEERING. By C. T. DENT. With Contributions by the Right Hon. J. BRYCE, M.P., Sir MARTIN CONWAY, D. W. FRESHFIELD, C. E. MATTHEWS, etc. With 13 Plates and 91 Illustrations in the Text. Crown 8vo., 10*s.* 6*d.*

POETRY OF SPORT (THE).—Selected by HEDLEY PEEK. With a Chapter on Classical Allusions to Sport by ANDREW LANG, and a Special Preface to the BADMINTON LIBRARY by A. E. T. WATSON. With 32 Plates and 74 Illustrations in the Text. Crown 8vo., 10*s.* 6*d.*

RACING AND STEEPLE-CHASING. By the EARL OF SUFFOLK AND BERKSHIRE, W. G. CRAVEN, the Hon. F. LAWLEY, ARTHUR COVENTRY, and A. E. T. WATSON. With Frontispiece and 56 Illustrations in the Text. Crown 8vo., 10*s.* 6*d.*

RIDING AND POLO. By Captain ROBERT WEIR, J. MORAY BROWN, T. F. DALE, THE LATE DUKE OF BEAUFORT, THE EARL OF SUFFOLK AND BERKSHIRE, etc. With 18 Plates and 41 Illustrations in the Text. Crown 8vo., 10*s.* 6*d.*

ROWING. By R. P. P. ROWE and C. M. PITMAN. With Chapters on Steering by C. P. SEROCOLD and F. C. BEGG; Metropolitan Rowing by S. LE BLANC SMITH; and on PUNTING by P. W. SQUIRE. With 75 Illustrations. Crown 8vo., 10*s.* 6*d.*

SEA FISHING. By JOHN BICKERDYKE, Sir H. W. GORE-BOOTH, ALFRED C. HARMSWORTH, and W. SENIOR. With 22 Full-page Plates and 175 Illustrations in the Text. Crown 8vo., 10*s.* 6*d.*

Sport and Pastime—*continued.*

THE BADMINTON LIBRARY—*continued.*

SHOOTING.

Vol. I. FIELD AND COVERT. By LORD WALSINGHAM and Sir RALPH PAYNE-GALLWEY, Bart. With Contributions by the Hon. GERALD LASCELLES and A. J. STUART-WORTLEY. With 11 Plates and 95 Illusts. in the Text. Cr. 8vo., 10s. 6d.

Vol. II. MOOR AND MARSH. By LORD WALSINGHAM and Sir RALPH PAYNE-GALLWEY, Bart. With Contributions by LORD LOVAT and Lord CHARLES LENNOX KERR. With 8 Plates and 57 Illustrations in the Text. Crown 8vo., 10s. 6d.

SKATING, CURLING, TOBOGGANING. By J. M. HEATHCOTE, C. G. TEBBUTT, T. MAXWELL WITHAM, Rev. JOHN KERR, ORMOND HAKE, HENRY A. BUCK, etc. With 12 Plates and 272 Illustrations in the Text. Crown 8vo., 10s. 6d.

SWIMMING. By ARCHIBALD SINCLAIR and WILLIAM HENRY, Hon. Secs. of the Life-Saving Society. With 13 Plates and 112 Illustrations in the Text. Cr. 8vo., 10s. 6d.

TENNIS, LAWN TENNIS, RACKETS AND FIVES. By J. M. and C. G. HEATHCOTE, E. O. PLEYDELL-BOUVERIE, and A. C. AINGER. With Contributions by the Hon. A. LYTTELTON, W. C. MARSHALL, Miss L. DOD, etc. With 12 Plates and 67 Illustrations in the Text. Cr. 8vo., 10s. 6d.

YACHTING.

Vol. I. CRUISING, CONSTRUCTION OF YACHTS, YACHT RACING RULES, FITTING-OUT, etc. By Sir EDWARD SULLIVAN, Bart., THE EARL OF PEMBROKE, LORD BRASSEY, K.C.B., C. E. SETH-SMITH, C.B., G. L. WATSON, R. T. PRITCHETT, E. F. KNIGHT, etc. With 21 Plates and 93 Illustrations in the Text. Crown 8vo., 10s. 6d.

Vol. II. YACHT CLUBS, YACHTING IN AMERICA AND THE COLONIES, YACHT RACING, etc By R. T. PRITCHETT, THE MARQUIS OF DUFFERIN AND AVA, K.P., THE EARL OF ONSLOW, JAMES MCFERRAN, etc. With 35 Plates and 160 Illustrations in the Text. Crown 8vo., 10s. 6d.

FUR, FEATHER, AND FIN SERIES.

Edited by A. E. T. WATSON.

Crown 8vo., price 5s. each Volume, cloth.

*** *The Volumes are also issued half-bound in Leather, with gilt top. The price can be had from all Booksellers.*

THE PARTRIDGE. Natural History, by the Rev. H. A. MACPHERSON; Shooting, by A. J. STUART-WORTLEY; Cookery, by GEORGE SAINTSBURY. With 11 Illustrations and various Diagrams in the Text. Crown 8vo., 5s.

THE GROUSE. Natural History, by the Rev. H. A. MACPHERSON; Shooting, by A. J. STUART-WORTLEY; Cookery, by GEORGE SAINTSBURY. With 13 Illustrations and various Diagrams in the Text. Crown 8vo., 5s.

THE PHEASANT. Natural History, by the Rev. H. A. MACPHERSON; Shooting, by A. J. STUART-WORTLEY; Cookery, by ALEXANDER INNES SHAND. With 10 Illustrations and various Diagrams. Crown 8vo., 5s.

THE HARE. Natural History, by the Rev. H. A. MACPHERSON; Shooting, by the Hon. GERALD LASCELLES; Coursing, by CHARLES RICHARDSON; Hunting, by J. S. GIBBONS and G. H. LONGMAN; Cookery, by Col. KENNEY HERBERT. With 9 Illustrations. Crown 8vo, 5s.

RED DEER.—Natural History, by the Rev. H. A. MACPHERSON; Deer Stalking, by CAMERON OF LOCHIEL; Stag Hunting, by Viscount EBRINGTON; Cookery, by ALEXANDER INNES SHAND. With 10 Illustrations. Crown 8vo., 5s.

THE SALMON. By the Hon. A. E. GATHORNE-HARDY. With Chapters on the Law of Salmon Fishing by CLAUD DOUGLAS PENNANT; Cookery, by ALEXANDER INNES SHAND. With 8 Illustrations. Cr. 8vo., 5s.

THE TROUT. By the MARQUESS OF GRANBY. With Chapters on the Breeding of Trout by Col. H. CUSTANCE; and Cookery, by ALEXANDER INNES SHAND. With 12 Illustrations. Crown 8vo., 5s.

THE RABBIT. By JAMES EDMUND HARTING. With a Chapter on Cookery by ALEXANDER INNES SHAND. With 10 Illustrations. Crown 8vo., 5s.

PIKE AND PERCH. By W. SENIOR, JOHN BICKERDYKE and ALEXANDER INNES SHAND. [*Nearly ready.*

Sport and Pastime—*continued.*

Bickerdyke.—*DAYS OF MY LIFE ON WATERS FRESH AND SALT, AND OTHER PAPERS.* By JOHN BICKERDYKE. With Photo-etching Frontispiece and 8 Full-page Illustrations. Crown 8vo., 6*s*.

Blackburne. — *MR. BLACKBURNE'S GAMES AT CHESS.* Selected, Annotated and Arranged by Himself. Edited, with a Biographical Sketch and a brief History of Blindfold Chess, by P. ANDERSON GRAHAM. 8vo., 7*s*. 6*d*. net.

Cawthorne and Herod.—*ROYAL ASCOT:* its History and its Associations. By GEORGE JAMES CAWTHORNE and RICHARD S. HEROD. With 32 Plates and 106 Illustrations in the Text. Demy 4to., 31*s*. 6*d*. net.

Dead Shot (The): or, Sportsman's Complete Guide. Being a Treatise on the Use of the Gun, with Rudimentary and Finishing Lessons in the Art of Shooting Game of all kinds. Also Game-driving, Wildfowl and Pigeon-shooting, Dog-breaking, etc. By MARKSMAN. With numerous Illustrations. Crown 8vo., 10*s*. 6*d*.

Ellis.—*CHESS SPARKS;* or, Short and Bright Games of Chess. Collected and Arranged by J. H. ELLIS, M.A. 8vo., 4*s*. 6*d*.

Folkard.—*THE WILD-FOWLER:* A Treatise on Fowling, Ancient and Modern, descriptive also of Decoys and Flight-ponds, Wild-fowl Shooting, Gunning-punts, Shooting-yachts, etc. Also Fowling in the Fens and in Foreign Countries, Rock-fowling, etc., etc., by H. C. FOLKARD. With 13 Engravings on Steel, and several Woodcuts. 8vo., 12*s*. 6*d*.

Ford.—*THE THEORY AND PRACTICE OF ARCHERY.* By HORACE FORD. New Edition, thoroughly Revised and Re-written by W. BUTT, M.A. With a Preface by C. J. LONGMAN, M.A. 8vo., 14*s*.

Ford.—*MIDDLESEX COUNTY CRICKET CLUB*, 1864-1899. Written and Compiled by W. J. FORD. With Photogravure Portrait of V. E. Walker. 8vo., 10*s*. net.

Francis.—*A BOOK ON ANGLING:* or, Treatise on the Art of Fishing in every Branch; including full Illustrated List of Salmon Flies. By FRANCIS FRANCIS. With Portrait and Coloured Plates. Crown 8vo., 15*s*.

Gibson.—*TOBOGGANING ON CROOKED RUNS.* By the Hon. HARRY GIBSON. With Contributions by F. DE B. STRICKLAND and 'LADY-TOBOGANNER'. With 40 Illustrations. Crown 8vo., 6*s*.

Graham.—*COUNTRY PASTIMES FOR BOYS.* By P. ANDERSON GRAHAM. With 252 Illustrations from Drawings and Photographs. Crown 8vo., 3*s*. 6*d*.

Hutchinson.—*THE BOOK OF GOLF AND GOLFERS.* By HORACE G. HUTCHINSON. With Contributions by Miss AMY PASCOE, H. H. HILTON, J. H. TAYLOR, H. J. WHIGHAM, and Messrs. SUTTON & SONS. With 71 Portraits, etc. Large crown 8vo., 7*s*. 6*d*. net.

Lang.—*ANGLING SKETCHES.* By ANDREW LANG. With 20 Illustrations. Crown 8vo., 3*s*. 6*d*.

Lillie (ARTHUR).

CROQUET: its History, Rules and Secrets. With 4 Full-page Illustrations by LUCIEN DAVIS, 15 Illustrations in the Text, and 27 Diagrams. Crown 8vo., 6*s*.

CROQUET UP TO DATE. Containing the Ideas and Teachings of the Leading Players and Champions. With 19 Illustrations (15 Portraits), and numerous Diagrams. 8vo., 10*s*. 6*d*. net.

Longman.—*CHESS OPENINGS.* By FREDERICK W. LONGMAN. Fcp. 8vo., 2*s*. 6*d*.

Madden.—*THE DIARY OF MASTER WILLIAM SILENCE:* a Study of Shakespeare and of Elizabethan Sport. By the Right Hon. D. H. MADDEN, Vice-Chancellor of the University of Dublin. 8vo., 16*s*.

Maskelyne.—*SHARPS AND FLATS:* a Complete Revelation of the Secrets of Cheating at Games of Chance and Skill. By JOHN NEVIL MASKELYNE, of the Egyptian Hall. With 62 Illustrations. Crown 8vo., 6*s*.

Moffat.—*CRICKETY CRICKET:* Rhymes and Parodies. By DOUGLAS MOFFAT, with Frontispiece by the late Sir FRANK LOCKWOOD, and 53 Illustrations by the Author. Crown 8vo, 2*s*. 6*d*.

Park.—*THE GAME OF GOLF.* By WILLIAM PARK, Jun., Champion Golfer, 1887-89. With 17 Plates and 26 Illustrations in the Text. Crown 8vo., 7*s*. 6*d*.

Sport and Pastime—*continued.*

Payne-Gallwey (Sir Ralph, Bart.).

Letters to Young Shooters (First Series). On the Choice and use of a Gun With 41 Illustrations. Crown 8vo., 7*s*. 6*d*.

Letters to Young Shooters (Second Series). On the Production, Preservation, and Killing of Game. With Directions in Shooting Wood-Pigeons and Breaking-in Retrievers. With Portrait and 103 Illustrations. Crown 8vo., 12*s*. 6*d*.

Letters to Young Shooters. (Third Series.) Comprising a Short Natural History of the Wildfowl that are Rare or Common to the British Islands, with complete directions in Shooting Wildfowl on the Coast and Inland. With 200 Illustrations. Crown 8vo., 18*s*.

Pole—*The Theory of the Modern Scientific Game of Whist.* By William Pole, F.R.S. Fcp. 8vo., 2*s*. 6*d*.

Proctor.—*How to Play Whist: with the Laws and Etiquette of Whist.* By Richard A. Proctor. Crown 8vo., 3*s*. 6*d*.

Ribblesdale.—*The Queen's Hounds and Stag-Hunting Recollections.* By Lord Ribblesdale, Master of the Buckhounds, 1892-95. With Introductory Chapter on the Hereditary Mastership by E. Burrows. With 24 Plates and 35 Illustrations in the Text. 8vo., 25*s*.

Ronalds.—*The Fly-Fisher's Entomology.* By Alfred Ronalds. With 20 coloured Plates. 8vo., 14*s*.

Wilcocks.—*The Sea Fisherman:* Comprising the Chief Methods of Hook and Line Fishing in the British and other Seas, and Remarks on Nets, Boats, and Boating. By J. C. Wilcocks. Illustrated. Cr. 8vo., 6*s*.

Mental, Moral, and Political Philosophy.

LOGIC, RHETORIC, PSYCHOLOGY, &C.

Abbott.—*The Elements of Logic.* By T. K. Abbott, B.D. 12mo., 3*s*.

Aristotle.

The Ethics: Greek Text, Illustrated with Essay and Notes. By Sir Alexander Grant, Bart. 2 vols. 8vo., 32*s*.

An Introduction to Aristotle's Ethics. Books I.-IV. (Book X. c. vi.-ix. in an Appendix). With a continuous Analysis and Notes. By the Rev. E. Moore, D.D. Crown 8vo. 10*s*. 6*d*.

Bacon (Francis).

Complete Works. Edited by R. L. Ellis, James Spedding and D. D. Heath. 7 vols. 8vo., £3 13*s*. 6*d*.

Letters and Life, including all his occasional Works. Edited by James Spedding. 7 vols. 8vo., £4 4*s*.

The Essays: with Annotations. By Richard Whately, D.D. 8vo., 10*s*. 6*d*.

The Essays: with Notes. By F. Storr and C. H. Gibson. Cr. 8vo, 3*s*. 6*d*.

The Essays: with Introduction, Notes, and Index. By E. A. Abbott, D.D. 2 Vols. Fcp. 8vo., 6*s*. The Text and Index only, without Introduction and Notes, in One Volume. Fcp. 8vo., 2*s*. 6*d*.

Bain (Alexander).

Mental and Moral Science: a Compendium of Psychology and Ethics. Crown 8vo., 10*s*. 6*d*.

Or separately,

Part I. *Psychology and History of Philosophy.* Crown 8vo., 6*s*. 6*d*.

Part II. *Theory of Ethics and Ethical Systems.* Crown 8vo., 4*s*. 6*d*.

Senses and the Intellect. 8vo., 15*s*.

Emotions and the Will. 8vo., 15*s*.

Logic. Part I. *Deduction.* Crown 8vo., 4*s*. Part II. *Induction.* Crown 8vo., 6*s*. 6*d*.

Practical Essays. Cr. 8vo., 2*s*.

Bray.—*The Philosophy of Necessity:* or, Law in Mind as in Matter. By Charles Bray. Crown 8vo., 5*s*.

Crozier (John Beattie).

Civilisation and Progress: being the Outlines of a New System of Political, Religious and Social Philosophy. 8vo., 14*s*.

History of Intellectual Development: on the Lines of Modern Evolution.

Vol. I. Greek and Hindoo Thought; Græco-Roman Paganism; Judaism; and Christianity down to the Closing of the Schools of Athens by Justinian, 529 A.D. 8vo., 14*s*.

Mental, Moral and Political Philosophy—*continued.*

LOGIC, RHETORIC, PSYCHOLOGY, &C.

Davidson.—*The Logic of Definition*, Explained and Applied. By William L. Davidson, M.A. Crown 8vo., 6s.

Green (Thomas Hill).—The Works of. Edited by R. L. Nettleship.

Vols. I. and II. Philosophical Works. 8vo., 16s. each.

Vol. III. Miscellanies. With Index to the three Volumes, and Memoir. 8vo., 21s.

Lectures on the Principles of Political Obligation. With Preface by Bernard Bosanquet. 8vo., 5s.

Gurnhill.—*The Morals of Suicide.* By the Rev. J. Gurnhill, B.A. Crown 8vo., 6s.

Hodgson (Shadworth H.).

Time and Space: A Metaphysical Essay. 8vo., 16s.

The Theory of Practice: an Ethical Inquiry. 2 vols. 8vo., 24s.

The Philosophy of Reflection. 2 vols. 8vo., 21s.

The Metaphysic of Experience. Book I. General Analysis of Experience; Book II. Positive Science; Book III. Analysis of Conscious Action; Book IV. The Real Universe. 4 vols. 8vo., 36s. net.

Hume.—*The Philosophical Works of David Hume.* Edited by T. H. Green and T. H. Grose. 4 vols. 8vo., 28s. Or separately, Essays. 2 vols. 14s. Treatise of Human Nature. 2 vols. 14s.

James.—*The Will to Believe*, and Other Essays in Popular Philosophy. By William James, M.D., LL.D., etc. Crown 8vo., 7s. 6d.

Justinian.—*The Institutes of Justinian*: Latin Text, chiefly that of Huschke, with English Introduction, Translation, Notes, and Summary. By Thomas C. Sandars, M.A. 8vo., 18s.

Kant (Immanuel).

Critique of Practical Reason, and other Works on the Theory of Ethics. Translated by T. K. Abbott, B.D. With Memoir. 8vo., 12s. 6d.

Fundamental Principles of the Metaphysic of Ethics. Translated by T. K. Abbott, B.D. Crown 8vo, 3s.

Introduction to Logic, and his Essay on the Mistaken Subtilty of the Four Figures.. Translated by T. K. Abbott. 8vo., 6s.

Kelly.—*Government or Human Evolution.—Justice.* By Edmond Kelly, M.A., F.G.S. Cr. 8vo., 7s. 6d. net.

Killick.—*Handbook to Mill's System of Logic.* By Rev. A. H. Killick, M.A. Crown 8vo., 3s. 6d.

Ladd (George Trumbull).

A Theory of Reality: an Essay in Metaphysical System upon the Basis of Human Cognitive Experience. 8vo., 18s.

Elements of Physiological Psychology. 8vo., 21s.

Outlines of Descriptive Psychology: a Text-Book of Mental Science for Colleges and Normal Schools. 8vo., 12s.

Outlines of Physiological Psychology. 8vo., 12s.

Primer of Psychology. Cr. 8vo., 5s. 6d.

Lecky.—*The Map of Life*: Conduct and Character. By William Edward Hartpole Lecky. 8vo., 10s. 6d.

Lutoslawski.—*The Origin and Growth of Plato's Logic.* With an Account of Plato's Style and of the Chronology of his Writings. By Wincenty Lutoslawski. 8vo., 21s.

Max Müller (F.).

The Science of Thought. 8vo., 21s.

The Six Systems of Indian Philosophy. 8vo., 18s.

Mill.—*Analysis of the Phenomena of the Human Mind.* By James Mill. 2 vols. 8vo., 28s.

Mill (John Stuart).

A System of Logic. Cr. 8vo., 3s. 6d.

On Liberty. Crown 8vo., 1s. 4d.

Considerations on Representative Government. Crown 8vo., 2s.

Utilitarianism. 8vo., 2s. 6d.

Examination of Sir William Hamilton's Philosophy. 8vo., 16s.

Nature, the Utility of Religion, and Theism. Three Essays. 8vo., 5s.

Monck.—*An Introduction to Logic.* By William Henry S. Monck, M.A. Crown 8vo., 5s.

Romanes.—*Mind and Motion and Monism.* By George John Romanes, LL.D., F.R.S. Cr. 8vo., 4s. 6d.

Stock.—*Lectures in the Lyceum*; or, Aristotle's Ethics for English Readers. Edited by St. George Stock. Crown 8vo., 7s. 6d.

Mental, Moral, and Political Philosophy—*continued.*

Sully (JAMES).

THE HUMAN MIND: a Text-book of Psychology. 2 vols. 8vo., 21s.

OUTLINES OF PSYCHOLOGY. Crown 8vo., 9s.

THE TEACHER'S HANDBOOK OF PSYCHOLOGY. Crown 8vo., 6s. 6d.

STUDIES OF CHILDHOOD. 8vo., 10s. 6d.

CHILDREN'S WAYS: being Selections from the Author's 'Studies of Childhood'. With 25 Illustrations. Crown 8vo., 4s. 6d.

Sutherland. — *THE ORIGIN AND GROWTH OF THE MORAL INSTINCT.* By ALEXANDER SUTHERLAND, M.A. 2 vols. 8vo, 28s.

Swinburne. — *PICTURE LOGIC:* an Attempt to Popularise the Science of Reasoning. By ALFRED JAMES SWINBURNE, M.A. With 23 Woodcuts. Cr. 8vo., 2s. 6d.

Webb.—*THE VEIL OF ISIS:* a Series of Essays on Idealism. By THOMAS E. WEBB, LL.D., Q.C. 8vo., 10s. 6d.

Weber.—*HISTORY OF PHILOSOPHY.* By ALFRED WEBER, Professor in the University of Strasburg. Translated by FRANK THILLY, Ph.D. 8vo., 16s.

Whately (ARCHBISHOP).

BACON'S ESSAYS. With Annotations. 8vo., 10s. 6d.

ELEMENTS OF LOGIC. Cr. 8vo., 4s. 6d.

ELEMENTS OF RHETORIC. Cr. 8vo., 4s. 6d.

Zeller (Dr. EDWARD).

THE STOICS, EPICUREANS, AND SCEPTICS. Translated by the Rev. O. J. REICHEL, M.A. Crown 8vo., 15s.

OUTLINES OF THE HISTORY OF GREEK PHILOSOPHY. Translated by SARAH F. ALLEYNE and EVELYN ABBOTT, M.A., LL.D. Crown 8vo., 10s. 6d.

PLATO AND THE OLDER ACADEMY. Translated by SARAH F. ALLEYNE and ALFRED GOODWIN, B.A. Crown 8vo., 18s.

SOCRATES AND THE SOCRATIC SCHOOLS. Translated by the Rev. O. J. REICHEL, M.A. Crown 8vo., 10s. 6d.

ARISTOTLE AND THE EARLIER PERIPATETICS. Translated by B. F. C. COSTELLOE, M.A., and J. H. MUIRHEAD, M.A. 2 vols. Crown 8vo., 24s.

MANUALS OF CATHOLIC PHILOSOPHY.

(*Stonyhurst Series.*)

A MANUAL OF POLITICAL ECONOMY. By C. S. DEVAS, M.A. Crown 8vo., 6s. 6d.

FIRST PRINCIPLES OF KNOWLEDGE. By JOHN RICKABY, S.J. Crown 8vo., 5s.

GENERAL METAPHYSICS. By JOHN RICKABY, S.J. Crown 8vo., 5s.

LOGIC. By RICHARD F. CLARKE, S.J. Crown 8vo., 5s.

MORAL PHILOSOPHY (ETHICS AND NATURAL LAW). By JOSEPH RICKABY, S.J. Crown 8vo., 5s.

NATURAL THEOLOGY. By BERNARD BOEDDER, S.J. Crown 8vo., 6s. 6d.

PSYCHOLOGY. By MICHAEL MAHER, S.J. Crown 8vo., 6s. 6d.

History and Science of Language, &c.

Davidson.—*LEADING AND IMPORTANT ENGLISH WORDS:* Explained and Exemplified. By WILLIAM L. DAVIDSON, M.A. Fcp. 8vo., 3s. 6d.

Farrar.—*LANGUAGE AND LANGUAGES.* By F. W. FARRAR, D.D., Dean of Canterbury. Crown 8vo., 6s.

Graham. — *ENGLISH SYNONYMS,* Classified and Explained: with Practical Exercises. By G. F. GRAHAM. Fcp. 8vo., 6s.

Max Muller (F.).

THE SCIENCE OF LANGUAGE.—Founded on Lectures delivered at the Royal Institution in 1861 and 1863. 2 vols. Crown 8vo., 10s.

BIOGRAPHIES OF WORDS, AND THE HOME OF THE ARYAS. Crown 8vo., 5s.

Roget.—*THESAURUS OF ENGLISH WORDS AND PHRASES.* Classified and Arranged so as to Facilitate the Expression of Ideas and assist in Literary Composition. By PETER MARK ROGET, M.D., F.R.S. With full Index. Crown 8vo., 10s. 6d.

Whately.—*ENGLISH SYNONYMS.* By E. JANE WHATELY. Fcp. 8vo., 3s.

Political Economy and Economics.

Ashley.—*English Economic History and Theory.* By W. J. Ashley, M.A. Cr. 8vo., Part I., 5s. Part II., 10s. 6d.

Bagehot.—*Economic Studies.* By Walter Bagehot. Crown 8vo., 3s. 6d.

Brassey.—*Papers and Addresses on Work and Wages.* By Lord Brassey. Edited by J. Potter, and with Introduction by George Howell. Crown 8vo., 5s.

Channing.—*The Truth about Agricultural Depression;* an Economic Study of the Evidence of the Royal Commission. By Francis Allston Channing, M.P., One of the Commission. Crown 8vo., 6s.

Devas.—*A Manual of Political Economy.* By C. S. Devas, M.A. Cr. 8vo., 6s. 6d. (*Manuals of Catholic Philosophy.*)

Jordan.—*The Standard of Value.* By William Leighton Jordan. Cr.8vo.,6s.

Leslie.—*Essays on Political Economy.* By T. E. Cliffe Leslie, Hon. LL.D., Dubl. 8vo., 10s. 6d.

Macleod (Henry Dunning).

Economics for Beginners. Crown 8vo., 2s.

The Elements of Economics. 2 vols. Crown 8vo., 3s. 6d. each.

Bimetalism. 8vo., 5s. net.

The Elements of Banking. Cr. 8vo., 3s. 6d.

The Theory and Practice of Banking. Vol. I. 8vo., 12s. Vol. II. 14s.

The Theory of Credit. 8vo. In 1 Vol., 30s. net; or separately, Vol. I., 10s. net. Vol. II., Part I., 10s. net. Vol II., Part II. 10s. net.

Mill.—*Political Economy.* By John Stuart Mill.

Popular Edition. Crown 8vo., 3s. 6d.
Library Edition. 2 vols. 8vo., 30s.

Mulhall.—*Industries and Wealth of Nations.* By Michael G. Mulhall, F.S.S. With 32 Diagrams. Cr. 8vo., 8s. 6d.

Stephens.—*Higher Life for Working People:* its Hindrances Discussed. An attempt to solve some pressing Social Problems, without injustice to Capital or Labour. By W. Walker Stephens. Cr. 8vo., 3s. 6d.

Symes.—*Political Economy.* With a Supplementary Chapter on Socialism. By J. E. Symes, M.A. Crown 8vo., 2s. 6d.

Toynbee.—*Lectures on the Industrial Revolution of the 18th Century in England.* By Arnold Toynbee. With a Memoir of the Author by Benjamin Jowett, D.D. 8vo., 10s. 6d.

Webb (Sidney and Beatrice).

The History of Trade Unionism. With Map and full Bibliography of the Subject. 8vo., 18s.

Industrial Democracy: a Study in Trade Unionism. 2 vols. 8vo., 25s. net.

Problems of Modern Industry: Essays. 8vo., 7s. 6d.

Wright.—*Outline of Practical Sociology.* With Special Reference to American Conditions. By Carroll D. Wright, LL.D. With 12 Maps and Diagrams. Crown 8vo., 9s.

Evolution, Anthropology, &c.

Clodd (Edward).

The Story of Creation: a Plain Account of Evolution. With 77 Illustrations. Crown 8vo., 3s. 6d.

A Primer of Evolution: being a Popular Abridged Edition of 'The Story of Creation'. With Illustrations. Fcp. 8vo., 1s. 6d.

Lang (Andrew).

Custom and Myth: Studies of Early Usage and Belief. With 15 Illustrations. Crown 8vo., 3s. 6d.

Myth, Ritual, and Religion. 2 vols. Crown 8vo., 7s.

Modern Mythology: a Reply to Professor Max Müller. 8vo., 9s.

Lubbock.—*The Origin of Civilisation,* and the Primitive Condition of Man. By Sir J. Lubbock, Bart., M.P. (Lord Avebury). With 5 Plates and 20 Illustrations. 8vo., 18s.

Romanes (George John).

Darwin, and after Darwin: an Exposition of the Darwinian Theory, and a Discussion on Post-Darwinian Questions.

Part I. The Darwinian Theory. With Portrait of Darwin and 125 Illustrations. Crown 8vo., 10s. 6d.

Part II. Post-Darwinian Questions: Heredity and Utility. With Portrait of the Author and 5 Illustrations. Cr. 8vo., 10s. 6d.

Part III. Post-Darwinian Questions: Isolation and Physiological Selection. Crown 8vo., 5s.

An Examination of Weismannism. Crown 8vo., 6s.

Essays. Edited by C. Lloyd Morgan, Principal of University College, Bristol. Crown 8vo., 6s.

Classical Literature, Translations, &c.

Abbott.—*HELLENICA*. A Collection of Essays on Greek Poetry, Philosophy, History, and Religion. Edited by EVELYN ABBOTT, M.A., LL.D. Crown 8vo., 7*s*. 6*d*.

Æschylus.—*EUMENIDES OF ÆSCHYLUS*. With Metrical English Translation. By J. F. DAVIES. 8vo., 7*s*.

Aristophanes. — *THE ACHARNIANS OF ARISTOPHANES*, translated into English Verse. By R. Y. TYRRELL. Crown 8vo., 1*s*.

Aristotle.—*YOUTH AND OLD AGE, LIFE AND DEATH, AND RESPIRATION*. Translated, with Introduction and Notes, by W. OGLE, M.A., M.D. 8vo., 7*s*. 6*d*.

Becker (W. A.), Translated by the Rev. F. METCALFE, B.D.

GALLUS: or, Roman Scenes in the Time of Augustus. With Notes and Excursuses. With 26 Illustrations. Crown 8vo., 3*s*. 6*d*.

CHARICLES: or, Illustrations of the Private Life of the Ancient Greeks. With Notes and Excursuses. With 26 Illustrations. Crown 8vo., 3*s*. 6*d*.

Butler.—*THE AUTHORESS OF THE ODYSSEY, WHERE AND WHEN SHE WROTE, WHO SHE WAS, THE USE SHE MADE OF THE ILIAD, AND HOW THE POEM GREW UNDER HER HANDS*. By SAMUEL BUTLER, Author of 'Erewhon,' etc. With 14 Illustrations and 4 Maps. 8vo., 10*s*. 6*d*.

Campbell.—*RELIGION IN GREEK LITERATURE*. By the Rev. LEWIS CAMPBELL, M.A., LL.D., Emeritus Professor of Greek, University of St. Andrews. 8vo., 15*s*.

Cicero.—*CICERO'S CORRESPONDENCE*. By R. Y. TYRRELL. Vols. I., II., III., 8vo., each 12*s*. Vol. IV., 15*s*. Vol. V., 14*s*. Vol. VI., 12*s*.

Hime.—*LUCIAN, THE SYRIAN SATIRIST*. By Lieut.-Col. HENRY W. L. HIME, (late) Royal Artillery. 8vo., 5*s*. net.

CONTENTS.—1. Life of Lucian—2. Classification of Lucian's Works—3. The Limits of Satire—4. Lucian's Philosophy and Religion—5. Characteristics. Appendix: Lucian's Knowledge of Latin.

Homer.

THE ILIAD OF HOMER. Rendered into English Prose for the use of those who cannot read the original. By SAMUEL BUTLER, Author of 'Erewhon,' etc. Crown 8vo., 7*s*. 6*d*.

THE ODYSSEY OF HOMER. Done into English Verse. By WILLIAM MORRIS. Crown 8vo., 6*s*.

Horace.—*THE WORKS OF HORACE, RENDERED INTO ENGLISH PROSE*. With Life, Introduction and Notes. By WILLIAM COUTTS, M.A. Crown 8vo., 5*s*. net.

Lang.—*HOMER AND THE EPIC*. By ANDREW LANG. Crown 8vo., 9*s*. net.

Lucan.—*THE PHARSALIA OF LUCAN*. Translated into Blank Verse. By Sir EDWARD RIDLEY. 8vo., 14*s*.

Mackail.—*SELECT EPIGRAMS FROM THE GREEK ANTHOLOGY*. By J. W. MACKAIL. Edited with a Revised Text, Introduction, Translation, and Notes. 8vo., 16*s*.

Rich.—*A DICTIONARY OF ROMAN AND GREEK ANTIQUITIES*. By A. RICH, B.A. With 2000 Woodcuts. Crown 8vo., 6*s*. net.

Sophocles.—Translated into English Verse. By ROBERT WHITELAW, M.A., Assistant Master in Rugby School. Cr. 8vo., 8*s*. 6*d*.

Tyrrell. — *DUBLIN TRANSLATIONS INTO GREEK AND LATIN VERSE*. Edited by R. Y. TYRRELL. 8vo., 6*s*.

Virgil.

THE ÆNEID OF VIRGIL. Translated into English Verse by JOHN CONINGTON. Crown 8vo., 6*s*.

THE POEMS OF VIRGIL. Translated into English Prose by JOHN CONINGTON. Crown 8vo., 6*s*.

THE ÆNEIDS OF VIRGIL. Done into English Verse. By WILLIAM MORRIS. Crown 8vo., 6*s*.

THE ÆNEID OF VIRGIL, freely translated into English Blank Verse. By W. J. THORNHILL. Crown 8vo., 6*s*. net.

THE ÆNEID OF VIRGIL. Translated into English Verse by JAMES RHOADES.

Books I.-VI. Crown 8vo., 5*s*.

Books VII.-XII. Crown 8vo., 5*s*.

THE ECLOGUES AND GEORGICS OF VIRGIL. Translated into English Prose by J. W. MACKAIL, Fellow of Balliol College, Oxford. 16mo., 5*s*.

Wilkins.—*THE GROWTH OF THE HOMERIC POEMS*. By G. WILKINS. 8vo., 6*s*.

Poetry and the Drama.

Armstrong (G. F. Savage).

Poems: Lyrical and Dramatic. Fcp. 8vo., 6s.

King Saul. (The Tragedy of Israel, Part I.) Fcp. 8vo., 5s.

King David. (The Tragedy of Israel, Part II.) Fcp. 8vo., 6s.

King Solomon. (The Tragedy of Israel, Part III.) Fcp. 8vo., 6s.

Ugone: a Tragedy. Fcp. 8vo., 6s.

A Garland from Greece: Poems. Fcp. 8vo., 7s. 6d.

Stories of Wicklow: Poems. Fcp. 8vo., 7s. 6d.

Mephistopheles in Broadcloth: a Satire. Fcp. 8vo., 4s.

One in the Infinite: a Poem. Crown 8vo., 7s. 6d.

Armstrong.—*The Poetical Works of Edmund J. Armstrong.* Fcp. 8vo., 5s.

Arnold.—*The Light of the World*: or, The Great Consummation. By Sir Edwin Arnold. With 14 Illustrations after Holman Hunt. Crown 8vo., 6s.

Barraud.—*The Lay of the Knights.* By the Rev. C. W. Barraud, S.J., Author of 'St. Thomas of Canterbury, and other Poems'. Crown 8vo., 4s.

Bell (Mrs. Hugh).

Chamber Comedies: a Collection of Plays and Monologues for the Drawing Room. Crown 8vo., 6s

Fairy Tale Plays, and How to Act Them. With 91 Diagrams and 52 Illustrations. Crown 8vo., 3s. 6d.

Coleridge.—*Selections from.* With Introduction by Andrew Lang. With 18 Illustrations by Patten Wilson. Crown 8vo., 3s. 6d.

Goethe.—*The First Part of the Tragedy of Faust in English.* By Thos. E. Webb, LL.D., sometime Fellow of Trinity College; Professor of Moral Philosophy in the University of Dublin, etc. New and Cheaper Edition, with *The Death of Faust*, from the Second Part. Crown 8vo., 6s.

Gore-Booth.—*Poems.* By Eva Gore-Booth. Fcp. 8vo., 5s.

Ingelow (Jean).

Poetical Works. Complete in One Volume. Crown 8vo., 6s. net.

Lyrical and other Poems. Selected from the Writings of Jean Ingelow. Fcp. 8vo., 2s. 6d. cloth plain, 3s. cloth gilt.

Lang (Andrew).

Grass of Parnassus. Fcp. 8vo., 2s. 6d. net.

The Blue Poetry Book. Edited by Andrew Lang. With 100 Illustrations. Crown 8vo., 6s.

Layard and Corder.—*Songs in Many Moods.* By Nina F. Layard; *The Wandering Albatross*, etc. By Annie Corder. In One Volume. Crown 8vo., 5s.

Lecky.—*Poems.* By the Right Hon. W. E. H. Lecky. Fcp. 8vo., 5s.

Lytton (The Earl of), (Owen Meredith).

The Wanderer. Cr. 8vo., 10s. 6d.

Lucile. Crown 8vo., 10s. 6d.

Selected Poems. Cr. 8vo., 10s. 6d.

Macaulay.—*Lays of Ancient Rome, with 'Ivry' and 'The Armada'.* By Lord Macaulay.

Illustrated by G. Scharf. Fcp. 4to., 10s. 6d.

——— Bijou Edition. 18mo., 2s. 6d. gilt top.

——— Popular Edition. Fcp. 4to., 6d. sewed, 1s. cloth.

Illustrated by J. R. Weguelin. Crown 8vo., 3s. 6d.

Annotated Edition. Fcp. 8vo., 1s. sewed, 1s. 6d. cloth.

Poetry and the Drama—*continued.*

MacDonald (GEORGE, LL.D.).

A BOOK OF STRIFE, IN THE FORM OF THE DIARY OF AN OLD SOUL: Poems. 18mo., 6*s.*

RAMPOLLI: GROWTHS FROM A LONG-PLANTED ROOT: being Translations, New and Old (mainly in verse), chiefly from the German; along with 'A Year's Diary of an Old Soul'. Crown 8vo., 6*s.*

Moffat.—*CRICKETY CRICKET:* Rhymes and Parodies. By DOUGLAS MOFFAT. With Frontispiece by the late Sir FRANK LOCKWOOD, and 53 Illustrations by the Author. Crown 8vo, 2*s.* 6*d.*

Moon.—*POEMS OF LOVE AND HOME,* etc. By GEORGE WASHINGTON MOON, Hon. F.R.S.L., Author of 'Elijah,' etc. 16mo., 2*s.* 6*d.*

Morris (WILLIAM).

POETICAL WORKS—LIBRARY EDITION.

THE EARTHLY PARADISE. 4 vols. Crown 8vo., 5*s.* net each.

THE LIFE AND DEATH OF JASON. Crown 8vo., 5*s.* net.

THE DEFENCE OF GUENEVERE, and other Poems. Crown 8vo., 5*s.* net.

THE STORY OF SIGURD THE VOLSUNG, AND THE FALL OF THE NIBLUNGS. Cr. 8vo., 5*s.* net.

POEMS BY THE WAY, AND LOVE IS ENOUGH. Crown 8vo., 5*s.* net.

THE ODYSSEY OF HOMER. Done into English Verse. Crown 8vo., 5*s.* net.

THE ÆNEIDS OF VIRGIL. Done into English Verse. Crown 8vo., 5*s.* net.

THE TALE OF BEOWULF, SOMETIME KING OF THE FOLK OF THE WEDERGEATS. Translated by WILLIAM MORRIS and A. J. WYATT. Crown 8vo., 5*s.* net.

Certain of the POETICAL WORKS may also be had in the following Editions:—

THE EARTHLY PARADISE.

Popular Edition. 5 vols. 12mo., 25*s.*; or 5*s.* each, sold separately.

The same in Ten Parts, 25*s.*; or 2*s.* 6*d.* each, sold separately.

Cheap Edition, in 1 vol. Crown 8vo., 6*s.* net.

POEMS BY THE WAY. Square crown 8vo., 6*s.*

*** For Mr. William Morris's Prose Works, see pp. 22 and 31.

Nesbit.—*LAYS AND LEGENDS.* By E. NESBIT (Mrs. HUBERT BLAND). First Series. Crown 8vo., 3*s.* 6*d.* Second Series. With Portrait. Crown 8vo., 5*s.*

Riley (JAMES WHITCOMB).

OLD FASHIONED ROSES: Poems. 12mo., 5*s.*

THE GOLDEN YEAR. From the Verse and Prose of JAMES WHITCOMB RILEY. Compiled by CLARA E. LAUGHLIN. Fcp. 8vo., 5*s.*

Romanes.—*A SELECTION FROM THE POEMS OF GEORGE JOHN ROMANES, M.A., LL.D., F.R.S.* With an Introduction by T. HERBERT WARREN, President of Magdalen College, Oxford. Crown 8vo., 4*s.* 6*d.*

Russell.—*SONNETS ON THE SONNET:* an Anthology. Compiled by the Rev. MATTHEW RUSSELL, S.J. Crown 8vo., 3*s.* 6*d.*

Samuels.—*SHADOWS, AND OTHER POEMS.* By E. SAMUELS. With 7 Illustrations by W. FITZGERALD, M.A. Crown 8vo., 3*s.* 6*d.*

Shakespeare.

BOWDLER'S FAMILY SHAKESPEARE. With 36 Woodcuts. 1 vol. 8vo., 14*s.* Or in 6 vols. Fcp. 8vo., 21*s.*

SHAKESPEARE'S SONNETS. Reconsidered, and in part Rearranged, with Introductory Chapters and a Reprint of the Original 1609 Edition, by SAMUEL BUTLER, Author of 'Erewhon'. 8vo., 10*s.* 6*d.*

THE SHAKESPEARE BIRTHDAY BOOK. By MARY F. DUNBAR. 32mo., 1*s.* 6*d.*

Wagner.—*THE NIBELUNGEN RING.* Done into English Verse by REGINALD RANKIN, B.A. of the Inner Temple, Barrister-at-Law. Vol. I. Rhine Gold and Valkyrie. Fcp. 8vo., 4*s.* 6*d.*

Wordsworth.—*SELECTED POEMS.* By ANDREW LANG. With Photogravure Frontispiece of Rydal Mount. With 16 Illustrations and numerous Initial Letters. By ALFRED PARSONS, A.R.A. Crown 8vo., gilt edges, 3*s.* 6*d.*

Wordsworth and Coleridge.—*A DESCRIPTION OF THE WORDSWORTH AND COLERIDGE MANUSCRIPTS IN THE POSSESSION OF MR. T. NORTON LONGMAN.* Edited, with Notes, by W. HALE WHITE. With 3 Facsimile Reproductions. 4to., 10*s.* 6*d.*

Fiction, Humour, &c.

Anstey.—*VOCES POPULI.* Reprinted from 'Punch'. By F. ANSTEY, Author of 'Vice Versâ'. First Series. With 20 Illustrations by J. BERNARD PARTRIDGE. Crown 8vo., 3*s.* 6*d.*

Beaconsfield (THE EARL OF).

NOVELS AND TALES. Complete in 11 vols. Crown 8vo., 1*s.* 6*d.* each.

Vivian Grey.	Sybil.
The Young Duke, etc.	Henrietta Temple.
Alroy, Ixion, etc.	Venetia.
Contarini Fleming, etc.	Coningsby.
	Lothair.
Tancred.	Endymion.

Birt.—*CASTLE CZVARGAS:* a Romance. Being a Plain Story of the Romantic Adventures of Two Brothers, Told by the Younger of Them. Edited by ARCHIBALD BIRT. Crown 8vo., 6*s.*

'Chola.'—*A NEW DIVINITY, AND OTHER STORIES OF HINDU LIFE.* By 'CHOLA'. Crown 8vo., 2*s.* 6*d.*

Churchill.—*SAVROLA:* a Tale of the Revolution in Laurania. By WINSTON SPENCER CHURCHILL. Crown 8vo., 6*s.*

Diderot. — *RAMEAU'S NEPHEW:* a Translation from Diderot's Autographic Text. By SYLVIA MARGARET HILL. Crown 8vo., 3*s.* 6*d.*

Dougall.—*BEGGARS ALL.* By L. DOUGALL. Crown 8vo., 3*s.* 6*d.*

Doyle (A. CONAN).

MICAH CLARKE: A Tale of Monmouth's Rebellion. With 10 Illustrations. Cr. 8vo., 3*s.* 6*d.*

THE CAPTAIN OF THE POLESTAR, and other Tales. Cr. 8vo., 3*s.* 6*d.*

THE REFUGEES: A Tale of the Huguenots. With 25 Illustrations. Cr. 8vo., 3*s.* 6*d.*

THE STARK MUNRO LETTERS. Cr. 8vo, 3*s.* 6*d.*

Farrar (F. W., DEAN OF CANTERBURY).

DARKNESS AND DAWN: or, Scenes in the Days of Nero. An Historic Tale. Cr. 8vo., 6*s.* net.

GATHERING CLOUDS: a Tale of the Days of St. Chrysostom. Cr. 8vo., 6*s.* net.

Fowler (EDITH H.).

THE YOUNG PRETENDERS. A Story of Child Life. With 12 Illustrations by Sir PHILIP BURNE-JONES, Bart. Crown 8vo., 6*s.*

THE PROFESSOR'S CHILDREN. With 24 Illustrations by ETHEL KATE BURGESS. Crown 8vo., 6*s.*

Francis.—*YEOMAN FLEETWOOD.* By M. E. FRANCIS, Author of 'In a North-country Village,' etc. Crown 8vo., 6*s.*

Froude.—*THE TWO CHIEFS OF DUNBOY:* an Irish Romance of the Last Century. By JAMES A. FROUDE. Cr. 8vo., 3*s.* 6*d.*

Gurdon.—*MEMORIES AND FANCIES:* Suffolk Tales and other Stories; Fairy Legends; Poems; Miscellaneous Articles. By the late LADY CAMILLA GURDON, Author of 'Suffolk Folk-Lore'. Crown 8vo., 5*s.*

Haggard (H. RIDER).

BLACK HEART AND WHITE HEART, AND OTHER STORIES. With 33 Illustrations. Crown 8vo., 6*s.*

SWALLOW: a Tale of the Great Trek. With 8 Illustrations. Crown 8vo., 6*s.*

DR. THERNE. Crown 8vo., 3*s.* 6*d.*

HEART OF THE WORLD. With 15 Illustrations. Crown 8vo., 3*s.* 6*d.*

JOAN HASTE. With 20 Illustrations. Crown 8vo., 3*s.* 6*d.*

THE PEOPLE OF THE MIST. With 16 Illustrations. Crown 8vo., 3*s.* 6*d.*

MONTEZUMA'S DAUGHTER. With 24 Illustrations. Crown 8vo., 3*s.* 6*d.*

SHE. With 32 Illustrations. Crown 8vo., 3*s.* 6*d.*

ALLAN QUATERMAIN. With 31 Illustrations. Crown 8vo., 3*s.* 6*d.*

MAIWA'S REVENGE. Cr. 8vo., 1*s.* 6*d.*

COLONEL QUARITCH, V.C. With Frontispiece and Vignette. Cr. 8vo., 3*s.* 6*d.*

CLEOPATRA. With 29 Illustrations. Crown 8vo., 3*s.* 6*d.*

BEATRICE. With Frontispiece and Vignette. Cr. 8vo., 3*s.* 6*d.*

ERIC BRIGHTEYES. With 51 Illustrations. Crown 8vo., 3*s.* 6*d.*

NADA THE LILY. With 23 Illustrations. Crown 8vo., 3*s.* 6*d.*

ALLAN'S WIFE. With 34 Illustrations. Crown 8vo.. 3*s.* 6*d.*

THE WITCH'S HEAD. With 16 Illustrations. Crown 8vo., 3*s.* 6*d.*

MR. MEESON'S WILL. With 16 Illustrations. Crown 8vo., 3*s.* 6*d.*

DAWN. With 16 Illustrations. Cr. 8vo., 3*s.* 6*d.*

Haggard and Lang.—*THE WORLD'S DESIRE.* By H. RIDER HAGGARD and ANDREW LANG. With 27 Illustrations. Crown 8vo., 3*s.* 6*d.*

Fiction, Humour, &c.—*continued.*

Harte.—*In the Carquinez Woods.* By Bret Harte. Crown 8vo., 3s. 6d.

Hope.—*The Heart of Princess Osra.* By Anthony Hope. With 9 Illustrations. Crown 8vo., 3s. 6d.

Jerome.—*Sketches in Lavender: Blue and Green.* By Jerome K. Jerome. Crown 8vo., 3s. 6d.

Joyce.—*Old Celtic Romances.* Twelve of the most beautiful of the Ancient Irish Romantic Tales. Translated from the Gaelic. By P. W. Joyce, LL.D. Crown 8vo., 3s. 6d.

Lang.—*A Monk of Fife;* a Story of the Days of Joan of Arc. By Andrew Lang. With 13 Illustrations by Selwyn Image. Crown 8vo., 3s. 6d.

Levett-Yeats (S.).

The Chevalier D'Auriac. Crown 8vo., 3s. 6d.

The Heart of Denise, and other Tales. Crown 8vo., 6s.

Lyall (Edna).

The Autobiography of a Slander. Fcp. 8vo., 1s., sewed.
Presentation Edition. With 20 Illustrations by Lancelot Speed. Crown 8vo., 2s. 6d. net.

The Autobiography of a Truth. Fcp. 8vo., 1s., sewed; 1s. 6d., cloth.

Doreen. The Story of a Singer. Crown 8vo., 6s.

Wayfaring Men. Crown 8vo., 6s.

Hope the Hermit: a Romance of Borrowdale. Crown 8vo., 6s.

Mason and Lang.—*Parson Kelly.* By A. E. W. Mason and Andrew Lang. Crown 8vo., 6s.

Max Müller.—*Deutsche Liebe (German Love):* Fragments from the Papers of an Alien. Collected by F. Max Müller. Translated from the German by G. A. M. Crown 8vo., 5s.

Melville (G. J. Whyte).

The Gladiators.	Holmby House.
The Interpreter.	Kate Coventry.
Good for Nothing.	Digby Grand.
The Queen's Maries.	General Bounce.

Crown 8vo., 1s. 6d. each.

Merriman.—*Flotsam:* A Story of the Indian Mutiny. By Henry Seton Merriman. Crown 8vo., 3s. 6d.

Morris (William).

The Sundering Flood. Cr. 8vo., 7s. 6d.

The Water of the Wondrous Isles. Crown 8vo., 7s. 6d.

The Well at the World's End. 2 vols. 8vo., 28s.

The Story of the Glittering Plain, which has been also called The Land of the Living Men, or The Acre of the Undying. Square post 8vo., 5s. net.

The Roots of the Mountains, wherein is told somewhat of the Lives of the Men of Burgdale, their Friends, their Neighbours, their Foemen, and their Fellows-in-Arms. Written in Prose and Verse. Square crown 8vo., 8s.

A Tale of the House of the Wolfings, and all the Kindreds of the Mark. Written in Prose and Verse. Square crown 8vo., 6s.

A Dream of John Ball, and a King's Lesson. 12mo., 1s. 6d.

News from Nowhere; or, An Epoch of Rest. Being some Chapters from an Utopian Romance. Post 8vo., 1s. 6d.

The Story of Grettir the Strong. Translated from the Icelandic by Eiríkr Magnússon and William Morris. Cr. 8vo., 5s. net.

*** For Mr. William Morris's Poetical Works, see p. 20.

Newman (Cardinal).

Loss and Gain: The Story of a Convert. Crown 8vo. Cabinet Edition, 6s.; Popular Edition, 3s. 6d.

Callista: A Tale of the Third Century. Crown 8vo. Cabinet Edition, 6s.; Popular Edition, 3s. 6d.

Fiction, Humour, &c.—*continued.*

Phillipps-Wolley.—*SNAP: a Legend of the Lone Mountain.* By C. PHILLIPPS-WOLLEY. With 13 Illustrations. Crown 8vo., 3s. 6d.

Raymond (WALTER).

TWO MEN O' MENDIP. Cr. 8vo., 6s.

NO SOUL ABOVE MONEY. Cr. 8vo., 6s.

Reader.—*PRIESTESS AND QUEEN:* a Tale of the White Race of Mexico; being the Adventures of Ignigene and her Twenty-six Fair Maidens. By EMILY E. READER. Illustrated by EMILY K. READER. Crown 8vo., 6s.

Sewell (ELIZABETH M.).

A Glimpse of the World	Amy Herbert
Laneton Parsonage.	Cleve Hall.
Margaret Percival.	Gertrude.
Katharine Ashton.	Home Life.
The Earl's Daughter.	After Life.
The Experience of Life.	Ursula. Ivors.

Cr. 8vo., 1s. 6d. each cloth plain. 2s. 6d. each cloth extra, gilt edges.

Somerville and Ross.—*SOME EXPERIENCES OF AN IRISH R.M.* By E. Œ. SOMERVILLE and MARTIN ROSS. With 31 Illustrations by E. Œ. SOMERVILLE. Crown 8vo., 6s.

Stebbing.—*PROBABLE TALES.* Edited by WILLIAM STEBBING. Crown 8vo., 4s. 6d.

Stevenson (ROBERT LOUIS).

THE STRANGE CASE OF DR. JEKYLL AND MR. HYDE. Fcp. 8vo., 1s. sewed. 1s. 6d. cloth.

THE STRANGE CASE OF DR. JEKYLL AND MR. HYDE; WITH OTHER FABLES. Crown 8vo., 3s. 6d.

MORE NEW ARABIAN NIGHTS—THE DYNAMITER. By ROBERT LOUIS STEVENSON and FANNY VAN DE GRIFT STEVENSON. Crown 8vo., 3s. 6d.

THE WRONG BOX. By ROBERT LOUIS STEVENSON and LLOYD OSBOURNE. Crown 8vo., 3s. 6d.

Suttner.—*LAY DOWN YOUR ARMS* (*Die Waffen Nieder*): The Autobiography of Martha von Tilling. By BERTHA VON SUTTNER. Translated by T. HOLMES. Cr. 8vo., 1s. 6d.

Taylor.—*EARLY ITALIAN LOVE-STORIES.* Taken from the Originals by UNA TAYLOR. With 13 Illustrations by HENRY J. FORD. Crown 4to., 15s. net.

Trollope (ANTHONY).

THE WARDEN. Cr. 8vo., 1s. 6d.

BARCHESTER TOWERS. Cr. 8vo., 1s. 6d.

Walford (L. B.).

MR. SMITH: a Part of his Life. Crown 8vo., 2s. 6d.

THE BABY'S GRANDMOTHER. Cr. 8vo., 2s. 6d.

COUSINS. Crown 8vo., 2s. 6d.

TROUBLESOME DAUGHTERS. Cr. 8vo., 2s. 6d.

PAULINE. Crown 8vo., 2s. 6d.

DICK NETHERBY. Cr. 8vo., 2s. 6d.

THE HISTORY OF A WEEK. Cr. 8vo. 2s. 6d.

A STIFF-NECKED GENERATION. Cr. 8vo. 2s. 6d.

NAN, and other Stories. Cr. 8vo., 2s. 6d.

THE MISCHIEF OF MONICA. Cr. 8vo., 2s. 6d.

THE ONE GOOD GUEST. Cr. 8vo. 2s. 6d.

'PLOUGHED,' and other Stories. Crown 8vo., 2s. 6d.

THE MATCHMAKER. Cr. 8vo., 2s. 6d.

THE INTRUDERS. Crown 8vo., 2s. 6d.

LEDDY MARGET. Crown 8vo., 2s. 6d.

IVA KILDARE: a Matrimonial Problem. Crown 8vo., 2s. 6d.

Ward.—*ONE POOR SCRUPLE.* By Mrs. WILFRID WARD. Crown 8vo., 6s.

Weyman (STANLEY).

SOPHIA. With Frontispiece. Crown 8vo., 6s.

THE HOUSE OF THE WOLF. With Frontispiece and Vignette. Crown 8vo., 3s. 6d.

A GENTLEMAN OF FRANCE. With Frontispiece and Vignette. Cr. 8vo., 6s.

THE RED COCKADE. With Frontispiece and Vignette. Crown 8vo., 6s.

SHREWSBURY. With 24 Illustrations by CLAUDE A. SHEPPERSON. Cr. 8vo., 6s.

Popular Science (Natural History, &c.).

Beddard. — *THE STRUCTURE AND CLASSIFICATION OF BIRDS.* By FRANK E. BEDDARD, M.A., F.R.S., Prosector and Vice-Secretary of the Zoological Society of London. With 252 Illustrations. 8vo., 21*s.* net.

Butler.—*OUR HOUSEHOLD INSECTS.* An Account of the Insect-Pests found in Dwelling-Houses. By EDWARD A. BUTLER, B.A., B.Sc. (Lond.). With 113 Illustrations. Crown 8vo., 3*s.* 6*d.*

Furneaux (W.).

THE OUTDOOR WORLD; or The Young Collector's Handbook. With 18 Plates (16 of which are coloured), and 549 Illustrations in the Text. Crown 8vo., 6*s.* net.

BUTTERFLIES AND MOTHS (British). With 12 coloured Plates and 241 Illustrations in the Text. Crown 8vo., 6*s.* net.

LIFE IN PONDS AND STREAMS. With 8 coloured Plates and 331 Illustrations in the Text. Crown 8vo., 6*s.* net.

Hartwig (DR. GEORGE).

THE SEA AND ITS LIVING WONDERS. With 12 Plates and 303 Woodcuts. 8vo., 7*s.* net.

THE TROPICAL WORLD. With 8 Plates and 172 Woodcuts. 8vo., 7*s.* net.

THE POLAR WORLD. With 3 Maps, 8 Plates and 85 Woodcuts. 8vo., 7*s.* net.

THE SUBTERRANEAN WORLD. With 3 Maps and 80 Woodcuts. 8vo., 7*s.* net.

HEROES OF THE POLAR WORLD. With 19 Illustrations. Cr. 8vo., 2*s.*

WONDERS OF THE TROPICAL FORESTS. With 40 Illustrations. Cr. 8vo., 2*s.*

WORKERS UNDER THE GROUND. With 29 Illustrations. Cr. 8vo., 2*s.*

MARVELS OVER OUR HEADS. With 29 Illustrations. Cr. 8vo., 2*s.*

SEA MONSTERS AND SEA BIRDS. With 75 Illustrations. Cr. 8vo., 2*s.* 6*d.*

DENIZENS OF THE DEEP. With 117 Illustrations. Cr. 8vo., 2*s.* 6*d.*

Hartwig (DR. GEORGE)—*continued.*

VOLCANOES AND EARTHQUAKES. With 30 Illustrations. Cr. 8vo., 2*s.* 6*d.*

WILD ANIMALS OF THE TROPICS. With 66 Illustrations. Cr. 8vo., 3*s.* 6*d.*

Helmholtz.—*POPULAR LECTURES ON SCIENTIFIC SUBJECTS.* By HERMANN VON HELMHOLTZ. With 68 Woodcuts. 2 vols. Cr. 8vo., 3*s.* 6*d.* each.

Hudson (W. H.).

NATURE IN DOWNLAND. With 12 Plates and 14 Illustrations in the Text by A. D. MCCORMICK. 8vo., 10*s.* 6*d.* net.

BRITISH BIRDS. With a Chapter on Structure and Classification by FRANK E. BEDDARD, F.R.S. With 16 Plates (8 of which are Coloured), and over 100 Illustrations in the Text. Cr. 8vo., 6*s.* net.

BIRDS IN LONDON. With 17 Plates and 15 Illustrations in the Text, by BRYAN HOOK, A. D. MCCORMICK, and from Photographs from Nature, by R. B. LODGE. 8vo., 12*s.*

Proctor (RICHARD A.).

LIGHT SCIENCE FOR LEISURE HOURS. Familiar Essays on Scientific Subjects. Vol. I. Crown 8vo., 3*s.* 6*d.*

ROUGH WAYS MADE SMOOTH. Familiar Essays on Scientific Subjects. Crown 8vo., 3*s.* 6*d.*

PLEASANT WAYS IN SCIENCE. Crown 8vo., 3*s.* 6*d.*

NATURE STUDIES. By R. A. PROCTOR, GRANT ALLEN, A. WILSON, T. FOSTER and E. CLODD. Crown 8vo., 3*s.* 6*d.*

LEISURE READINGS. By R. A. PROCTOR, E. CLODD, A. WILSON, T. FOSTER and A. C. RANYARD. Cr. 8vo., 3*s.* 6*d.*

*** For Mr. Proctor's other books see pp. 13 and 28, and Messrs. Longmans & Co.'s Catalogue of Scientific Works.*

Stanley.—*A FAMILIAR HISTORY OF BIRDS.* By E. STANLEY, D.D., formerly Bishop of Norwich. With 160 Illustrations. Cr. 8vo., 3*s.* 6*d.*

Popular Science (Natural History, &c.)—*continued.*

Wood (Rev. J. G.).

Homes without Hands: A Description of the Habitations of Animals, classed according to the Principle of Construction. With 140 Illustrations. 8vo., 7s. net.

Insects at Home: A Popular Account of British Insects, their Structure, Habits and Transformations. With 700 Illustrations. 8vo., 7s. net.

Out of Doors; a Selection of Original Articles on Practical Natural History. With 11 Illustrations. Cr. 8vo., 3s. 6d.

Strange Dwellings: a Description of the Habitations of Animals, abridged from 'Homes without Hands'. With 60 Illustrations. Cr. 8vo., 3s. 6d.

Wood (Rev. J. G.)—*continued.*

Petland Revisited. With 33 Illustrations. Cr. 8vo., 3s. 6d.

Bird Life of the Bible. With 32 Illustrations. Cr. 8vo., 3s. 6d.

Wonderful Nests. With 30 Illustrations. Cr. 8vo., 3s. 6d.

Homes under the Ground. With 28 Illustrations. Cr. 8vo., 3s. 6d.

Wild Animals of the Bible. With 29 Illustrations. Cr. 8vo., 3s. 6d.

Domestic Animals of the Bible. With 23 Illustrations. Cr. 8vo., 3s. 6d.

The Branch Builders. With 28 Illustrations. Cr. 8vo., 2s. 6d.

Social Habitations and Parasitic Nests. With 18 Illustrations. Cr. 8vo., 2s.

Works of Reference.

Gwilt.—*An Encyclopædia of Architecture.* By Joseph Gwilt, F.S.A. With 1700 Engravings. Revised (1888), with Alterations and Considerable Additions by Wyatt Papworth. 8vo., 21s. net.

Maunder (Samuel).

Biographical Treasury. With Supplement brought down to 1889. By Rev. James Wood. Fcp. 8vo., 6s.

Treasury of Geography, Physical, Historical, Descriptive, and Political. With 7 Maps and 16 Plates. Fcp. 8vo., 6s.

The Treasury of Bible Knowledge. By the Rev. J. Ayre, M.A. With 5 Maps, 15 Plates, and 300 Woodcuts. Fcp. 8vo., 6s.

Treasury of Knowledge and Library of Reference. Fcp. 8vo., 6s.

Historical Treasury. Fcp. 8vo., 6s.

Maunder (Samuel)—*continued.*

Scientific and Literary Treasury. Fcp. 8vo., 6s.

The Treasury of Botany. Edited by J. Lindley, F.R.S., and T. Moore, F.L.S. With 274 Woodcuts and 20 Steel Plates. 2 vols. Fcp. 8vo., 12s.

Roget. — *Thesaurus of English Words and Phrases.* Classified and Arranged so as to Facilitate the Expression of Ideas and assist in Literary Composition. By Peter Mark Roget, M.D., F.R.S. Recomposed throughout, enlarged and improved, partly from the Author's Notes, and with a full Index, by the Author's Son, John Lewis Roget. Crown 8vo., 10s. 6d.

Willich.—*Popular Tables* for giving information for ascertaining the value of Lifehold, Leasehold, and Church Property, the Public Funds, etc. By Charles M. Willich. Edited by H. Bence Jones. Crown 8vo., 10s. 6d.

Children's Books.

Buckland.—*Two Little Runaways.* Adapted from the French of Louis Desnoyers. By James Buckland. With 110 Illustrations by Cecil Aldin. Cr. 8vo., 6s.

Crake (Rev. A. D.).

Edwy the Fair; or, The First Chronicle of Æscendune. Cr. 8vo., 2s. 6d.

Alfgar the Dane; or, The Second Chronicle of Æscendune. Cr. 8vo. 2s. 6d.

Crake (Rev. A. D.)—*continued.*

The Rival Heirs: being the Third and Last Chronicle of Æscendune. Cr. 8vo., 2s. 6d.

The House of Walderne. A Tale of the Cloister and the Forest in the Days of the Barons' Wars. Crown 8vo., 2s. 6d.

Brian Fitz-Count. A Story of Wallingford Castle and Dorchester Abbey. Cr. 8vo., 2s. 6d.

Children's Books—*continued.*

Henty (G. A.).—EDITED BY.

YULE LOGS: A Story-Book for Boys. By VARIOUS AUTHORS. With 61 Illustrations. Crown 8vo., 6*s.*

YULE TIDE YARNS: a Story-Book for Boys. By VARIOUS AUTHORS. With 45 Illustrations. Crown 8vo., 6*s.*

Lang (ANDREW).—EDITED BY.

THE BLUE FAIRY BOOK. With 138 Illustrations. Crown 8vo., 6*s.*

THE RED FAIRY BOOK. With 100 Illustrations. Crown 8vo., 6*s.*

THE GREEN FAIRY BOOK. With 99 Illustrations. Crown 8vo., 6*s.*

THE YELLOW FAIRY BOOK. With 104 Illustrations. Crown 8vo., 6*s.*

THE PINK FAIRY BOOK. With 67 Illustrations. Crown 8vo., 6*s.*

THE BLUE POETRY BOOK. With 100 Illustrations. Crown 8vo., 6*s.*

THE BLUE POETRY BOOK. School Edition, without Illustrations. Fcp. 8vo., 2*s.* 6*d.*

THE TRUE STORY BOOK. With 66 Illustrations. Crown 8vo., 6*s.*

THE RED TRUE STORY BOOK. With 100 Illustrations. Crown 8vo., 6*s.*

THE ANIMAL STORY BOOK. With 67 Illustrations. Crown 8vo., 6*s.*

THE RED BOOK OF ANIMAL STORIES. With 65 Illustrations. Crown 8vo., 6*s.*

THE ARABIAN NIGHTS ENTERTAINMENTS. With 66 Illustrations. Cr. 8vo., 6*s.*

Meade (L. T.).

DADDY'S BOY. With 8 Illustrations. Crown 8vo., 3*s.* 6*d.*

DEB AND THE DUCHESS. With 7 Illustrations. Crown 8vo., 3*s.* 6*d.*

THE BERESFORD PRIZE. With 7 Illustrations. Crown 8vo., 3*s.* 6*d.*

THE HOUSE OF SURPRISES. With 6 Illustrations. Crown 8vo. 3*s.* 6*d.*

Praeger (ROSAMOND).

THE ADVENTURES OF THE THREE BOLD BABES: HECTOR, HONORIA AND ALISANDER. A Story in Pictures. With 24 Coloured Plates and 24 Outline Pictures. Oblong 4to., 3*s.* 6*d.*

THE FURTHER DOINGS OF THE THREE BOLD BABIES. With 24 Coloured Pictures and 24 Outline Pictures. Oblong 4to., 3*s.* 6*d.*

Stevenson.—*A CHILD'S GARDEN OF VERSES.* By ROBERT LOUIS STEVENSON. Fcp. 8vo., 5*s.*

Upton (FLORENCE K. AND BERTHA).

THE ADVENTURES OF TWO DUTCH DOLLS AND A 'GOLLIWOGG'. With 31 Coloured Plates and numerous Illustrations in the Text. Oblong 4to., 6*s.*

THE GOLLIWOGG'S BICYCLE CLUB. With 31 Coloured Plates and numerous Illustrations in the Text. Oblong 4to., 6*s.*

THE GOLLIWOGG AT THE SEASIDE. With 31 Coloured Plates and numerous Illustrations in the Text. Oblong 4to., 6*s.*

THE GOLLIWOGG IN WAR. With 31 Coloured Plates. Oblong 4to., 6*s.*

THE VEGE-MEN'S REVENGE. With 31 Coloured Plates and numerous Illustrations in the Text. Oblong 4to., 6*s.*

The Silver Library.

CROWN 8VO. 3*s.* 6*d.* EACH VOLUME.

Arnold's (Sir Edwin) Seas and Lands. With 71 Illustrations. 3*s.* 6*d.*

Bagehot's (W.) Biographical Studies. 3*s.* 6*d.*

Bagehot's (W.) Economic Studies. 3*s.* 6*d.*

Bagehot's (W.) Literary Studies. With Portrait. 3 vols, 3*s.* 6*d.* each.

Baker's (Sir S. W.) Eight Years in Ceylon. With 6 Illustrations. 3*s.* 6*d.*

Baker's (Sir S. W.) Rifle and Hound in Ceylon. With 6 Illustrations. 3*s.* 6*d.*

Baring-Gould's (Rev. S.) Curious Myths of the Middle Ages. 3*s.* 6*d.*

Baring-Gould's (Rev. S.) Origin and Development of Religious Belief. 2 vols. 3*s.* 6*d.* each.

Becker's (W. A.) Gallus: or, Roman Scenes in the Time of Augustus. With 26 Illus. 3*s.* 6*d.*

Becker's (W. A.) Charicles: or, Illustrations of the Private Life of the Ancient Greeks. With 26 Illustrations. 3*s.* 6*d.*

Bent's (J. T.) The Ruined Cities of Mashonaland. With 117 Illustrations. 3*s.* 6*d.*

Brassey's (Lady) A Voyage in the 'Sunbeam'. With 66 Illustrations. 3*s.* 6*d.*

Churchill's (W. S.) The Story of the Malakand Field Force, 1897. With 6 Maps and Plans. 3*s.* 6*d.*

Clodd's (E.) Story of Creation: a Plain Account of Evolution. With 77 Illustrations. 3*s.* 6*d.*

Conybeare (Rev. W. J.) and Howson's (Very Rev. J. S.) Life and Epistles of St. Paul. With 46 Illustrations. 3*s.* 6*d.*

Dougall's (L.) Beggars All: a Novel. 3*s.* 6*d.*

The Silver Library—*continued.*

Doyle's (A. Conan) Micah Clarke. A Tale of Monmouth's Rebellion. With 10 Illusts. 3*s*. 6*d*.

Doyle's (A. Conan) The Captain of the Polestar, and other Tales. 3*s*. 6*d*.

Doyle's (A. Conan) The Refugees: A Tale of the Huguenots. With 25 Illustrations. 3*s* 6*d*.

Doyle's (A. Conan) The Stark Munro Letters. 3*s*. 6*d*.

Froude's (J. A.) The History of England, from the Fall of Wolsey to the Defeat of the Spanish Armada. 12 vols. 3*s*. 6*d*. each.

Froude's (J. A.) The English in Ireland. 3 vols. 10*s*. 6*d*.

Froude's (J. A.) The Divorce of Catherine of Aragon. 3*s*. 6*d*.

Froude's (J. A.) The Spanish Story of the Armada, and other Essays. 3*s*. 6*d*.

Froude's (J. A.) Short Studies on Great Subjects. 4 vols. 3*s*. 6*d*. each.

Froude's (J. A.) Oceana, or England and Her Colonies. With 9 Illustrations. 3*s*. 6*d*.

Froude's (J. A.) The Council of Trent. 3*s*. 6*d*.

Froude's (J. A.) The Life and Letters of Erasmus. 3*s*. 6*d*.

Froude's (J. A.) Thomas Carlyle: a History of his Life.
1795-1835. 2 vols. 7*s*. 1834-1881. 2 vols. 7*s*.

Froude's (J. A.) Cæsar: a Sketch. 3*s*. 6*d*.

Froude's (J. A.) The Two Chiefs of Dunboy: an Irish Romance of the Last Century. 3*s*. 6*d*.

Gleig's (Rev. G. R.) Life of the Duke of Wellington. With Portrait. 3*s*. 6*d*.

Greville's (C. C. F.) Journal of the Reigns of King George IV., King William IV., and Queen Victoria. 8 vols., 3*s*. 6*d*. each.

Haggard's (H. R.) She: A History of Adventure. With 32 Illustrations. 3*s*. 6*d*.

Haggard's (H. R.) Allan Quatermain With 20 Illustrations. 3*s*. 6*d*.

Haggard's (H. R.) Colonel Quaritch, V.C.: a Tale of Country Life. With Frontispiece and Vignette. 3*s*. 6*d*.

Haggard's (H. R.) Cleopatra. With 29 Illustrations. 3*s*. 6*d*.

Haggard's (H. R.) Eric Brighteyes. With 51 Illustrations. 3*s*. 6*d*.

Haggard's (H. R.) Beatrice. With Frontispiece and Vignette. 3*s*. 6*d*.

Haggard's (H. R.) Allan's Wife. With 34 Illustrations. 3*s*. 6*d*.

Haggard (H. R.) Heart of the World. With 15 Illustrations. 3*s*. 6*d*.

Haggard's (H. R.) Montezuma's Daughter. With 25 Illustrations. 3*s*. 6*d*.

Haggard's (H. R.) The Witch's Head. With 16 Illustrations. 3*s*. 6*d*.

Haggard's (H. R.) Mr. Meeson's Will. With 16 Illustrations. 3*s*. 6*d*.

Haggard's (H. R.) Nada the Lily. With 23 Illustrations. 3*s*. 6*d*.

Haggard's (H. R.) Dawn. With 16 Illusts. 3*s*. 6*d*.

Haggard's (H. R.) The People of the Mist. With 16 Illustrations. 3*s*. 6*d*.

Haggard's (H. R.) Joan Haste. With 20 Illustrations. 3*s*. 6*d*.

Haggard (H. R.) and Lang's (A.) The World's Desire. With 27 Illustrations. 3*s*. 6*d*.

Harte's (Bret) In the Carquinez Woods and other Stories. 3*s*. 6*d*.

Helmholtz's (Hermann von) Popular Lectures on Scientific Subjects. With 68 Illustrations. 2 vols. 3*s*. 6*d*. each.

Hope's (Anthony) The Heart of Princess Osra. With 9 Illustrations. 3*s*. 6*d*.

Hornung's (E. W.) The Unbidden Guest. 3*s*. 6*d*

Howitt's (W.) Visits to Remarkable Places. With 80 Illustrations. 3*s*. 6*d*.

Jefferies' (R.) The Story of My Heart: My Autobiography. With Portrait. 3*s*. 6*d*.

Jefferies' (R.) Field and Hedgerow. With Portrait. 3*s*. 6*d*.

Jefferies' (R.) Red Deer. With 17 Illusts. 3*s*. 6*d*.

Jefferies' (R.) Wood Magic: a Fable. With Frontispiece and Vignette by E. V. B. 3*s*. 6*d*.

Jefferies (R.) The Toilers of the Field. With Portrait from the Bust in Salisbury Cathedral. 3*s*. 6*d*.

Kaye (Sir J.) and Malleson's (Colonel) History of the Indian Mutiny of 1857-8. 6 vols. 3*s*. 6*d*. each.

Knight's (E. F.) The Cruise of the 'Alerte': the Narrative of a Search for Treasure on the Desert Island of Trinidad. With 2 Maps and 23 Illustrations. 3*s*. 6*d*.

Knight's (E. F.) Where Three Empires Meet: a Narrative of Recent Travel in Kashmir, Western Tibet, Baltistan, Gilgit. With a Map and 54 Illustrations. 3*s*. 6*d*.

Knight's (E. F.) The 'Falcon' on the Baltic: a Coasting Voyage from Hammersmith to Copenhagen in a Three-Ton Yacht. With Map and 11 Illustrations. 3*s*. 6*d*.

Köstlin's (J.) Life of Luther. With 62 Illustrations and 4 Facsimiles of MSS. 3*s*. 6*d*.

Lang's (A.) Angling Sketches. With 20 Illustrations. 3*s*. 6*d*.

Lang's (A.) Custom and Myth: Studies of Early Usage and Belief. 3*s*. 6*d*.

Lang's (A.) Cock Lane and Common-Sense. 3*s*. 6*d*.

Lang's (A.) The Book of Dreams and Ghosts. 3*s*. 6*d*.

Lang's (A.) A Monk of Fife: a Story of the Days of Joan of Arc. With 13 Illustrations. 3*s*. 6*d*.

Lang's (A.) Myth, Ritual, and Religion. 2 vols. 7*s*.

Lees (J. A.) and Clutterbuck's (W. J.) B. C. 1887, A Ramble in British Columbia. With Maps and 75 Illustrations. 3*s*. 6*d*

Levett-Yeats' (S.) The Chevalier D'Auriac. 3*s*. 6*d*.

Macaulay's (Lord) Complete Works. 'Albany' Edition. With 12 Portraits. 12 vols. 3*s*. 6*d*. each.

Macaulay's (Lord) Essays and Lays of Ancient Rome, etc. With Portrait and 4 Illustrations to the 'Lays'. 3*s*. 6*d*.

The Silver Library—*continued.*

Macleod's (H. D.) Elements of Banking. 3*s.* 6*d.*

Marbot's (Baron de) Memoirs. Translated. 2 vols. 7*s.*

Marshman's (J. C.) Memoirs of Sir Henry Havelock. 3*s.* 6*d.*

Merivale's (Dean) History of the Romans under the Empire. 8 vols. 3*s.* 6*d.* each.

Merriman's (H. S.) Flotsam: A Tale of the Indian Mutiny. 3*s.* 6*d.*

Mill's (J. S.) Political Economy. 3*s.* 6*d.*

Mill's (J. S.) System of Logic. 3*s.* 6*d.*

Milner's (Geo.) Country Pleasures: the Chronicle of a Year chiefly in a Garden. 3*s.* 6*d.*

Nansen's (F.) The First Crossing of Greenland. With 142 Illustrations and a Map. 3*s.* 6*d.*

Phillipps-Wolley's (C.) Snap: a Legend of the Lone Mountain With 13 Illustrations. 3*s.* 6*d.*

Proctor's (R. A.) The Orbs Around Us. 3*s.* 6*d.*

Proctor's (R. A.) The Expanse of Heaven. 3*s.* 6*d.*

Proctor's (R. A.) Light Science for Leisure Hours. First Series. 3*s.* 6*d.*

Proctor's (R. A.) The Moon. 3*s.* 6*d.*

Proctor's (R. A.) Other Worlds than Ours. 3*s.* 6*d.*

Proctor's (R. A.) Our Place among Infinities: a Series of Essays contrasting our Little Abode in Space and Time with the Infinities around us. 3*s.* 6*d.*

Proctor's (R. A.) Other Suns than Ours. 3*s.* 6*d.*

Proctor's (R. A.) Rough Ways made Smooth. 3*s.* 6*d.*

Proctor's (R. A.) Pleasant Ways in Science. 3*s.* 6*d.*

Proctor's (R. A.) Myths and Marvels of Astronomy. 3*s.* 6*d.*

Proctor's (R. A.) Nature Studies. 3*s.* 6*d.*

Proctor's (R. A.) Leisure Readings. By R. A. Proctor, Edward Clodd, Andrew Wilson, Thomas Foster, and A. C. Ranyard. With Illustrations. 3*s.* 6*d.*

Rossetti's (Maria F.) A Shadow of Dante. 3*s.* 6*d.*

Smith's (R. Bosworth) Carthage and the Carthaginians. With Maps, Plans, etc. 3*s.* 6*d.*

Stanley's (Bishop) Familiar History of Birds. With 160 Illustrations. 3*s.* 6*d.*

Stephen's (L.) The Playground of Europe (The Alps). With 4 Illustrations. 3*s.* 6*d.*

Stevenson's (R. L.) The Strange Case of Dr. Jekyll and Mr. Hyde; with other Fables. 3*s.* 6*d.*

Stevenson (R. L.) and Osbourne's (Ll.) The Wrong Box. 3*s.* 6*d.*

Stevenson (Robert Louis) and Stevenson's (Fanny van de Grift) More New Arabian Nights.—The Dynamiter. 3*s.* 6*d.*

Trevelyan's (Sir G. O.) The Early History of Charles James Fox. 3*s.* 6*d.*

Weyman's (Stanley J.) The House of the Wolf: a Romance. 3*s.* 6*d.*

Wood's (Rev. J. G.) Petland Revisited. With 33 Illustrations. 3*s.* 6*d.*

Wood's (Rev. J. G.) Strange Dwellings. With 60 Illustrations. 3*s.* 6*d.*

Wood's (Rev. J. G.) Out of Doors. With 11 Illustrations. 3*s.* 6*d.*

Cookery, Domestic Management, &c.

Acton. — *Modern Cookery.* By Eliza Acton. With 150 Woodcuts. Fcp. 8vo., 4*s.* 6*d.*

Ashby.—*Health in the Nursery.* By Henry Ashby, M.D., F.R.C.P., Physician to the Manchester Children's Hospital. With 25 Illustrations. Crown 8vo., 3*s.* 6*d.*

Buckton.—*Comfort and Cleanliness:* The Servant and Mistress Question. By Mrs. Catherine M. Buckton. With 14 Illustrations. Crown 8vo., 2*s.*

Bull (Thomas, M.D.).

Hints to Mothers on the Management of their Health during the Period of Pregnancy. Fcp. 8vo., 1*s.* 6*d.*

The Maternal Management of Children in Health and Disease. Fcp. 8vo., 1*s.* 6*d.*

De Salis (Mrs.).

Cakes and Confections à la Mode. Fcp. 8vo., 1*s.* 6*d.*

Dogs: A Manual for Amateurs. Fcp. 8vo., 1*s.* 6*d.*

Dressed Game and Poultry à la Mode. Fcp. 8vo., 6*d.*

De Salis (Mrs.).—*continued.*

Dressed Vegetables à la Mode. Fcp. 8vo., 1*s* 6*d.*

Drinks à la Mode Fcp. 8vo., 1*s.* 6*d.*

Entrées à la Mode. Fcp. 8vo., 1*s.* 6*d.*

Floral Decorations. Fcp. 8vo., 1*s.* 6*d.*

Gardening à la Mode. Fcp. 8vo. Part I., Vegetables, 1*s.* 6*d.* Part II., Fruits, 1*s.* 6*d.*

National Viands à la Mode. Fcp. 8vo., 1*s.* 6*d.*

New-laid Eggs. Fcp. 8vo., 1*s.* 6*d.*

Oysters à la Mode. Fcp. 8vo., 1*s.* 6*d.*

Soups and Dressed Fish à la Mode. Fcp. 8vo., 1*s.* 6*d.*

Savouries à la Mode. Fcp. 8vo., 1*s.* 6*d.*

Puddings and Pastry à la Mode. Fcp. 8vo., 1*s.* 6*d.*

Sweets and Supper Dishes à la Mode. Fcp. 8vo., 1*s.* 6*d.*

Tempting Dishes for Small Incomes. Fcp. 8vo., 1*s.* 6*d.*

Wrinkles and Notions for Every Household. Crown 8vo., 1*s.* 6*d.*

Cookery, Domestic Management, &c.—*continued.*

Lear.—*Maigre Cookery.* By H. L. Sidney Lear. 16mo., 2*s.*

Mann.—*Manual of the Principles of Practical Cookery.* By E. E. Mann. Crown 8vo. 1*s.*

Poole.—*Cookery for the Diabetic.* By W. H. and Mrs. Poole. With Preface by Dr. Pavy. Fcp. 8vo., 2*s.* 6*d.*

Walker.—*A Book for Every Woman.* By Jane H. Walker.

Part I., The Management of Children in Health and out of Health. Crown 8vo., 2*s.* 6*d.*

Part II. Woman in Health and out of Health. Crown 8vo., 2*s.* 6*d.*

Miscellaneous and Critical Works.

Armstrong.—*Essays and Sketches.* By Edmund J. Armstrong. Fcp. 8vo., 5*s.*

Bagehot.—*Literary Studies.* By Walter Bagehot. With Portrait. 3 vols. Crown 8vo., 3*s.* 6*d.* each.

Baring-Gould.—*Curious Myths of the Middle Ages.* By Rev. S. Baring-Gould. Crown 8vo., 3*s.* 6*d.*

Baynes. — *Shakespeare Studies*, and other Essays. By the late Thomas Spencer Baynes, LL.B., LL.D. With a Biographical Preface by Professor Lewis Campbell. Crown 8vo., 7*s.* 6*d.*

Boyd (A. K. H.) ('**A.K.H.B.**').

And see MISCELLANEOUS THEOLOGICAL WORKS, *p.* 32.

Autumn Holidays of a Country Parson. Crown 8vo., 3*s.* 6*d.*

Commonplace Philosopher. Cr. 8vo., 3*s.* 6*d.*

Critical Essays of a Country Parson. Crown 8vo., 3*s.* 6*d.*

East Coast Days and Memories. Crown 8vo., 3*s.* 6*d.*

Landscapes, Churches, and Moralities. Crown 8vo., 3*s.* 6*d.*

Leisure Hours in Town. Crown 8vo., 3*s.* 6*d.*

Lessons of Middle Age. Crown 8vo., 3*s.* 6*d.*

Our Little Life. Two Series. Crown 8vo., 3*s.* 6*d.* each.

Our Homely Comedy: and Tragedy. Crown 8vo., 3*s.* 6*d.*

Recreations of a Country Parson. Three Series. Crown 8vo., 3*s.* 6*d.* each.

Butler (Samuel).

Erewhon. Crown 8vo., 5*s.*

The Fair Haven. A Work in Defence of the Miraculous Element in our Lord's Ministry. Cr. 8vo., 7*s.* 6*d.*

Life and Habit. An Essay after a Completer View of Evolution. Cr. 8vo., 7*s.* 6*d.*

Evolution, Old and New. Cr. 8vo., 10*s.* 6*d.*

Alps and Sanctuaries of Piedmont and Canton Ticino. Illustrated. Pott 4to., 10*s.* 6*d.*

Luck, or Cunning, as the Main Means of Organic Modification? Cr. 8vo., 7*s.* 6*d.*

Ex Voto. An Account of the Sacro Monte or New Jerusalem at Varallo-Sesia. Crown 8vo., 10*s.* 6*d.*

Selections from Works, with Remarks on Mr. G. J. Romanes' 'Mental Evolution in Animals,' and a Psalm of Montreal. Crown 8vo., 7*s.* 6*d.*

The Authoress of the Odyssey, where and when She wrote, who She was, the Use She made of the Iliad, and how the Poem grew under Her hands. With 14 Illustrations. 8vo., 10*s.* 6*d.*

The Iliad of Homer. Rendered into English Prose for the use of those who cannot read the original. Crown 8vo., 7*s.* 6*d.*

Shakespeare's Sonnets. Reconsidered, and in part Rearranged, with Introductory Chapters and a Reprint of the Original 1609 Edition. 8vo.

Miscellaneous and Critical Works—*continued.*

Calder.—*Accident in Factories:* its Distribution, Causation, Compensation, and Prevention. A Practical Guide to the Law and to the Safe-Guarding, Safe-Working, and Safe-Construction of Factory Machinery, Plant, and Premises. With 20 Tables and 124 Illustrations. By John Calder. Crown 8vo., 7*s.* 6*d.* net.

Charities Register, The Annual, *and Digest:* being a Classified Register of Charities in or available in the Metropolis. With an Introduction by C. S. Loch, Secretary to the Council of the Charity Organisation Society, London. 8vo., 4*s.*

Comparetti. — *The Traditional Poetry of the Finns.* By Domenico Comparetti. Translated by Isabella M. Anderton. With Introduction by Andrew Lang. 8vo., 16*s.*

Dickinson.—*King Arthur in Cornwall.* By W. Howship Dickinson, M.D. With 5 Illustrations. Crown 8vo., 4*s.* 6*d.*

Evans.—*The Ancient Stone Implements, Weapons and Ornaments of Great Britain.* By Sir John Evans, K.C.B., D.C.L., LL.D., F.R.S., etc. With 537 Illustrations. Medium 8vo., 28*s.*

Haggard. — *A Farmer's Year:* being his Commonplace Book for 1898. By H. Rider Haggard. With 36 Illustrations by G. Leon Little. Crown 8vo., 7*s.* 6*d.* net.

Hamlin.—*A Text-Book of the History of Architecture.* By A. D. F. Hamlin, A.M. With 229 Illustrations. Crown 8vo., 7*s.* 6*d.*

Haweis.—*Music and Morals.* By the Rev. H. R. Haweis. With Portrait of the Author, and numerous Illustrations, Facsimiles, and Diagrams. Cr. 8vo., 6*s.* net.

Hodgson.—*Outcast Essays and Verse Translations.* By Shadworth H. Hodgson, LL.D. Crown 8vo., 8*s.* 6*d.*

Hoenig. — *Inquiries concerning the Tactics of the Future.* Fourth Edition, 1894, of the 'Two Brigades'. By Fritz Hoenig. With 1 Sketch in the Text and 5 Maps. Translated by Captain H. M. Bower. 8vo., 15*s.* net.

Hullah.—*The History of Modern Music.* By John Hullah. 8vo., 8*s.* 6*d.*

Jefferies (Richard).

Field and Hedgerow: With Portrait. Crown 8vo., 3*s.* 6*d.*

The Story of My Heart: my Autobiography. With Portrait and New Preface by C. J. Longman. Cr. 8vo., 3*s.* 6*d.*

Jefferies (Richard)—*continued.*

Red Deer. With 17 Illustrations. Crown 8vo., 3*s.* 6*d.*

The Toilers of the Field. With Portrait from the Bust in Salisbury Cathedral. Crown 8vo., 3*s.* 6*d.*

Wood Magic: a Fable. With Frontispiece and Vignette by E. V. B. Crown 8vo., 3*s.* 6*d.*

Jekyll (Gertrude).

Wood and Garden: Notes and Thoughts, Practical and Critical, of a Working Amateur. With 71 Illustrations from Photographs by the Author. 8vo., 10*s.* 6*d.* net.

Home and Garden: Notes and Thoughts, Practical and Critical, of a Worker in both. With 53 Illustrations from Photographs by the Author. 8vo., 10*s.* 6*d.* net.

Johnson.—*The Patentee's Manual:* a Treatise on the Law and Practice of Letters Patent. By J. & J. H. Johnson, Patent Agents, etc. 8vo., 10*s.* 6*d.*

Joyce.—*The Origin and History of Irish Names of Places.* By P. W. Joyce, LL.D. 2 vols. Crown 8vo., 5*s.* each.

Kingsley.—*A History of French Art,* 1100-1899. By Rose G. Kingsley. 8vo., 12*s.* 6*d.* net.

Lang (Andrew).

Letters to Dead Authors. Fcp. 8vo., 2*s.* 6*d.* net.

Books and Bookmen. With 2 Coloured Plates and 17 Illustrations. Fcp. 8vo., 2*s.* 6*d.* net.

Old Friends. Fcp. 8vo., 2*s.* 6*d.* net.

Letters on Literature. Fcp. 8vo., 2*s.* 6*d.* net.

Essays in Little. With Portrait of the Author. Crown 8vo., 2*s.* 6*d.*

Cock Lane and Common-Sense. Crown 8vo., 3*s.* 6*d.*

The Book of Dreams and Ghosts. Crown 8vo., 3*s.* 6*d.*

Macfarren. — *Lectures on Harmony.* By Sir George A. Macfarren. 8vo., 12*s.*

Marquand and Frothingham.—*A Text-Book of the History of Sculpture.* By Allan Marquand, Ph.D., and Arthur L. Frothingham, Junr., Ph.D., Professors of Archæology and the History of Art in Princetown University. With 113 Illustrations. Crown 8vo., 6*s.*

Miscellaneous and Critical Works—*continued.*

Max Müller (The Right Hon. F.).

India: What can it Teach Us? Crown 8vo., 5*s*.

Chips from a German Workshop.

Vol. I. Recent Essays and Addresses. Crown 8vo., 5*s*.

Vol. II. Biographical Essays. Crown 8vo., 5*s*.

Vol. III. Essays on Language and Literature. Crown 8vo., 5*s*.

Vol. IV. Essays on Mythology and Folk Lore. Crown 8vo., 5*s*.

Contributions to the Science of Mythology. 2 vols. 8vo., 32*s*.

Milner.—*Country Pleasures:* the Chronicle of a Year chiefly in a Garden. By George Milner. Crown 8vo., 3*s*. 6*d*.

Morris (William).

Signs of Change. Seven Lectures delivered on various Occasions. Post 8vo., 4*s*. 6*d*.

Hopes and Fears for Art. Five Lectures delivered in Birmingham, London, etc., in 1878-1881. Cr 8vo., 4*s*. 6*d*.

An Address delivered at the Distribution of Prizes to Students of the Birmingham Municipal School of Art on 21st February, 1894. 8vo., 2*s*. 6*d*. net.

Art and the Beauty of the Earth: a Lecture delivered at Burslem Town Hall, on October 13, 1881. 8vo., 2*s*. 6*d*. net.

Some Hints on Pattern-Designing: a Lecture delivered at the Working Men's College, London, on 10th December, 1881. 8vo., 2*s*. 6*d*. net.

Arts and Crafts Essays. By Members of the Arts and Crafts Exhibition Society. With a Preface by William Morris. Crown 8vo., 2*s*. 6*d*. net.

Pollock.—*Jane Austen:* her Contemporaries and Herself. An Essay in Criticism. By Walter Herries Pollock. Crown 8vo., 3*s*. 6*d*. net.

Poore (George Vivian, M.D., F.R.C.P.).

Essays on Rural Hygiene. With 13 Illustrations. Crown 8vo., 6*s*. 6*d*.

The Dwelling House. With 36 Illustrations. Crown 8vo., 3*s*. 6*d*.

Richter. — *Lectures on the National Gallery.* By J. P. Richter. With 20 Plates and 7 Illustrations in the Text. Crown 4to., 9*s*.

Rossetti.—*A Shadow of Dante:* being an Essay towards studying Himself, his World and his Pilgrimage. By Maria Francesca Rossetti. With Frontispiece by Dante Gabriel Rossetti. Crown 8vo., 3*s*. 6*d*.

Soulsby (Lucy H. M.).

Stray Thoughts on Reading. Small 8vo., 2*s*. 6*d*. net.

Stray Thoughts for Girls. 16mo., 1*s*. 6*d*. net.

Stray Thoughts for Mothers and Teachers. Fcp. 8vo., 2*s*. 6*d*. net.

Stray Thoughts for Invalids. 16mo., 2*s*. net.

Southey.—*The Correspondence of Robert Southey with Caroline Bowles.* Edited, with an Introduction, by Edward Dowden, LL.D. 8vo., 14*s*.

Stevens.—*On the Stowage of Ships and their Cargoes.* With Information regarding Freights, Charter-Parties, etc. By Robert White Stevens, Associate-Member of the Institute of Naval Architects. 8vo., 21*s*.

Turner and Sutherland.—*The Development of Australian Literature.* By Henry Gyles Turner and Alexander Sutherland. With Portraits and Illustrations. Crown 8vo., 5*s*.

Van Dyke.—*A Text-Book on the History of Painting.* By John C. Van Dyke, Professor of the History of Art in Rutgers College, U.S. With 110 Illustrations. Crown 8vo, 6*s*.

Warwick.—*Progress in Women's Education in the British Empire:* being the Report of Conferences and a Congress held in connection with the Educational Section, Victorian Era Exhibition. Edited by the Countess of Warwick. Cr. 8vo. 6*s*.

White.—*An Examination of the Charge of Apostacy against Wordsworth.* By W. Hale White, Editor of the 'Description of the Wordsworth and Coleridge MSS. in the Possession of Mr. T. Norton Longman'. Crown 8vo., 3*s*. 6*d*.

Willard. — *History of Modern Italian Art.* By Ashton Rollins Willard. With Photogravure Frontispiece and 28 Full-page Illustrations. 8vo., 18*s*. net.

Miscellaneous Theological Works.

*** *For Church of England and Roman Catholic Works see* MESSRS. LONGMANS & CO.'s *Special Catalogues.*

Balfour. — *THE FOUNDATIONS OF BELIEF*: being Notes Introductory to the Study of Theology. By the Right Hon. ARTHUR J. BALFOUR, M.P. 8vo., 12*s*. 6*d*.

Boyd (A. K. H.) ('A.K.H.B.').

COUNSEL AND COMFORT FROM A CITY PULPIT. Crown 8vo., 3*s*. 6*d*.

SUNDAY AFTERNOONS IN THE PARISH CHURCH OF A SCOTTISH UNIVERSITY CITY. Crown 8vo., 3*s*. 6*d*.

CHANGED ASPECTS OF UNCHANGED TRUTHS. Crown 8vo., 3*s*. 6*d*.

GRAVER THOUGHTS OF A COUNTRY PARSON. Three Series. Crown 8vo., 3*s*. 6*d*. each.

PRESENT DAY THOUGHTS. Crown 8vo., 3*s*. 6*d*.

SEASIDE MUSINGS. Cr. 8vo., 3*s*. 6*d*.

'*TO MEET THE DAY*' through the Christian Year: being a Text of Scripture, with an Original Meditation and a Short Selection in Verse for Every Day. Crown 8vo., 4*s*. 6*d*.

Campbell.—*RELIGION IN GREEK LITERATURE.* By the Rev. LEWIS CAMPBELL, M.A., LL.D., Emeritus Professor of Greek, University of St. Andrews. 8vo., 15*s*.

Davidson.—*THEISM*, as Grounded in Human Nature, Historically and Critically Handled. Being the Burnett Lectures for 1892 and 1893, delivered at Aberdeen. By W. L. DAVIDSON, M.A., LL.D. 8vo., 15*s*.

Gibson.—*THE ABBÉ DE LAMENNAIS. AND THE LIBERAL CATHOLIC MOVEMENT IN FRANCE.* By the Hon. W. GIBSON. With Portrait. 8vo., 12*s*. 6*d*.

Lang. — *MODERN MYTHOLOGY*: a Reply to Professor Max Müller. By ANDREW LANG. 8vo., 9*s*.

MacDonald (GEORGE).

UNSPOKEN SERMONS. Three Series. Crown 8vo., 3*s*. 6*d*. each.

THE MIRACLES OF OUR LORD. Crown 8vo., 3*s*. 6*d*.

Martineau (JAMES).

HOURS OF THOUGHT ON SACRED THINGS: Sermons, 2 vols. Crown 8vo., 3*s*. 6*d*. each.

ENDEAVOURS AFTER THE CHRISTIAN LIFE. Discourses. Crown 8vo., 7*s*. 6*d*.

THE SEAT OF AUTHORITY IN RELIGION. 8vo., 14*s*.

ESSAYS, REVIEWS, AND ADDRESSES. 4 Vols. Crown 8vo., 7*s*. 6*d*. each.

HOME PRAYERS, with *TWO SERVICES* for Public Worship. Crown 8vo., 3*s*. 6*d*.

Max Müller (F.).

THE SIX SYSTEMS OF INDIAN PHILOSOPHY. 8vo., 18*s*.

CONTRIBUTIONS TO THE SCIENCE OF MYTHOLOGY. 2 vols. 8vo., 32*s*.

THE ORIGIN AND GROWTH OF RELIGION, as illustrated by the Religions of India. The Hibbert Lectures, delivered at the Chapter House, Westminster Abbey, in 1878. Crown 8vo., 5*s*.

INTRODUCTION TO THE SCIENCE OF RELIGION: Four Lectures delivered at the Royal Institution. Crown 8vo., 5*s*.

NATURAL RELIGION. The Gifford Lectures, delivered before the University of Glasgow in 1888. Crown 8vo., 5*s*.

PHYSICAL RELIGION. The Gifford Lectures, delivered before the University of Glasgow in 1890. Crown 8vo., 5*s*.

ANTHROPOLOGICAL RELIGION. The Gifford Lectures, delivered before the University of Glasgow in 1891. Cr. 8vo., 5*s*.

THEOSOPHY, OR PSYCHOLOGICAL RELIGION. The Gifford Lectures, delivered before the University of Glasgow in 1892. Crown 8vo., 5*s*.

THREE LECTURES ON THE VEDÂNTA PHILOSOPHY, delivered at the Royal Institution in March, 1894. 8vo., 5*s*.

RÂMAKRISHNA: HIS LIFE AND SAYINGS. Crown 8vo., 5*s*.

Romanes.—*THOUGHTS ON RELIGION.* By GEORGE J. ROMANES, LL.D., F.R.S. Crown 8vo., 4*s*. 6*d*.

Vivekananda.—*YOGA PHILOSOPHY*: Lectures delivered in New York, Winter of 1895-96, by the SWAMI VIVEKANANDA, on Raja Yoga; or, Conquering the Internal Nature; also Patanjali's Yoga Aphorisms, with Commentaries. Crown 8vo, 3*s*. 6*d*.

Williamson. — *THE GREAT LAW*: A Study of Religious Origins and of the Unity underlying them. By WILLIAM WILLIAMSON. 8vo., 14*s*.

10,000/7/00.